FINANCIAL MANAGEMENT

FINANCIAL MANAGEMENT

Edited by
R.K. Malhotra
Nachhattar Singh
S.D. Sharma

ANMOL PUBLICATIONS PVT. LTD.
NEW DELHI - 110 002 (INDIA)

ANMOL PUBLICATIONS PVT. LTD.
4374/4B, Ansari Road, Daryaganj
New Delhi - 110 002
Ph.: 23261597, 23278000
Visit us at: www.anmolpublications.com

PRINTED IN INDIA

Published by J.L. Kumar for Anmol Publications Pvt. Ltd., New Delhi - 110 002 and Printed at Mehra Offset Press, Delhi.

CONTENTS

PREFACE

A major trend virtually in all areas of business is the increasing utilisation of 'management science' concepts, models, techniques and approaches in the organisations. Rapid advances in management concepts and techniques and changes in the climate in which business organisations, institutional enterprises and governments operate call for a more comprehensive and authoritative information on all modern arts and science of management. The Encylopaedia of Modern Management is an attempt in this direction. The encyclopaedia is designed on the lines of systematic reading—a programmed reading of subjects in a planned sequence.

It is more than a reference work covering over 1000 topics related to management. Each topic has been selected carefully and recognition has been given to new development and innovative approaches. In addition to the new dimensions in the information processing and communications technology, the changes in taxation, employee-employer relations, mergers and acquisitions, enhanced moral responsibilites regarding environment and acceptable norms of business, modern techniques in production, marketing and office administration and new insights of the behavioural sciences into human motivations and group effectiveness are some of the topics covered. Elaborate discussions and illustrations have been given as the complexity of the subject matter demands. The book has been designed so that it may be used by top management, department management, executive, executive aspirant, accountant, teacher, student of business and management and, indeed, all those concerned with the conduct of business. The scope of this treatise differs in many respects from any reference books, handbooks and deskbooks dealing with business management.

The writing effort has been assited by many individuals. We gratefully acknowledge all the contributions made by various individuals which made this encyclopaedia possible. Constructive suggestions to help improve the book are welcome.

Editors

1

NATURE OF FINANCIAL MANAGEMENT

OVER the past several years, the role of financial management in the business organization has substantially changed. In the early half of the century the job of the financial manager was largely confined to the acquisition of funds. For the most part, the use of those funds within the organization was not the manager's concern. As business firms continued to expand their markets, however, and organizations became larger and more diversified, greater control of the financial operation became necessary. The function of financial management accordingly underwent significant change. From concern merely with the acquisition of funds, financial management has evolved into an integrated approach which encompasses all aspects of acquiring and utilizing means of financial support for the firm's activities.

Today, financial managers are asked to respond to such issues as: How large should the firm be? What should its asset composition be? How should its capital structure be divided?

A firm must constantly consider the means by which it will generate sales growth in future years. The role of financial management in this process is to determine whether growth should be generated internally, via the research and development route, or the firm should look to potential mergers and acquisitions for its future growth. When developing plans for future growth the firm must decide the amount of fixed and current assets that is going to be needed to support that growth. Once such issues are resolved, it must decide how to raise the necessary funds to acquire the needed assets.

The financial manager is involved in all of these decisions, from the planning of future growth and asset acquisition to the task of raising funds via debt or equity instruments.

An overriding concern is the effect of his or her decisions on the trade-off of risk and profitability. All policy decisions involve this trade-off, and it is the responsibility of the financial manager to be sure that the ultimate decision will have the most favorable impact on the goal structure of the firm.

GOALS OF THE FIRM

The financial manager must keep the goal structure and objectives of the firm clearly in mind in order to operate within an efficient decision-making framework. Much has been written recently about the goals of the firm and how the firm's value or worth is determined. Most financial experts today agree that the primary goal of the firm should be to maximize the value of the company through maximizing the wealth of its share-holders. In this light, *value* refers to the market value of the owners' equity, which can be represented by common stock for a corporation, as share in a partnership, or the owner's interest in a sole proprietorship. The maximum value of owner's equity is directly influenced by how investment, financing, dividend, and current asset management decisions are handled in the firm.

The Profit Goal

Maximization of profits is often considered as either the sole goal or an alternative goal of the firm. This concept is a narrow one compared to the goal of maximizing the *value* of the firm. The maximization of profits as reflected through earnings per share is not an adequate goal for three reasons.

First, it does not take into consideration the time value of money, a concept which states that a rupee today is worth more than a rupee tomorrow. For example, an individual offered a choice of receiving a sum of Rs 1,000 today or waiting two years and receiving a larger sum of Rs 1,500 would have to analyze the decision to determine what the future sum would be worth in today's rupees and compare it to the Rs 1,000 that could be received today. Another approach would be to see which income alternative would be worth more if the Rs 1,000 that would be received today were invested for two years. Obviously, the individual would want to select the income alternative that would yield the most money. The analysis must evaluate the comparative value of a sum being received today versus a sum to be received in two years. This problem concerns the time value of money.

The business community faces essentially the same type of problem when it makes a selection from among investment proposals. A firm may have an investment opportunity that will return Rs 1 million six years from now, but if it also has an investment opportunity that would have returns commencing in Years 1–6, the analysis might indicate a preference for the second proposal, depending upon the time value of money for the firm and the shareholders.

The second reason the maximization of earnings per share is not an acceptable goal is that it does not consider the risk of alternative earnings streams. One project may have an earning stream that will attain the goal of maximum earnings per share, but the risk involved may make this alternative totally unacceptable to a stockholder group which is adverse to risk.

The third failing is that the earnings per share maximization concept does not take into account the impact of the dividend policy on the market price or the value of the firm. Theoretically, a firm would never pay a dividend if the objective were to maximize earnings per share. Rather, it would reinvest all earnings in order to generate still greater earnings in the future. Observations in the marketplace indicate that the value or market price of the firm is maximized by balancing retained earnings with dividends to shareholders.

The Growth of Wealth Goal

One of the basic assumptions in the operation of any business is that *it is being operated for the benefit of the owners.* In a company the *owners* are the common shareholders; in a partnership the *owners* are the individual partners; and in a proprietorship the *owner* is the individual proprietor. The individual owner's goals and lifestyles can be quite diverse. However, we can generalize that any owner will attempt to maximize the utility or satisfaction level to be gained by an interest in a particular business. Greater satisfaction is achieved through increases in the owner's wealth.

In essence, the maximization of the individual's utility or satisfaction is achieved through (and is thus equivalent to) the maximization of wealth. If the firm sets as its goal the maximization of the wealth of its share-holders the individual owners will be in a position to maximize their own utility function. This means that they can convert part of their holdings into cash for purposes of current consumption or they can make the decision to forego current for future consumption by saving and reinvesting. No matter what their utility function or preference structure, the individual owners can make varying adjustments within the wealth constraint until they are fully satisfied. Thus the greater their wealth, the greater will be their flexibility in varying their consumptive patterns.

For the owners of common stock in a company, their wealth is maximized when the price of the common stock is maximized. This is achieved when the management of the firm operates efficiently and makes optimal decisions in the areas of capital investments, financing, dividends, and current asset management. If the owner's interest is in a partnership or sole proprietorship, the objective of management should be to operate in such a manner that the owners can obtain a maximum price in the marketplace for their interest.

Conflict of Objectives

In business operations conflicts often arise between management, shareholders, and others concerning how the objectives of the firm are to be achieved. Because of this, there is often a discrepancy between the stated goal of maximizing the value of the firm through maximizing the wealth of the shareholders and actual corporate behavior.

One of the best ways to illustrate the conflicting objectives of various groups is in the area of dividend policy. What may be considered good for the shareholders may not be considered good for the managers or directors of the firm. And what is good for some shareholders of a firm may not be good for other shareholders.

Managers and the directors of the company may come into conflict with the general stockholders on the issue of how much of the earnings should be reinvested in the company. They may both agree that the value of the firm and the wealth of the shareholders are maximized through maximizing the price of the stock, but they may be in conflict over how this wealth maximization is to be achieved. The managers and directors may view the reinvestment of earnings as an important contribution to the financing of asset investments and a way to broaden the equity base of the firm, which would help support future debt. They might feel that this would lead to future operating efficiencies that would be reflected in future earnings and would help to maximize the price of the stock in the long run. The common shareholders, on the other hand, may feel strongly that a current return through paying out earnings in dividends would have a much more favorable impact on the maximization of the price of the stock. The tools of financial theory may indeed support the manager group but the general weight of the shareholder body in terms of voting power may force it to bend to their wishes. Financial theorists may criticize a firm for not operating in the most efficient manner to maximize the value of the firm in the long run, but they also must recognize the pressures that can be brought to bear by a stockholder group. Stockholder's opposition could be reflected in a decline in the stock price because they sell their stock, or they could utilize their voting power to vote out the existing directors.

There may also be clashes between owners. In middle-size companies it is not uncommon for management to maintain control of the common stock of the firm by owning 51 per cent of it. If these managers are in a high income tax bracket, they might prefer to have the earnings reinvested rather than paying taxes on the dividends, while the rest of the shareholder group may want dividends. In this instance, after analyzing the firm a financial theorist might agree with the shareholders that the value of the firm would be maximized, as reflected in the maximization of the price of the stock, through the payment of the dividends. The result of management's preference for reinvestment of earnings could be a decline in the price of the stock, as other shareholders sell. In this instance, corporate behavior may deviate from the primary objective of the firm: maximizing the wealth of the shareholders.

INTEGRATED FINANCIAL POLICY DECISION FRAMEWORK

Considering the types of operational functions that involve the financial manager, the trade-offs between risk and profitability, the influence of the external environment on the firm, and the maximization of the value of the firm through its market price as the primary goal of the firm, a framework of financial management can be presented as in Figure 1.

To achieve the goal of maximizing the wealth of shareholders commensurate with the associated risk, three stratagems are suggested. These concern decisions relating to long-term investments, changes in the liquidity position of the firm, and changes in the debt composition or financial structure of the firm. Each of these policy decisions involves the financial manager, and each will have a direct impact on the value of the firm through the inherent risk-return trade-offs.

Many of the decisions financial managers must make involve risk- return trade-offs. A measure of return and a feeling for the level of risk involved in a particular item under consideration may by itself not be difficult to acquire. But as the number of items under consideration by the decision maker increases, the task of making decisions becomes more complex. Not only does the volume of work increase, but the risk-return relationships are viewed differently by different persons. As a result, the trade- off process must be somewhat subjective. One decision maker may feel that a particular project has an acceptable measure of return for the level of risk involved in other words, he or she is satisfied with the risk-return trade-off. Another may feel that the risk exposure in that project is too great. Because perceptions of risk are individual in nature, financial managers must not only evaluate their own perceptions of risk and return on an issue, they also must be aware of other managers' views and incorporate them into the analysis.

One decision demonstrating the interrelationship between risk and return might be whether or not to add a new product into the product list of the firm. To produce this product, the firm would have to increase its equipment and plant commitment substantially. Market surveys indicate that the product is in great demand and will substantially add to the profitability of the firm. The risk factor that must be considered is that the sales forecast may be in error, or the cost structure of producing the product may be under-

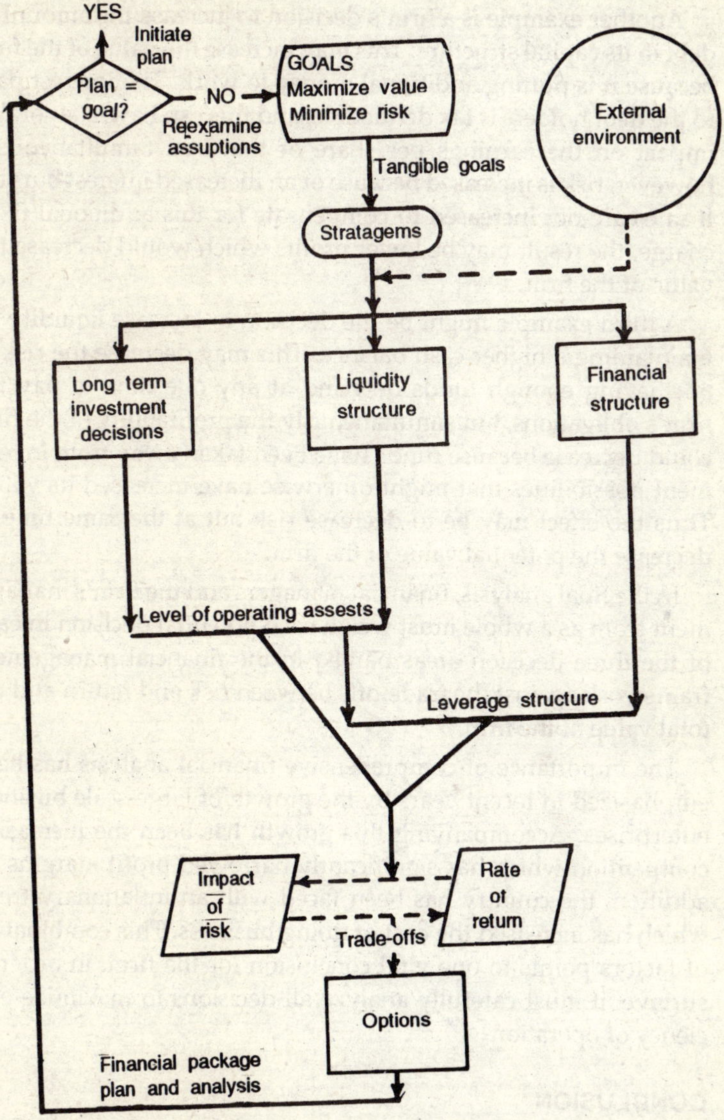

Fig. 1. Framework of Financial Management.

stated. If either of these occur, the firm could be making a commitment that could prove very unprofitable.

Another example is a firm's decision to increase the amount of debt in its capital structure. This may increase the value of the firm because it is putting additional money to work. The interest paid to the debt holders is tax deductible, and this can have a favorable impact on the earnings per share of the firm. Simultaneously, however, risk is increased because of an increased interest burden. If sales are not increased to compensate for this additional fixed charge, the result may be lower profits which would decrease the value of the firm.

A third example might be the decision to increase liquidity by maintaining a higher cash balance. This may decrease the risk of not having enough funds on hand at any one time to pay the firm's obligations, but simultaneously the profitability of the firm could decrease because funds have been taken away from investment possibilities that might otherwise have increased its value. Thus the effect may be to decrease risk but at the same time to decrease the potential value of the firm.

In the final analysis, financial managers and the firm's management team as a whole must weigh each potential decision in each of the three decision areas named in the financial management framework against the trade-offs between risk and return and the total value of the firm.

The importance of comprehensive financial analysis has been emphasized in recent years by the growth of large-scale business enterprises. Accompanying this growth has been the increasing competition which has significantly narrowed profit margins. In addition, the country has been faced with an inflationary trend which has increased the cost of doing business. This combination of factors points to one vital conclusion for the firm: in order to survive, it must carefully analyze all decisions to maximize efficiency of operation.

CONCLUSION

In today's world, the financial manager plays a vital role in the overall managerial decision-making process. Whether working for a large or small firm, this manager is responsible for analyzing, planning and controlling the firm's resources so they can be employed in the most efficient manner.

Formerly serving solely as the individual responsible for the acquisition of funds, the financial manager now typically is much more involved in the control of all resources and decisions of the firm. His or her role in this decision process can be summarized in a single diagram which shows the trade-off of risk and return as related to the policy decisions of the firm.

Besides a working knowledge of finance, the financial manager must also be familiar with such areas as accounting, economics, and quantitative analysis in order to be of maximum value to the firm. He should also be familiar with the external environment influencing business and industry. Although a detailed description and analysis of business external environment is out of scope of this treatise, albiet Figure 2 shows it in brief. Note how such external factors are inter-related with each other.

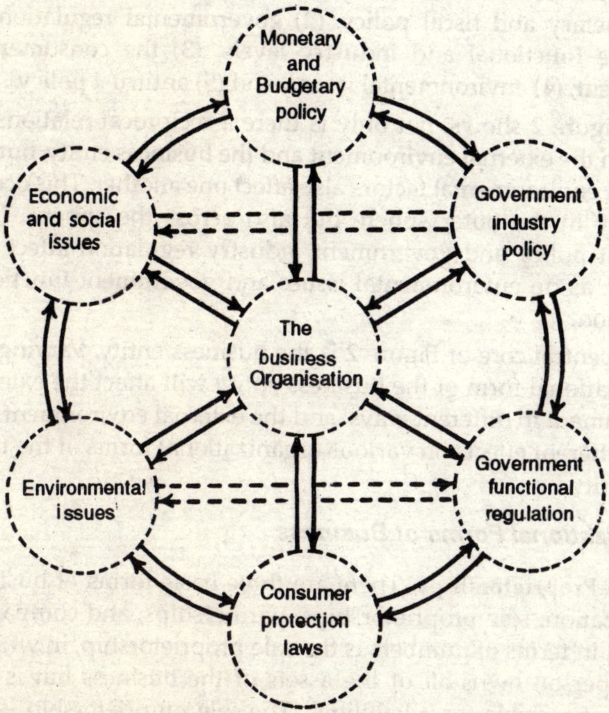

Fig. 2. Business and its External Environment.

EXTERNAL ENVIRONMENT OF BUSINESS

The financial manager who is to be successful must be familiar with the external environment of business. Those who deal with the financial aspects of a firm must be aware of its relationship to its environment and be prepared to deal with these implications.

There is a host of external factors that can influence business. In this text, however, the emphasis will be on those facets of the environment that have a direct bearing on the financial aspects of the firm.

Figure 2 illustrates the interface that exists between the external environment and the business world. Each of the factors surrounding the business entity influences its decisions, and the resulting decisions in turn influence the surrounding environment. The issues that directly affect the finance function are (1) monetary and fiscal policy, (2) governmental regulation, at both the functional and industry levels, (3) the consumerism movement, (4) environmental issues, and (5) antitrust policy.

As Figure 2 shows, not only is there a reciprocal relationship between the external environment and the business entity, but the external environmental factors also affect one another. This occurs not only in the outer sphere but also across the sphere. Thus antitrust policy and government industry regulation affect one another, as do environmental issues and government functional regulation.

The central core of Figure 2 is the business entity. Varying the organizational form of the business entity will affect the external environment in different ways, and the external environment will have different effects on various organizational forms of the business entity.

Organizational Forms of Business

Sole Proprietorships. There are three basic forms of business organization: sole proprietorships, partnerships, and companies. Largest in terms of numbers is the sole proprietorship, in which a single person owns all of the assets of the business but is also solely responsible for it liabilities. The sole proprietorship is historically the oldest business form. Its greatest virtue is its simplicity; its chief disadvantage is that an individual must provide all the assets of the organization as well as his or her own personal assets in the event of a suit. In other words, the proprietor has unlimited liability. A sole proprietorship is probably in the small business category and could have difficulty in obtaining capital for business operations. Also, the duration of the firm usually is limited to the life of the owner.

Partnerships. In many respects the partnership form of organization is similar to the sole proprietorship, except that there is more than one owner. A *general partnership* is a form in which all partners have unlimited liability. It is important that the partners be carefully selected, since any one can bind the partnership with liabilities. Generally there is a partnership agreement which spells out how profits will be distributed, how much capital will be invested by each partner, how new partners will be admitted, and how the partnership will be reconstituted in the event of the death or withdrawal of one or more partners. By legal definition, the partnership is dissolved if one partner withdraws or dies. Since the reconstitution of the partnership is somewhat complex, many individuals view this form of business organization unacceptable.

Another form of partnership which is permitted in several cases is the *limited partnership*. In this situation the individual partner is limited in terms of liability by the amount of capital he or she has invested. However, with this form of partnership, there must be at least one general partner whose liability is unlimited. Limited partners cannot participate in the operations of the business. Their primary function is to provide needed investment capital, and they share in the profits and losses according to the partnership agreement. This form of organization is used extensively in real estate syndications.

Companies. In today's business world, the corporate form of organization is one of the most important. By definition, a company is a legal entity created by law that can engage in the ownership of assets and the incurrence of liabilities. One of the main features of the company is that it stands apart from the ownership, thus allowing an owner to have limited liability up to the amount of his or her investment. The concept of limited liability can represent a distinct advantage over the sole proprietorship and the partnership forms of organization. The function of raising capital can be performed in the company's name, thus protecting the owners from the dangers of unlimited liability, since their personal assets cannot be used in the settlement of claims against the company. In many small, privately held companies, however, personal as well as corporate assets must be used as collateral in order to raise funds. In this manner, many lending institutions bypass the corporate veil.

In public company, ownership is divisible into shares of stock. The fact that these shares can be transferred constitutes a major advantage for the corporate form of organization. In the event that one stockholder dies or wishes to sell stock, the company will continue as a business entity. With private company, the owners often will create what is termed a *buy-sell agreement*. This establishes a market value for the organization so that in the event an owner dies or desires to sell, the remaining owner or owners has a determined base for the buy or sell decision.

A group of individuals who want to form a company, must incorporate within some state and must file an application with a state official, generally the Company Law Board. In the application form, the applicant must list the title of the organization, the location of business, the names of all owners and directors, the purpose of the business, the amount of shares that will be initially authorized, and the amount of paid-up capital.

The company has become a very popular form of organization, principally because of the advantages it offers of limited liability, transferability of ownership, and ease of raising capital. Even with the disadvantages of incorporation fees and the length of time necessary to form a company, the tremendous demands for capital experienced by many firms in recent years have made this form of organization by far the most important.

2

FINANCIAL RATIOS

THE success of an organization often lies upon the information given in a Financial Manager's plan for future performances. Not only must the future be planned with forecasts and budgets, but there must be continual evaluation of the performance of the firm in comparison with past forecasts. One of the building blocks of an accurate forecast is ratio analysis, a technique which enables the financial manager to gain a perspective on the firm.

Financial ratios portray relationship that exist between various items appearing in balance sheets and income accounts and occasionally other items. They may be expressed in simple mathematical terms (e.g., three to one), in percentages, or in other terms which make them more readily comprehensible (e.g., man hours costs per production unit). They are used to measure and evaluate the financial condition and operating effectiveness of a business.

Many different ratios are commonly used and new ones are constantly being devised to serve more specific purposes. Some of those commonly used portray the following relationships:

- ☐ Net profit on sales.
- ☐ Net profit on tangible net worth.
- ☐ Current assets to current liabilities.
- ☐ Current liabilities to tangible net worth.
- ☐ Net fixed assets to tangible net worth.

- Sales to inventories.
- Sales to receivables (expressed in days' sales)
- Operating profits to interest charges.

Need of Standards

In order to have significance, the ratios of a specific company must be compared with a norm. Since different types of industries have different characteristics, the typical ratios in one line of business tend to be different from those in another and, therefore, sets of typical ratios for each line of industry are desirable. The availability of these is steadily increasing, particularly as more and more trade associations develop statistics for their members.

Financial Analysis

Techniques of use vary somewhat and some skill is desirable. Even without training, however, a businessman can usually arrive at some worthwhile conclusions regarding the financial condition and operating effectiveness of a concern by the use of ratios, provided a set of standard ratios of that line is available. A comparison of the ratios of the company being analyzed with the appropriate standard ratios shows in what respects that company is typical of superior to or inferior to representative companies in its industry.

The financial condition (as distinguished from the operating effectiveness) can be determined basically from five ratios:

Net Fixed Assets to Tangible Net Worth. When this ratio is significantly above the norm, it indicates a potentially top heavy investment in fixed assets, possibly an excessively high breakeven point in sales, and is frequently accompanied by a shortage of working capital.

What the proper ratio should be depends, of course, on the line of business. Near one extreme are such concerns as finance companies and wholesalers, which generally operate in leased quarters, do no manufacturing, and have no need of fixed assets beyond necessary office equipment. Such concerns rarely have more than about 10% of their tangible net worth invested in net fixed assets. At the other extreme will generally be found the public utilities, which must have large investments in plant assets. Such concerns may have an investment in net fixed assets equivalent to 300% of tangible net worth. Despite these extremes, it is generally true in most lines of business that the investment in net fixed assets tends to range between 30% and 60% of tangible net worth.

The business which invests too high a proportion of its capital in fixed assets may easily find itself with insufficient money left over with which to conduct operations. This rule applies to every concern, whether a small retailer or a giant manufacturer. So long as the company is adequately equipped for its operational needs, there is no danger in too small an investment in net fixed assets. Generally speaking, a low fixed investment leaves the greater part of the invested capital free for other purposes.

Sales to Net Working Capital. This measures the adequacy of working capital for the volume transacted. A ratio which is significantly higher than the norm indicates inadequate working capital and reflects an excessive risk of financial embarrassment.

Simply stated, this ratio is important because it takes capital to finance the day-to-day operations of a business. Again, what the relationship should be depends on the line of business. Near one extreme are such concerns as whole-salers of cigarettes and confectionery, which are usually close to their sources of supply so that they can obtain frequent and quick replenishment of their inventories. They are not required to process their inventories except to break large incoming lots into smaller quantities for delivery to their customers. And since selling terms are either cash or on a load-to-load basis, collections are prompt. As a result, cash is received sufficiently rapidly to meet obligations punctually.

Generally speaking, those industries in which inventory turnover is relatively rapid and in which selling terms are short can and usually do have a higher turnover of net working capital than others not so situated. Dealers in perishables and style goods particularly have a high turnover of net working capital—and among such lines, an annual sales volume equivalent to from eight to fifteen times net working capital is typical.

Near the other extreme are industries in which the inventory turnover is necessarily low or in which selling terms are long. Thus, net working capital in substantial amounts is required for meeting maturing obligations while the company waits for its inventories to be processed or aged, as the case may be, before they are delivered to customers, and while it waits for collections on its receivables. Here annual sales may be equivalent to only once or twice the net working capital. Distillers of whiskey and manufacturers of tobacco produces, for example, must age their merchandise for extended periods. Furniture retailers and others selling on installment terms require substantial amounts of new working capital to carry their receivables.

The lines of industry in which the extremes of either a high or a low net working capital turnover appear are in the minority. In the great majority of cases, sound financial policy requires that management provide net working capital equivalent to at least one sixth to one fourth of annual sales. Failure to preserve this ratio usually indicates that the company is undercapitalized, and that it must "overtrade." It will be straining its resources and undergoing the risk that maturing obligations may not be met promptly, that creditors may take temporary control, or, worst of all, that the company will be in too weak a condition to withstand any unexpected loss without going into bankruptcy.

Inventory to Net Working Capital. With the exception of relatively few lines of business (e.g., retail shoes, retail drugs) inventories typically are equivalent to less than 100% of net working capital and are generally in the 60%–80% range. The importance of this ratio comes from the fact that as long as inventories are equivalent to less than 100% of the net working capital, it is simultaneously true that cash and receivables cover the current liabilities. Above 100% cash and receivables fail to cover the current debt. In times of economic stress the ability to meet maturing obligations promptly is predicated largely on the liquidity of the current assets, and the so-called "acid test" of liquidity is met when cash and receivables cover the current debt. Inventories are unlike cash and receivables in that the former are worth only; what they will bring when they are sold. Whereas the latter are already in definite rupee amounts. the desirability of maintaining cash and receivables at least equivalent to the current liabilities is thus apparent, and this objective is always attained so long as inventories are less than net working capital.

A high ratio of inventory to net working capital does not necessarily indicate that inventories are excessive. The basic weakness may be that net working capital is inadequate. Whether the latter is true can be determined by studying the net working capital turnover, as discussed above in connection with Ratio No. 2.

Sales to Receivables. This ratio is commonly expressed in number of days' sales represented by the receivables. The number of days is called the *collection period*, and measures the liquidity of the receivables. Cash sales are eliminated in making this calculation, since cash sales do not generate receivables.

A quick method to determine the over-all quality of the receivables is to examine the receivables in the light of credit terms extended by the company. For example, if the terms of sale provide for payment in thirty days, then, barring seasonal factors, there should be approximately thirty days' credit sales in receivables at any given time. The analysis calls for dividing annual credit sales by 365 to determine average credit sales per day. The resulting figure is then divided into total receivables, the answer being the numbers of days' sales in receivables or the average collection period. If the collection period is substantialy longer than the period provided by the terms of sale, the company faces a potentially serious financial situation..

Sales to Inventory. By indicating the rapidity with which the inventory turns, this ratio indicates its liquidity. A low ratio suggests slow-moving items and a lack of inventory control.

Other Ratios

Because the five ratios discussed above are basic, they tend to control other balance sheet ratios. If these five are normal, other ratios such as *Current and/or Total Debt to Tangible Net Worth* and the *Current Ratio* (current assets to current liabilities) will likewise be normal. Conversely, a heavy debt-to-worth ratio or a low current ratio is invariably caused by the fact that one or more of the five basic ratios are out of line.

Whatever may be the real cause of business failures, there is one thing which is common to them all, and that is debts—debts which could not be paid. One of the best means of telling whether debts are excessive is to compare them with the tangible net worth. The relationships vary considerably from one line of industry to another, but a dependable rule of thumb is that current liabilities should generally not exceed 50% or 60% of tangible net worth. Generally, most financially sound enterprises operate with current liabilities equivalent to not much more than 40% of the tangible net worth, except for those concerns in certain lines (e.g., finance companies, wholesalers of cigarettes) in which wide seasonal fluctuations are inevitable. Total debts, including both current liabilities and funded debt, should generally be not more than 70% or 80% of the tangible net worth; and another good general rule is that a funded debt should not be greater than net working capital.

Operating Effectiveness can be determined by the use of ratios developed from items in the income statements. The simplest are those of net profits in relation to sales and to tangible net worth. When these are low, a more detailed analysis is required to determine the cause, which may be one or a combination of things. Causes of low earnings may be found in inadequate gross profit margins, excessive rent, excessive salaries, raw material costs, or any of the other items of expense.

Analysis by means of financial ratios becomes more valuable when a comparison is made between specific ratios in successive years. For example, a steady reduction in gross profit margin should constitute a warning of potential danger. Or a steady reduction in turn-over of receivables or inventory may point out the need for prompt remedial steps Conversely, a reduction in the ratio of debt to net worth or an increase in the current ratio would suggest that the financial condition is becoming stronger.

RATIO ANALYSIS

As a tool for evaluating a firm's performance, the calculation of ratios by itself is not very meaningful. For example, if two specific pieces of information are taken from the balance sheet and a ratio is made of their relationship, the results say little. But when this result is utilized with other information, such as industry data, ratio analysis has considerable power in evaluating the performance of a firm. The best method for this analysis is to compare the ratios of a firm with the industry averages over a period of time, such as five or ten years. This provides a fairly accurate picture of how the firm has performed, not only as compared to its own past performance but also as compared to industry norms. To be effective, the ratio analysis of a firm must be used in conjunction with industry data, and the analysis must be constructed over a specific period of time.

While ratio analysis is a powerful tool of financial analysis, it has some limitations. One of the basic problems is the compatibility of the results gained by comparing firm against firm or firm against industry. Following are some of the areas in which the problem of compatibility can occur. It is assumed that the reader is familiar with the common statements of financial information such as Balance Sheet, Profit and Loss Account, Profit and Loss Appropriation Account etc.

The review of the basic depreciation techniques in Volume 2, *The Economic Aspects of Management*, of this treatise should make it possible to visualize the effects on the balance sheet and income statement, if one company uses an accelerated form (also called diminishing balance) and another uses straight line. If all data for both companies are the same except for the depreciation figures, the following would result. The firm using the accelerated depreciation methods would have a higher cost of goods sold (COGS), lower gross profit, and lower net income. The net fixed assets on the balance sheet also would be less. The opposite effects would hold for the other firm. If we did not recognize these differences, we might conclude in a ratio analysis that the first did not perform as well as the second.

Another illustration concerns methods of inventory valuation and varying price-level changes. Assume we are in a period of rising prices. With a LIFO (Last-In, First-Out) inventory method, the firm will have a higher COGS figure, lower gross profit, lower tax burden, and lower net income. The balance sheet would show a lower inventory figure. If we compare this firm with a second whose data are exactly the same but which uses a FIFO (First-In, First-Out) inventory method, a clear distortion will occur. In periods of rising prices, the Fifo will give lower COGS and higher gross profits, taxes, and net income figures. The balance sheet will also show a higher inventory value. In periods of declining price levels, the opposite effects would occur for the two firms. We must consider this possibility in utilizing ratio analysis and be aware of the distortions that could occur.

Distortions can also occur in ratio analysis for firms that evaluate assets in different ways. Two companies with the same assets but which utilize different asset valuation techniques will have different asset values, assuming all other financial data are the same. Ratio analysis which utilizes this information without taking this differences into account will be distorted.

The same problem arises with a comparison of firms that file consolidated and nonconsolidated statements. A clear distortion of data would exist, and a ratio analysis would not reflect a true comparison of the companies.

Another example is companies that capitalize leases and those that do not. Capitalized leases will affect the fixed assets and leverage position of the firm. A comparison of two companies, one that capitalizes leases and another that does not, will lead to a distortion of all ratios that utilize these data.

The many different methods of accounting utilized by various firms can produce widely different results for the same ratio. Are the results favorable or unfavorable when compared to industry figures? The distortion must be taken into consideration when making such comparisons, but the task is difficult because we do not know the magnitude of the effect that these differences in accounting procedures will have on the financial statements of a firm. They all may be working together to lower the tax burden of the firm, or they could be pulling against each other and thus will negate any effect on the financial statements. And, of course, in many instances the individual doing the analysis does not have the data available to restructure all of the financial statements so that the analysis will be equally comparable among all firms.

Another issue that can have a significant impact on financial statements is inflation accounting. The purpose of this technique is to permit the various accounts to reflect changes in the general purchasing power of the rupee. Many companies have eliminated this problem with inventories by valuing them at current costs, but it still holds for depreciation. The contention is that historical cost depreciation does not reflect current replacement costs accurately. During periods of high inflation, this situation can lead to an overstatement of profits. As the inflation rate continues, the gap between historical costs and current costs may widen, and this would present a distorted picture of the firm under analysis.

In some industries, the newly developed inflation data are comparable among firms. In the cement, trucking, and airline industries, the assets are similar, and in one study these firms reported coordinating their approach to replacement-cost valuation. Other industries with similar assets reporting some efforts at coordination were railroads, utilities, textiles, aerospace, lodging, retail, and automotive.

The inflation-accounting approach to reporting financial information will make company/company and company/industry analysis over time much more difficult. This is because companies differ in their implementation of these requirements, and historical analysis will not have included inflation accounting. Thus if we were trying to see what trends might be developing, the results would change when we came to the present year's data.

All of these factors make the job of the financial analyst much more difficult. We cannot rely solely on the ratios to provide an accurate picture but must look behind the actual calculations to the data base and the way in which it was constructed. Only in this way can we make accurate conclusions from financial ratio analysis.

TYPES OF FINANCIAL RATIOS

To evaluate the financial condition of a firm properly, the financial manager could commence with a ratio analysis. This process basically involves selecting two pieces of financial data and constructing a ratio or index concerning their relationship. An analysis of a number of ratios or indexes will provide a skilled analyst with a good picture of the past financial performance of the firm.

Generally, ratio analysis can be divided into four categories:

1. *Liquidity ratios* help measure the firm's ability to meet its current obligations.
2. *Leverage ratios* measure the degree to which the firm has utilized debt financing and, sometimes, preferred, stock financing in its financial structure.
3. *Activity ratios* measure how efficiently the firm is utilizing its resources.
4. *Profitability ratios* measure the overall operating effectiveness of the firm.

To illustrate the use of financial ratio analysis, we will examine each of these categories of ratios for the ABC Co. (a hypothetical firm) for the years ending March 31, 1983-87. Tables 1 and 2 present balance sheet and income statement data for this period.

Liquidity Ratios

One of the first concerns of a financial manager should be the ability of the firm to meet its current obligations, such as taxes, credit from suppliers, and short-term loans from the bank. Although a cash budget would be required to show in detail the monthly flow of funds into and out of the firm, ratio analysis can quickly point out any weakness in the firm concerning this area.

1. Current Ratio. This ratio is calculated by taking the sum of current assets and dividing by the sum of current liabilities. Current assets consist of cash, marketable securities, accounts receivable, and inventories. Current liabilities generally consist of accounts payable, short-term notes, the current maturity on long-term debt, accrued income taxes, and other accrued expenses such as wages. The current ratio is the most frequently used ratio in determining a firm's liquidity, for it shows the extent to which the claims of the short-term creditors are covered by the liquid assets of the firm. In the case of ABC Co., the current ratio is:

$$\text{Current ratio} = \frac{\text{Current assets}}{\text{Current liabilities}} = \frac{\text{Rs. } 987{,}775}{\text{Rs. } 497{,}086} = 1.99 \text{ times.}$$

For 1987, the firm is providing relatively less protection for its current creditors than the industry average. However, it still provides a margin of safety for the current creditors of the firm in the sense that the liquidity position of the firm (current assets) could decrease by approximately 50 per cent before the current creditors would just have enough current assets to cover their claims. If a bank or supplier were thinking of extending further credit or were interested in determining the degree of protection it holds in the firm, it would utilize the current ratio as a measure.

2. Quick Ratio or Acid Test. The acid-test ratio is calculated by deducting inventory from the current asset figure and dividing the result by current liabilities. Inventories typically are the least liquid current asset and as such are subject to the greatest risk of loss in case of liquidation. As a result, many short-term creditors will calculate the quick ratio in addition to the current ratio. For ABC Co., the quick, or acid-test, ratio is calculated as follows:

Table 1

ABC Co.

Consolidated Balance Sheet as on March 31, 1983-1987

(*Rs. in thousand*)

	1983	*1984*	*1985*	*1986*	*1987*
Assets					
Cash	56,666	46,864	39,843	48,066	44,221
Marketable securities	24,906	27,188	384	9,600	29,428
Receivables, net	198,937	198,026	219,146	256,329	275,738
Inventories	530,667	536,838	557,984	574,488	638,388
Total Current Assets	811,176	808,916	817,357	888,483	987,775
Other investments, at cost	15,301	14,430	19,715	21,547	56,829
Other assets	9,468	9,680	11,724	4,547	39,576
Plant and equipment, net	336,682	347,823	358,254	383,298	366,248
Prepaid expenses	8,164	7,121	10,260	9,100	1,200
Total Assets	1,180,791	1,187,970	1,217,310	1,306,975	1,451,628
Liabilities and Stockholders' Equity					
Accounts payable	84,994	99,077	105,088	160,697	201,155
Notes payable	66,516	63,064	91,418	170,957	238,359
Accrued taxes	42,947	45,397	33,163	34,823	37,742
Current portion of long-term debt	6,136	6,910	14,740	6,475	8,984
Other current liabilities	4,653	4,200	4,536	5,498	10,846
Total Current Liabilities	205,246	218,648	248,945	378,450	497,086
Long-term debt	183,984	153,822	142,514	91,023	114,047
Common stock (no par)	396,800	396,800	396,800	396,800	396,800
Retained earnings	394,761	418,700	429,051	440,702	443,695
Total Stockholders' Equity	791,561	815,500	825,851	837,502	840,495
Total Liabilities and Stockholders' Equity	1,180,791	1,187,970	1,217,310	1,306,975	1,451,628

Table 2

ABC Co.

Consolidated Profit and Loss Statements
For the Years Ended December 31,1983-1987

(Rs. in thousands)

	1983	1984	1985	1986	1987
Sales	1,549,821	1,525,138	1,523,984	1,591,696	1,626,921
Cost of sales	1,250,255	1,243,580	1,257,946	1,326,201	1,352,479
General and administrative expenses	98,685	101,726	104,485	107,897	111,601
Selling expenses	67,790	65,817	71,657	69,931	76,401
Profit from Operations	133,091	114,015	89,896	87,667	86,440
Other income	17,909	20,859	20,233	24,759	25,748
Total income	151,000	134,874	110,129	112,426	112,188
Interest	13,561	13,950	14,775	17,848	25,984
Other expenses	13,987	23,284	23,817	28,421	30,097
Net Profit before Income Taxes	123,452	97,640	71,537	66,157	56,107
Incomes taxes	58,635	43,941	31,426	24,746	23,354
Net Profit	54,817	53,699	40,111	41,411	32,753
Retained earnings, beginning	358,464	394,761	418,700	429,051	440,702
Dividends	28,520	29,760	29,760	29,760	29,760
Retained earnings, ending	394,761	418,700	429,051	440,702	443,695

$$\text{Quick ratio} = \frac{\text{Current assets} - \text{Inventory}}{\text{Current liabilities}}$$

$$= \frac{\text{Rs. } 349{,}387}{\text{Rs. } 497{,}086} = 0.7 \text{ times.}$$

Since the industry average is 1.1, the firm is in an unsatisfactory position.

The liquidity category of ratios shows that ABC Co. is below the industry average. This deficiency could be a signal of continued liquidity problems, but to draw any further conclusions, trend analysis, which is discussed in a later section of this chapter, would be necessary.

Leverage Ratios

Leverage, by definition, is the employment of another person's money to run the firm (in addition to equity capital). The degree to which leverage is utilized in the firm can be measured by leverage ratios. Unlike equity capital, debt financing involves a contractual arrangement, which can have an interest obligation attached. Thus an analyst interested in evaluating a firm's performance will usually examine one or more leverage ratios. If it is determined that the degree of leverage is too large, the analyst may foresee the increased risk which often accompanies the contractual payment of interest and thus anticipate the possibility of an earnings instability which would render the firm unable to meet the interest payments.

In general, firms with low leverage have reduced the risk of not being able to meet their cash outflows in times of economic downturns, but, at the same time, they forego the opportunity of large gains through the use of leverage in periods of economic upswings. This is one reason why leverage is called a double-edged sword.

The measurement of the degree of leverage can generally be approached in two ways. The first method examines ratios from the balance sheet, while the second examines the fixed contractual obligations of the firm from the income statement.

3. Debt to Total Assets. The ratio of debt to total assets measures the extent to which creditor capital has supplied funding for asset investment, relative to the contribution of the equity holders. Those firms subject to a larger degree of instability in earnings before interest and taxes (EBIT) will have smaller debt to total asset ratios than others with a small degree of earnings instability.

In discussing a debt to total asset ratio, it is important to keep in mind the definition of debt. Many ratios can be altered in terms of their definition, and leverage ratios fit this situation. For some purpose the ratio of total debt to total assets, which would include current liabilities as well as all long-term debt, might be of interest. An equity investor might want to know this type of leverage ratio to get an overall perception of the risk exposure. The long-term debt to total asset ratio also might be measured. Institutions or persons participating in long-term debt financing might be interested in this type of ratio to get a perspective of the relative collateral-available base and long-term interest obligations of the firm. Or, the interest might be only with interest-bearing debt, including long-term as well as short-term interest-bearing debt. A bank or other lending institutions would be interested in this ratio as a measure of the total interest burden of the company.

Problems often arise when the definition of debt is not clear. It is imperative to have a specific definition in mind when making comparisons, and it is equally important to provide a definition of the debt ratio so that others can effectively utilize the analysis.

In the case of ABC Co., the ratio of total debt to total assets is:

$$\text{Debt to total assets} = \frac{\text{Total debt}}{\text{Total assets}} = \frac{\text{Rs. } 611{,}133}{\text{Rs. } 1{,}451{,}628} = 42.1\%.$$

Industry average = 41.0%

The firm's ratio of 42.1 per cent, compared with the industry average of 41 per cent, indicates that the firm slightly exceeds the industry norm. There are two implications of this positions. If the firm wishes future financing and goes to the debt market, it may be turned away or may be forced to pay a much higher interest rate for the debt, a reflection of the perceived increase in risk due to the fact that the firm would further exceed the industry norm. A second implication is that if they need financing in the future and cannot utilize the debt market or the equity market (due perhaps to a substantial drop in the entire market or just in their own stock) they will find themselves in an undesirable position. Since the industry debt norm often plays an important role in determining the debt limit of any firm within that industry, it is important to try to maintain that balance of debt in the capital structure.

4. Debt to Net Worth. Another ratio that measures the utilization of debt is the comparison of debt to net worth. This ratio shows the direct relationship between the debt contribution to the capital structure of the firm and the equity contribution. In some instances the debt contribution is substantially greater than the equity contribution to the capital structure.

For ABC, this ratio again demonstrates that the firm exceeds the industry norm:

$$\text{Debt to net worth} = \frac{\text{Total debt}}{\text{Net worth}} = \frac{\text{Rs. } 611{,}133}{\text{Rs. } 840{,}495} = 72.7\%.$$

Industry average = 69.5%.

5. Times Interest Earned. The times interest earned ratio is the first present which utilized information from the income statement. From the example in Table 2, it is defined as earnings before interest and taxes (EBIT), divided by the interest charges. The reason for using income *before* taxes is simple: Interest expense is deductible for tax purposes and will thus have a definite effect on the tax liability of the firm. In financial terms, the ratio tells a banker or other interested parties how much the earnings could decrease before the firm would not be able to meet its debt obligations.

$$\text{Times interest earned} = \frac{\text{Earnings before interest and taxes (EBIT)}}{\text{Interest charges}}$$

$$= \frac{\text{Rs. } 56{,}107 + \text{Rs. } 25{,}984}{\text{Rs. } 25{,}984}$$

$$= \frac{\text{Rs. } 82{,}091}{\text{Rs. } 25{,}984} = 3.16 \text{ times.}$$

Industry average = 4.8 times.

This ratio shows that the firm can cover its interest charges 3.16 times before taxes. However, the industry average is 4.8 times, which would indicate that bankers and others who might lend to this company would think seriously about the ability of the firm to service its existing debt, much less attempt to service a *greater* level of debt. The lack of adequate coverage results when interest charges are too great relative to the operating income level. This ratio shows why the industry average is 41 per cent in terms of debt to total assets. The instability of EBIT in the industry is such that a higher level of debt may be undesirable in terms of interest coverage for various groups of creditors.

If there are several interest-bearing securities in a firm's structure, we may be interested in calculating a cumulative times interest earned figure. This is done by calculating the times interest earned figure on the first issue and then consecutively adding the interest figures to the calculations until all of the issues are considered. This would finally give us the interest coverage on all of the issues. The calculation process is shown in Table 3. We are assuming that the level of EBIT is Rs 3 million. The first issue of 5 per cent mortgage bonds for Rs 10 million has an annual interest amount of Rs 500,000. This provides an interest coverage of 6 times. With the 7 per cent debentures of Rs 5 million, providing an additional Rs 350,000 interest, the total interest coverage has dropped to 3.53 times. When the 8 per cent subordinated debentures are included, the total interest is Rs 1,090,000, which provides an interest coverage of 2.75 times.

Table 3

Illustration of Cumulative Times Interest Earned

Issue	*Amount*	*Annual interest*	*Cumulative interest*	*Cumulative times interest earned*
5% mortgage bonds	10 million	500,000	500,000	6.00
7% debentures	5 million	350,000	850,000	3.53
8% Subordinated debentures	3 million	240,000	1,090,000	2.75
	18 million	1,090,000		2.75

Thus one of the advantages in examining the times interest earned ratio on a cumulative basis is that we can see how each component of the debt structure affects the interest coverage.

6. Fixed Charge Coverage. The fixed charge coverage ratio is also used to determine the ability of the firm to meet the obligations of the creditors, but it is more comprehensive than the *times interest earned ratio* since it considers all fixed charges including lease payments. Lease commitments are a fixed charge because they are contractual but do not appear on the balance sheet as building or equipment items. The ratio is found by dividing income before charges by fixed charges. Fixed charges generally consist of interest, lease, and rent payments as well as the before-tax funds required for any sinking fund payments. Preferred dividends are also considered by most financial managers as the equivalent to a fixed charge, particularly if the dividend is cumulative. In the formula for fixed charge coverage, ABC has no leases and no preferred stock outstanding, so the values of these two factors are zero.

$$\text{Fixed charge coverage} = \frac{\text{Income available for meeting fixed charges}}{\text{Fixed charges}}$$

$$= \frac{\text{Earnings before tax + Interest + Office rent}}{\text{Interest + Leases + rent + Before–tax sinking fund + Before tax preferred stock dividends}}$$

$$= \frac{\text{Rs. }56{,}107 + \text{Rs. }25{,}984 + \text{Rs. }5{,}000}{\text{Rs. }25{,}984 + 0 + \text{Rs. }5{,}000 + 5{,}263 + 0} = \frac{\text{Rs. }87{,}091}{\text{Rs. }36{,}247}$$

$$= 2.4 \text{ times.}$$

$$\text{Industry average} = 5.0 \text{ times.}$$

ABC has a fixed charge coverage of 2.4 times, and this does not compare favorably with the industry average. As mentioned above, the firm might have difficulty raising further debt through banking institutions or other means because of this apparent inability to service its fixed charges currently in a manner relative to that of the rest of the industry.

The four leverage ratios indicate that ABC Co. is running out of debt capacity. From the balance sheet, the ratios indicate that the firm is just at or close to the industry norm. From the income statement they indicate poor performance. More meaningful analysis can be done with trend analysis, which shows the firm's position relative to the industry over time.

Activity Ratios

The activity category of ratios measures the firm's ability to utilize its resources effectively. These ratios are compiled with information from both the balance sheet and the income statement.

7. Total Asset Turnover. The total asset turnover ratio measures over-all effectiveness in the utilization of the firm's resources. It is found by dividing sales by total assets. For ABC, this ratio is:

$$\text{Total asset turnover} = \frac{\text{Sales}}{\text{Total assets}} = \frac{\text{Rs. } 1{,}626{,}921}{\text{Rs. } 1{,}451{,}628} = 1.12 \text{ times.}$$

Industry average = 1.51 times.

This indicates ABC is somewhat sluggish in terms of effective utilization of its assets. Two possibilities may account for this: One is that the firm has too many assets for the level of sales it is generating, but if this is simply a temporary situation because the firm has hit a low sales point, there is no cause for concern. The second is that the firm is utilizing its assets inefficiently; an inefficient location for the warehouse, for example, can create a need for more trucks to transfer goods back and forth.

At this point, we would look further into the asset base to see what specific category of assets is causing the problem. We could next examine the turnover ratios for inventory, fixed assets, and accounts receivable.

8. Inventory Turnover. This turnover ratio is calculated by dividing cost of goods sold by inventory. This ratio for ABC Co. is:

$$\text{Inventory turnover} = \frac{\text{Cost of goods sold}}{\text{Inventory}} = \frac{1{,}352{,}479}{638{,}388} = 2.12 \text{ times.}$$

Industry average = 3.40 times.

ABC's inventory turnover of 2.12 does not compare as favorably as it should with the industry ratio of 3.4 times. This may be just a temporary situation, but it is a warning sign that the firm should keep abreast of the situation to see if it continues.

Two problems exist in the calculation and analysis of this ratio. First, there is the conflict between market price and cost. Should sales or cost of goods sold be used in the numerator? Sales are listed at market price, while inventory is usually listed at cost, thus it is more appropriate to use the cost of goods sold figure in place of sales in the numerator. However, many industry sources of information, such as Dun and Bradstreet use sales to inventory with inventory listed at cost. For compatibility with the industry source, the inventory turnover ratio may have to be calculated using sales rather than cost of goods sold.

The second problem involves the use of information from both the balance sheet and the income statement to construct a ratio. Basically the sales figure from the income statement is considered to be a *flow statement* which summarizes the sales from the first day of the period to the last. The balance sheet reflects data at one point in time and is considered to be a stock *statement*. If the business of the firm is highly seasonal or if the firm's sales are subject to wide fluctuations during the course of a year, then a balance sheet inventory for one point in time does not properly reflect the activity in that account during the whole period. It is therefore suggested that an average inventory figure be taken to reflect that activity over the whole year. This is done by taking the figures for the beginning and end of the period, summing them, and dividing by two. It should be remembered, however, that one important factor in ratio analysis is compatibility with industry data. If the industry data do not use an average inventory figure, then the comparison is meaningless unless the ratio is constructed in exactly the same fashion. Since the industry data do not use average inventory, the analysis does not consider it but simply uses inventory for the end of the year.

9. Fixed Asset Turnover. The fixed asset turnover ratio measures the turnover of plant and equipment owned by the firm and evaluates whether the firm has too much plant and equipment on hand for the existing sales level, or whether it is using the existing plant and equipment inefficiently. For ABC, this ratio is:

$$\text{Fixed asset turnover} = \frac{\text{Sales}}{\text{Fixed assets}}$$

$$= \frac{\text{Rs. } 1{,}626{,}921}{\text{Rs. } 366{,}248}$$

$$= 4.44 \text{ times.}$$

$$\text{Industry average} = 6.10 \text{ times.}$$

As the other turnover ratios indicate, ABC is well below the industry average. If this represents a permanent leveling off of sales, it may indicate that the firm should dispose of some of its fixed assets. This ratio clearly indicates that the firm is not operating near its plant and equipment capacity.

10. Average Collection Period. The average collection period ratio measures the average number of days sales are tied up in receivables. It is calculated by dividing the annual receivables figures by total annual credit sales per day. Assuming that all of the sales of ABC are credit sales, this ratio for the firm is:

$$\text{Average-collection period} = \frac{\text{Receivables}}{\frac{\text{Annual credit sales}}{360}}$$

$$= \frac{\text{Rs. } 275{,}738}{\frac{\text{Rs. } 1{,}626{,}921}{360}}$$

$$= \frac{\text{Rs. } 275{,}738}{\text{Rs. } 4{,}519}$$

$$= 61 \text{ days.}$$

$$\text{Industry average} = 55 \text{ days.}$$

It is obvious that ABC is slightly lagging the industry in terms of turning receivables into cash so that the funds can be turned back into the production cycle. The accounts receivable turnover ratio can easily be calculated from the above information by taking 360 days in the year and dividing it by the collection period of 61 days. Thus the turnover ratio is 5.9 times.

Although the average collection period ratio is an important tool, it is still only an average of the entire collection schedule of the firm. In reality, there is no substitute for examining the collection schedule (which is called the *accounts receivable aging schedule*) to keep track of those accounts that are seriously behind in their payments. An accounts receivable aging schedule breaks down the total receivables by 30-day time periods and presents these as a per cent of the total accounts receivable. For ABC, the aging schedule as of December 31, 1987 was:

Aging of accounts (days)	*Aging as a per cent of total*
0–30	40
31–60	26
61–90	15
91–120	11
Over 121	8

It is apparent that a considerable number of accounts receivable are overdue beyond 90 days. The longer these receivables stay uncollected, the more the firm will find itself in a cash crisis, because it must use its own funds to pay its suppliers and other creditors. If the firm ever needs a loan from a bank which agrees to use the accounts receivable as collateral, it is quite likely that no accounts receivable over 90 days will be accepted. This would severely limit the amount the firm could borrow from the bank. In addition, whenever accounts receivable lag beyond 90 days, the probability of ever collecting them is substantially decreased. Typically, the financial manager provides an estimate of the probability of noncollection which, when summed, equals the allowance for doubtful accounts.

The activity ratios for ABC Co. indicate that the firm does not perform very well compared to the industry. A general analysis (total asset turnover) found that the firm was below the industry norm. This problem was centered in the inventory and fixed asset categories. Only in the accounts receivable area did the firm surpass industry averages. More specific conclusions can be stated when the performance of the firm is examined over time.

Profitability Ratios

Profitability ratios measures the overall efficiency of the firm and reflect to a degree all of the other measures of performance that have thus far been examined. Profitability ratios can be measured from the viewpoint of both the relation to sales and the relation to owner's investment.

11. Profit Margins on Sales. Two ratios describe the relative profitability of the firm after deducting certain cost items. The first is the *gross profit margin*, which shows the relative profitability after the cost of goods sold has been deducted from sales. This ratio indicates the operating efficiency in terms of production as well as the efficient pricing of the firm's products. For ABC Co., this ratio is:

$$\text{Gross profit margin} = \frac{\text{Sales less cost of goods sole}}{\text{Sales}}$$

$$= \frac{\text{Rs. } 274{,}442}{\text{Rs. } 1{,}626{,}921} = 16.9\%.$$

Industry average = 24.4%.

ABC's gross profit margin is below the industry average of 24 per cent. Either the firm's cost of production is higher than that in the industry, or its products are underpriced compared to the industry average.

Another measure of profitability in relation to sales is the *net profit margin.* For ABC, this is:

$$\text{Net profit margin} = \frac{\text{Net profit after taxes}}{\text{Sales}}$$

$$= \frac{\text{Rs. } 32{,}753}{\text{Rs. } 1{,}626{,}921} = 2\%.$$

Industry average = 3.4%.

ABC's nět profit margin also is below the industry average. Many firms may have a reasonable gross profit margin and a low net profit margin, primarily due to high operating costs, such as executive salaries or other fixed costs. Both ratios are important to consider in keeping the costs of production and general operations under control.

12. Return on Total Assets. The ratio of return on total assets measures the return available on the assets employed by the firm. Traditionally it is defined as in this ratio for ABC:

$$\text{Net return on total assets} = \frac{\text{Net profit after taxes}}{\text{Total assets}}$$

$$= \frac{\text{Rs. } 32{,}753}{\text{Rs. } 1{,}451{,}628} = 2.3\%.$$

Industry average = 4.0%.

This ratio can be interpreted in a second way. Since total assets (the left side of the balance sheet) equals total liabilities and equities (the right side of the balance sheet), this ratio can also measure the return on invested capital (ROI). Thus it can measure the return to both debt holders and stockholders. The answer would be the same as above; the only difference is that the denominator would be total liabilities and equities instead of total assets.

If a company has significant interest charges, the ratio used above, with net profit after taxes as the numerator, is not appropriate. This is because the return to the debtholders is not being measured. In this case the more appropriate ratio is one that utilizes earnings before interest and taxes (EBIT) in the numerator. This ratio can be called the *net operating return on assets.* For ABC Co., it is:

$$\text{Net operating return on total assets} = \frac{\text{Earnings before interest and taxes (EBIT)}}{\text{Total assets}}$$

$$= \frac{\text{Rs. } 56{,}107 + \text{Rs. } 25{,}984}{\text{Rs. } 1{,}451{,}628}$$

$$= \frac{\text{Rs. } 82{,}091}{\text{Rs. } 1{,}451{,}628} = 5.7\%.$$

Industry average = 7.0%.

Again, ABC is below the industry norm. This ratio could also be called the *net operating return on investment.*

13. Return on net worth. The ratio for return on net worth measures the rate of return available to common shareholders when preferred stock is purposely deleted. It is measured by dividing net earnings available to common shareholders (EAC) by the net worth of the firm. For ABC, this is:

$$\text{Return on net worth} = \frac{\text{Earnings available common shareholders}}{\text{Net worth}}$$

$$= \frac{\text{Rs. } 32{,}753}{\text{Rs. } 840{,}495} = 3.9\%.$$

Industry average = 8.8%.

ABC Co. is again below the industry average of 8.8 per cent. The reasons for this are the same as those for the low return on total assets, that is: the low gross profit margin, and the low turnover of assets.

The profitability ratios have demonstrated that ABC Co. is not performing well when compared to the industry. More conclusions will be discussed in the sections on ratio summary and trend analysis, which follow:

Trend Analysis

Ratio analysis consists of two basic forms of analysis. First, the financial manager can compare a recent ratio with one or several other ratios in the past or with forecast ratios. When ratios are calculated over a number of periods and years, we can actually map the performance of the company over time. This form of analysis is referred to as *trend analysis.* It provides a means to determine whether the company's financial picture is deteriorating or improving.

The second method of comparison involves the use of industry data by which we can compare a particular firm's performance to that of a number of firms in the same industry. A partial trend analysis comparing past performance for both ABC and the industry is presented in Figure 1. In this example, four ratios—one from each category—are presented for the period 1983-87. In terms of liquidity, ABC has substantially deteriorated in its position com-

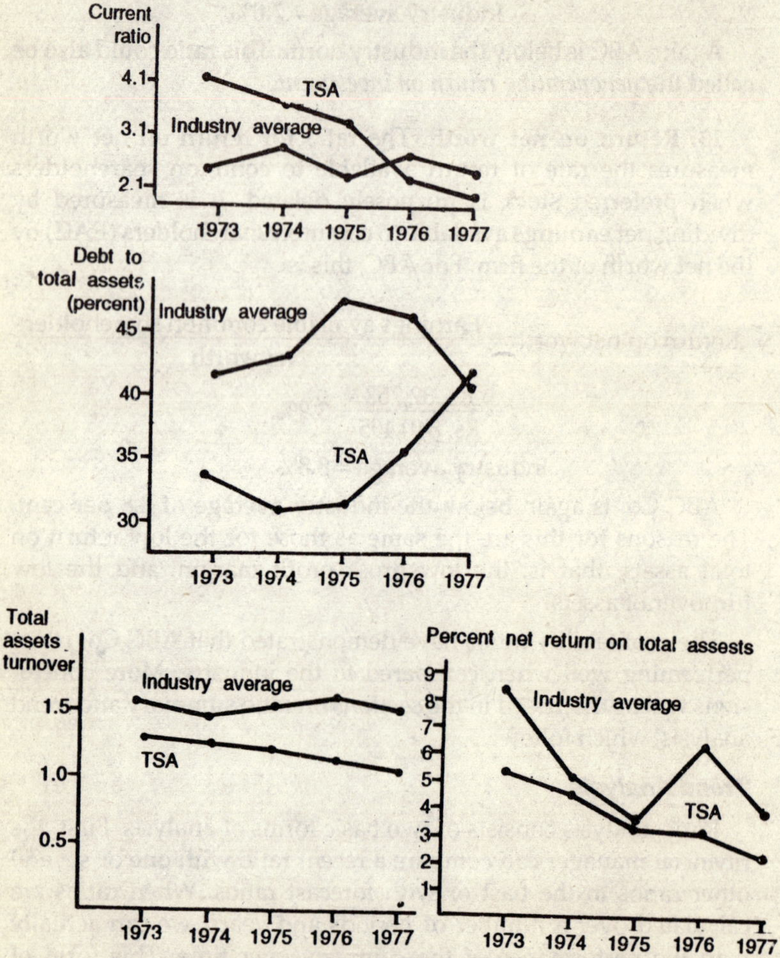

Fig. 1. ABC Co. (Trend Analysis)

pared to the industry. The leverage ratio of debt to total assets indicates that the firm started increasing its leverage position in 1983 and has steadily increased it, up to 42 per cent. The industry, on the other hand, has decreased its leverage position to around 41 per cent.

In terms of total asset turnover, the firm's position has declined since 1983, while the industry also declined in its position but then turned upward in 1986. Note that this decline in turnover coincides with the increased leverage position of the firm. It is possible that the firm increased its leverage position to support the purchase of more equipment for an expected increase in the level of sales. It appears however, that the increase in sales never occurred.

The lack of the expected increase in sales is evident in the return on total assets. While the industry's position slightly increased in 1986, the firm's position deteriorated from 5.6 per cent in 1983 to its current level of 2.3 per cent.

From the analysis presented, it is clear that ABC Co. must take immediate steps to halt the deterioration of its profits position. Its ability to raise additional capital is clearly impaired by the high degree of leverage that currently exists. If sales are not expected to increase immediately, it would be wise for the firm to dispose of some of its assets. This would increase the turnover position and help the profit picture substantially.

EARNING POWER

The relationship between turnover and profitability ratios was mentioned in terms of overall efficiency in the operation of a firm. This relationship is called *earning power*. It clearly demonstrates how too large an asset or investment (liabilities) and stockholder's equity base in relation to a specific sales level can seriously impair profitability.

The relationship is generated by utilizing the total asset or total investment turnover ratio and the profit margin on sales:

$$\text{Earning power} = \frac{\text{Sales}}{\text{Total assets or investment}} \times \frac{\text{Net profit after taxes}}{\text{Sales}}$$

$$= \frac{\text{Net profit after taxes}}{\text{Total assets or investment}}$$

For ABC Co., the relationship is shown as:

$$\text{Earning power} = \frac{\text{Rs. } 1{,}626{,}921}{\text{Rs. } 1{,}451{,}628} \times \frac{\text{Rs. } 32{,}753}{\text{Rs. } 1{,}626{,}921} = \frac{\text{Rs. } 32{,}753}{\text{Rs. } 1{,}451{,}628}$$

$$= 2.3\%.$$

In essence, the two ratios combined have more significance than when they are separated. The total asset or investment turnover ratio by itself ignores profitability, while the profitability ratio ignores the efficient utilization of resources.

The firm could increase its earning power in two ways. First it could increase its turnover ratio by either increasing the sales level or decreasing the asset or investment structure necessary to support the existing level of sales. Either of these suggestions would increase the turnover relation and increase the earning power of the firm. The second method is to increase the profit margin on sales by increasing the net income figure relative to sales. This can be done by increasing the price, decreasing costs, or decreasing the leverage position, which would lower interest expenses.

In general, different kinds of industries will have different relationships between the profit margin on sales and the tangible asset turnover ratios. For example, a firm with a high asset or investment requirement, such as a large industrial firm, will undoubtedly have a low turnover ratio compared to other firms. To continue to be competitive with other firms in attracting investors interested in high earning-power relationships, the firm must compensate for the low turnover ratio with a high profit margin on sales. Other firms, such as those in the retail trade category, will have low asset or investment requirement and a high turnover ratio. Thus they can afford to maintain a lower profit margin on sales and still have earning power that will attract investors.

COMMON-SIZE ANALYSIS

Another type of ratio analysis the financial analyst may find important is *common-size analysis*. This form of analysis examines the financial statements in *per cent form*; this allows us to make an evaluation of each item on the balance sheet and income statement. Table 4 presents a common-size analysis for ABC for 1987.

The analysis of the balance sheet presents each asset, liability, and equity figure as a per cent of total assets. With the income statement, each item is evaluated as a per cent of net sales. In a few instances, each item is evaluated as a per cent of gross income. This occurs when a firm obtains a substantial portion of its income from "other" sources. With a common-size analysis some of the ratios are immediately calculated, such as the debt to total asset ratio and the gross and net profit margins.

The advantage of this form of analysis is that when it is compared to industry data in the form of a common-size analysis, we can immediately compare each balance sheet and income statement item and determine if too many rupees are being invested or expended in a specific category as compared to the industry or other firms of similar asset size. For example, general and administrative expenses for ABC Co., are 7 per cent of sales; if it was determined from industry data that similar firms in the same industry or all firms in the same asset class had general and administrative expenses of only 4 per cent of sales, it would be clear that ABC is out of phase with the industry and should take steps to bring its cost structure in line. Another example might be that, for the industry, accounts receivable are 23 per cent of total assets, while for ABC they are only 19 per cent. This could mean that ABC is turning away a substantial volume of sales by a credit policy which does not extend enough credit to its customers.

Table 4

ABC Co.

Common-Size Analysis
Consolidated Balance Sheet
As on December 31, 1987

(Rs. in thousands)

	1987	*Common size (per cent)*
Assets		
Cash	44,221	3.1
Marketable securities	29,428	2.0
Receivables, net	275,738	19.0
Inventories	638,388	44.0
Total Current Assets	987,775	68.1

	1987	Common size (per cent)
Other investments, at cost	56,829	3.9
Other assets	39,576	2.7
Plant and equipment, net	366,248	25.2
Prepaid expenses and deferred charges	1,200	0.1
Total Assets	1,451,628	100.0
Liabilities and Stockholders' Equity		
Accounts payable	201,155	13.8
Notes payable	238,359	16.4
Accrued taxes	37,742	2.6
Current portion of long-term debt	8,984	0.6
Other current liabilities	10,846	0.8
Total Current Liabilities	497,086	34.2
Long-term debt	114,047	7.9
Common stock (no par)	396,800	27.3
Retained earnings	443,695	30.6
Total Stockholders' Equity	840,495	57.9
Total Liabilities and Stockholders' Equity	1,451,628	100.0

ABC Co.

Common-Size Analysis
Consolidated Profit and Loss Statements
For Year Ended December 11, 1987

(*Rs. in thousands*)

	1987	Common size (per cent)
Sales	1,626,921	100.0
Cost of sales	1,352,479	83.1
General and administrative expenses	111,601	6.9
Selling expenses	76,401	4.7
Profit from Operations	86,440	5.3
Other income	25,748	1.6
Total Income	112,188	6.9
Interest	25,984	1.6
Other expense	30,097	1.9
Net Profit before Income Taxes	56,107	3.4
Income taxes	23,354	1.4
Net Profit	32,753	2.0

This form of analysis can be a very powerful tool for financial analysts in evaluating a particular firm's performance in comparison with the industry or in evaluating similar firms with the same asset size. It is even more powerful when the analysis is extended over a number of years and a trend analysis is developed with the tool of common-size analysis.

UTILITY AND USERS OF FINANCIAL RATIO ANALYSIS

Ratio analysis is used by different persons for different purposes. A banker who is considering extending a loan to an organization will generally be interested in the liquidity and leverage ratios. The banker is interested in the firm's ability to cover its current liabilities and to service existing as well as future debt. A potential equity investor would be more interested in the profitability ratio, along with a measure of the degree of financial leverage in the firm. For internal control purposes, the firm would be interested in examining one or more ratios from each category to get a balanced perspective of its performance over a recent operating period.

If the analysis of a company shows any weak areas, instead of computing only a few ratios (such as one from each category), it would be wise to do a much more extensive ratio analysis. This could pinpoint exactly the areas of weakness in the firm.

In utilizing ratio analysis to measure a firm's relative performance over time, we must be aware that there are characteristics of a particular management or firm which can cause substantial differences in ratio results within an industry. Management's perceptions of the business environment will at times override a decision to utilize industry norms as a level of performance toward which the firm should strive. Management's perceptions are colored by the level of risk it is willing to accept. This issue was discussed in the first chapter in terms of the risk-return trade-offs that must be considered in making financial decisions.

One area where a firm's ratios can deviate from the industry norms because of its management characteristics is its debt capacity. Later in the text we will illustrate how the use of debt can add to a firm's profitability and reduce some of its cost of raising money. If, for example, the industry's debt to total asset ratio is 40 per cent and the firm's ratio is 25 per cent, it may be suggested that the firm should increase its amount of debt. However, the firm's management may be adverse to the risk in herent in increasing the amount of debt, which would increase the amount of fixed interest payments.

Liquidity is another area where a firm's ratio may deviated from the industry norm due to management's perception of risk. One firm may maintain a much larger rupee amount of liquid assets than would be indicated by the industry norm. When the current and quick ratios exceed the industry norms, this can provide the margin of liquidity protection the firm is seeking, but the result of this decision can be a decrease in profitability. High liquidity means that funds are lying idle and not being used for investment in other profitable areas. Also, the higher the operating assets figure is compared to sales, the lower will be the return on operating assets. In essence, the firm may have too large a current asset base for the level of sales it is generating.

Besides management characteristics that can lead to wide deviations in firm's ratios compared to the industry norms, there are characteristics of the firm that can lead to such deviations. One of the prime examples is the issue of size. Some industry sources of data average for the whole industry and do not break the analysis down by a firm's asset size. Small firms have much more difficulty in raising equity funds than large firms and their access to the bond and common stock markets as tools for financing may be limited or nonexistent. As a result, small firms utilize trade credit and bank loans to a much greater degree than large firms do. This can lead to a capital structure that is heavily debt oriented, and therefore smaller firms have leverage ratios that are larger than the industry norms.

In utilizing ratio analysis, therefore, we must incorporate both management and firm characteristics that may explain any deviations in a firm's performance as compared to the industry norm.

3

STATEMENTS OF FINANCIAL ANALYSIS AND FORECASTING

THE financial planning and analysis process is an integral part of the financial manager's job. The subsequent chapters, covering long-term debt and equity funds which are raised infrequently and in large amounts, primarily because the cost per money unit raised by selling such securities decreases as the size of the issue increases. Because of these considerations, it is important that the firm have a working estimate of its total needs for funds for the next few years. It is therefore useful to examine methods of forecasting the firm's overall needs for funds.

We must recognize that firms need assets to make sales; if sales are to be increased, assets must also be expanded. Growing firms require new investments—immediate investment in current assets and, as full capacity is reached, investment in fixed assets as well. New investments must be financed, and new financing carries with it commitments and obligations to service the capital obtained. A growing profitable firm is likely to require additional cash for investments in receivables, inventories, and fixed assets. Such a firm can, therefore, have a cash flow problem. The nature of such type problem, as well as the cause and effect relationship between assets and sales, is the subject matter of this chapter.

The analytical and control tools available to a financial manager provide ways to examine the flow of funds through an organization and certain aspects of financial forecasting. The statement of sources and uses of funds is an excellent tool which can be used on either a historical or a forecast basis to evaluate how the firm obtains sources of funds and where the funds are applied. Thus funds flow analysis is a valuable tool for financial planning beyond the short-run period.

Planning for future financial needs has become one of the most important jobs of the financial manager. The importance of this function is magnified by two factors. First, raising long-term funds through either the debt or equity markets is generally done infrequently and in large amounts, so planning the optimal time to place an issue before the open market is a vital consideration in minimizing the cost to the company. Second, during the course of the business cycle, there are times when money becomes extremely tight and banks are physically unable to lend to some of their customers. If this happens to a firm in a serious cash shortage position, it would be unable to continue operations unless it acquired funds from other sources. Proper financial planning can assist in determining financial needs and the proper time to acquire the funds.

The first part of any financial forecasting plan is establishment of the long-term percentage trends that exist between (1) sales and the balance sheet accounts and (2) sales and the other accounts of the income statement. This information can thus be utilized in a cash budgeting framework to establish short-term financial needs.

For every use of funds in the financial operations of a firm, there must be a corresponding source. While considering the relationship between the balance sheet and income and revenue statement, it could be said that the assets listed in the balance sheet support the sales of the firm, while the liability and equity sections of the balance sheet list the sources for financing the assets.

Figure 1 shows a flow-of-funds cycle that in a sense is never-ending. Before it can start production, a firm must have some cash input. This is usually obtained from an issue of common stock or by incurring some form of debt. The firm will then use some of the cash to acquire fixed assets to start production and to obtain trade credit to buy the raw materials used in the production cycle. It will

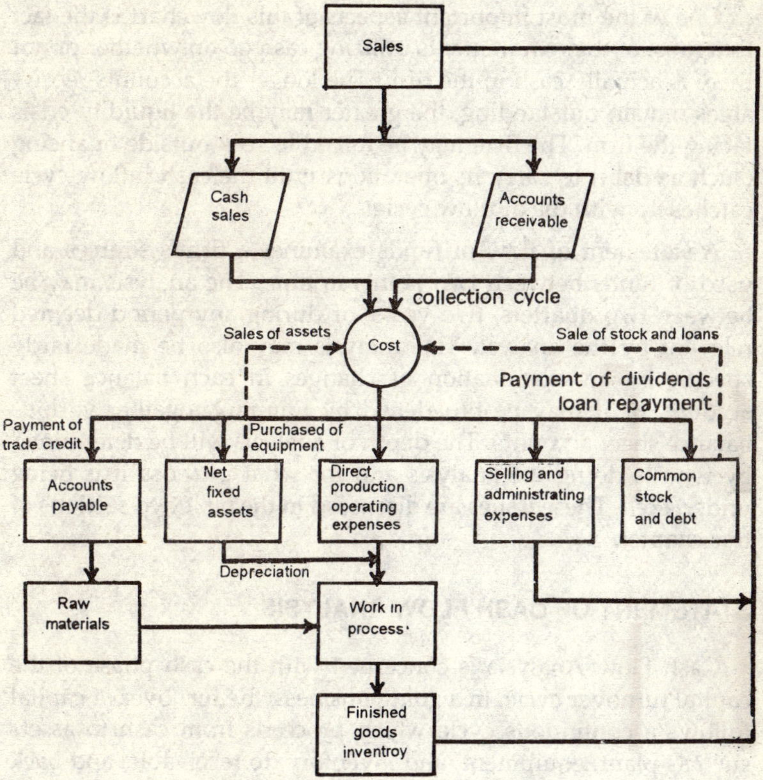

Fig. 1. Internal Funds Flow of a Firm.

use the raw materials and fixed assets, plus cash to pay for operating expenses, to produce a product which become part of the finished goods inventory. It will also use cash to pay for selling and administrative expenses to provide sales, which are in the form of cash or accounts receivable. The cash sales will immediately flow into the cash pool to start the next production cycle, while the accounts receivable will be turned into cash in accordance with the collection cycle of the firm. From the cash pool, the firm can pay its trade credit; buy more assets; apply more cash to operating, production, and selling or administrative expenses; or pay dividends. Thus the cycle continues. Another source of cash would be the sale of assets for cash which would flow back into the cash account.

One of the most important aspects of this flowchart is the fact that most of the requirements utilizing cash go on whether or not there is actually cash in the firm. The longer the accounts receivables remain outstanding, the greater may be the liquidity crisis facing the firm. The firm may be forced to seek outside financing (such as debt) to carry its operations until the cash inflow cycle catches up with the outflow cycle.

A statement of flow of funds examines a firm's sources and used of funds between two points in time. The analysis may be between two quarters, two years, or during any period deemed relevant by the analyst. The analysis may also be made fairly specific by an examination of changes in each balance sheet account, or it may be broadened by lumping together various balance sheet accounts. The depth of analysis will be determined by who is doing the analysis and for what purpose it is being undertaken. These issues are discussed in the next two sections of this chapter.

STATEMENT OF CASH FLOW ANALYSIS

Cash Flow Analysis is concerned with the cash phase of the capital turnover cycle. In a going business, the turnover of capital follows a continuous cycle which proceeds from cash to assets such as plant, equipment, and inventory; to receivable; and back to cash. Significant figures which describe the cash phase are (1) cash balance at any given time, (2) rate of cash flow (inflow, outflow, net increase or decrease) per unit of time, and (3) financial ratios which relate cash and cash flow figures to other associated indicators of financial position and performance.

Reasons

A company must have enough cash to meet obligations as they mature, and management has customarily met this problem by carrying cash balances supplemented by sources of credit which experience has shown to be adequate for the purpose. In recent years, emphasis has been placed on cash flow to guide management in deploying its liquid capital resources most effectively. Financial management has become increasingly aware that, while capital in the form of cash or equivalent assets can earn a return, this rate of return is generally much below the rate that can be earned from investments in other types of business assets. Also, in a period of inflation, holding cash entails a loss of purchasing power. Hence cash balances are held at minimum levels consistent with anticipated requirements in order that cash in excess of such requirements can be promptly invested.

Cash flow has also come into widespread use by investors as an indicator of credit worthiness, as an index of management's opportunity to shift a company's capital into areas offering the most attractive rates of return, and as a measure of ability to pay dividends when undivided profits are available. Interest in cash flow analysis reflects a business environment characterized by rapid technological change and growth. It also reflects wider divergence between cash flow and periodic net profits as accounting methods have become increasingly affected by tax considerations.

Cash may be defined as "capital in the form of cash or equivalent assets available at management's discretion for meeting obligations as they mature or for investment in operating assets." Usually included are temporary investments made to hold cash, provided such investments can be converted to cash without material delay or loss when needed for disbursements. Excluded are assets such as plant, equipment, and inventories which cannot be converted into cash for making current disbursements without impairing future revenues. The definition reflects the intent to measure funds available for disbursement in the immediate or near future.

Cash Forecasts

Management needs reliable information about cash balances and cash flow to guide financial planning and current administration of cash assets. Since decisions relate to the future, forecasts of cash movements constitute the principal sources of data for the purpose. Historical data are useful only insofar as they give an insight into the future. Some of the information needed in management of cash may be developed in the processes of budgeting and accounting, but additional procedures are required.

Three distinct patterns are distinguishable in cash forecasts:

(1) Forecasts of cash receipts and disbursements by days or weeks for periods ranging from one to six weeks ahead. These

forecasts show adequacy of cash balances to meet disbursements, guide transfers of cash between company locations and bank accounts, and show how much cash is available for temporary investment on a day-by-day basis. Anticipated cash collections and scheduled disbursements constitute the basic data for these short period forecasts. Ordinarily they are used only by financial management.

(2) Forecasts of cash flows and balances for the coming year by months and quarters. The principal purposes served by monthly forecasts are to disclose periods of cash shortage in time for loans to be arranged and to show when excess cash will be available for temporary investment. Knowing when cash will be available and when it will be needed, investment media and maturities can be selected to obtain the best available yields together with the desired degree of liquidity. Forecasting proceeds by scheduling receipts and disbursements, or more commonly, by adjusting budgeted income to an approximate cash basis.

(3) Long-range forecasts of cash flow covering periods of several years in advance. Such forecasts serve primarily to indicate amounts and timing of internally generated cash available for capital expenditures or the amounts of additional cash which must be provided to support a given program. The long-range cash forecast is an aspect of over-all long-range financial planning.

The purpose of a funds flow statement on a cash basis is to verify the changes that have occurred in the cash account. A statement of flow of funds on a cash basis is prepared by (1) examining the changes in the balance sheet accounts that increase and decrease cash, (2) examining the factors in the income statement that increase and decrease cash and (3) consolidating the data into statement of sources and uses of funds. *Sources of funds* arise from the following changes:

1. Net decreases in any non-cash asset.
2. Net increases in any liability account.
3. Proceeds from the sale of any stock.
4. Cash provided from operations.

Uses of funds consist of the following items:

1. Net increases in any noncash asset.
2. Net decreases in any liability account.

3. A gross increase in fixed assets.
4. Retirement of stock.
5. Cash dividends.

An example of the construction of a statement of sources and uses of funds on the cash basis is provide in Table 1. Using the hypothetical example of ABC Co. we can construct a statement of sources and uses of funds from the balance sheet and income statement information provided in previous chapter. Table 1 shows the sources and uses of funds for the firm's fiscal year ending March 31, 1987. When the uses are subtracted from the sources, the difference should be equal to the change in the cash position between the two statements.

Table 1

ABC Co.

Sources and Uses of Funds—Cash Basis
As of March 31, 1986 through March 31, 1987

(*Rs in thousands*)

Sources		*Uses*	
Funds from operation:		Dividends	29,760
Net profit	32,753	Fixed asset investment	8,450
Depreciation	25,500	Increase in marketable securities	19,828
Decrease in prepaid expenses	7,900		
Increase in accounts payable	40,458	Increase in receivables, net	19,409
Increase in notes payable	67,402	Increase in inventories	63,900
Increase in accrued taxes	2,919	Increase in other investments	35,282
Increase in current portion long-term debt	2,509	Increase in other assets	35,029
Increase in other current liabilities	5,348		
Increase in long-term debt	23,024		
Subtotal	207,813		
Decrease-Cash account	3,845		
	211,658		211,658

An examination of the ABC Co., data shows that the firm utilized funds to pay dividends, to increase its fixed asset investment, to increase marketable securities and accounts receivables, and to increase the other investment and asset accounts. Primary sources of funds came from operations, an increase in accounts payable, and an increase in short-term as well as long-term debt. As the uses slightly exceeded the sources of funds, there was a decrease in the cash position of Rs. 3.8 million.

It appears that some of the changes in the ABC balance sheet from 1986 to 1987 have contributed to the firm's poor financial performance. The largest single use of funds was for an increase in inventory. When this is related to the inventory turnover ratio, it helps explain why the firm is below the industry average. However, as outsiders utilizing this type of analysis, we cannot draw any value judgments from what we observe without first questioning management as to its motives for expanding the level of inventory. There was a substantial increase in other investment and other assets. These accounts are not defined to an outsider utilizing only published data on a company. Without inside information as to what comprises these accounts, no evaluation should be made. A substantial amount was paid out in dividends. Any comments related to this item must be put into perspective with the firm's and industry's dividend history.

It appears from that a substantial part of the sources of funds for ABC in 1986–87 came from increases in the liability portion of the balance sheet. It would be expected that an increase in inventories would be financed to a large extent by an increase in accounts payable; this appears to be verified in Table 1. The total impact of the increase in the amount of debt is reflected in the leverage ratios. The firm has exceeded the industry norm for both the debt to total asset and the debt to net worth ratios. Of greater concern, however, is the substantial increase in interest-bearing debt shown in Table 1.

FUNDS FLOW STATEMENT

An analyst preparing a financial statement may only be interested in analyzing changes in working capital as a general category, rather than considering each asset and liability account separately. By combining the net changes in the current asset and current liability accounts, we can obtain a statement of sources and uses of funds on a working capital basis. (see Table 2) The only difference between the two statements is that this one lumps together the current asset and current liability accounts; the analysis of the statement remains basically the same.

Table 2

ABC Co.

Sources and Uses of Funds—Working Capital Basis
As of December 31, 1986 through December 31, 1987

(*Rs. in thousands*)

Sources	*Amount*	*Uses*	*Amount*
Funds provided by operations:		Dividends	29,760
Net profit	32,753	Fixed asset investment	8,450
Depreciation	25,500	Increase in other investments	35,282
Increase in long-term debt	23,024	Increase in other assets	35,029
Decrease in prepaid expenses and deferred charges	7,900		
Decrease in working capital*	19,344		
	108,521		108,521

* Reconciliation with sources and uses of funds on cash basis

Net change in current assets	99,292
Net change in current liabilities	118,636
Decrease in working capital	(19,344)

Bankers and other credit analysts who are interested in determining whether an applicant can maintain a specified minimum working capital position would be examples of particular groups interested in a funds flow analysis on a working capital basis.

Flow of Funds Analysis

As an analytical tool for the financial analyst, the flow-of- funds analysis provides a great deal of information on the financial operating aspects on the firm. It can be used as a historical tool to examine several statements over time in order to determine how the uses of funds relate to the goal of utilizing the firm's resources efficiently, and whether asset balances have been maintained beyond the amount necessary to support existing sales levels.

In addition, it can be used to trace financing sources to determine the relationship between internal and external financing and to decide whether or not shifts need to be made to secure the financial future of the firm. Flow-of-funds analysis can also used to examine the future position of the firm by constructing statements of sources and uses of funds from pro forma financial statements. By utilizing this tool in a forecasting framework, management can determine not only the future financial needs of the firm but also how they should be allocated among financing sources.

LONG-RANGE FINANCIAL PLANNING

Long-Range Planning is a systematic process for purposefully directing and controlling the future activities of the enterprise for periods extending beyond one year. It does more than merely predict the future, for it is above all a program of intended action and desired result.

Unlike *forecasting* which is restricted to predicting the future, the fundamental aim of all business *planning* is to exercise some degree of control over the business and its environment in order to exert a favorable influence over future events.

The distinctive feature of long-range planning is the aim of imposing before-the-fact control over the results of events that may take place as much as 5, 10, or even 25 years ahead. The choice of the time span for the plan is often influenced by the special characteristics of the company and its industry. For example, a public utility company with a large investment in capital equipment may plan 25 years ahead; whereas a lumber company may have a 50 or 100-year reforestation program; and conversely, a small firm manufacturing consumer products may need to plan no more than two years ahead. But a cursory survey of actual practice indicates that the time span in long-range planning typically ranges from two to ten years, with a decided preference for a five-year period. A period longer than five or ten years is seldom used, apparently because of the extreme uncertainty inherent in planning for more extended time periods.

Ideally the long-range plan should be both an operational and a strategic plan, integrated with short-range planning so that each year the first year of the long-range plan becomes the basis for the current year's financial operating plan. The formal planning document expressing the actions and results that have been preplanned should be kept current, so that it will always correspond with corporate objectives. A suitable means for making changes in the plan is to put it on a "rolling base" so that this can be updated and extended every twelve months by dropping the immediately past year and replacing it with a further annual period.

For the conventional five-year plan, the key objectives are usually future profitability and company growth. But it should not be overlooked that in some instances the long-range plan may be in effect, a plan for survival (as a necessary pre-condition to making profit in some later period).

The long-range plan is an *overall* plan for the company, which encompasses all areas of company activity (e.g. marketing, manufacturing, finance) and integrates the subordinate plans for each individual department, function or activity, etc. Therefore while there will be separate plans for research and development, capital facilities, acquisitions and diversifications, product development, etc., each is nonetheless only one aspect of the overall company plan. The financial long-range plan translates these other plans into the common language of finance, and quantifies the projected results in financial terms.

Acceptance

Over the past fifteen years or so, long-range financial planning has been rapidly accepted into the repertory of modern professional management. With its growing popularity, the enthusiasm of its proponents and a large body of professional literature on the subject, it is now widely used by many companies of varying size. In fact, it has successfully moved into the mainstream of management practice as a vital and highly regarded disciplinary tool to optimize long-term results.

There is a crucial need for long-range planning because a growing proportion of total costs now is of the *fixed* type and represents the *continuing costs* of having capacity and maintaining an organization in readiness to manufacture and sell. Greater expenditures for fixed investment in plant and equipment, an increasing number of persons employed on a salary basis, and continuing large-scale long-term commitments for research facilities, training centers, and headquarters staff are indicative of this type of situation. It follows, then, that companies are typically faced with a situation where many of the day-to-day operating decisions are constrained within the framework of managerial decisions made long ago, because the earlier decisions involved forward commitments having long-term implications or payout. Under such circumstances long-range planning becomes not only desirable but mandatory if a company is to grow and prosper.

Processes and Techniques

Long-range planning comprises processes and techniques that are already known and understood: *forecasting, planning, analyzing, controlling*, and *coordinating* are not new in themselves. But in the past these techniques had often been treated as individual managerial tools to be used independently of one another, instead of being used in conjunction or combined in an integrated program for planning and controlling future operations. What is new is the concept of a comprehensive planning program, motivated by profit and geared to the long-term future, and making use of the other known managerial techniques as instruments to help in attaining specific planned objectives.

Stages of Long-Range Planning

Stage I—Long-Range Economic Forecasting. In order to have basic data that will serve as guides in setting company goals it is necessary to forecast the basic overall characteristics of the environment within which business operations will be conducted. It will be prudent to predict prospective *economic, political, sociological, technological, competitive* and other relevant conditions in order to formulate the key assumptions upon which long-range strategy and planning should be based. Some typical factors to be forecast include population, income levels, and buying habits. Such factors are analyzed to outline the prospective developments that will influence the market during the planning period. These long-range economic foreeasts do not in themselves constitute firm plans, but serve instead as guides for planning and policy making, and in the preparation of plans and budgets. (See Business Forecasting.) Company long-range strategy goals, financial objectives, and product strategy are all conditioned by and influenced by this prediction of the future and the eventual estimation as to what the *optimum attainable results* would be.

Stage II—Determining Long-Range Goals. Having determined the basic features of the future environment (including estimated size of the overall market, nature of competition, potential market share, etc.) management formulates overall company policy for the intended future development of the business; establishes long-range goals; and determines the basic strategies (e.g. diversification, acquisition, research) for achieving them. These goals, which are expressed in terms of markets to be served, products to be sold, and targets for sales and profit performance, etc., will be ultimately translated into specific objectives.

Stage III—Specific Planning Objectives and Sales Forecasting. The specific planning objectives identify the business operations, plus the key sales and profit results desired. The next stage therefore is the preparation of long-range sales revenue forecasts reflecting the planned level of operations. Such forecasts will specify and identify (both in total and by interim time segment) the rupee amount, physical volume, product mix, market mix, market share, and other relevant sales details.

It may also be necessary to translate the overall company plan into individual plans for the major components of company activity. Thus there will be separate but coordinated individual specialized plans for such areas as: *Marketing*, and related advertising, promotion, and distribution activities; *Production*, and related manufacturing, organization, and manpower activities; *Engineering*, and related design, styling and testing activities.

Stage IV—Organization and Facilities Planning. This stage involves the planning of the level and type of organization and facilities that will be needed. The principal purposes of the facilities plan are:

(1) Determination of the amount, type, and desired timing of future requirements for physical facilities, manpower, etc.

(2) Provision of the lead-time necessary to construct facilities, develop an organization, and arrange necessary financing.

(3) Determination of priorities for the allocation of funds.

(4) Provision of the proper capacity at a minimum of expense.

(5) Optimum use of capacity.

Since these requirements for facilities etc. imply expenditures for future years, the plans should be expressed in terms of the money needed to provide the facilities so that the capital budget may be prepared from these data.

Stage V—Capital Budgeting. Data prepared for the facilities plan form the basis for preparing a program of projected capital investments, and for drawing up the capital budget for the related capital expenditures. Planning and control of expenditures for investment in plant and equipment are achieved through the capital budget, which provides a means for the comparative evaluation of investment projects, the selection of those with the highest priorities, and the forecasting of cash disbursements.

Stage VI—Long-Range Cash Forecasting. Forecasts of cash flows are important in the financial planning of capital expenditures and for working capital for future operations because they have an important role in:

(1) Selecting investment projects.

(2) Determining the amount and timing of the cash needed.

(3) Forecasting the time when cash can be recovered for reinvestment, payment of debts, dividends etc.

State VII—Other Planning. Consistent with other areas of financial planning, and coordinated with all functions and activities that are planned, it is also necessary to plan company capital structure and financial position, profits and return on capital employed, etc. Expenses must be budgeted; shorter-range plans must be prepared and integrated with the long-range plan; financial results must be projected and measured; and all relevant financial aspects must ultimately find their expression in the long-range planning document.

LONG-TERM FINANCIAL FORECASTING TECHNIQUES

Following text examines several techniques by which valid sales forecasts can be generated and balance sheet relationships developed. To utilize these techniques effectively, it is important to obtain data on a company for a number of years so that proper relationships can be developed.

Percent-of-Sales Method

Simply defined, the percent-of-sales method of forecasting develops a relationship between sales and some of the variable portions of the balance sheet and income statement. The success with which this method is applied depends entirely on the validity of the sales forecast. The next method of financial forecasting to be discussed (simple linear regression) assists in determining that forecast. For now assume that the forecast has been established and that sales are expected to increase from Rs. 1 million to Rs. 1.6 million over the next year.

Management of ADA Corporation, another hypothetical example, has observed that over a ten-year period the asset accounts of cash, accounts receivable, and inventories have varied directly with sales. On the liabilities side, accounts payable and accrued wages and taxes have been observed to vary directly with sales. Management also has concluded that the amount in each account represents an efficient level to support that particular sales level. Table 3 shows the exact percentage relationship, which represents a weighted average over the past ten years. In addition to the percentage relation between sales and the asset accounts, management also has determined that net income after taxes has been approximately 3 per cent of sales. It is assumed that there is enough fixed asset capacity to generate the new sales.

Table 3

Variable Portion of Balance Sheet Expressed as a Per cent of Sales for ADA Corporation

Assets		*Liabilities*	
Cash	5%	Accounts payable 15%	
Receivable (net)	15	Accrued taxes and wages	5
Inventories	20		
Total Variable Assets	40%	Total Variable Liabilities	20%
Net income as a percent of sales = 3%			

One of the key assumptions in the utilization of this concept is that management should strive for an optimal asset base to support a given level of sales. Once that optimal asset base has been reached, a firm will want to change its assets only if the level of sales has increased or decreased.

Table 4 shows the asset requirements necessary to support an increase in sales of Rs. 600,000, and the amount needed to finance the assets. For a Rs. 600,000 increase in sales, the assets that very directly with sales must increase by Rs. 240,000. Spontaneous sources of financing in the form of accounts payable and accruals will provide Rs. 120,000. Net income on total sales will provide Rs. 48.000. This leaves Rs. 72,000 to be financed from external sources.

Table 4

ADA Corporation
Forecasted External Financing Needs
(using percent-of-sales forecasting method)

Assets		*Liabilities*	
Cash	30,000	Accounts payable	90,000
Receivable (net)	90,000	Accrued taxes and wages	30,000
Inventories	120,000		
Total Variable Assets	240,000	Total Variable Liabilities	120,000

Increase in assets	240,000
Less: Spontaneous financing	120,000
Total Needed Financing	120,000
Less: Net income	48,000
Total Needed External Financing	72,000

Once the decision is made regarding the extent of the financing requirements, management can evaluate the alternatives available for raising the needed external capital. In this kind of analysis, it is important to leave the external sources of financing (such as notes payable and common stock) constant so that the internally generated analysis will determine the amount of external financing needed.

The percent-of-sales method of forecasting can assist management in determining the future financial position of the firm. However, the method is only as accurate as the estimated relationship over time between sales and the various income statement and balance sheet accounts.

A major objection to this technique is that it tends to view the firm in a static situation, with fixed relationships between sales and other accounts. If, for example, we examine the relationships between sales and the various income statement and balance sheet accounts over a ten-year period and find that there was not a constant relationship between these accounts, a real problem exists. How do you establish a single percentage relationship between sales and a particular account when for each of the ten years a different relationship may have existed? Or how would the situation be handled when a definite increasing or decreasing trend developed in the relationship? In the first instance, we might take a simple average of the data. But this does not allow us to consider relative magnitudes of change. In the latter case, we could take a weighted average, but then the problem arises as to the definition of the relative weights.

A second major objection to this technique is that it can provide biased results in terms of the forecast of the various balance sheet accounts. This issues will be discussed later in this chapter. To overcome the objections to the percent-of-sales method, some technique of forecasting that is considered to be more accurate can be used.

Simple Linear Regression

The linear regression method of forecasting determines the relationship between two variables through a mathematical process. We can utilize a computer, or we can determine the relationship graphically. This method is conceptualized in the equation:

$$y = a + bx,$$

where:

y = The dependent variable.

a = The intercept value, or constant term if using a computer.

b = The slope of the line, or regression coefficient if using a computer.

x = The independent variable.

This method is classified as *simple* because it considers only two variables—one independent and one dependent variable. It is *linear* because it assumes a linear relationship between the variables. It is a *regression* technique because it attempts to determine the nature of the relationship between the independent and dependent variables.

Forecasting Sales. In utilizing this method to develop pro forma statements, the first step would be to develop a sales forecast. This is done by developing a relationship between a firm's sales and some measure of aggregate economic activity. It might be felt that the company's sales are best related to gross national product; therefore we would collect data on the company's sales and GNP for a number of periods and either plot the relationship on a graph or feed the data into a computer. It is important that data be collected for a number of observable periods so that a proper relationship can be developed. Table 5 shows GNP and sales data for 13 past years for the Jones Corporation.

Table 5

GNP and Sales Data for Jones Corporation

	Sales (in millions)	*Gross National Product (in billions, current Rupees)*
1964	Rs. 1,000	Rs. 632
1965	1,120	685
1966	1,175	750
1967	1,225	794
1968	1,300	864
1969	1,370	930
1970	1,425	982
1971	1,450	1,054
1972	1,550	1,171
1973	1,620	1,306
1974	1,700	1,413
1975	1,800	1,516
1976	1,950	1,692

If we are using the graphic solution to this problem, the next step is to graph the data points over the past years, as shown in Figure 2. The third step is to use a ruler and draw a line of best fit through the data points such that the distance between the individual data points and the regression line is minimized. In essence, this is what a regression line accomplishes. This is shown in Figure 3. Note that in the example the measure of aggregate economic activity will be the independent variable, and the sales figures will be dependent upon changes in GNP.

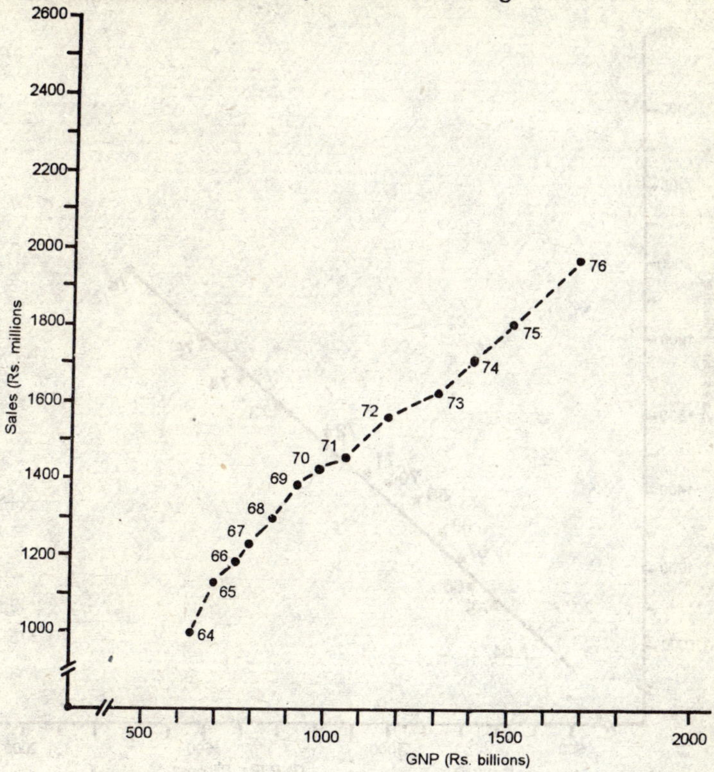

Fig 2. Plots of Sales and GNP, Jones Corporation.

Once the relationship has been established graphically, we can proceed to forecast sales. Government data provide forecasts of future GNP. To determine future sales, we extend or extrapolate the regression line, plot future GNP, and then read the future sales level from the regression line. These steps are shown in Figure 4.

If, for example, a 1980 forecast of GNP of Rs. 2.442 trillion were obtained, we could forecast 1980 sales at Rs. 2.56 billion. This is done by finding the GNP forecast, drawing a vertical line up to the regression line, and then drawing a horizontal line to the sales axis.

Graphic regression analysis illustrates the concept quite well. However, it could lead to a forecasting error if the line of best fit or regression line is not accurately drawn. This is why regression analysis is usually done with the aid of the computer. The data in

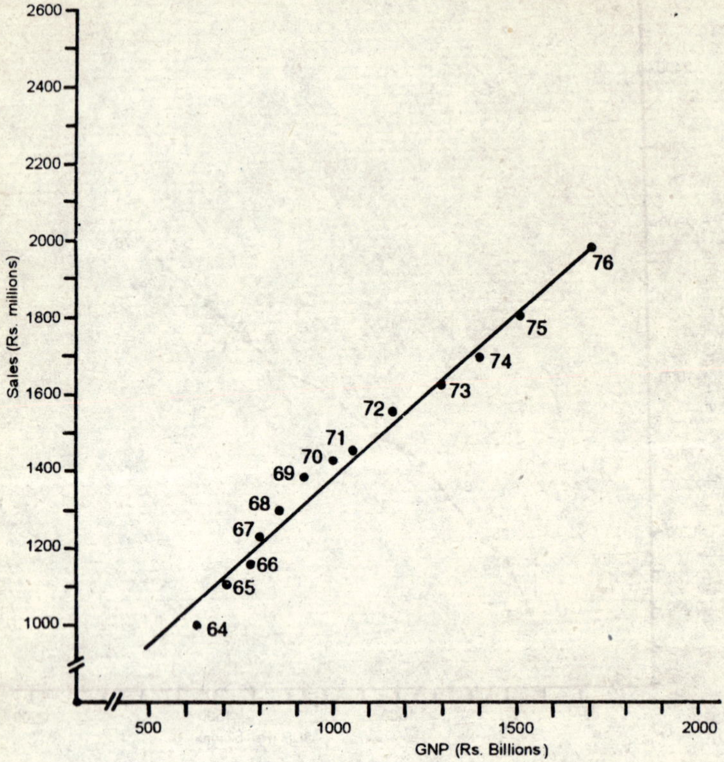

Fig. 3. Plot of Sales and GNP, with Regression Line, Jones Corporation.

Table 5 are fed into the computer, and the results are expressed in the format of Equation $y = a + bx$. For our example, the computer would give the following results:

$$y = 0.56174 + 0.00083 \text{ GNP}$$

If we wanted to forecast 1980 sales, we would input the forecasted GNP for 1980 (Rs. 2.442 trillion) and obtain the following results:

$$y = 0.56174 + 0.00083 \cdot \text{Rs. } 2.44 \text{ trillion}$$

$$y = 0.56174 + \text{Rs. } 2.0268 \text{ billion}$$

$$= \text{Rs. } 2.5886 \text{ billion}$$

The Rs. 2.59 billion sales forecast for 1990 with the computer is right or target with the graphic forecast of Rs. 2.6 billion. The only

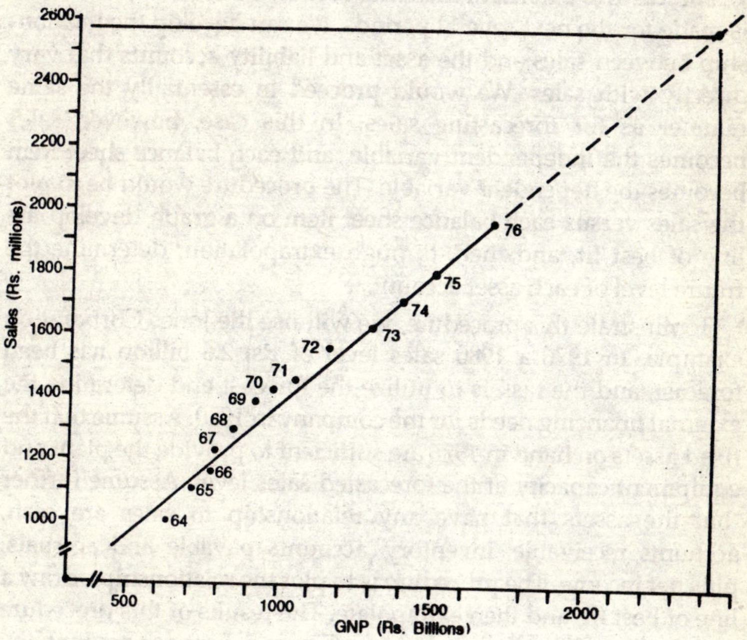

Fig. 4. Forecasting Future Sales, Jones Corporation.

problem with the graphic analysis is that there is no mechanism to indicate whether a good relationship between the independent and dependent variables has been developed. We can forecast with any relationship, but the question is whether or not the forecast is accurate.

The computer provides a measure of relative it called the *coefficient of determination.* This coefficient, which can have a value from 0 to 1.00, indicates numerically the strength of the relationship. In our example, the coefficient of determination (frequently called r^2) was equal to 0.985. This means that the independent variable explains 98.5 per cent of the variation in sales. Thus we do have a good fit and are provided with what appears to be a good forecast, assuming that the 9.6 per cent compound annual growth rate can be sustained in GNP.

Forecasting External Financing Needs. Once the sales forecast is made for the next several periods, we can develop the relationship between sales and the asset and liability accounts that vary directly with sales. We would proceed in essentially the same manner as for forecasting sales. In this case, however, sales becomes the independent variable, and each balance sheet item becomes the dependent variable. The procedure would be to plot the sales versus each balance sheet item on a graph develop the line of best fit, and then, through extrapolation, determine the future level of each asset account.

To illustrate this procedure, we will use the Jones Corporation example. In 1976 a 1980 sales level of Rs. 2.6 billion has been forecast, and the task is to utilize the forecast and determine the external financing needs for the company in 1980. Assume that the fixed assets on hand in 1976 are sufficient to provide the plant and equipment capacity at the forecasted sales level. Assume further that the assets that have any relationship to sales are cash, accounts receivable, inventory, accounts payable and accruals, plus net income. The procedure is to plot the relationships, draw a line of best fit, and then extrapolate. The results of this procedure and the line of best fit, are shown in Figure 5. For each account, the independent variable, sales, is shown on the horizontal axis, and the dependent variable is shown on the vertical axis. With a forecasted sales level of Rs. 2.6 billion, we find that point on the horizontal axis, draw a vertical line to the regression line, and then draw a horizontal line to the vertical axis. This gives the forecast of the dependent variable.

The next task is to utilize this information to determine the external financing needs for 1980. Table 6 presents the 1976 data of the Jones Corporation for the five balance sheet items in question. Table 7 shows the forecasted information for the same five balance sheet items in 1980, obtained from Figure 5. Table 8 shows the forecast financing external needs for the company in 1980. With an increase in sales, total increases in assets related to sales have amounted to Rs. 186 million. Spontaneous sources have increased by Rs. 57 million. Thus the total financing need is Rs. 129 million. Of this amount, net income after taxes is forecast to be Rs. 44

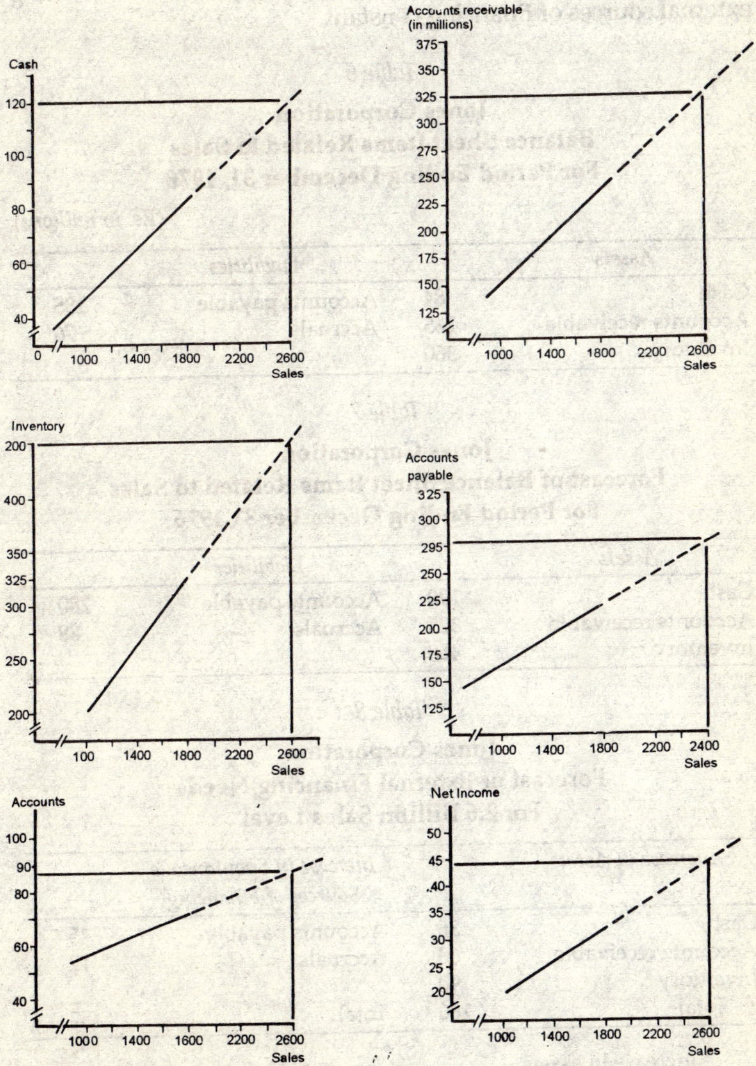

Fig. 5. Regression Results for Balance Sheet and Net Income Accounts, Jones Corporation (in millions).

million, which leaves Rs. 85 million to be financed externally. As with the percent-of-sales method, we always hold all existing external sources of financing constant.

Table 6

Jones Corporation
Balance Sheet Items Related to Sales
For Period Ending December 31, 1976

(Rs. in millions)

Assets		*Liabilities*	
Cash	84	Accounts payable	235
Accounts receivable	265	Accruals	76
Inventory	360		

Table 7

Jones Corporation
Forecast of Balance Sheet Items Related to Sales
For Period Ending December 31,1976

Assets		*Liabilities*	
Cash	120	Accounts payable	280
Accounts receivable	325	Accruals	88
Inventory	450		

Table 8

Jones Corporation
Forecast of External Financing Needs
For 2.6 Billion Sales Level

Increase in Assets		*Increase in Spontaneous Sources of Financing*	
Cash	36	Accounts payable	45
Accounts receivable	60	Accruals	12
Inventory	90		
Total	186	Total	57

Increase in assets	186
Less: Spontaneous financing	57
Total Needed Financing	129
Less: Net income*	44
Total Needed External Financing	85

* The net income figure is from the forecast in Figure 5.

Comparison of Percent-of-sales and Simple Linear Regression Methods: The simple linear regression technique of forecasting can be used to forecast sales as well as external financing needs. In this respect, it has an advantage over the percent-of-sales method. Also, from a mechanical point of view, the simple linear regression method makes it possible to develop a more realistic relationship between the independent and dependent variables. In terms of forecasting accuracy, the regression technique also has advantages.

Because the simple linear regression form of forecasting is more exact than the percent-of-sales method, it is less likely to create errors in the forecast as sales deviate from current levels. The greater error possible in the percent-of-sales method results from its basic assumption. Both methods assumes that the relationship between sales and a particular asset or liability account is linear, but the percent-of-sales method assumes that the linear relationship goes through the origin, as illustrated in Figure 6.

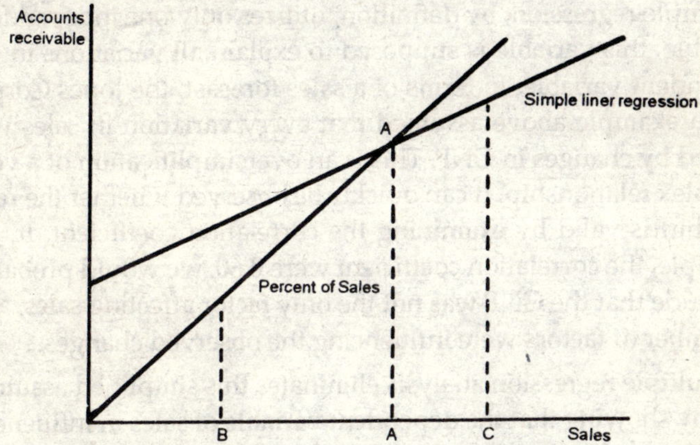

Fig. 6. Percent-of-Sales Versus Simple Linear Regression Methods.

It is unrealistic to assume that at a zero level of sales, there will be a zero balance of accounts receivable or any other asset or liability account. Yet this is the assumption of the percent- of-sales method of forecasting. The simple linear regression technique does not make this assumption. A comparison of sales and accounts receivable figures will show the increasing error of the percent-of-sales method. This error of forecasting is shown as the shaded part of Figure 6.

Point A in Figure 6 is associated with the current sales level. At this point, both methods provide the same results, which implies that there is no forecasting error. However, as sales deviate from this point, say to points B or C, the error increases. At point B, which would be associated with a forecast below the current levels, the percent-of-sales method would understate the true relationship between sales and accounts receivable. This would result in a forecast that underestimates the accounts receivable figure. At point C, the percent-of-sales method overstates the relationship between sales and accounts receivable. This occurs when the sales level is above the current level. The overstatement of the relationship would lead to an overestimate of the accounts receivable figure.

Given a choice of utilizing one or the other forecasting techniques, the simple linear regression method is to be preferred.

Multiple Regression Analysis

Simple regression, by definition, utilizes only one independent variable; this variable is supposed to explain all variations in the dependent variable. In terms of a sales forecast, the Jones Corporation example above assumed that every variation in sales was caused by changes in GNP. This is an oversimplification of a very complex relationship. It can quickly be observed whether the relationship is valid by examining the correlation coefficient. If, for example, the correlation coefficient were 0.60, we would probably conclude that the GNP was not the only factor affecting sales, and a number of factors were influencing the observed changes.

Multiple regression analysis eliminates this simplified assumption by showing that the dependent variable of sales in influenced by a host of independent variables. The equation form of this analysis is shown as:

$$y = f\,(bx_1 + cx_2 + dx_3 + \ldots\ldots + nx_n)\,,$$

where:

y = Dependent variable.

b through n = Coefficients of the independent variables.

x_1 through x_n = Values of the various independent variables.

f = Functional notation.

An example of the multiple regression technique can be demonstrated by the automobile industry, where there is a clean relationship between a number of independent variables and the demand for industry automobile sales. In the development of the demand equation for automobiles it is clear that sales are not related simply to personal income but rather to a number of different factors. An equation that would explain the demand for new domestic automobiles would be:

$$y = f(P, PDI, N, La, U, d, m, r)$$

where:

y = Industry automobile sales.
P = Per unit price.
PDI = Personal disposal income.
N = A measure of population growth such as the number of persons reaching the driving age.
La = Liquid assets of the country.
U = A measure of automobiles replacement demand such as used automobiles on the highway.
d = Required down payment for purchasing an automobile.
m = Loan maturity on automobile loans.
r = Interest rate applicable the automobile loan.

As each of these independent variables changes by either increasing or decreasing, it will have an influence on automobile demand. Negative influences on automobile demand are reflected by increases in the independent variables of price, used automobiles, required down payment, and interest rate. Positive influences are reflected by increases in personal disposable income, in the population growth measure, liquid assets, and the maturity of the loan. Thus the demand for automobiles is dependent not only on changes in personal income but also in price, liquid assets, replacement demand, population, down payment, maturity of loan, and interest rate.

Once developed, the relationship is tested through the use of a multiple regression computer program. As with simple regression, the model is tested by a collecting data on each of the variables over a number of years, placing the data in the computer and running the program. With more than two variables, we cannot graph the relationship in two-dimensional space. The computer output provides information by which the model can be evaluated. First, a coefficient of determination, which is the correlation coefficient squared, is given. This provides a measure of how well all the variables explain the variation in the industry sales. In addition, the specific regression coefficient for each independent variable is provided, along with a partial correlation coefficient that explains how each independent variable correlates to the dependent variable of industry sales. If the partial correlation coefficient is low, we can eliminate that variable, add another independent variable that is felt to influence sales, and run the model through the computer again to see if the revised model describes the variation in industry sales more accurately.

To develop a forecasting procedure fully, multiple regression may be utilized to first determine industry sales. We would then determine the firm's sales by applying our knowledge of the market share each firm holds within the industry. Once the firm's future sales are determined through this more sophisticated process, the simple linear regression method may be employed to determine the pro forma balance sheet and income statement. If it has been determined that some of the balance sheet items have other factors influencing changes in these accounts in addition to sales, it will be necessary to use the multiple regression method to develop these balance sheet items. This is done by setting the individual balance sheet items as the dependent variable and determining all of those factors that will influence changes in that account.

CASH FORECASTING

Once long-range forecasting have been developed, as illustrated in the 13-year forecast for Jones Corporation, it is important to examine the future of the company on a shorter term basis to define more explicitly, from month to month or quarter to quarter, its goals and financial needs. This task is accomplished through a budgeting framework such as that shown in Figure 7. Starting with the corporate goal structure, management will determine a long-term strategy for a given period (for example, five years). This phase would develop a product mix strategy, a long-term sales forecast, and possibly a long-term pro forma bal-

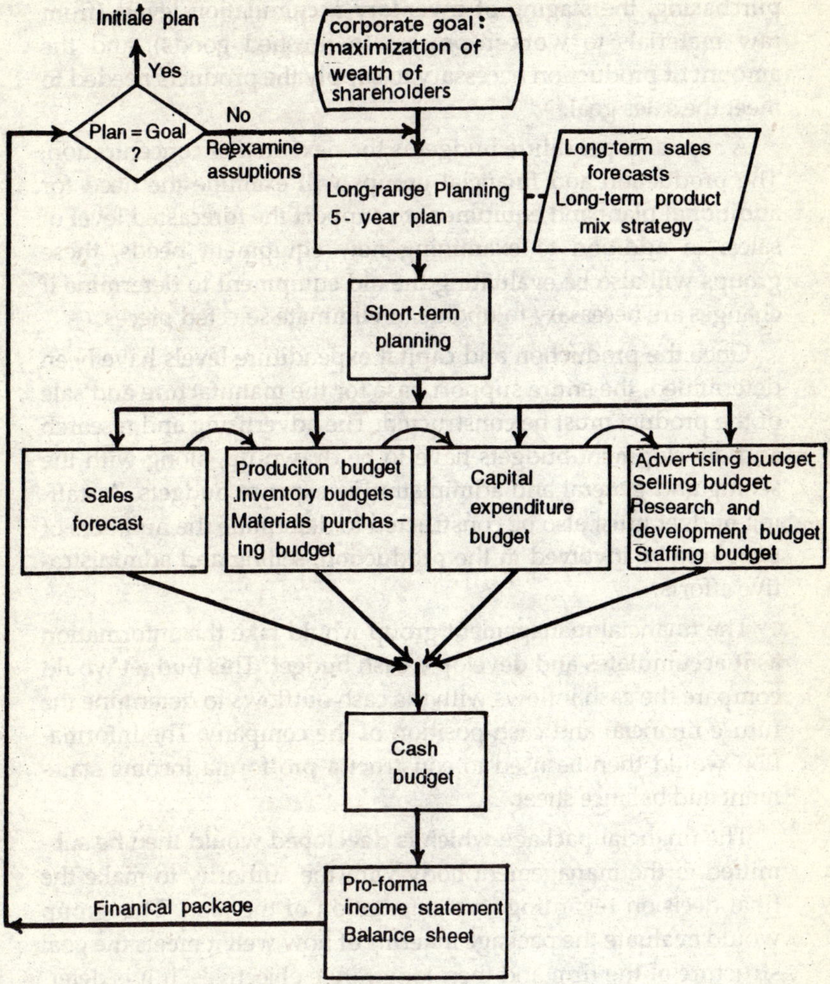

Figure. 7. Budgeting Framework for the Firm.

ance sheet and income statement. A short-term planning program may then be developed to determine the exact timing of the financial needs of the organization. A short-term sales forecast on a monthly or quarterly basis would first be developed for one or two years. From the short-term sales forecast, the production group will develop production, inventory, and material purchasing budgets. These budgets define the timing of raw materials purchasing, the staging of inventory accumulation levels (from raw materials to work-in-process to finished goods), and the amount of production necessary to supply the products needed to meet the sales goal.

A capital expenditure budget is the next area of concentration. The production and financial groups will examine the need for additional plant and equipment to support the forecasted level of sales. In addition to examining new equipment needs, these groups will also be evaluating the old equipment to determine if changes are necessary to update or eliminate selected pieces.

Once the production and capital expenditure levels have been determined, the entire support base for the manufacture and sale of the product must be constructed. The advertising and research and development budgets have to be drawn up, along with the selling and general and administrative expense budgets. A staffing budget must also be constructed to determine the numbers of people to be involved in the production, selling and administrative efforts.

The financial management group would take this information as it accumulates and develop a cash budget. This budget would compare the cash inflows with the cash outflows to determine the future financial and cash position of the company. The information would then be used to construct a pro forma income statement and balance sheet.

The financial package which is developed would then be submitted to the management body with the authority to make the final decision regarding implementation of the plan. This group would evaluate the package in terms of how well it meets the goal structure of the firm and their long-range objectives. If it is determined that the plan developed does meet the goal structure of the firm, it would be implemented. If on the other hand, the plan did not satisfy the management group, a re-evaluation process would be initiated to re-examine the underlying assumptions of the long-range planning. In addition, management may re-examine the corporate goal structure to see if any modifications should be considered. The result of this re- evaluation process would be a recycling of the whole planning and budgeting process. This would be continued until management is satisfied that the planning and budgeting package developed would meet corporate goals.

The Process of Cash Forecasting

The cash budget is stressed in this chapter because it is this budget that shows management not only the extent to which financing will be required but also the time of such financing. The cash budget makes a comparison between the cash recovery pattern of the monthly sales and the cash outflow requirements of the firm for a given month.

An example of the cash budget can be illustrated for the Davis Corporation. Table 9 shows the cash budget for the firm for the first six months of 1988. The firm has estimated that its sales will go from Rs. 80,000 to Rs. 120,000 over this period. Table 10 develop a breakdown of the cash recovery as generated by those sales. Historically, the firm's sales breakdown is 10 per cent cash and 90 per cent credit. Of the credit sales, 70 per cent are collected in the current period, 20 per cent in the following 30 days, and the remaining 10 per cent within 60 days.

The outflows for each month are listed in Table 9, using information supplied by the production and sales support groups. After the outflows have been totaled, they are subtracted from inflows to derive the cash from operations. Adding in the initial cash provides a cumulative operating monthly flow. Note that the initial cash balance for each month is simply the cumulative or ending cash balance from the previous month. For this firm, the cumulative cash balance, including the required minimum cash balance, was negative for the first two months. This means that the firm did not generate enough cash to cover the monthly cash outflows plus the minimum cash balance. In the final month the firm developed a Rs. 3,045 cash surplus above the minimum required cash need.

On the basis of these data, management must make a decision to defer some of the cash outflows until a positive cash flow is reached, or to seek external financing to assist during the cash deficit period.

After the cash budget has been developed, we can proceed to develop the income statement and balance sheet at the end of the budgeting period. Table 11 presents the balance sheet for Davis

Table 9

Davis Corporation—Six-month Cash Budget (for January-June 1978)

(*Rupees*)

	January	*February*	*March*	*April*	*May*	*June*	*Total*
Sales	80,000	90,000	100,000	100,000	110,000	120,000	600,000
Inflows:							
Monthly cash collections	79,295	86,850	96,400	99,100	107,300	116,400	585,345
Total Inflows	79,295	86,850	96,400	99,100	107,300	116,400	585,345
Outflows:							
Materials	30,000	33,000	36,000	36,000	39,000	42,000	216,000
Production salaries	50,000	52,000	54,000	55,000	57,000	59,000	327,000
Officer salaries	1,500	1,500	1,500	1,500	1,500	1,500	9,000
Office rent	1,500	1,500	1,500	1,750	1,750	1,750	9,750
Property tax	1,000	—	—	1,000	—	—	2,000
Advertising	250	250	300	300	300	300	1,700
Insurance	410	410	480	410	410	410	2,530
Selling expenses	1,000	1,000	1,000	1,000	1,000	1,000	6,000
Utilities	490	490	500	500	510	510	3,000
Legal and accounting	200	200	200	200	200	200	1,200
Automobile	415	415	420	420	425	425	2,520
Total Outflows	86,765	90,765	95,900	98,080	102,095	107,095	580,700
Cash from operations	7,470	3,915	500	1,020	5,205	9,305	4,645
Initial cash	400	7,070	10,985	10,485	9,465	4,260	400
Cumulative cash from operations	7,070	10,985	10,485	9,465	4,260	5,045	5,045
Minimal desired cash balance	2,000	2,000	2,000	2,000	2,000	2,000	2,000
Cash surplus or deficit above minimum need	9,070	12,985	12,485	11,465	6,260	3,045	3,045

Table 10

Davis Corporation—Accounts Receivable Collection Schedule

(Rupees)

	January	*February*	*March*	*April*	*May*	*June*	*July*	*August*
Cash sales, 10%	8,000	9,000	10,000	10,000	11,000	12,000		
Credit sales, 90%	72,000	81,000	90,000	90,000	99,000	108,000		
Current, 70%	50,400	56,700	63,000	63,000	69,300	75,600		
30 days, 20%	15,000 Dec.	14,400	16,200	18,000	18,000	19,800	21,600	
60 days, 10%	5,895 Nov.	6,750 Dec.	7,200	8,100	9,000	9,000	9,900	10,800
Monthly collection	79,295	86,850	96,400	99,100	107,300	116,400	31,500	10,800

Corporation as of December 31,1987. From this table, we can begin to construct the income statement for June 30, 1988 (Table 12). With consideration of the footnotes at the bottom of the projected income statement (which show the cash expenses and depreciation charges for the period), it can be concluded that the company will show a net profit after taxes of Rs. 39,932.

Table 11

Davis Corporation
Balance Sheet
For Year Ended December 31,1977

(*Rupees*)

Assets		*Liabilities*	
Cash	400	Notes payable	125,000
Account receivable	27,645		
Inventories	70,000		
Prepaid expenses	15,000		
Total Current Assets	113,045	Total Current Liabilities	125,000
Gross fixed assets	200,000	Common stock	55,000
Less accumulated depreciation	75,000	Retained earnings	58,045
Net fixed assets	125,000		
Total Assets	238,045	Total Liabilities and Equity	238,045

Table 12

Davis Corporation
Pro Forma Income Statements
For Six Months Ended June 30,1988

(*Rupees*)

Sales		600,000
Less cost of goods sold		
Add beginning inventory	70,000	
Materials purchases for items sold	216,000	
Direct labor for items sold	327,000	
Factory overhead for items sold	12,500	
Goods Available for Sale	625,500	
Less ending inventory (given)	111,930	513,570
Gross Profit		86,430
Selling expenses	10,220	

Operating expenses		
Officers salaries	9,000	
Rent	9,750	
Property tax and license	2,000	
Insurance	2,530	
Legal and accounting	1,200	
Utilities	900	35,600
Earnings before taxes		50,830
Income tax		10,898
Net Income after Taxes		39,932

Table 11 and 12 can be used to develop the projected balance sheet shown in Table 13. It is assumed that all cash above the Rs. 2,000 minimum is invested in marketable securities. The accounts receivable figure is developed from the collection cycle shown in Table 10. The inventory level is determined from the ending inventory figure in the projected income statement. Prepaid expenses are assumed constant. Net fixed have been decreased by the amount of depreciation for the period, Rs. 10,400. Total assets have increased to Rs. 288,875.

Table 13

Davis Corporation
Pro Forma Balance Sheet
For Six Months Ended June 30,1988

Assets		*Liabilities*	
Cash	2,000	Notes payable	125,000
Marketable securities	3,045	Accrued income taxes	10,898
Accounts receivable	42,300		
Inventories	111,930		
Prepaid expenses	15,000		
Total Current Assets	174,275	Total Current Liabilities	135,898
Gross plant and equipment	200,000	Common stock	55,000
Less: Accumulated depreciation	85,400	Retained earnings	97,977
Net Fixed Assets	114,600		
Total Assets	288,875	Total Liabilities and Equity	288,875

Evaluation of the Budgeting Process

There is no question that the budgeting process is very important as a means whereby the firm can continually evaluate its performance against its goal structure. However, in some instances there is too much reliance upon this process. One problem occurs when the budget systems grow so large and complex that they become essentially a meaningless tool. Another problem is that the budgeting process can be very costly in terms of both manpower and rupees. Management may become so involved in the budgeting process that it forgets the budget is only a mechanism by which to evaluate performance and not an end in itself. All managers should continually re-evaluate their expenditures to see how they can maintain efficiency in the cost structure of their divisions.

4

COST RELATIONSHIPS AND PROFIT PLANNING

COST BENEFIT AND COST EFFECTIVENESS ANALYSIS

COST-BENEFIT and Cost-Effectiveness Analysis are the quantitative examination of alternative ways to accomplish public goals as to their benefits, or effectiveness, to be gained and the costs to be incurred—for the purpose of identifying the preferred alternative.

In cost-benefit analysis, benefits are primarily expressed in monetary values. In cost-effectiveness analysis, benefits are primarily left in non-monetary units.

These analyses are of principal concern to managers of public agencies—whether Government, state, or local. Private (profit-motive), firms use their own version of cost-benefit analysis when they analyze alternative investment opportunities to maximize profits. The more complex cost-benefit and cost-effectiveness analysis approaches are needed for choices in the public sector because of the considerably more complex problems of determining benefits. Some private firms, however, are required to do these studies, for example, as part of their design of military hardware, or contract to do these types of studies for government agencies. Managers of such firms, thus, also need a basic understanding of them.

The term "cost" is used in the definition in its broad sense: Although currency units are the units most generally used in this type of analysis, any economic resource might, for a given problem, be the limiting factor—e.g.. personnel.

History

Though evaluations of public projects have doubtless occurred throughout history, the modern use of cost-benefit analysis (CBA) can be said to have begun in the 1930s with the United States Flood Control Act of 1936. Congress declared that benefits "to whomsoever they may accrue" of Federal projects should exceed costs. In the 1950s, the Inter-Agency Committee on Water Resource issued "Proposed Practices for Economic Analysis of River Basin Projects." known as the "Green Book." It suggested specific procedures that provided the seed for future work in water-resource projects. Major publications in the 1950s were Otto Eckstein's (1958) "Water Resources Development: The Economics of Project Evaluation" and Roland McKean's (1958) "Efficiency in Government Through Systems Analysis." As these titles indicate, the first major application of CBA was to aid in the selection of water-resources projects. This application continues to the present time with the Corps of Engineers as one of the major performers of CBA. Probably the second major application of CBA has been to the selection of major Transportation projects, e.g., highways, but application can be found in almost all areas of the public sector.

Cost-effectiveness analysis (CEA) blossomed at the RAND Corporation in the late 1950s and gained considerable momentum when the Secretary of Defense (Robert McNamara) appointed Charles Hitch, of RAND, as comptroller of the Department of Defense at the beginning of the 1960s. The just-published book of Hitch and McKean, "Economics of Defense in the Nuclear Age," became a best-seller and formed the basis for a major effort at the regular use of CEA in the Defense Department. In the mid-1960s President Lyndon Johnson mandated the use of the DOD analysis approach for non-defense agencies as part of the introduction of the Planning-Programming-Budgeting System (PPBS). Variations of CEA and CBA have since been used periodically by Federal agencies. These procedures have spread to state and local public agencies, though slowly. The more limited use in state and local agencies is due in large part to the more limited analytical resources available to those governments.

CEA has been used, particularly in military applications, to help determine the preferred "configuration" for specific equipment or systems, as well as to help determine which particular system is preferable.

Procedures

Cost-benefit and cost-effectiveness analyses are composed of six principal steps:

(1) **Description of Alternatives.** Each alternative must be identified and examined to identify the major characteristics that affect over-all system performance and generate costs. The major equipment, though of primary interest, should not be examined in isolation. All components of the system necessary to perform the desired mission (including facilities, equipment, personnel, and maintenance needs) should be included in the analysis.

(2) **Identification of Pertinent Measures of Effectiveness, i.e., Benefits.** The mission for which alternatives are being considered should be translated into specific quantifiable evaluation criteria. Sufficient attention to this vital step is necessary to avoid selections based upon inadequate criteria. The "criterion problem" is a particularly difficult one in these studies because of the usually ill-defined nature of public programs. Generally, for public sector progrmas, there will be multiple impacts, and so multiple evaluation criteria are needed. In addition, to be comprehensive, the analysis should consider possible unintended effects as well as those intended, for example, pollution resulting from a transportation system or displacement of families resulting from a housing program.

(3) **Expression of Both Mission Performance and Cost as Functions of the Characteristics of Each Alternative.** A mathematical model is developed to reflect the major relationships. The model will consist of both cost and performance relationships. Where the analysis involves alternatives that are only in conceptual or preliminary design states, the major elements determining these relationships will be the physical or performance specifications of the system. The primary cost and performance tradeoffs should be derived from the model. The mathematical formulation of the model may involve any of a number of quantitative tech-

niques, such as computer simulation or mathematical programming.

(4) Estimation of the Costs and Benefits for Each Alternative. Using the mathematical relationships developed in Step (3), the analysts then make estimates of the benefits and costs of each alternative. In analyzing public programs, an additional complication arises. Most programs affect different groups of citizens in different ways. Some programs will benefit different age groups, or different income groups, differently. Some programs will affect residents of some geographic areas in special ways but not residents of other areas. And so on. It is, therefore, necessary also to assess the "distributional" effects of each alternative program being considered.

(5) Valuation of the Benefits and Costs (for Cost-Benefit Analysis Only.): Cost-benefit analysis requires that rupees values be assigned to the benefits. For some benefits, such as added revenues that may occur with some of the alternatives being examined, this is relatively easy; however, in most cases the rupee values of benefits of public goods are by no means clear. For example, the value of improvements in client health, employment, faster and safer travel added recreational opportunities, and so on, are difficult to determine. Various methods of *imputing* values to such benefits have been used, such as estimating the change in earnings that families would incur if mortality or mobility rates were reduced, or using travel costs as an estimate of the value of an added recreational opportunity. With the highly subjective and intangible nature of many benefits, such imputations must generally be treated with some skepticism. (For example, in the example given earlier, what about the value of extending the life of a retire person, with no added earning power? Surely it has value!)

(6) Analysis and Presentation of Results. For cost-benefit analyses, the time flow of the costs and monetarized benefits are generally translated into "present-values" using an appropriate "discount" rate—to reflect the time value of money. For each alternative examined, the present value of the benefits can be compared to that of the costs, perhaps in the form of cost-benefit ratios.

For cost-effectiveness analysis, for each alternative, the values for each evaluation criteria (e.g., the estimated reduction in morbidity rates, or amount of reduction in travel time and number of persons affected) are displayed along with the estimated costs.

A highly simplified example of the outputs of a cost- effectiveness analysis is shown in Fig. 1. The problem in this hypothetical study is to select a system that will provide nation-wide weather observations. The Government is interested in determining which system it should put into development to get the most for its money. (An industrial concern might perform such a study to determine which of the alternatives it should emphasize in its internal research and development activities.) The graph on the top of Fig. 1 plots, for each of the three alternatives, total system cost against a single measure of effectiveness—the number of weather observations per week. Considerable information is provided even on such a simplified graph as this. First, the graph indicates for each effectiveness level (that is, for each number of achievable observations per week) which of the three systems is least costly and by approximately how much Second, the graph can be used to indicate for any specified budgetary limitation, what levels of effectiveness can be achieved. Third, it indicates the cost penalties associated with choosing an alternative other than the low-cost system. This would be of interest if, as frequently happens, other factors not included quantitatively in the analysis need to be considered.

It must be recognized that in a realistic situation more than one effectiveness criterion will probably have to be considered. In addition, various considerations may be involved that are difficult to quantify. The quantitative information must, of course, be placed in a proper perspective with the over-all requirements of the decision maker's problem.

The graph on the right in Fig. 1 indicates the manner in which each of the curves in the graph on the left might have been developed. In order to compare the three alternatives, it was necessary to determine or each alternative the "optimum" characteristics (that is, those characteristics that yield minimum cost) of the alternative for each effectiveness level. In this example, alternative No. 3 is a satellite system. and the satellite's weight is the primary characteristic that needs to be optimized. The graph indicates the

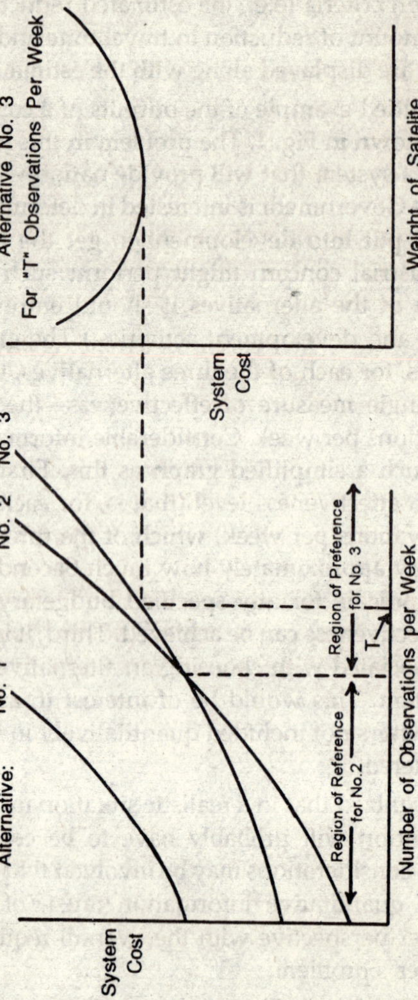

Fig. 1. Results of Hypothetical Cost-Effectiveness Analysis: Satellite Weather Observation System

preferred (i.e., lowest cost) weight of the weather satellite of alternative No. 3 for one specified level of effectiveness.

Cost-benefit analysis has the advantage of greatly simplifying (at least on the surface) the decision-maker's choice: for each alternative, the output of the analysis is a cost-benefit ratio or is the difference between rupees benefits and rupees costs. The choice becomes simply a matter of choosing that alternative with the best cost-benefit value. In cost-effectiveness analysis, especially those analyses with multiple evaluation criteria, the product of an analysis is a display presenting the cost and the various values of the evaluation criteria for each alternative. It is left completely up to the decision-maker how to value the various criteria. The disadvantage of cost-benefit analysis is that this very simplicity can hide, or at least mask, the many assumptions and judgments used to input monetary values to each evaluation criteria.

Major Applications

The information that can be obtained from these analyses has the following major uses:

(1) To aid decision makers, in situations where funds or other economic resources are a significant constraint, in making, improved choices among alternative systems.

(2) To indicate the preferred characteristics of the alternative systems. (That is, the analysis requires "sub- optimization" of the major characteristics of each alternative. In the example of Fig. 1, information was provided as to the preferred weight of the satellite.)

(3) To provide indications as to specific areas to further study or research in which funds might be applied to bring over-all system savings or to reduce critical areas of uncertainty. (For example, in the weather satellite illustration, the analytical results might indicate the over-all savings that would probably result from improved reliability of the major satellite components. The amount of such savings would suggest the magnitude of effort that could profitably be expanded to improve component reliability.)

(4) To suggest, in certain situations, additional alternatives that would fare will in the face of the major difficulties of the examined alternatives and that, therefore, might be preferable.

(5) To indicate, for industrial users, the magnitude of the potential business for major components of the preferred system—at least for specific effectiveness levels.

Subject Branchings

Two areas of special technique development have been given impetus by cost-benefit and cost-effectiveness analysis: *cost analysis*, and *analysis of uncertainty*.

Cost Analysis. With rupees cost normally being used as one of the main selection criteria accuracy in cost estimation become of considerable importance. Cost analysis, or cost estimation, has developed into a field, and perhaps a profession, of its own, especially for analyzing military weapon systems. Special techniques in addition to those traditionally used in corporate product cost estimating are needed. Some of the techniques in use are:

(1) *Statistical Regression Analysis.* For use in estimating costs for proposed items that are generally similar but have somewhat different characteristics from those on which direct cost experience is available. A distinctive feature of the resulting estimating equations is that they relate selected physical or performance characteristics of the item to cost.

(2) *Learning Curve Analysis.* For use in estimating future hardware costs in those instances where varying the quantity requirements appears likely to produce a significantly different *unit* cost. (The terms "learning curve," "progress curve," and "improvement curve" are used synonymously to indicate the cost-quantity relationship. The basic shape of this curve is generally represented as a downward sloping straight line where both the vertical and horizontal axes, representing respectively unit costs and cumulative quantity, are logarithmic scales.)

(3) *Engineering Analysis.* To provide the basic information for describing the cost-generating characteristics of any new or future components.

The primary concern of cost analysis is the development of relationships between a system's cost (to include research and development, investment, and operating costs as appropriate) and its physical and performance characteristics.

Analysis of Uncertainty. There are inherent uncertainties in the information and in the resulting data used in these analyses. Careful investigation may reduce this uncertainty somewhat, but can never eliminate it. Therefore, it appears desirable for decision makers to be aware of the approximate nature and magnitude of the uncertainties in order to evaluate the risks inherent in their decisions. Two approaches to this problem can be identified. The first is most frequently referred to as *sensitivity analysis.* In this approach, those equation parameters believed to be subject to the greatest uncertainty and to be of the most significance to the study are given more than one value. The calculations called for by the model are performed for each value of the parameter. The results indicate the sensitivity of the selection criteria to the value of the parameter. The computational problem, unfortunately, soon becomes great as more alternate values are examined. This greatly restricts the amount of sensitivity analysis that can be performed.

The effect of applying sensitivity analysis to a cost- effectiveness study is shown in Fig. 2. This presents the same study shown in Fig. 1, but with the addition of sensitivity analysis. Bands are now used rather than single lines to express the cost versus effectiveness relationships. The upper boundary of each band represents those events which would result in the most expensive conditions; the lower boundary, the least expensive conditions. It is to be noted that even with the range of uncertainties considered, alternative No. 1 is completely "dominated" by the other alternatives. It is also apparent that the decision maker's problem is more complex. There now exists a large overlapping region between alternatives No. 2 and No. 3. In addition to considering specific levels of effectiveness and cost, it is now also necessary to consider the likelihoods of the various conditions that determine the uncertainty.

It must be emphasized that the basic problem itself has not been made more complex. *Uncertainties that were always present have merely been explicitly and quantitatively expressed.* The complexity of the problem reflected in Fig. 2 is probably much closer to "reality" than the more simplified analysis of Fig. 1.

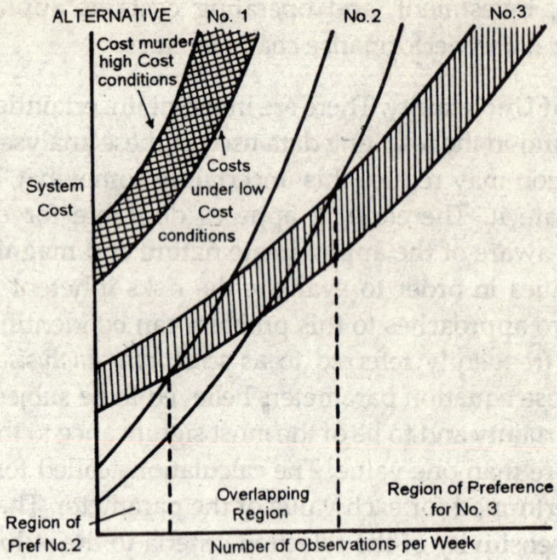

Fig. 2. A Cost-Effectiveness Analysis with Sensitivity Analysis Applied: Weather Observation System.

Fig. 2 illustrates a primary consideration of cost-benefit and cost-effectiveness analysis—namely, to seek "dominant" solutions or, at least, solutions that are preferred over a wide range of possible conditions.

The second approach to analyzing uncertainty can be described by the term *subjective confidence limits.* This statistical technique serves to complement sensitivity analysis. Whereas sensitivity analysis indicates the impact of a change in the value of a parameter, it says nothing about the *likelihood* of occurrence of the various values. In the subjective confidence limits technique, the analyst provides a range of values for any parameter whose value is considered to be subject to significant uncertainty. These ranges of values are somewhat subjective, thereby giving rise to the use of the terms "subjective" in describing the procedure. The range of values for each such parameter is assumed to conform to a particular probability distribution. The statistical expected value and variance for each parameter can then be calculated and combined as called for by the equations of the model in order to estimate an expected value and variance for the total system. This is done for each alternative system to provide unexpected value with confidence limits for each. This approach is similar to that used in PERT analyses is estimating the time requirements for a given network of activities.

Acceptance and Potential

The application of cost-benefit and cost-effectiveness analysts by industry and Government to assist in the evaluation of military and other Government sponsored projects has been considerable. These approaches appear likely to continue to be used on a wide scale to help make choices of Federal programs. They are likely to gain more usage by state and local public agencies, especially as public agencies are increasingly required to justify their programs and as staff becomes more familiar, through education, with these approaches.

COST-VOLUME-PROFIT ANALYSIS

Cost-Volume-Profit analysis is a micro-economic technique used for measuring the functional relationships between the major factors affecting profits, and for determining the profit structure of the firm. The basic methodology involved is fundamental to the use of financial data to guide managerial decision-making in a wide variety of business situation.

Fixed and Variable Costs

An understanding of cost-volume-profit relationships is predicated upon the acceptance of certain basic concepts of cost behavior regarding the manner in which costs respond to changing volume. Some costs vary quite closely with changes in volume whereas others remain unchanged in total amount regardless of changes in rate of activity. Costs which vary with volume are ordinarily called *variable costs* which those costs which do not vary with volume are called *fixed costs.* Inherently, costs are neither fixed nor variable, but acquire such characteristics as a result of management policies and decisions. They are classified as "fixed" or "variable" for analytical purposes.

Typically, fixed costs originate from the provision of capacity in readiness to do business, and in the short run they tend to remain constant in total amount irrespective of fluctuations in production or sales volume. Since such costs are fixed for a given period of time they are also termed *period, standby,* or *capacity* costs. Rent, depreciation, property taxes, insurance, and the salaries of key executive and supervisory personnel, are all typical examples of fixed costs. Conversely, the variable costs usually represent the factors of cost which increase or decrease proportionately with actual volume of production or sales. Usually raw materials and certain kinds of labor, supplies, and services are variable costs (also called *direct costs*), because the amount of total cost varies directly with volume of activity.

In analyzing cost-volume-profit relationships, the first step is to study the behavior of costs under conditions of changing volume, and to divide costs into fixed and variable components. The next step is to determine the total amount of fixed cost and the rates at which variable costs and profit change in response to volume. Within the context of given conditions, these figures are constants, and together they describe the profit structure of the company and measure the functional relationships between costs, volume, and profit.

Volume is a key factor in profit planning, because most managerial decisions are affected, in part at least, by the changes in costs and sales income which accompany changes in volume. Therefore cost-volume-profit analysis as a highly useful management technique for studying business problems, and has many practical applications in connection with planning and control. The information derived from this type of analysis provides a suitable basis both for projecting profits under alternative proposed combinations of costs and volumes, and also for evaluating the profit consequences of alternative decisions. In particular, the principles of cost-volume-profit relationships have been implicitly accepted and systematically applied in connection with direct costing, profit planning, break-even analysis, marginal analysis, flexible budgeting, and pricing policy.

Marginal Analysis

Derived from economic theory, marginal analysis is an analytical technique for measuring the financial consequences of a given action. For the purposes of marginal analysis, only those cost and revenue elements affected by the action are considered: all others are irrelevant and therefore excluded. What matters here are only the amounts of change in the totals of these elements, i.e., the difference or increments to total cost or revenue that stem from the action. For this reason the technique has also been termed *incre-*

mental cost (or profit) analysis, differential cost (or profit) analysis, or marginal cost (or income) analysis. Irrespective of the term used, the concept is the same: namely, to identify and quantify the financial effect of the action or forward decision. This analysis can be applied to a variety of situations, involving either past or future actions. However, it is most commonly used in industry in connection with profit planning and for guiding managerial decision-making involving alternative choices.

Some typical applications requiring the evaluation of alternative course of action and the measurement of potential results include:

(1) Make-or-buy decisions.
(2) Capital investment decisions.
(3) Product-mix problems.
(4) Adding or deleting a product.
(5) Expanding or contracting sales volume.
(6) Pricing decisions.

It should be remembered that while marginal analysis does represent a considerable advance in the methodology of modern management, it should not be treated as the sole and infallible basis or decision making. While it provides a reliable means for measuring and comparing the economic worth of proposed projects, or alternative courses of action, there are often other important factors which management must take into consideration before reaching a decision. Since some factors, such as public relations, customers good will, or risk, are seldom succeptible to accurate measurement, the results of the analysis should be used with sophistication.

Break-Even Analysis

This is a technique of financial analysis for investigating the functional relationships between the rate of activity and costs, revenue, and profits. Specifically, Break-Even Analysis focuses attention on anticipated profit behavior in response to changes in underlying conditions by predicting the profit consequences of changes in sales volume, rate of output, selling prices, or product costs, etc.

A specialized form of profit graph, called the break-even chart, is frequently used to present diagrammatically significant cost-volume-profit relationships; relating total costs at various sales volumes to the expected revenue and profit (or loss) at each alternative volume. The break-even chart is also used for determining the break-even point. Since the break- even point identifies the volume of activity where revenue exactly equals total costs, both fixed and variable, it thus indicates that combination of sales (i.e., the volume) at which operations "break even" and yield neither a profit nor a loss. At sales levels below the break-even point, operations will result in a loss; and above this point they will contribute profits.

The chart has been known to accountants for a long time prior to widespread discussions in industrial engineering and manufacturing management literature, as evidenced by the appearance of an illustration and an explanation of methods for preparing such a chart in the "Encyclopedia of Accounting" edited by George Lisle and published in Edinburgh and London in 1904.

Knowledge of the break-even point and the underlying functional relationships between costs, volume and profit is particularly useful for the purposes of profit forecasting and planning. Some typical managerial application of this technique would include:

(1) Predicting profits at alternatives sales volumes.

(2) Predicting costs and revenues at alternative levels of output.

(3) Measuring the effect of price changes on total profit.

(4) Measuring the effect on total profit of changes in product-mix.

(5) Measuring the effect of cost changes on break-even point.

OPERATING-MARGIN ANALYSIS

Operating-Margin Analysis has been advanced by Hodgson and Uyterhoeven as on effective technique for evaluating opportunities in foreign operations. However, it should provide useful insights in corporate planning where new industries are to be entered, whether in domestic or foreign markets.

Operating margin in a business is defined as the difference between sales price and the cost of materials purchased. For example, if a manufacturer pays Rs. 66 for materials going into a refrigerator which sells for Rs. 101, his operating margin amounts to

Rs. 35. It is the margin within which he will have to operate, e.g., manufacture, sell, pay for research, conduct all other corporate activities, and make a profit.

Operating-margin analysis enables management to reconcile its basic manufacturing, marketing and growth plans within the price- materials cost limits imposed by competitive environments.

The writers quoted express the operating margin as a percentage of the cost of materials purchased. Thus, the operating margin for the refrigerator in the above example would be Rs. 35, Rs. 66 or 53%.

The operating-margin concept is not new, for it is the economist's concept of "value added." However, it should not be confused with a common accounting usage, in which operating margin constitutes the difference between sales prices and cost of goods sold. What is novel about the concept is the framework in which its proponents suggest that it be used: It defines the condition of an *industry* and not just an individual firm. The margin limits are almost identical for all competing participants in a given industry (or in a given country) because each sells his products competitively and buys his materials at approximately the same price. Variations in margin within the same product line do not hinder the approach, but invite investigation as to the reasons for the difference. Likewise different degrees of integration among companies can be reduced to a common denominator by using one of the least-integrated firms as a base, and segregating the additional activities of the other participants as separate "business."

The operating-margin concept is also helpful because it keeps management from placing excessive emphasis on the accounting statements of established firms. Accounting principles, give companies great flexibility, especially in allocating expenses, thus making "true" profits a rather elastic notion. (The correct profit figure becomes even more elusive in foreign countries with their different accounting practices, tax laws, disclosure regulations, etc.) The operating margin as here conceived is highly exact because its two basic points always remain unobscured and untouched by either accounting convention or company practices. Both the selling price and the cost of materials purchased can be determined objectively. In most cases they are common knowledge. If not, they can readily be determined either through trade channels or with the help of an engineer familiar with the product requirements.

Treatment of Costs

Under operating-margin analysis, two totally different components are analyzed: *involuntary cost* and *discretionary expenses.* Involuntary expenses arise from the nature of a firm's business, its scale of manufacturing, the types of processes used; and the degree of product specialization or standardization achieved. They consist mainly of minimum manufacturing costs, and cannot be eliminated unless a firm cuts production. Therefore, they have to be insured by everyone in the industry.

Involuntary expenses normally constitute the difference between cost of goods sold and cost of materials purchased. However, there are exceptions: Tooling expenses, though usually included in the costs of goods sold, are in reality discretionary expenses. Manufacturing costs which are not absolutely necessary, but which may add desirable features to the product line, are also discretionary, even though included in the costs of goods sold.

Discretionary expenses allow a company to fulfill its marketing and development objectives. Within the framework of competitive conditions, a firm has a certain latitude in determining which and how many discretionary expenses it wants to incur. Thus one corporate strategy may call for large profit distributions to stockholders, or for retention to finance expansion or diversification. Another firm may direct discretionary expenses towards product development, upgrading of quality, and tooling for frequent model changes. Or it may strengthen its marketing position by establishing distribution outlets, creating brand loyalty, improving service to customers, etc. Still another firm may surrender discretionary money to reduce prices.

Discretionary expenses often qualify as true economic investments and should be considered as such even though they are entered into accounting statements as expenses and not as assets. In terms of a company's long-term competitive strength, money invested in building up the distribution position or in creating product differentiation may be no less important than money invested in fixed plant and machinery. During, periods of rapid growth, management often emphasizes increases in productive capacity while ignoring discretionary expenses of an investment nature. With the maturity of an industry, however, the emphasis usually shifts from the "capacity to make" to the "ability to sell," thus penalizing companies which in earlier years ignored discretionary expenses for marketing.

Because discretionary expenses of an investment nature in a firm's income statement (in contrast to fixed-asset investment) reduce current profits substantially, a careful analysis of these costs is needed if low profits, or even accounting losses, in growth industries are to be interpreted correctly.

Appraising Competition

An enterprise must be able to live within the prices imposed by competition and still generate a sufficiently wide operating margin to achieve growth. For this reason, in determining entry and participation requirements of a foreign venture (or entry into a new domestic field) it is vital to analyze the company's probable position relative to the industry leaders. By considering the involuntary costs and discretionary expenses of the leaders, management can predict future price trends. It can then assess its relative capacity to compete and estimate its ability to pay for the necessary discretionary expenses of an investment nature that will be needed to achieve a strong position in the industry. Such an analysis will permit an estimate of the extent to which industry leaders may be able to cut prices. These reductions will primarily hinge on (1) the lowering of their involuntary costs: and (2) as an industry moves to maturity, the extent to which achievement of product and marketing objectives allows the leaders to lower their discretionary expenses.

Lowering Involuntary Costs

In a dynamic industry, volume is the prime determinant of the operating margin. Larger scales of production reduce involuntary costs, enabling industry leaders to lower prices. The extent as well as the timing of price reductions can be fairly accurately predicted by analyzing the leader's involuntary costs and by establishing a schedule of his costs for various increases in volume that can be anticipated with market growth. Price declines will often depend not only on increases in the scale of manufacture of a single product, but also on increased production volumes of similar products. In such cases an appraisal should include those products as well as the one of main concern.

A manufacturer contemplating entry into an industry in a less mature stage of development must anticipate the conditions under which he could be the victim of a price-cost squeeze. This contingency will occur if prices drop faster than a company's ability-to lower costs, which could happen if the industry leaders grow faster than anyone else. Thus management may have to incur losses and match the price reduction in order to maintain its relative market share. Otherwise it may not achieve sales levels which justify increasing its plant scale to the point where this would ultimately bring the venture's costs in line with the costs of industry leaders.

It is therefore essential to establish entry goals, such as market-share objectives, and to decide what production and sales efforts are necessary to achieve them. This will help to ensure that the venture will generate adequate resources at least to sustain its position relative to the industry leaders.

Cuts in Discretionary Expenses

During rapid growth periods, companies are likely to make substantial discretionary expenses of an investment nature—e.g., outlays to establish the product, to strengthen distribution, and to finance expansion. As the growth slackens or its objectives are achieved, fewer discretionary expenses of this type will be required, thus freeing the money for price reductions. The magnitude of this drop can also be predicted through operating-margin analysis, although it is more difficult to foresee its timing. High discretionary margins are also vulnerable when competitors lower their profit margins or undertake less expensive marketing methods and resort to price cutting in order to gain a larger market share.

During periods of substantial excess capacity, the temptation may develop to make sales so long as these will cover out-of-pocket costs, resulting in a major price break. Such conditions, however, cannot last indefinitely. As demand catches up with capacity, prices will usually return to a level at which the most efficient industry leaders can still make a reasonable return on their investment

Conditions of Entry into a Market

A wide operating margin indicates that a new venture can incur high levels of involuntary and discretionary costs. A margin tend to be wide when even the industry leaders have a comparatively low scale of output; when the industry leaders have high discretionary expenses or cash requirements for marketing, product development, construction of new capacity, or diversification programs; when there is insufficient competition; when the industry leaders have priced their products to maximize their profits even though this induces smaller competitors to use minor price reductions as a competitive weapon; or when the leaders are inefficient manufacturers or marketers.

A tight industry will be characterized by relatively low profits for the industry leader, while loose competitive conditions permit satisfactory profits to both leaders and followers. It is important to recognize, however, that both loose and tight conditions are possible under a wide as well as a narrow operating margin.

In sum, Hodgson and Uyterhoeven submit that opportunities and difficulties in *entering* an industry are more a function of the magnitude of the operating margin than of the profitability of industry members. A wide operating margin can provide a better opportunity for entry than a narrow operating margin *whether the industry leaders are profitable or not.* On the other hand, a profitable industry with narrow operating margins may be very difficult to enter.

PRICE-EARNING ANALYSIS

A glance through the price-earnings ratios distributed to newspapers by the Associated Press along with stock tables shows that the PE range on the New York Stock Exchange reaches from 2 to about 735. Thus if one knows that a company's earnings per share are Re. 1, he can conclude with confidence only that the price of its stock will be between Rs. 2 a share and Rs. 735 a share!

Though even so cursory an examination might lead to the suspicion that there must be other important things, much of the financial and business world revolves around earnings per share, or EPS. Yet in fact determining the merit of corporate policies by their impact on per-share earnings is fraught with danger. EPS is too often a misleading indicator that can result in costly decisions that frequently short-change the common shareholders.

The EPS criterion confuses investment decisions with financing policies. Substandard projects can appear desirable simply because of the way in which they are financed. Furthermore, a large body of empirical evidence indicates (as the range in PE ratios suggests) that the market is not primarily interested in earnings or in EPS per se.

There are many reasons why management and the financial community would be well advised to abandon EPS as an analytical tool. This is particularly true for acquisition pricing and financing and capital structure planning. Both executives and analysts need to take a closer look at the key elements that determine the price of a company's stock.

Acquisition Analysis

The rhetoric we read in many business publications about acquisition analysis is misleading. Commonly, for instance, we are told that companies should make acquisitions because of the "earnings leverage" that will result.

As an example, let us assume that company A sells as a price-earnings multiple of 20 and that company B sells at a PE of 10. Often, we are told that company A can offer B's shareholders a PE of, say, 15—a premium of 50%—and that A can still increase its EPS. For each rupee of earning A is buying, it only has to give up shares earnings 75 paise. Thus, if A uses its shares to buy B and form a new company, AB, AB's EPS will always exceed A's EPS. Hence, we are told that the acquisition of B is good for A's shareholders. And, obviously, it is good for B's shareholders since they obtain a 50% premium above the market price of their shares.

But if we turn the example around, the danger in using EPS becomes obvious. If B buys A to form BA, B will pay at least A's PE of 20. But now BA's EPS will be less than B's because the company with the lower PE must offer more shares per rupee of acquired earnings.

The same people who tell us that AB is good for A's shareholders tell us that BA is bad for B's shareholders, even though AB and BA are the same company, most often with the same assets and earnings expectations and, even, the same management. Should we expect AB and BA to sell at different prices in the market when they are really the same company?

A's acquisition of B or B's acquisition of A is in fact good for the buyer's shareholders only if synergism is expected. And the synergism must be at least large enough to justify the premium paid above the seller's current share price. Thus, it is illogical to claim that IBM, for example, can afford to pay more for B than could the Chase Manhattan Bank because IBM sells at a much higher PE than Chase. If Chase can expect to generate larger synergism than IBM with the acquisition of B, shouldn't Chase be able to offer a greater price for B?

Furthermore, the business writer fails to realize that if IBM (or any firm selling at a high PE) were to acquire firms for which it paid full value (i.e., there is no added benefit to the buyer's shareholders), IBM's PE would fall to offset the gain in EPS. Empirical evidence supports this position.

Investment and Financing

Another pitfall in using EPS as a guide for acquisition policy is confusing investment with financing. In one case the president of a well diversified manufacturer selling at 16 times earnings wanted to acquire a small, but exceptionally profitable, engineering consulting firm for a PE of 25. An equity swap would "dilute" the pro forma EPS. Facetiously, we suggested that he sell his company to the engineering firm, even though the latter was only about 10% as large as the manufacturer, so that the EPS would rise. He suggested an alternative; use debt to finance the acquisition. The anticipated profits from the acquisition would more than cover his company's out-of-pocket cost of interest on debt. Thus his company's income would rise while the number of outstanding shares would remain constant. He was right, the pro forma EPS would rise.

However, there is conceptual problem with his suggestion. Since the pro forma EPS can be enhanced simply by employing debt, bad investments can appear to be good investments because the management can lever the firm and increase the EPS at the time the investment is undertaken. Furthermore, the management can increase the EPS without making any investment by borrowing to retire common shares. So there are many ways financing decisions can affect EPS, though they cannot change the intrinsic desirability of the acquisition, which is simply a multiplant decision. This means the investment decision must be made independently of the financing decision, or in other words, on the basis of considerations other than the effect on EPS.

Thus, there are two distinct shortcomings to employing EPS as an analytical tool in acquisition pricing. First, the existing EPS of the buyer and seller determine the decision, so that synergism may be excluded from consideration. Second, EPS can lead the decision-maker to believe that bad investments are good investments; simply lever the firm sufficiently at the time an investment is undertaken and EPS can be enhanced to any level desired by management.

The Benefits of Debt Financing

An emphasis on EPS not only misdirects management in selecting and pricing acquisitions, it also leads to ridiculous conclusions on the balance between debt and equity in a company's financial structure. Depending on the PE multiple, mechanical dependence on EPS would lead to the expansion of debt to cover dubious projects, or to the elimination of all debt by issuing common shares. While in most cases an increase in the amount of debt in relation to equity will enhance EPS, in fact the benefits to a company's market value derived from its financing policies have nothing to do with EPS.

A company can use debt to increase its EPS so long as its after-tax return on fixed capital is larger than its after-tax interest costs. Today high-grade bonds cost the firm less than 4.5% after taxes. Thus, corporate investments in new plant and equipment yielding more than 4.5% after taxes would appear desirable to analysts emphasizing EPS. It is certainly not difficult to imagine the likely direction of IBM's share price if projects were undertaken earning a mere 5% on fixed capital, even if the EPS were rising.

The market will not ignore the fact that an increase in debt forces the common shareholder to assume greater financial risk, in the form of higher fixed costs due to interest expense. Without some factor to offset part of this new risk, the price-earnings multiple will decline. So the price of the common shares would remain unchanged despite the added EPS.

At the other extreme, the EPS criterion would dictate that high PE firms issue shares to retire debt. As it works out mathematically, EPS can be increased by issuing shares to retire debt so long as the price-earnings ratio is larger than the reciprocal of the after-tax borrowing rate. If a company's after-tax cost of borrowed funds is 4.5%, the reciprocal is one divided by 4.5% or 22.2. Whenever the PE exceeds 22.2, management can increase the EPS simply by issuing equity to retire debt. Hence, supporters of EPS maximization would recommend that companies selling at very high PEs be debt free, a policy that would hardly be beneficial to the common shareholders.

There is considerable evidence that debt financing does add to the market value of a firm's common equity. Of course, the reason is that there is a factor that reduces part of the financial risk created by the fixed interest expense. The Federal Government bears a large portion of the financial risk—up to 48%, the corporate income tax rate. The deductibility of interest expense in calculating taxable income means that the company's earnings are reduced by up to only 52% of the cost of debt.

A large body of empirical evidence clarifies our intuition about borrowed capital, namely, that investors do not expect management to reduce debt. As it comes due they expect management to refinance and, hence, maintain a particular target debt ratio. A target debt ratio implies that investors expect the annual tax saving to continue forever.

The present value of this perpetual stream is simply the corporate income tax rate multiplied by the amount of interest- bearing debt that is anticipated by the market. As long as the level of debt does not exceed prudent limits, the market value of a firm's common shares will rise 48 paise for each rupees of interest-bearing debt in its target capital structure. Thus, the real benefit of debt financing to the common shareholders is not the added EPS; it is the tax saving.

Price Determination Factors

It is clear that an EPS criterion frequently misallocates valuable corporate resources and shortchange; the shareholders. Nor, to judge by market behavior, is EPS the criterion that impresses investors, especially the sophisticated investors who really determine share prices.

Investors do not discount earnings *per se*. Consider two companies, X and Y. Assume that all we know is that their profits are expected to increase at identical annual rates of 15%. At this stage, a foolish question would be: which company should sell at a higher price, X or Y? Of course, the obvious answer is that we would expect X and Y to sell at an identical price, since, in the absence of additional information, X and Y are the same company.

However, with the addition of one other item about the two companies we must conclude that X would command the greater market value: X requires almost no investment in new capital to increase its profits 15% annually, whereas Y requires a rupee of additional capital for each incremental rupee of sales. X sells at the higher price and price-earnings multiple because it requires less capital to grow at a given rate despite the fact that X and Y are expected to have identical future profits. That is, X has a larger expected rate of return on incremental capital. The key determinant of market value in this case is the expected return on incremental capital.

The implication we can draw from this example is that investors do not simply discount expected earnings; rather, investors discount anticipated earnings net of the amount of capital required to be invested in order to maintain an expected rate of growth in profits. This concept can be referred to as the expected future "Free Cash Flow." It is expected cash flow that is above and beyond the anticipated investment requirement of the business.

The key to successful acquisition analysis and capital structure planning is to focus on the determinants of market value that are employed by sophisticated investors. The pricing mechanism is to calculate the current value of the expected future free cash flow. The resulting EPS is unimportant.

5

CAPITAL BUDGETING

BUDGETING is an important—and, in any, operation of si[illegible] icant size and complexity, an indispensable—[illegible] agement planning and control. Its objectives ar[illegible]

(1) To determine the input of planning, in terms o[illegible] ne[illegible] agreed upon activities and expectable levels of those ac[illegible] m[illegible] well as expected revenues, if any, resulting from thos[illegible]

(2) To warn decision-makers and responsible managers [illegible] significant departures from planned cost inputs and revenues occur; and

(3) To develop a responsive, cooperative work force in the matter of fiscal control.

A comprehensive budget may be defined as a forecast of all of the transactions of an organization for a stipulated period, organized in such a way as to bring to the attention of specific managers the financial results of those activities over which they have control, and to enable the preparation of financial statements such as the budgeted income statement, balance sheet, and cash flow statement.

The budgeting process itself is an extensive one, and consists of the preparation of individual budgets by those departments (or persons) best in a position to do so—for example, the sales budget by the production department, the production budget by the production department, the purchases budget by the purchasing agent, and so on. The preparation of some of these budgets, for example, the manufacturing overhead and selling expense budgets, is expedited by a well developed system of flexible budgets. Standard cost data are also of help in providing information as to hours or quantities needed for manufacture at any given level of activity. In turn, the budgeting process itself may lead to the revision of flexible budgets and the updating of standard costs.

A relatively recent development that has attracted wide attention is Zero-Base Budgeting.

The timing and detailed preparation of each of the various budgets which in total form the master budget are usually the responsibility of a budget director, who in turn may have the help and authoritative back-up of a budget committee. The budget committee may be composed of the top executives of the firm, ...uding the president, controller, and budget director.

...HE CAPITAL BUDGETING PROCESS

The capital budgeting process involves the selection of those ...w investment proposals presented to a firm that will contribute ...ost to the wealth maximization of the shareholders. To continue ...sful a firm may have to engage in a continual search ...vestment proposals to add to its profit stream.

The product life cycle for a firm's output consists of three phases. The first phase is called the experimentation stage, in which the production processes and other aspects of the product are refined and the product is introduced to the market. During the second stage, sales increase rapidly. They continue to grow until the third phase, the maturity stage, is reached, after which they start to decline. If a firm is not looking for new products to supplement and eventually replace the income stream provided by present products, in time it will cease to exist. This is why the proper selection of new investment proposals is so important.

The selection of long-term investment are to be as important a strategy the firm as the selection of the proper liquidity balance and the proper funding mix. The selection of new investment proposals will have an impact on the firm's profitability and the level of operating assets as well as the funding mix. The new investments will not only influence the firm's rate of return but will also have trade-off implications for risk. Financial management's selection process provides a package of investment selections. Top management then evaluates the impact of the financial package on the goal structure of the firm. If it meets the goal structure the package is initiated; if it does not, the basic underlying assumptions of the investment alternatives must be re-examined, and the whole loop starts again.

The capital budgeting process involves four different types of investment alternatives:

1. The firm can replace existing assets and thus reduce the cost structure of the firm.
2. The firm can provide new products or services that have been developed through its research and development efforts.
3. The firm can add new product or service lines by acquiring other firms.
4. The firm can evaluate other uses for funds, such as investing in the securities markets.

In any evaluation process, the first job is to evaluate the cost-benefit structure of a proposal. Revenue and expense forecasts must be made to determine the net revenue structure of the proposal. In addition, the proposal may necessitate enlargement of the asset base of the firm to support a new sales level. In many instances, this will entail new asset investments. When this information is developed into a cash budget, the net cash flow structure of the project has been determined.

As important as development of the net cash flow data for a project is selection of the technique to be used to compare one project to another in terms of their ability to maximize the wealth of shareholders. Five alternative methods for ranking investment proposals will be discussed later in this treatise.

Once the net cash flows have been determined and the ranking method has been chosen, the ranking technique can be used to develop a measure of return and risk for each project. Under conditions of certainty, there is no measure of risk since all future net cash flows generated from a prospective investment are assumed to be known with certainty. However, when future net cash flows are not known with 100 per cent certainty, the concepts of probability and utility theory can be used to assist management in outlining the trade-offs between the rate of return and the measure of risk for each proposal. The risk structure that is apparent in any selection process basically revolves around what is termed *business risk.* When future cash flows are not known with certainty, an error can arise in the selection of future sales or future costs associated with a project.

Management next must evaluate the risk-return trade-offs of the various investment proposals. Relevant inputs into the capital budgeting system will be the amount of rupees available to invest and the selection of an investment cutoff point. The selection of an investment cutoff point is quite important, since the capital budgeting process does not always tell an analyst which projects to accept or reject. Rather, it presents the analyzed investments in an array of profitability as measured by the rate of return.

After all the elements of the capital budgeting system have been analyzed, a selection of investments is made and presented as the firm's financial package. This subsystem then enters the main framework of financial management, leading to the part where the whole package is evaluated in terms of the goal structure of the firm.

SOME MATHEMATICS FOR MANAGEMENT

Capital budgeting analysis, including the evaluation of investment alternatives, is based on certain mathematical techniques. Here we discuss the concepts of compound value and present value, which are used later in investment analysis under conditions of certainty.

COMPOUND VALUE

Simply defined, *compound value* examines the effect of depositing money for a period of time and watching it grow at a certain rate of interest. A lump-sum can be deposited and its value determined at some future point in time, or a stream of money can be deposited over a period of time and its expansion noted. In the first case, the compound value of a lump sum of money is being analyzed, while in the second case, it is the compound value of an annuity stream of money that is being analyzed.

Suppose a person deposited Rs. 10,000 in a time deposit at a commercial bank or in a passbook account at a savings and loan institution which was paying an annual interest rate of 6 per cent on the deposited funds. We can view the growth of this money over time through the formula:

$$S_t = D\,(1 + i)^t,$$

where:

S = Value of the sum of money at the end of t years.
D = Initial deposit.
i = Interest rate.
t = Number of years the money is left in the account.

If the funds were left in the account for one year, the value of the money would be equal to:

$$S_1 = \text{Rs. } 10{,}000\,(1 + .06)^1 = \text{Rs. } 10{,}000\,(1.06) = \text{Rs. } 10{,}600.$$

If the money were deposited for two years, the equation would be:

$$S_2 = \text{Rs. } 10{,}000\,(1.06)^2 = \text{Rs. } 10{,}000\,(1.1236) = \text{Rs. } 11{,}236.$$

The amount by which the Rs. 10,000 will grow as it remains in the financial institution year after year is shown in Table 1. After the first year, the Rs. 10,600 will become the beginning balance for the second year—with interest being earned not only on the base amount of Rs. 10,000 but also on the Rs. 600 of interest that was earned during the previous year. If the Rs. 10,000 plus accrued interest were left in the bank for six years, the amount would have grown to Rs. 14,185.

Table 1

Illustration of Compound Value at 6 Per cent

Year	*Beginning amount (0)*	×	1 + *i*	=	*Ending sum (S_t)*
1	10,000		1.06		10,6000
2	10,600		1.06		11,236
3	11,236		1.06		11,910
4	11,910		1.06		12,625
5	12,625		1.06		13,382
6	13,382		1.06		14,185

Table 2 illustrates how a lump-sum investment can grow over time. Table 2 calculates the value of Re. 1 growing at different interest rates and for different time periods. Each of the factors in the table represents a specified $(1 + i)^t$ rate of interest. For example, if Rs. 10,000 were deposited in a bank which was paying 6 per cent on a time deposit, how much would the money be worth at the end of ten years? Stating the equation for the compound sum as:

Sum = Initial deposit times the appropriate table value,

we simply have to find the table value interest factor of 6 per cent for ten years and multiply that value by Rs. 10,000.

The table value is equal to 1.791, which represents the value of Re. 1 growing at 6 per cent for ten years. Multiplying by the initial deposit of Rs. 10,000, we can determine that the funds have grown to Rs. 17,910. If we continued the analysis by hand, by the time we reached the tenth year the same results would be achieved by using Table 1 as by using Table 2.

Table 2

Values of Compound Sum of Re. 1

Year	*1%*	*2%*	*3%*	*4%*	*5%*	*6%*	*7%*	*8%*	*9%*	*10%*
1	1.010	1.020	1.030	1.040	1.050	1.060	1.070	1.080	1.090	1.100
2	1.020	1.040	1.061	1.082	1.102	1.124	1.145	1.166	1.188	1.210
3	1.030	1.061	1.093	1.125	1.158	1.191	1.225	1.260	1.295	1.331
4	1.041	1.082	1.126	1.170	1.216	1.262	1.311	1.360	1.412	1.464
5	1.051	1.104	1.159	1.217	1.276	1.338	1.403	1.469	1.539	1.611
6	1.062	1.126	1.194	1.265	1.340	1.419	1.501	1.587	1.677	1.772
7	1.072	1.149	1.230	1.316	1.407	1.504	1.606	1.714	1.828	1.949
8	1.083	1.172	1.267	1.369	1.477	1.594	1.718	1.851	1.993	2.144
9	1.094	1.195	1.305	1.423	1.551	1.689	1.838	1.999	2.172	2.358
10	1.105	1.219	1.344	1.480	1.629	1.791	1.967	2.159	2.367	2.594
11	1.116	1.243	1.384	1.539	1.710	1.898	2.105	2.332	2.580	2.853
12	1.127	1.268	1.426	1.601	1.796	2.012	2.252	2.518	2.813	3.138
13	1.138	1.294	1.469	1.665	1.886	2.133	2.410	2.720	3.066	3.452
14	1.149	1.319	1.513	1.732	1.980	2.261	2.579	2.937	3.342	3.797
15	1.161	1.346	1.558	1.801	2.079	2.397	2.759	3.172	3.642	4.177

Accumulation of a Future Sum With Annual Payments

An individual or a corporation may want to make a payment sometime in the future by setting aside a specified amount each year. Suppose, for example, a corporation agreed to pay another corporation Rs 20,000 three years hence for services rendered. The question is how much the corporation must put away each year to accumulate the sum. If the money were going to be put into a savings and loan institution paying 6 per cent, we could solve this problem by using compound value of an Annuity of Re. 1 for *N* years, which gives the compound sum of an annuity. The annual deposit is found by the formula:

$$\text{Annual deposit} = \frac{\text{Sum to be accumulated}}{\text{Table value for compound sum of annuity}}.$$

Semiannual, Quarterly, and Daily Compounding

Many savings and loan institutions state that more can be earned with the semiannual, quarterly, or even daily compounding they provide than in institutions that compound only annually. The shorter the compounding period, the greater will be the yield at the end of the year, for the initial deposit is earning interest on all the interest that has been paid prior to the end of the year.

This concept can be demonstrated with following equation, which shows the value of Re. 1 compounded on an annual basis:

$$S_t = D\,(1 + i)^t.$$

With more frequent compounding, the formula is slightly altered by the addition of another term, p, which refers to the number of times the sum is compounded in a year. This is shown below:

$$S_t = D\left(1 + \frac{i}{p}\right)^{pt}.$$

If, for example, we deposited Rs. 10,000 in a savings and loan institution paying 6 per cent, and the amount were compounded on an annual basis, then the value at the end of one year would be:

$$S_1 = \text{Rs. } 10{,}000\,(1 + 0.06)^1 = \text{Rs. } 10{,}000\,(1.06) = \text{Rs. } 10{,}600.$$

If the Rs. 10,000 were deposited in an institution paying 6 per cent and compounding semiannually, the amount at the end of the year would be Rs. 10 greater:

$$S_1 = \text{Rs. } 10{,}000\left(1 + \frac{.06}{2}\right)^{2\times 1} = \text{Rs. } 10{,}000\,(1.03)^2$$

$$= \text{Rs. } 10{,}000\,(1.061) = \text{Rs. } 10{,}610$$

If the Rs. 10,000 were deposited in an institution paying 6 per cent and compounded quarterly, the amount would be even greater:

$$S_1 = \text{Rs. } 10{,}000\left(1 + \frac{.06}{4}\right)^{4\times 1} = \text{Rs. } 10{,}000\,(1.015)^4$$

$$= \text{Rs. } 10{,}000\,(1.0614) = \text{Rs. } 10{,}614.$$

As the compounding increases from quarterly to daily, *p* increases from 4 to 365. Thus, the greater the number of times the lump sum or an annuity is compounded, the greater will be the ending amount, because interest is earned on interest already paid during the year.

In the above example, the results were shown in the equation format. Note that the interest rate was cut from 6 to 3 to 1.5 per cent, while the periods were increased from 1 to 2 to 4. It should be pointed out that the period values do not refer just to years but to any period of compounding, whether it be years, quarters, months or days.

PRESENT VALUE

In making decisions between alternative investment proposals, one of the problems is how to evaluate the merits of the various projects. There must be some basis by which each investment can be put on an equal weighting scale, which an analyst can use to state definitely that one project is superior to another. When projects have different cash outlays and different revenue lives, the analysis is quite complex. One way this problem is simplified is with the concept of present value (PV). Essentially, this concept evaluates the earnings of the project in a time framework and evaluates the future earnings stream in terms of its present worth. When this is done for all projects being considered, there is a common base from which the selection decision can be made. The concept of present value can be considered in terms of both annuities and lump-sum amounts.

Present Value of a Lump Sum

The concept of *present value of a lump* examines the current value of a future payment. The concept recognizes that a Rupee today is worth more than a Rupee in the future. If someone offered you a choice of either Rs. 1,000 today or Rs. 1,700 five years hence, which should you take? The question can be answered in two ways. The first is to determine the value of Rs. 1,000 five years hence by using the concept of the compound sum of Re. 1. If we know that the interest rate available on a so-called secure investment is 5 per cent, then we could either compound the Rs. 1,000 or find the current value of the Rs. 1,700 future sum by discounting that sum back to the present. Utilizing Table 3 we find that the table factor is 0.784. By plugging it into the formula shown below, it can be determined that the value is Rs. 1,333:

$$\text{Present value} = \text{Rs. } 1{,}700 \times 0.784 = \text{Rs. } 1{,}333.$$

Note that, as with other concepts, the table value is multiplied by the rupee value. From the above analysis, it is clear that you should prefer the Rs. 1,700 five years hence. In essence we are saying that if the Rs. 1,000 were invested at 5 per cent far five years, a value of Rs. 1,276 would be obtained. Thus the sum given today is worth less.

The concept of present value is simply the opposite of compounding. Instead of finding the future value of a stated amount, we are interested in finding the current value of a future sum. This relationship can be expressed as:

$$\text{Present value} = PV = \frac{S}{(1+i)^n},$$

where:

PV = Present value of the sum.

S = Future sum being discounted.

i = Interest rate used as the discount rate.

n = Number of years.

If the numbers were substituted into the equation, we would have:

$$PV = \frac{\text{Rs. } 1{,}700}{(1.05)^5} = \text{Rs. } 1{,}700\left(\frac{1}{(1.05)^5}\right)$$

$$= \text{Rs. } 1{,}700\ (0.784) = \text{Rs. } 1{,}332.80$$

$$= \text{Rs. } 1{,}700\left(\frac{1}{1.276}\right) \text{from Table 2}$$

$$= \text{Rs. } 1{,}700\ (0.784) \text{ from Table 3}$$

$$= \text{Rs.} 1{,}332.80.$$

Present Value of an Annuity

Often we are interested in finding the present value of a whole series of payments. If you were offered a choice of a lump-sum payment of Rs. 2,000 or an annuity of Rs. 800 a year for three years, how large would the lump sum have to be to make you indifferent between the two alternatives? If we knew that we could invest the lump sum at 5 per cent, we could use this as the

Table 3

Present Value of Re. 1

Year	1%	2%	3%	4%	5%	6%	7%	8%	9%	10%	12%	14%	15%
1	.990	.980	.971	.962	.952	.943	.935	.926	.917	.909	.893	.877	.870
2	.980	.961	.943	.925	.907	.890	.873	.857	.842	.826	.797	.769	.756
3	.971	.942	.915	.889	.864	.840	.816	.794	.772	.751	.712	.675	.658
4	.961	.924	.889	.855	.823	.792	.763	.735	.708	.683	.636	.592	.572
5	.951	.906	.863	.822	.784	.747	.713	.681	.650	.620	.567	.519	.497
6	.942	.888	.838	.790	.746	.705	.666	.630	.596	.564	.507	.456	.432
7	.933	.871	.813	.760	.711	.665	.623	.583	.547	.513	.452	.400	.376
8	.923	.853	.789	.731	.677	.627	.582	.540	.502	.467	.404	.351	.327
9	.914	.837	.766	.703	.645	.592	.544	.500	.460	.424	.361	.308	.284
10	.905	.820	.744	.676	.614	.558	.508	.463	.422	.386	.322	.270	.247

discount factor and determine in today's rupees what the annuity is worth.

The solution to the problem can be expressed in the following formula:

Present value of an annuity = PV_A

$$= R_1\left(\frac{1}{1+i}\right)^1 + R_2\left(\frac{1}{1+i}\right)^2 + \ldots\ldots + R_n\left(\frac{1}{1+i}\right)^n,$$

where:

PV_A = Present value of the annuity.

R_n = Yearly sum to be received.

i = Interest rate.

n = Number of years being considered.

Since we are concerned only with three years, the formula is:

$$PV_A = R_1\left(\frac{1}{1+i}\right)^1 + R_2\left(\frac{1}{1+i}\right)^2 + R_3\left(\frac{1}{1+i}\right)^3.$$

And, since the annuity stream is constant at Rs. 800 per year, the formula can be simplified to:

$$PV_A = R\left[\frac{1}{(1+i)^1} + \frac{1}{(1+i)^2} + \frac{1}{(1+i)^3}\right]$$

$= R$ (Present value of an annuity factor found in Table 4).

Utilizing Table 4, which shows the present value factors for an annuity of Re. 1, we can determine that the value of the annuity is Rs. 2,178.40. This is shown in Equation.

PV_A = Rs. 800 × 2.723 = Rs. 2,178.40.

If it is known that the lump sum to be received is Rs. 2,000, and it could be invested at the same interest rate as the annuity, you should definitely prefer the annuity because the present value of the Rs. 800 annuity stream of income is much more than the lump-sum payment today Rs. 2,000.

Annual Receipt from an Annuity

The concept of an annual receipt from an annuity is used by the insurance and securities industries to establish retirement plans for corporate employees and individuals. The concept can be illustrated by the following example.

Table 4

Present Value of an Annuity of Re. 1

Year	1%	2%	3%	4%	5%	6%	7%	8%	9%	10%
1	0.990	0.980	0.971	0.962	0.952	0.943	0.935	0.926	0.917	0.909
2	1.970	1.942	1.913	1.886	1.859	1.833	1.808	1.783	1.759	1.736
3	2.941	2.884	2.829	2.775	2.723	2.673	2.624	2.577	2.531	2.487
4	3.902	3.808	3.717	3.630	3.546	3.465	3.387	3.312	3.240	3.170
5	4.853	4.713	4.580	4.452	4.329	4.112	4.100	3.993	3.890	3.791
6	5.795	5.601	5.417	5.242	5.076	4.917	4.766	4.623	4.486	4.355
7	6.728	6.472	6.230	6.002	5.786	5.582	5.389	5.206	5.033	4.868
8	7.652	7.325	7.020	6.733	6.463	6.210	6.971	5.747	5.535	5.335
9	8.566	8.162	7.786	7.435	7.108	6.802	6.515	6.247	5.985	5.759
10	9.471	8.983	8.530	8.111	7.722	7.360	7.024	6.710	6.418	6.145

An executive considering retirement learns that an investment he made years ago and had completely forgotten is now worth Rs. 40,000. The original sum had been invested in a security that has been growing at approximately 9 per cent per year and is expected to grow at the same rate for the next ten years. The executive is interested in determining how much can be withdrawn over the next ten years in equal installments such that, at the end of the period, the balance will be zero.

The solution to this problem is to find the annual withdrawal payment which would result in a zero balance at the end of ten years. Knowing that the present value of the annuity stream is Rs. 40,000 and that the interest rate is 9 per cent, it is a simple task to adjust equation,

$$PV_A = R \times IF,$$

to solve for the amount of the annual withdrawal. This is shown in Equation

$$R = \frac{PV_A}{IF},$$

where

PV_A = Annuity stream (Rs. 40,000).

R = Unknown receipt stream.

IF = Interest factor for the present value of an annuity.

We know that the interest factor for ten years at 9 per cent is 6.418, from the present value of an annuity table. Therefore we solve the equation:

$$R = \frac{\text{Rs. } 40{,}000}{6.418} = \text{Rs. } 6{,}232.47.$$

Thus the executive can receive Rs. 6,233 a year for ten years before exhausting the Rs. 40,000 sum. Even though there are annual withdrawals from the sum, the remaining balance is still growing at 9 per cent, which will yield considerably more than the original sum of Rs. 40,000.

Present Value of an Uneven Receipt Stream

In the discussion of the present value of an annuity concept, it was pointed out that a constant stream of income was being received each year. In many instances, however, a constant annual sum is unrealistic. When firms evaluate future investment alternatives, it is very unlikely that in future years the investment will return a constant annual amount; rather, a uneven stream of earnings is probable.

HOW CERTAINTY CONDITIONS AFFECT CAPITAL BUDGETING?

The consideration of the formal process of capital budgeting analysis by examining it under conditions of certainty is the theme of this section. By certainty we mean that the forecast of future cash flows a project may create is known with 100 per cent accuracy. No element of risk need be considered when examining the capital budgeting process under conditions of certainty.

The general goal in evaluating investment proposals is to judge them on the basis of the return they will yield and compare that to what investors might demand in terms of a return. The measure of return on the project should be equal to or greater than what the investors require. The measure of the rate of return is the key to determining the effect of the investment of the market price of the common stock. This is of vital importance, since we have defined as the primary goal of the firm the maximization of the value of the firm. This is achieved through the maximization of the wealth of the shareholders, and this is reflected in the price of the common stock.

Firstly, we examine the process involved in gathering the relevant data necessary to evaluate the profitability of one project versus another. This includes the definition of cash flows and an illustration of how a determination of future cash flow estimates is arrived at. When we estimate the benefits to be received from a project, we are interested in the cash flows the project will generate rather than an estimate of future net income. This is because cash in essence is critical to all decisions of the firm. The firm is committing cash now in the form of an investment in the hopes of receiving cash in the future that will be in excess of that investment. In the final analysis, it is cash and only cash that can be reinvested in the firm or distributed to the shareholders in the form of dividends. This is why, in the capital budgeting process, we are interested in cash flows rather than net income.

Later we shall examine some different methods for ranking investment alternatives and then consider which ranking technique is the best to use for capital budgeting analysis.

Determination of Cash Flows

One of the primary tasks in the evaluation of investment alternatives is the determination of the net cash flow stream. This task must be accomplished for all investment proposals under consideration. This determination is very important, because the profitability analysis of alternatives depends on the accuracy of the net cash flow information.

Prospective investments which compete with one another in terms of the functions they perform are classified as *mutually exclusive;* if you accept one you must automatically reject the other. Investments which do not compete in terms of their function are classified as *non mutually exclusive* investments. When the cash flows generated from one project are contingent upon other projects, these investments are classified as *contingent cash flow* streams. If the cash flows of a project do not depend upon any other project, they are termed *independent*.

METHODS FOR RANKING INVESTMENT PROPOSALS

This section will present five methods of ranking alternative investment proposals. Each attempts to determine analytically an array of investment opportunities which would be profitable for the firm. In today's world, many capital decisions are made only out of necessity, without any consideration given to profitability. Many firms have no formal evaluation process by which future investment alternatives that may add to the wealth of the firm and to the wealth of the shareholders can be examined. Instead, management is so involved in the day-to-day operations of the firm that it loses sight of its goal structure and makes investment decisions solely on what is termed the *degree of necessity.* This situation can arise when repairs are necessary on the equipment or the plant, or major alterations in a product line are needed to keep revenues coming in. In these situations, management leaves no room to consider the contribution of the equipment, plant, or product line to the overall goal and profit structure of the firm.

Rather, it makes these decisions to keep sales revenues coming in to meet immediate cash needs.

In a time of narrowing profit margins and increasing competition, it is essential for any firm wishing to achieve its goal structure to employ a formalized capital budgeting process which continually evaluates all aspects of the organization and future investment opportunities. Ideally, this evaluation process should utilize some of the suggested techniques outlined below.

Payback Method

The payback method of ranking investment alternatives is defined as the number of years it takes to recoup the initial investment for a project. The technique gives preference to investment proposals with the earliest payback periods. It utilizes net cash flow data, as illustrated in Table 5. Both projects A and B require an initial outlay of Rs. 1,200. The net cash flows shown in Table 5 indicate that project A would have a payback period of two years, while project B would have a payback period of three years. This was determined by counting the number of years it takes to recover the initial outlay of Rs. 1,200 through the net cash flows. The data in the above example indicate that project A is preferable to Project B because the payback period is shorter.

Table 5

Illustration of the Payback Technique for Rs. 1,200 Investment

Year	*Net cash flows*	
	Project A	*Project B*
1	Rs. 700	Rs. 200
2	500	400
3	300	600
4	100	800
5		1,000

Though this technique is utilized frequently in American business, it has two major drawbacks. The first is that it does not take into account the earnings over the entire life of the project. In the above example, project A was preferred to project B, yet the revenue pattern for A stopped after the fourth year, while that of B continued, with net cash flows increasing through the fifth year. The second drawback is that the pay-back method does not consider the time value of money. Though the technique does favor the earliest recapture of the investment, there is no formal process by which weights can be assigned to the cash flow stream, as is done in the concept of present value. As a result, we cannot design a preference structure which shows that rupees today are worth more than dollars in the future.

In the past, defense of the payback method has centered around the fact that revenue streams in the future face great uncertainty, and projects that return an early payback eliminate some of that uncertainty. Another defense of the payback method is that the immediate need for cash to keep the firm running, automatically gives preference to earlier payback projects. In reality these are not valid defenses but rather excuses for not utilizing a more sophisticated procedure for running the firm. There are numerous techniques for handling the problem of uncertainty in cash flow streams, which will be discussed later in this chapter. In addition, better forecasting and budgeting procedures are needed so that the firm can be aware of future cash squeezes in advance and not be forced to accept projects solely for their immediate cash contribution.

Average Rate of Return

One method of ranking investment alternatives is primarily an accounting method consisting of a ratio of the average annual profit after taxes to the average net investment. Table 6 presents income data for projects C and D, which will be utilized in the calculation of the average rate of return (ARR).

Table 6

Illustration of the Average Rate of Return

Year	*Income data*	
	Project C	*Project D*
0 Initial outlay	Rs. 20,000	Rs. 30,000
1 Net income	500	1,750
2 Net income	750	1,500
3 Net income	1,000	1,250
4 Net income	1,250	1,000
5 Net income	1,500	750

Following equation shows the format for solving the average rate of return.

$$\text{Average rate of return} = \frac{\dfrac{\text{Total net income}}{\text{Number of years}}}{\dfrac{\text{Initial investment} + \text{Ending book value}}{2}}$$

Solving, we obtain an average rate of return of 10 per cent for project C and 8.3 per cent for project D.

$$ARR_C = \frac{\dfrac{\text{Rs. }5{,}000}{5}}{\dfrac{\text{Rs. }20{,}000}{2}} = \frac{\text{Rs. }1{,}000}{\text{Rs. }10{,}000} = 10\%$$

$$ARR_D = \frac{\dfrac{\text{Rs. }6{,}250}{5}}{\dfrac{\text{Rs. }30{,}000}{2}} = \frac{\text{Rs. }1{,}250}{\text{Rs. }15{,}000} = 8.33\%$$

On the basis of this analysis, project C is preferable to project D.

One advantage of this method over the payback method of ranking investment alternatives is that the average rate of return does consider the earnings over the entire life of the project. However, there are two strong criticisms of the average rate of return. The first is that the concept does not take into account the time value of money. This is clearly evident by the fact that project C is preferred to project D, yet project D is the one with heavier inflows during the early life of the project. The second criticism is that the technique utilizes profit after taxes as an accounting concept and does not consider the net cash flows of the project.

Thus the average rate of return, like the payback method, leaves much to be desired as a technique by which to evaluate alternative investment proposals.

Internal Rate of Return

The internal rate of return (IRR) method of ranking alternative investment proposals is the first method we will be discussing which incorporates the concept of the time value of money. Recognizing that a rupee today is worth more than a rupee tomorrow, this technique utilizes the concept of present value in the calculation process. Thus the concepts of the present value of a lump sum and the present value of an annuity discussed earlier are applied to the IRR ranking method.

Formally defined, the internal rate of return is that rate of discount which *equates the present value of the net cash flows with the present value of the investment*. The equation for the internal rate of return can be shown as:

$$\text{Present value of investment} = \frac{R_1}{(1+r)^1} + \frac{R_2}{(1+r)^2} + \ldots\ldots + \frac{R_n}{(1+r)^n} = \sum_{t=1}^{n} \frac{R_t}{(1+r)^t},$$

where:

R_t = Annual net cash flows to be received from the investment proposal

$(1 + r)^t$ = Discount rate applied to the net cash flow stream.

If an even series of net cash flows is being dealt with, solving for r is fairly simple. Assume we are interested in determining the internal rate of return for a project that cost Rs. 15,000 today and is expected to return Rs. 5,000 in net cash flows each year for four years. The format for this problem is shown in following equation.

$$\text{Rs. } 15{,}000 = \frac{\text{Rs. } 5{,}000}{(1+r)^1} + \frac{\text{Rs. } 5{,}000}{(1+r)^2} + \frac{\text{Rs. } 5{,}000}{(1+r)^3} + \frac{\text{Rs. } 5{,}000}{(1+r)^4}$$

To find the internal rate of return, we divide the cost by the annual net cash flows and obtain the table interest factor (Rs. 15,000/Rs. 5,000 = 3). Then we look in the present value of an annuity table under the row of present value factors for four years and read across the row until we find the closest interest factor calculated in this table. Then read up the column to the top where the discount factors are listed. The internal rate of return is close to 12 per cent. The steps outlined show how to interpolate to find the exact rate of return, which is 12.6 per cent.

6

FINANCING AND INVESTMENT DECISIONS

THE FINANCIAL STRUCTURE OF THE COMPANY

THE following text focuses on the financing instruments that are available to a firm for use on a short-term or intermediate-term basis. The purpose is to identify these instruments and to indicate when they should be utilized. This decision involves an evaluation of short- and intermediate-term instruments as contrasted with long-term instruments.

In terms of the financial management framework (see Chapter 1,) we will be discussing the implications that funding mix decisions can have for the goals and the value (worth) of the firm. In Figure 1 the funding mix decision is shown as an aspect of financial structure, one of the three major corporate stratagems. As they affect the leverage structure of the firm, decisions as to which financing instrument to use will be subject to an analysis of the risk-return trade-offs. The options selected to comprise the financial package will be evaluated by upper level management to determine if the proposed financial plan meets the goal structure of the firm.

Figure 2 illustrates the facets of analysis that are involved when a firm makes a decision as to what type of financing instrument it

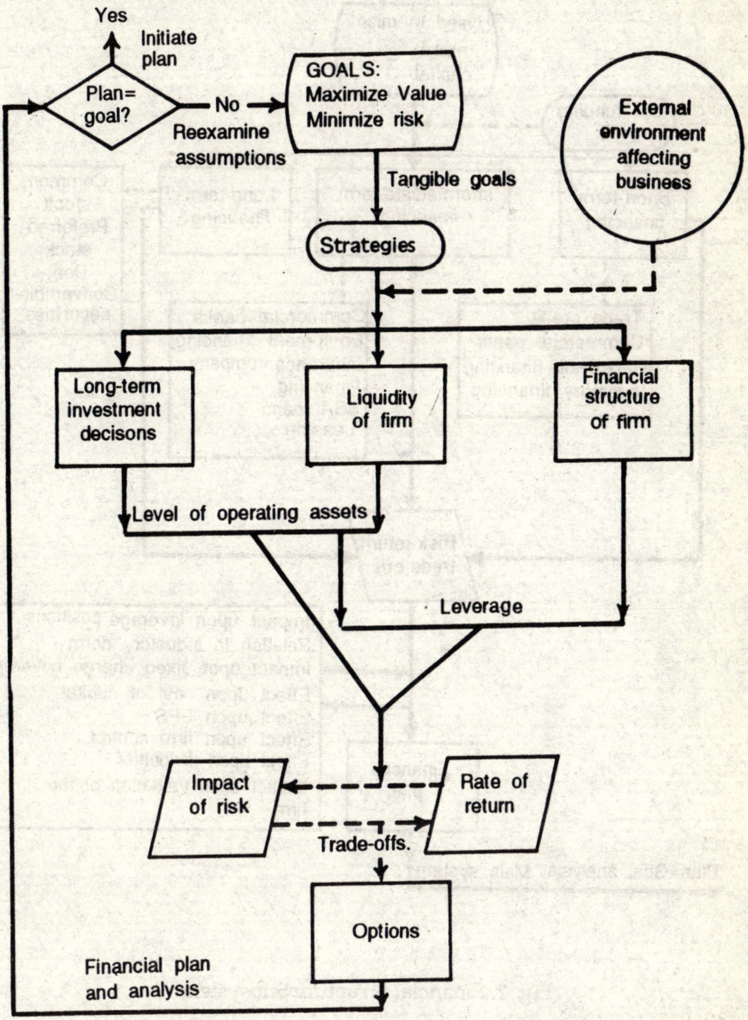

Fig. 1. Financial Management Framework.

should utilize. The old funding mix enters the flow as an input into the system. Short- intermediate-, and long-term financing

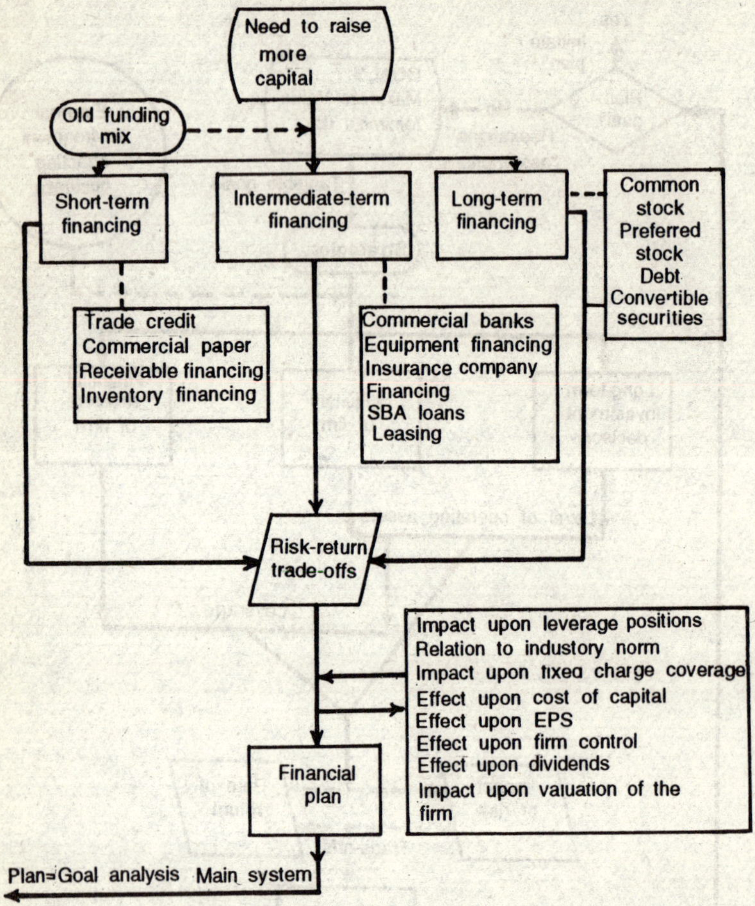

Fig. 2. Financial Structure Subsystem.

sources are available for consideration. However, associated with each alternative financing source are the considerations of the risk-return trade-offs. The analyst must make the financing decision in light of its possible effects for the leverage position of the firm, the cost of capital, the earnings per share, and the value of the firm. Once a decision is made, given the risk-return trade-offs, the financial package is completed and enters the main system leading to the plan-equals-goal analysis.

Of the various decisions the financial manager must make, the financing decision is one of the most important. The incurrence of a financing liability requires the periodic payment of interest and, upon maturity, payment of the principal. This obligation becomes a fixed burden for the corporation. Failure to make these payments can place it in bankruptcy.

SHORT-TERM FINANCING

Here the emphasis is on short-term financing such as trade credit, commercial paper, and other forms of instruments with a maturity structure of one year or less. Generally, management of the firm will make a decision as to the distribution between short- and long-term financing. An accepted rule is that short- term needs should be financed by short-term sources and long-term needs by long-term sources. This is why inventories and accounts receivable generally are financed by accounts payable and short-term bank lines of credit.

One source of short-term financing we will not discuss is accrued expenses, which frequently are referred to as spontaneous sources of financing. Accrued wages, taxes, and other expenses do provide a short breathing space for many firms, but because of the contractual nature of the obligation there is not a large degree of flexibility in adjusting the payment pattern. Though it is a major part of the current liability picture it is not a viable decision variable.

Trade Credit

Trade credit has become one of the most common forms of short-term financing available to business today. For business establishments, it is the form most often used. When a firm buys supplies or merchandise, the supplier will generally grant a period of time for the firm to pay for the goods even after it has already received them. At no explicit interest cost, this is a very attractive means of obtaining goods. Today suppliers are much more liberal than financial institutions in the granting of credit. For small firms that have limits as to the amount of borrowing that can be obtained from a financial institution, trade credit is not only attractive but is a vital form of financing.

Trade credit can assume three different forms: open account, notes payable, and trade acceptances. The most common is the *open account,* whereby a customer receives shipment of the goods and an invoice which details the price, quantity, and description of the goods, along with a specified time for payment. The term *open account* comes from the fact that no written agreement other than verification of receipt of shipment is required. Such credit is extended after the supplier has checked the credit worthiness of the customer.

The second form of trade credit is *notes payable.* If a customer has slipped behind on payments or if a supplier simply wants formal recognition of the obligation, it may ask the buyer to sign a note which officially recognizes the debt obligation of the buyer. The note will specify when the payment is due. Promissory notes are frequently used in lieu of open accounts in the fur and jewelry industries.

The third form of trade credit is *trade acceptances.* In this situation, the seller draws a document calling for the payment for goods at some future date. The seller will not release the goods until the buyer has formally accepted the draft, and has designated a bank to be the recipient of the payment when it becomes due. At that point it becomes a trade acceptance and, if the buyer has a good credit reputation, may have a degree of marketability. If it is marketable, the seller can discount the trade acceptance and receive immediate funds in payment of the goods. When the trade acceptance finally matures, the holder of the acceptance presents it to the designated bank for collection.

The Cost of Trade Credit

Because trade credit is one form that does not have an explicit rate of interest attached, many businessmen feel that it is free credit. This is true in terms of not having to pay any additional interest above the face value of the goods. However, in terms of maximizing the value of the firm, there is a definite cost associated with trade credit. If cash discounts are offered and not taken, there is a definite opportunity cost or implicit rate of interest associated with the face amount of credit. By not taking the cash discount, the firm foregoes the opportunity of getting a reduction on the face value of the purchased merchandise. It then foregoes the opportunity of profitability utilizing this savings elsewhere.

This situation can be illustrated by an example of a firm that is offered credit terms of 2/10, net 30 and does not utilize the cash discount. The formula utilized to calculate the implicit interest cost is:

$$\frac{\text{Per cent cash discount}}{1 - \text{Per cent cash discount}} \times \frac{360}{\substack{\text{Net credit period} \\ (30\text{ days} - 10\text{ days})}}$$

Applying the credit-term data of 2/10, net 30, yields:

$$\frac{2}{98} \times \frac{360}{20} = 0.0204 \times 18 = 36.73\%.$$

Thus the annual interest cost of not taking cash discounts amounts to 36.73 per cent.

As the net credit period lengthens, the annual cost of not taking the cash discount declines. If the net credit period were 30 in the above example, the number of times this period occurs during a year would decline in Equation. When multiplied by the discount period, this would reduce the annual interest cost to:

$$\frac{2}{98} \times \frac{360}{30} = 0.0204 \times 12 = 24.5\%.$$

Continuing with the assumption of 2/10 discount terms, the relationship between the annual interest cost and the net credit period can be shown in Figure 3. This illustrates the fact that as the net period increases, the cost of interest decreases. By the same token, if the cash discount is not taken, it is imperative that the firm efficiently manages the cash position and does not pay the bill until the net period elapses. If the bill is paid before the net period elapses, the effective interest rate increases.

To illustrate this last point, assume that the credit terms are 2/10, net 30. The firm does not take the cash discount, but instead of waiting until the 30 days elapses to pay the bill it historically pays by the 15th day. The annual opportunity cost is substantially increased:

$$\frac{2}{98} \times \frac{360}{15 - 10} = 0.0204 \times 72 = 146.9\%.$$

The reason why the interest cost or opportunity cost has increased to such a large degree is that the customer, by choice, has decreased the net 30-day period to a net of 15 days. Thus the net

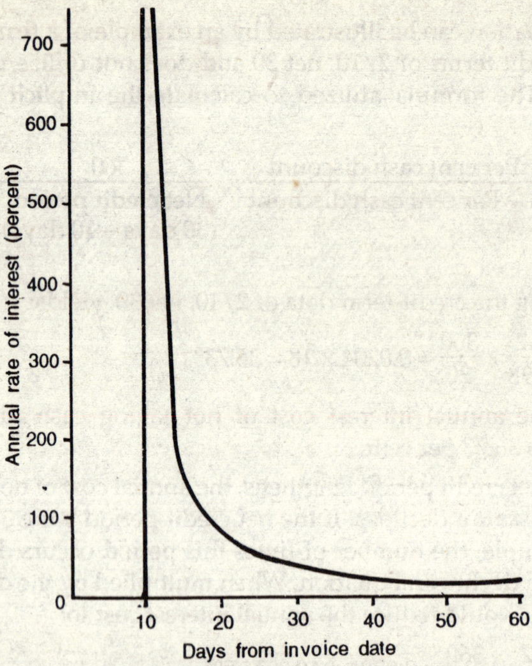

Fig. 3. Annual Rate of Interest on Accounts Payable (with terms of 2/10, net 30)

credit period after the cash discount period of 10 days has been reduced from 20 to 5 days. It is clear that there is a considerable opportunity cost associated with a decision not to take cash discounts offered by suppliers.

Advantages and Disadvantages of Trade Credit

There are several advantages associated with the use of trade credit. The greatest is that this source of credit is readily available for most firms. No formal credit application is required each time it is utilized. Only in the initial application does a buyer go through a credit check by the supplier. If a firm has been taking cash discounts and a liquidity problem arises, additional credit is available by allowing the payables to lapse until the end of the net period. Generally, there are no restrictions associated with trade credit such as those that are common with other forms of short-term lending. The only specific restriction pertains to the amount of trade credit that will be extended at any particular time.

Trade credit is particularly important to small firms which have difficulty receiving loans from financial institutions due to their lack of credit worthiness as viewed by these institutions. In a period of tight money where the availability of loanable funds becomes limited, trade credit is an even greater source of financing for the small firm.

Associated with the use of trade credit are two distinct disadvantages which can become costly for a firm. The first relates to stretching the accounts payable beyond the credit period. Frequently firms feel that since they regard trade credit as a free source of financing, they can stretch the accounts payable and no harm will be done. This is a very dangerous assumption. Most firms have an accounts payable aging schedule in which accounts payable are due within 30 days, 60 days, 90 days, and beyond. The longer the aging schedule, the more difficult it is for a firm to pay off overdue bills. If they go to banks for financing, banks will require that payables be current within 60 days. If there is a significant percentage which goes beyond this period, the bank will require that part of the loan proceeds be used to bring the payable current. A firm's response to a liquidity crisis is often to lengthen its payables. If this continues, however, its suppliers will no doubt cut the line of credit.

The second disadvantage of trade credit concerns firms that extend this form of credit and thereby record accounts receivables. If it does not receive immediate cash, a firm extending trade credit may have to look to other sources of financing to underwrite the production cycle. The longer customers take to pay their accounts payable, which are the suppliers' receivables, the more critical the cash shortage becomes. Frequently, a firm extending trade credit will have to slow down on the payment of its own accounts payable when there is a significant lengthening in its accounts receivable aging schedule. This in turn can jeopardize the firm's credit relationship with its suppliers.

Commercial Paper

Commercial paper is a form of financing which consists of short-term promissory notes which are unsecured and are sold in the money market. They are issued by large companies and primarily sold to other business firms, insurance companies, pension funds, and banks. Because they are unsecured and are sold in the money market, they are restricted in use to the most credit-worthy of the large companies. Though the commercial paper market has a long history, much of its tremendous growth has occurred in recent years with increases in the installment financing of automobiles and other consumer durable goods. As credit tightens in terms of the banks' ability to make loans, the commercial paper market increases. Many of the companies that issue these notes now look at this market as an alternative source of financing.

The Commercial Paper Market

The commercial paper market includes a dealer distribution system and a system of direct placement. Most industrial firms, utilities, and medium-size finance companies utilize the dealer market to place their commercial paper. Five major dealers comprise the market, which purchases the paper from firms and then sells it to investors. Denominations of commercial paper range from Rs. 25,000 to several rupees, and maturity runs from about two to six months, with an average of five months. The cost of this paper is from 0.5 to 1 per cent below the prime lending rate. Considering that there are no compensating balance requirements, the rate differential is still more significant. The commission on the sale of paper runs from 0.125 of 1 per cent. Many firms are looking at this source of financing more in terms of a permanent source than as the traditional seasonal instrument.

Appraisal of the Commercial Paper Market

Commercial paper is a much cheaper source of financing than short-term bank financing, as we have noted. Many companies are considering commercial paper as a supplement to bank credit. A company could make use of the paper market when the interest rate differential was large and borrow from the bank when the gap narrowed. This would result in the lowest borrowing cost to the firm in the short term.

Evidence has indicated that it is imperative for a firm not to impair its relations with a bank by using its services only during periods of extremely tight money, however. It is often suggested that a firm should have a backup line of credit with a bank to cover its borrowing position in the commercial paper market.

One factor which has helped the growth of the commercial paper market is a regulation that the maximum loan a national bank can make to a single borrower is 10 per cent of the bank's capital and surplus. It is the perpetual need of short-term capital that has helped the commercial paper market to boom.

UNSECURED SHORT-TERM BANK LOANS

Short-term bank financing plays a key role in the growth of a firm. Frequently during the course of a year there is a period in which cash inflows are not sufficient to meet cash outflow demands. Short-term bank financing is one important vehicle by which a firm can be carried through such periods. This form of financing appears as a note payable on the balance sheet at a specific rate of interest. It is second only to trade credit in importance.

Types of Unsecured Bank Loans

Unsecured bank loans usually take the form of a line of credit, a revolving credit agreement, or a transaction loan.

Cash Credit Limit. A limit of credit usually sets an upper limit as to the amount a firm can borrow on an unsecured basis. It is usually set for one year and is subject not only to an annual cleanup but also to an annual review before renewal. This review consists of an examination of an audited annual report. The line of credit is established after the bank has evaluated the credit worthiness and financial needs of the borrower.

Usually this form of financing is considered to be a temporary source which carries a firm through a seasonal low in terms of cash inflows. A cash budget is frequently drawn up to show the estimated cash inflow and outflow pattern over the next year. It may be that in 3 of the 12 months a negative cash flow pattern emerges; this can be handled by a line of credit. The required clean-up period usually extends for 30 days out of the year. When a firm is unable to clean up its line of credit, it is an indication to the bank that a more permanent source of financing may be needed.

Revolving Credit Arrangement. Unlike the line of credit, which does not involve a legal commitment on the part of the bank, the revolving credit agreement is a formal commitment by the bank to lend up to a specified amount at the wishes of the borrower. In essence, this is a guaranteed line of credit issued by the banks. Negotiations between bank and borrower will determine the maximum amount of commitment. If, for example, the firm borrowed Rs. 1.3 million four months ago from a Rs. 2 million revolving credit agreement, it can borrow the remaining amount at any time. For this privilege of having a guaranteed line of credit, the firm must pay a commitment fee on the unused portion of the revolving credit.

Transaction Loans. Certain types of business firms do not need a line of credit or a revolving credit agreement but may need short-term capital for a specific use. A good example is in the construction industry, in which firms often need funds to complete jobs. After the contractor receives payment for a job it can repay the bank. Banks examine each request on an individual basis. The ability of the borrower to repay the loan through projected cash flows is quite important in this type of arrangement.

Compensating Balance Requirements

Banks will not only charge interest on a short-term line of credit; in addition, they will require the borrower to maintain a demand deposit balance. This balance is calculated in direct proportion to the amount of the borrowed funds.

Demand-deposit requirements are called compensating balances and will usually run from between 10 to 20 percent of the loan balance. If the loan is for Rs. 100,000 and there is a 20 percent compensating balance requirement. Rs. 20,000 must be kept in deposits at the bank. If this required balance is above the balance that the firm normally maintains at the bank for operation needs, the effect is to raise the effective rate of interest on the loan.

The bank usually views the compensating balance requirement as a means of increasing the general liquidity of the borrower. In addition, it provides the bank with a margin of safety in case the firm defaults on its repayment.

SECURED FORMS OF CREDIT

Borrowing on an unsecured basis would always be the best method for a firm to use in obtaining bank financing. This provides a wide latitude of operation, for at a later date the existing collateral can be utilized for more debt financing. In addition, record keeping for collateralized loans is costly and time-consuming.

However, banks often require a form of security to be put up as collateral to protect the lender in the case of default. This requirement means the firm can obtain capital when it would otherwise be impossible. Sometimes the collateralization of a loan will lead the lending institution to quote a lower interest rate, which over time can be of considerable advantage to the borrower.

Security to collateralize a loan can take many forms. Marketable securities, land, buildings, equipment, and inventory are all possible sources of collateral. Marketable securities, which appears to be the best form of collateral, are usually in short supply for firms needing capital. Land, buildings, and equipment are usually used as security devices for long-term forms of lending. Most of the collateral used for short-term financing needs, therefore, is supplied by accounts receivable and inventories.

BILLS RECEIVABLE FINANCING

One of the more liquid assets on a firm's balance sheet that is assignable for collateral is its accounts receivable. As such, they are a prime lending vehicle. There are two methods by which a firm can utilize the accounts receivable in obtaining short- term financing. It can either *pledge its receivables* as collateral against a loan, or it can *sell its receivables*, which is called *factoring*.

Pledging Bills Receivable

When a firm pledges its accounts receivable, the lending institution has a lien on them. If any receivables default, the firm which pledged them is responsible and must take the loss. When a firm utilizes this form of collateral, the organization that originally purchased the goods on credit is not notified. Commercial banks and the larger sales finance companies are the organizations that typically lend on this form of collateral.

In establishing this form of financing, the lender and the borrower sign legally binding documents which set forth the obligations of each party. Once this is done, whenever the borrower obtains a large enough amount of receivables they are taken to the lending institution for evaluation. The lender screens the receivables, weeding out those that are unacceptable. Usually the lending institution will advance funds up to 75 to 80 per cent of the face value of the receivables. This provides a margin of safety for the lending institution in case of default on the payment of any receivables. This also forces the borrower to take a so-called equity position in the receivables. The lender will always try to get as wide a margin of safety as possible on the collateral. Many times the lending institution will demand recourse to the borrowing firm if the customer defaults on receivables.

The interest rate on this type of financing usually runs about 3 percentage points above the prime lending rate. If the receivables do not meet the quality requirements of traditional lending institutions, such as banks and large finance companies, there are other companies which lend on receivables that are perceived to have higher risk. The interest rates charged are usually quite high compared to the traditional lender's rates, however.

Factoring Accounts Receivable

When a firm factors its account receivable, it actually sells them to a factor who actually buys the receivables. This may be done with or without recourse. With recourse, the factor can look to the seller of receivables for payment if there is a default on the payment of the receivable. Without recourse, the factor cannot look to the seller of the receivables for collection in case of default.

The factor maintains a credit department which can undertake a credit check of a customer. If a firm sells without recourse, utilization of this service can allow it to forego the cost of maintaining a credit department of its own. In this case, the factor assumes risk and bad-debt losses and all expenses associated with collecting slow accounts. The customer of the firm who is factoring the receivables may or may not be told of the factor agreement; this decision is made between the lender and the seller of the receivables.

Associated with the assumption of risk and servicing of the receivables is an added cost to the seller. Usually a fee is attached which runs from 1 to 3 per cent of the face value of the receivables. In addition, there will be interest charges for funds that are advanced before collection by the factor.

The cost of using a factor can be illustrated with the following example. A firm factors on the average Rs. 100,000 per month for a year. The factor will lend 80 per cent of the face value of the receivables and will charge a factoring fee of 1 per cent of that face value. In addition, the factor charges 1 per cent interest per month on the amount borrowed. The interest cost and the factoring fee are taken out in advance of all funds given to the firm. Assume that the firm borrows the full amount each month. We can calculate the annual cost to the firm of utilizing the factoring service as shown in following equation.

$$\text{Actual cost} = \frac{\text{Interest cost} + \text{Factoring fee}}{\text{Actual rupees received}}$$

In this example, the factor fee of 1 per cent of Rs. 100,000 amounts to Rs. 1,000. If the firm borrowed Rs. 80,000 per month at 1 per cent, the monthly interest would be Rs. 800. If the interest and factoring cost are deducted before the firm receives any funds, the actual cost would be:

$$\text{Actual cost (per month)} = \frac{\text{Rs. } 800 + \text{Rs. } 1{,}000}{\text{Rs. } 80{,}000 - \text{Rs. } 800 - \text{Rs. } 1{,}000}$$

$$= \frac{\text{Rs. } 1{,}800}{\text{Rs. } 78{,}200} = 2.3\%$$

On an annual basis, this would amount to 27.6 per cent (2.3 per cent times 12).

INVENTORY FINANCING

Inventory is another asset that has considerable merit as collateral for short-term financing. The lender usually will advance only a specified percentage against the face value of the inventory. This loanable value is based on the type of inventory being considered and the ability of the lender to dispose of it in case of default. The more specialized the inventory and the market for the product, the more unwilling is the lender to advance a large percentage of the face value. The more standard and salable the inventory, the higher the loan percentage. Frequently lenders will loan 90 per cent of the face value when they feel the inventory is standard and has a ready market, apart from the marketing organization of the borrower.

Lenders usually consider such items as marketability, perishability, market price stability, and difficulty in liquidating the inventory in determining the percentage value that they are willing to advance on an inventory loan. The most important aspect of a lender's analysis is to substantiate that there is enough liquidating value in the inventory to cover the loan and accrued interest in case of default on the part of the borrower. In addition, the lender must determine the ability of the borrower to service the debt by examining the cash flow structure of the firm. There are several ways in which inventory can be collateralized; these methods are discussed below.

Floating Lien

A feature of the Uniform Commercial Code permits a borrower to pledge inventory "in general" as collateral against a loan, without specifying the inventory involved. This allows the lender to obtain a floating lien or claim against all of the borrower's inventory. This type of arrangement is very difficult to police, and in general it is made only to provide extra security for a loan. A floating lien can cover both receivables and inventory; thus it allows a lender to obtain a lien on the major part of the current assets of a firm. The floating lien also can cover both present and future inventory.

Chattel Mortgage

A chattel mortgage provides for the borrower's inventory to be identified specifically by a serial number or some other means. The borrower still holds title to the goods, but the lender has a lien or claim on the inventory. Under this arrangement, the lender has to give his consent before the inventory can be sold. Any inventory that has a rapid turnover or is not readily identifiable would not be suited for this type of lien arrangement. Capital asset items such as machine tools and other heavy equipment are well suited for a chattel mortgage.

Trust Receptions

With a trust receipt loan, the borrower holds both the inventory and the proceeds from the sale of inventory in trust for the lender. Consumer durable goods, automobiles, and equipment are good examples of the types of inventory that are well suited to serve as this form of collateral.

The automobile dealership system is an excellent example of how a trust receipt collateral system works. When automobiles are shipped to the dealer from the manufacturer, the lending institution will pay the manufacturer under an arrangement made with the dealer. The dealer in turn signs a trust receipt agreement which specifies the handling of the inventory. The dealer is allowed to sell the cars and must turn the proceeds over to the lender. Under the trust receipt arrangement, the inventory is serialized and is periodically audited by the lender. The purpose of the audit is to determine if any cars have been sold without the proceeds of the sale being remitted to the lender.

Each time a new batch of cars is acquired from the manufacturer, a new trust receipt agreement is signed to take account of the new inventory. Though this method provides a wider margin of safety than a floating lien arrangement, there is always the possibility that a dealer will sell cars and not remit the proceeds to the lender in payment of the funds advanced.

Terminal Warehouse Receipt Loans

Under another arrangement for using inventory as collateral for a loan, the borrower's inventory is housed in a public, or terminal, warehouse company. A warehouse receipt which specifies the inventory located there provides the lender with a security interest in the inventory. Because the goods in inventory can only be released on authorization by the lender, it can maintain strict control over the inflow and outflow of inventory. In addition, an insurance policy is usually issued which contains a loss-payable clause for the benefit of the lender.

The warehouse receipt can be in a negotiable or nonnegotiable form. If it is negotiable, the receipt can be transferred from one party to another by endorsement, but before the goods can be released the receipt must be presented to the warehouse man. A nonnegotiable warehouse receipt is issued in favour of the lender, which has title to the goods and is the only one that can release them. The nonnegotiable receipt arrangement provides that the release of goods must be authorized in writing. Most arrangements are of the nonnegotiable form.

Field Warehouse Receipt Loans

With the form of collateralization known as the field warehouse receipt loan, the inventory remains on the property of the borrower. A field warehouse company sets off a specific part of the borrower's storage area in which to locate the inventory being used as collateral. Often this area is physically fenced off and only the field warehouse company has access to it. Once the collateral value of the inventory is verified by the field warehouse company, the lender advances the funds. This arrangement is desirable when there is great expense involved in locating the inventory elsewhere, especially true when the borrower has a high inventory turnover ratio.

There is no question that the cost of this form of collateral financing is very high. This is primarily due to the cost of the warehouse company which acts as a third party in this arrangement. The evidence of collateral is only as good as the warehouse company issuing the receipt. Historically there has been evidence indicating fraud in terms of the validity of the inventory actually being stored in a particular spot.

INTERMEDIATE-TERM FINANCING

Short-term debt, as noted in previous pages, exists for less than a year and is used to finance seasonal and temporary needs; lending institutions like to see short-term debt cleaned off the books for at least 30 days during the course of a year. Intermediate-term debt, the subject of this chapter, is used more for equipment purchases and permanent build-ups in accounts receivable and inventory. Cash flows generated from future operations are used to repay these loans through periodic payments of principal and interest. Usually the payment period or term is on a monthly basis and ranges from two to ten years. The length of a term loan is a function of the cash flow generated by the assets purchased with the borrowed funds.

The major sources of intermediate-term financing—bank term loans, insurance company loans, equipment financing, and lease financing—are discussed in this chapter.

TERM LOANS

Term loans written by banks represent one of the most vital financing resources for a firm. A bank term loan is for a period of maturity of more than one year. It consists of a formal loan agreement signed by borrower and lender, and in most instances it is collateralized by some of the firm's assets.

Usually the loan agreement will specify how a term loan is to be repaid. The most frequent method is through monthly payments consisting of interest and principal. Some term loans are written in such a way that there is a large final payment at the end. This has the advantage of reducing the monthly payments, but it increases the overall interest payments and may create a financial burden for a firm trying to obtain the funds for the final payment. A term loan may be paid off before maturity, but this is usually accompanied by a prepayment penalty as fixed by the lending institution at the time of prepayment.

Maturity. Term loans can be written for from two to ten years. In previous years, banks were reluctant to lend beyond four to six years, because the estimated cash flow uncertainty of the borrower was considered to be very dangerous. Now however, maturities frequently run up to seven years and in some instances are as long as ten years.

Collateral. Commercial banks usually require a firm seeking a term loan to put up as collateral stocks, bonds, machinery, or equipment. Banks require collateral on about 90 per cent of loans.

Warrant positions. In recent years, many institutional investors, including bank subsidiaries, have not only required the fixed periodic repayment of a term loan but have also been taking an equity position in the company as additional compensation. This usually takes the form of warrants which give the lending institution an option to purchase a specified quantity of the company's common stock at some future date. Investors who have made this arrangement with a firm that later becomes dynamic in sales performance have had an opportunity for substantial yield, provided a good secondary market develops in the common stock.

Interest. The interest cost on a term loan is usually higher than for short-term loans. On a short-term basis, a firm may be able to borrow at the prime rate. A term loan for the same firm may range from 0.25 to 0.50 per cent higher. Term loans may be written on a fixed interest rate base, which is set at the beginning of the life of the loan and is effective throughout its life, and on a variable rate, which can be adjusted to changes in the prime lending rate. For the variable rate, the usual procedure is to set floor and ceiling levels which the interest rate cannot exceed but can fluctuate within. In addition to the explicit interest cost, there is an implicit cost in terms of required compensating balances.

Advantages. Term loans provide a great deal of flexibility to the borrower. The firm deals directly with the lending institution, and the loan is tailored to its needs. When the firm develops a strong banking relationship over the years, its own bank can be the source of a term loan. If conditions change during the life of the loan, its structure can be altered or revised. Term loans provide a source of debt capital for small firms that do not have access to the large capital markets and for large firms the need to obtain capital quickly and do not want to go through the lengthy process of a public issue.

Limitations. One of the more significant limitations of a bank term loan is the length of time it can cover (maximum ten years) and the limited amount that can be lent. If more capital is needed, the firm must negotiate with more than one lender; this is when an insurance company may participate in the loan with the bank. Another limitation is the restrictive covenants that can accompany a term loan; however, these would undoubtedly also be encountered with insurance company term loans as well as bond issues. Another limitation is the issue of warrants which give the lending institution an equity position in the firm, which may be undesirable from the shareholders' point of view.

Characteristics of the Loan Agreement

The term loan provides the borrower with a guaranteed source of capital for a longer period than a 90-day bank loan can. The firm does not have to continually renew the loan and submit it to review to determine if it should be renewed. If the position of the company has deteriorated, the bank may not renew a short-term loan. These factors are not present in a term loan. However, restrictive covenants usually are associated with a term loan agreement, due to the long-term commitment by the bank and its desire to protect its position. Several of these restrictions are identified below.

Working Capital Position. Usually a bank or lending institution will require a firm seeking a term loan to maintain a minimum working capital position. In relation to the current ratio, a relationship of 2 : 1 or 3 : 1 is frequently required.

Fixed Asset Requirements. Lenders will frequently place restrictions on the amount of additional fixed assets that may be purchased by the borrower after the loan has been obtained. While some fixed assets are often purchased with part of the loan proceeds, this restriction refers to additional purchases. This fixed-asset requirement is designed to keep the borrower from undertaking commitment beyond what is considered prudent by the lender.

Additional Long-term Debt. Frequently there are prohibitions to prevent the firm from acquiring additional long-term debt without the permission of the lending institution, in order to protect the lender's claim against the assets used as collateral. This is frequently not a problem, because most lenders do not like to take second positions on a firm's assets. The loan agreement may also prohibit a firm from assuming any contingent liabilities, such as subsidiary guarantees, and there may be a clause prohibiting long-term leases above a specified amount.

Management. The loan agreement may also specify that there may not be a major change in management personnel without the permission of the lender. Usually the lender will require that there be life insurance on the key individuals within the firm to protect the lender in the event of loss of services of a management figure due to death.

Financial Statements. Always, the lender will require the firm to submit quarterly financial statements for review. This allows it to observe the financial performance of the firm continually and to try to forestall a financial problem that may be observed on the horizon.

All of these restrictions are aimed at protecting the interest of the lender. It is important that the collateral assigned to the loan be completely guaranteed in terms of the lender's claim to them in case of liquidation. It is also important that the firm maintains an adequate cash flow structure so that the repayment schedule can be secured. Therefore the lender tries to make sure that the firm does not undertake any fixed commitments that could jeopardize the cash flow structure.

Insurance Company Loans

Like commercial banks, insurance companies have become very active in lending. However, insurance companies are generally interested in making loan commitments that have a maturity structure in excess of ten years. The explicit interest cost may be higher on insurance company loans due to the fact that there are no compensating balance requirements. However, the implicit interest cost might very well be similar to that of a term loan from a commercial bank.

The investment in a term loan must yield a sufficient return to make it competitive with alternative investment decisions for an insurance company. Prepayment penalties are associated with insurance company loans because these firms like to invest for longer periods of time without interruption. Associated with the loans are restrictive covenants on working capital, fixed asset acquisition, long-term debt, and management activities similar to those for term loans from commercial banks.

Frequently, a bank and an insurance company will share in the same loan. The bank will participate for from five to seven years, with the insurance company participating in the remaining life of the loan; both will draw up a single loan agreement. This financial combination is a distinct advantage to the firm because it can help service both its intermediate- and long-term financial requirements. In fact, the bank and the insurance company complement each other in the lending arena.

In India such intermediate term financing is not very common. Insurance companies are more known for Housing development loans and such. These are more regulated by the Govt. policies compared to traditional lending institutions.

EQUIPMENT FINANCING

When equipment is pledged for collateral, it is usually for intermediate-term loans to finance purchase of the equipment. The most important consideration for a lender utilizing new equipment as collateral is to set up a repayment schedule that is a direct function of the estimated cash flow to be generated from the equipment. The loan repayment schedule will also be tied to the estimated economic life of the equipment.

It is important for a lending institution to have a margin of safety in using equipment as collateral. This is why the estimated market value will always be greater than the actual loan value. This margin of safety can assist a lending institution when it must liquidate the equipment and settle for less than Re. 1 for every rupee of stated equipment value. Frequently liquidation settlements will run down to 70 or 60 cents on the rupee. The loan advance against equipment that is readily salable will be much greater than for more specialized equipment.

To determine a fair value for the equipment, the lender or the borrower will have an independent appraisal made which will give not only an itemized figure on the market value of the equipment but also an estimate of the liquidation value. In addition to considering the actual amount realizable from selling the equipment, the lender must also consider the costs involved in physically disposing of it. All of these factors enter into the decision as to how much will be advanced against the equipment as collateral.

Sources of Equipment Financing

Commercial banks, finance companies, and equipment manufacturers or sellers are actively involved in the financing of equipment. Commercial banks will lend at a lower rate than finance companies. In india these are regulated by the guidelines of the Reserve Bank of India. The latter should be used only as a last resort. The finance companies usually do not finance the full amount from their own resources but get the same re-financed from a commercial bank or such lending institution such as IDBI, IFCI or ICICI, etc. The seller of the equipment may act as a financing source; it can hold the paper or dispose of it by selling it to a captive finance company. In many cases where heavy equipment is involved, the manufacturer or seller is the only source of financing its purchase. In practice this is done through a separate company practically owned by the manufacturer or seller. This is one reason why many heavy equipment manufacturers have formed captive finance companies. Chattel mortgages and conditional sales contracts are two methods by which these loans can be secured.

FINANCING OF SMALL SCALE SECTOR

There are various programmes in force for financing small business, usually known as small scale industries. For example these include Prime Minister Rozgar Yojna, Women entrepreneur financing programme, shree shakti programme of SBI, etc.

An industrial unit is defined as one engaged in the manufacturing, processing and/or preservation of goods. Additionally, units engaged in repairs and servicing are also deemed to be industrial units.

What is a Small Scale Industry

The definition of Small Scale Industries has undergone changes from time to time. It is linked to the investment in plant and machinery by the unit. At present, a SSI unit is defined as one which is engaged in a manufacturing, processing, preservation of goods or repairing (or certain specific items) and its investment in the plant and machinery is not more than Rs. 3 million 500 thousand. An ancillary unit is basically a Small Scale Industrial Unit of which supplies or proposes to supply more than 50% of its products to one or more parent units (which may or may not be SSI units) for production of other articles.

Tiny Industry

The concept of Tiny Industry is rather recent. It is a small scale industrial unit which is situated at centres having population of 50,000 and the investment in the plant and machinery is not over Rs 200 thousand.

District Industries Centre

In every district there is a 'District Industries Centre' to cater to the needs of Small and Village Industries. The centre provides, under one roof, all the services and support required by Small Scale, Village and Cottage Industries such as supply of raw material, machinery and equipment, credit facilities, marketing research, etc. There is a separate wing with the centre to deal with cottage and household sector.

Approach of Banks

The basic approach of the banks towards financing of small scale industries is to encourage its growth by meeting all its need-based financial requirements. Financing of small scale sector got an impetus with the nationalisation of Imperial Bank of India in 1955, which was then renamed as State Bank of India. State Bank took up financing of small scale industrial units in the 1956 as a pilot project in a few selected centres in the country. The experience gained by the SBI in this area proved to be a trend- setter and provided valuable inputs to the banking sector as a whole for intensive financing of this sector. SBI's record in the financing of small scale industries, where it has proved itself to be the unquestioned pioneer in the country, set the tone for the other banks in this field. Right from the initial stages, it was stressed that the purpose of the loan and the viability of the project are of much greater consequence, than the security furnished. While at subsequent stages, all the banks framed their own schemes, these are governed by the norms stipulated by the Reserve Bank of India (RBI) from time to time.

Due to certain inherent weakness, the small scale industries cannot face the competition offered by the large industries. Hence, the bank decided to provide credit facilities to small scale industries on liberalised terms. The scheme was introduced by SBI in the year 1956 on pilot scheme basis in 22 districts of the country later on its area of operation was extended to the entire country. The scheme envisages relaxation in the norms of financing as also grant of some additional facilities.

Liberalisation

Under the Liberalised Schemes of Assistance to Small Scale Industries the relaxations are permitted in the following areas:

Approach. The approach is need based and not security oriented.

Security. SBI meets genuine credit needs of SSI units and stress is not on the security, the borrower is in a position of offer. Collateral/additional securities is not a rigid requirement.

Margin. In case of Small Scale Industrial advances, lower margin is retained which normally varies from 20 to 40%. Whereas in other advances, normally higher margins are required. The margins can be further reduced in deserving cases

Rate of Interest. Bank charges lower rate of interest from the small scale industries borrowers and follow differential pattern of interest. These are governed by the RBI's directives from time to time. At present it is as low as 10% for loan of Rs 7,500, for Rs 100 thousand the rate is 15%.

Additional Facility. Additional facilities like Special hypothecation, Trust letter, Trust receipt, Contingent limit, etc. are provided to small scale industrial units.

Entrepreneur Scheme of SBI

This is a scheme specially designed for technically qualified persons or those having business qualifications who are unable to meet even the minimum margin requirements of the bank, i.e., those unable to provide even 15% of the project cost from their own sources. Technically qualified persons include those having degrees/diplomas in any technical field of study, with or without experience, as also craftsmen with adequate experience in the line of proposed manufacture. For the purpose of the scheme, business qualifications would mean having a degree/diploma in business management from a recognised and approved institution or being a qualified Cost/Chartered Accountant.

As in the case of the liberalised schemes, all the activities covered by the credit guarantee scheme of the Reserve Bank of India are eligible for finance under the scheme. Originally ceiling of Rs. 200 thousand was applied to the quantum of finance permissible under this scheme, which has subsequently been raised to Rs. 1 million. Under this scheme, under appropriate circumstances, the bank may finance the entire requirements of the unit by waiving the margin contribution of the unit in full, i.e., there is no minimum margin requirement to be met by the unit. In respect of interest rates also, some further concessions are also made to units financed under this scheme.

Stree Shakti (Women Power) ***Package of SBI***

This is a complete range of assistance developed by the SBI specially for women entrepreneurs. All small scale and small business activities are covered—be it a handloom weaving unit, handicrafts, pickle/paper making, garments or SSI unit. To qualify as a women entrepreneur, the person shall own at least 51% of the enterprise and at least 50% of the work-force/employees engaged by the enterprise should be women. Besides concessions in margins and interest, from time to time, SBI holds special Entrepreneurial Development Programme for such women entrepreneurs, who have no formal training or exposure to business.

Equity Fund Scheme of SBI

Generally funds are supplied by the promoters in the form of equity (own capital) and by the financial institutions and other sources by way of loans. Further, some minimum funds are required, say 25% of the project cost, as equity capital before these financial institutions give loans to new unit. However, for some entrepreneurs it is difficult to bring the minimum equity capital.

The problem could be solved by reducing the minimum equity capital requirement, i.e., reducing margin from 25% to some lower amount, say 15% and meet the shortfall by additional loan. This is one possible solution but it affects the viability of the project adversely, as costs increase on account of interest burden affecting the profits and secondly, the cushion of equity available to absorb shocks in case of emergencies is reduced. In short, the unit will suffer from a low equity base problem.

To obviate this and meet all genuine needs of the entrepreneur without affecting the viability of the projects, State Bank of India has introduced a novel scheme of financing which is known as the Equity Fund Scheme under which long term interest free loans are given to eligible small scale entrepreneurs.

Source of Fund for Equity Fund Scheme. Funds for assistance under the scheme are provided by appropriating a certain amount of the profits earned by the bank. The fund has been created with a view to bringing about rapid development and industrialisation to enable the bank to meet its social commitments.

Eligibility. Any one who fulfils the following criteria is eligible for assistance under the scheme:

1. The applicant should be taking up the venture for the first time.
2. The applicant(s) should devote direct and full attention to the unit, and should not be associated with any other unit in any capacity.

3. The applicant should confine borrowings to State Bank of India only. In case the applicant has availed term loan from State Financial Corporation, exception would be made if all other borrowings are confined to the State Bank of India.
4. The cost of project should be not less than Rs. 25,000.
5. The applicant should be eligible for finance under our normal schemes for financing of SSI.
6. The applicant should not propose an activity which comes under Selective Credit Control of RBI.
7. The applicant should be atleast a matriculate.

Investment

(The applicant) is required to invest as much as you can, as a larger equity base would strengthen the project. However, the minimum requirement is as follows:

1. 10% of the project cost when considered for finance in Liberalised Scheme.
2. 5% of the project cost if the applicant is trained under the Bank's Entrepreneurial Development Programme and financed under our Liberalised Scheme.
3. 'Nil' when financed under Entrepreneur Scheme.

Equity Assistance

The actual amount of the assistance will be the difference between 25% of the project cost and the equity capital available with the applicant, subject to a minimum Rs. 5000 and a maximum Rs. 0.1 million (the amount of assistance would be rounded off to the nearest thousand).

Interest Rate and Re-payment

No interest will be charged by the Bank on the assistance provided under Equity Fund Scheme. However, on the other loans interest would be charged at usual rates. Further, in the event of misutilisation/non-compliance of stipulated terms etc., the Bank reserves the right to charge interest at normal rate for the entire period for which equity assistance is availed. Keeping in view the need to conserve resources in the initial period, normally no repayment is stipulated for 5–7 years. Thereafter, the loan is to be repaid in 5–7 years in convenient monthly/quarterly/half yearly instalments. The repayment will be fixed according to the surplus generation capacity of the unit.

Security Requirements

As equity fund assistance is a part of the total financial assistance, no additional security is needed. The security provided for the other loans will stand extended to cover the assistance under Equity Fund Scheme.

The securities are of two types:

Primary Security. When charges by way of hypothecation or pledge or mortgage are created over the assets acquired out of the bank's finance, such securities are primary.

Collateral Security: It is known as secondary or additional security also. When charges are created over the assets other than those procured out of the bank's finance, such securities are by way of secondary securities.

For example, a term loan is granted for purchase of a tractor and the tractor is hypothecated to the bank. The agricultural land of ten acres is also mortgaged to the bank in addition to the hypothecation of the tractor. The hypothecation of the tractor will be primary security and mortgage of land will be treated as collateral security.

LEASE FINANCING

Lease financing has become one of the most important sources of financing for a firm. It is a method of obtaining use of buildings and equipment without purchasing them. Before 1950 the concept concerned the lease of only land and buildings. Today, almost any asset can be leased.

In a lease arrangement, the *lessee*—one who leases from others—obtains most of the values that are associated with ownership of the asset, while the *lessor*—one who leases to others—retains title to the asset. The obligations of the lessor and lessee are detailed in a lease contract. The contract establishes the *lease period* in which the contract is noncancelable and the *lease payments*, which consist of periodic payments for the use of the asset. It also details the *lease options*, which specify how the lease can be renewed or how the asset can be purchased at the end of the lease period. Finally, the lease contract establishes whether the agreement is a net lease or maintenance lease. Under a *net lease*, the lessee pays all the cost of maintenance, repairs, taxes, insurance, and other expenses. Under a *maintenance lease*, the lessor has the responsibility of maintaining the asset and paying all insurance expenses.

Types of Leases

Leasing is similar to borrowing in that a lease contract provides the firm with financial leverage. One feature of leases is that the full amount is deductible for income tax purposes, but the Internal Revenue Service must agree that the contract is a genuine lease. There are several factors that should be specified in the lease agreement to demonstrate to the IRS that the contract is a viable lease agreement. First, the terms of the lease must be less than 30 years, or the lease will be considered as a form of sale. Second, the rent payments must represent a reasonable return to the lessor, which would be in the range of 7 to 12 per cent. Third, the renewal option must be a bona fide arrangement which can be met by giving the lessee the first option to meet an outside bid.

Service Leases. Operating and service leases include provisions for both financing and maintenance. Computers, automobiles, and trucks usually are in this category of leases. Because frequently the lease contract will not return the full value of the asset to the lessor, it is usually written for a period of time less than the economic life of the asset. The lessor obtains the rest of the funds by a renewal from another party or by selling the property.

Under this arrangement, the lease payments include a fee for the service and maintenance of the property. A service lease will also include a clause that gives the lessee the right to cancel the agreement and return the property before the expiration date. This has the advantage of allowing the lessee to consider new property if the property becomes obsolete.

Financial Leases. Strict financial leases require the lessee to maintain and service the property. It cannot cancel the lease, and the lessee must fully amortize the lease so that rental payments equal the full price of the property.

A firm seeking new equipment under a financial lease will first select the equipment and negotiate a price and delivery terms with the manufacturer. Then the firm will contact a bank or leasing company which will buy the equipment from the manufacturer or distributor and then lease it to the firm that wants to use it. Simultaneously, a lease agreement is written between the user and the lessor which consists of the terms previously specified in a lease contract. The lessee can renew the lease but cannot cancel it without paying the lessor fully the value of the equipment.

This contract is basically the same as that used in the sale and leaseback agreement. Thus a sale and leaseback arrangement can be considered as a special type of financial lease.

Sale and Leaseback. In a sale and leaseback arrangement, a party owning land, buildings, or equipment will sell the property to another party with the capacity to execute an agreement which allows the seller to lease the property back for a specified period of time. In the case of land and buildings, life insurance companies are the prime lessors, while in the case of equipment, commercial banks, insurance companies, or specialized leasing companies are usually contacted.

The major advantage to such an arrangement is that the seller immediately receives cash for the property which it can utilize elsewhere but still has the use of the property. In addition, the lease payments are 100 per cent tax deductible, whereas a loan on the facilities only creates a tax shield in terms of the interest payments.

Leasing or Borrowing

The decision as to whether an asset should be leased or purchased depends on the cash outflows involved and the opportunity cost of funds for the firm. There are several techniques to assist in the analysis. Among these more popular are: These have been discussed in detail in *The Economic Aspects of Management*, vol. 3 of this treatise the present value and internal rate of return methods.

Availability of Leasing Services

In general, a lease contract can be arranged for any asset which has sufficient value to justify the paperwork involved and sufficient durability to permit the lessor to realize salvage value should the lessee fail to fulfill his contract. It is difficult to find a lessor who will provide leasing service for an asset which retails at less than Rs. 5000, it may be quite easy to find a lessor for an asset costing several million rupees. Assets which are commonly leased include aircraft, computers, business machines, material handling equipment, machine tools, trucks, automobiles, and railroad cars.

Sources of Lease Financing

As time goes on, more and more entrepreneurs have begun to recognize profit potential through offering leasing service. The potential lessee must use great caution in selecting his lessor, so that he can sure that the lessor will continue in business during the lease term.

Manufacturers may offer a lease plan to their customers directly or through an associated captive finance company. If the manufacturer wishes to emphasize greater distribution of his product, he may be content with his normal profit margin on the "sale" to the lesser and thus price his leasing service at very reasonable rates.

The finance companies may offer leasing service as well as their standard services of accounts-receivable financing, chattel-mortgage financing, and conditional-sale financing. However, as competition from other lessors has intensified, many finance companies have been unable to secure their desired return on investment through offering leasing service, and this part of their operation has been de-emphasized.

Many leasing companies offer their services through direct mail, magazine, and newspaper advertising. They may work closely with a manufacturer, train salesmen in leasing techniques, and provide outside financing to carry the leases produced by the manufacturer's sales department. Where such liaison exists, the manufacturer may arrange to market used equipment returned from the leases.

Commercial banks now offer leasing service to their customers, since regulating authorities authorized them to become outright owners of leased equipment. The banks find that their return on investments in leased property may exceed that of mortgaged property. Sometimes banks furnish capital for leases to their customers; a leasing company may handle a administration of the leases.

Lease brokers act as intermediaries between lenders, leasing companies, and leasing users. The broker determines the need of the prospective lessee and solicits bids from banks, leasing companies, and other financing sources. The broker is compensated for his services by the organization furnishing the financing, or he may be paid as a consultant by the lessee.

Investment bankers and the tax departments of large accounting firms may assist a prospective lessee in finding leasing service through private placement of the lease with syndicates of wealthy investors or with corporate customers with available cash reserves. Many limited partnerships have been formed which permit the partners to use depreciation on leased assets and the investment tax credit as deductions against taxable income. As income requirements of such investors may be minimal, the rates for this type of leasing service may be below those otherwise available. Similarly, the manufacturer wishing to lease equipment may form his own subsidiary leasing company which may secure financing on its own credit standing or on the guarantee of its parent. Careful legal work must be done to insure that such an organization is a separate entity for tax purposes.

Trends in the Leasing Industry

In earlier years, many small organizations with less than first-grade credit standing were successful in leasing assets, although the rates charged were very high. Such leasing service is now more difficult to locate, as lessors generally require a good credit standing for long-term leasing. There has been high mortality among smaller leasing companies which were unable to secure the needed capital for equipment purchasing as their marketing activities expanded. Many such companies were merged with larger firms. Thus, the trend in the industry is toward consolidation, with the larger firms surviving.

Banks are becoming more and more aggressive in direct leasing. As the smaller leasing companies secure their financing from banks, frequently banks used by their lessee, the banks control money costs to the lessor. When a bank enters the leasing industry directly. It eliminates the leasing company's mark-up on the cost of borrowed funds and thus decreases the cost of leasing to the user. Thus, growing bank leasing involvement is accelerating the consolidation of small leasing organizations into larger, well-financed firms.

As users of leasing have become more sophisticated, they have insisted that their financial officers solicit several bids for substantial leasing requirements. Rate competition among major lessors is very common. This competition has decreased the profitability of leasing achievable by the smaller leasing organization.

For several years, such specialized leasing companies offered computer leases at rates less than those charged by the computer manufacturers. These were non-pay-out leases. The lessor felt he could re-market the used computer at the end of the lease term. To offset this competition with their own leasing plans, manufacturers reduced rates and likewise removed "software" services from leases undertaken by the computer leasing companies.

While early leases may have averaged three years in length, there is a trend toward lengthening the lease to an approximation of a normal depreciable life of the asset as allowed by Government schedules. This is done to counteract the Government's effort to disallow short-term leases on the ground that they are disguised contracts of conditional sale.

Because of wide fluctuations in interest rates, there is a growing trend to negotiate a floating financing rate which is tied to the prime rate as set by major banks.

Thus, the lessee may wish to negotiate with the lessor for a pass-through of the credit. He may benefit by securing an immediate deduction from taxes without having made an outlay for the entire purchase price of the asset acquired.

Advantages to the Lessor of Equipment

Increased Sales for Manufacturers. As leasing service is widely available from the sources mentioned earlier any manufacturer can offer a leasing plan to his customers without investment of his own capital in these long-term receivables. Consequently, his marketing is made more effective through his offering of the leasing plan.

Stabilizing Business Cycles. Lease receivables billed on a monthly or quarterly basis provide a determinable future income on which cash utilization projections can be made. A company which manufactures on a seasonal basis may find that leasing will assist in spreading sales income more evenly throughout the year.

Forced Obsolescence. As all lease contracts have a basic lease term, the manufacturer's or leasing company's marketing department has an opportunity to approach the lesser toward the end of the basic lease to suggest that an improved machine be leased to replace the current machine. Such a marketing program can have substantial impact on the regular introduction of new products.

Profit on Resale or Re-Lease of Used Equipment. Where there is residual value left in equipment at the end of a lease, it may be diverted to a secondary market at considerable profit to the lessor.

Profit on Financing. The lessor always has the opportunity to increase his financing rate sufficiently to return a profit on the financing of the lease, in addition to the profit to be realized on salvage value of the asset at the end of the lease.

Discount from Manufacturer. The lessor operating independently may be able to negotiate a purchase of the asset at a discount from the manufacture, and then charge the lessee rentals based on the full retail price.

Profit on Renewals and Purchase Options. The lease may include such provisions and if the lessee exercises them additional profit comes to the lessor.

Retention of Investment Tax Credit. The lessor may have the right to retain the investment tax credit. Individuals and non-corporate lessors may claim the ITC only if they manufactured the leased assets, or are in the business of offering "short"–term leases, or are able to meet certain difficult-to-pass mechanical tests. Large lessors in a profit position may find the credit very useful in reducing income taxes.

The Lessor's Problem of Financing

As mentioned earlier, there has been considerable mortality among leasing companies because of cash flow problems. An aggressive marketing staff constantly brings new leases to the financial officer. He must constantly tap new sources of financing to secure the money required to purchase the equipment needed by the lessee. Organizations planning to enter leasing should enlist help from their accountants in charting anticipated cash requirements. Lessees selecting leasing organizations should be sure to choose one with proper financing and with the needed managerial skills.

Contractual Arrangements

Leases normally are written for a basic term of an agreed number of months or years. Renewal options may be negotiated by the lessee. Purchase options may likewise be negotiated. Some leases provide for substitution of later-designed equipment and return of original equipment. The rates for leasing service are usually expressed in percentages of total equipment cost paid on a monthly or quarterly basis. The effective add-on interest rate can be determined by multiplying the amount of the monthly leasing payment by the number of months in the basic period, and then comparing that total to the quoted retail purchase price of the asset being leased.

For leases of smaller rupee amounts to companies of less than first-grade credit standing, effective interest rates may range from 12% to 18%, or higher. For large companies, typical rates may be expressed as additions to the prime rate of interest, perhaps 2% to 3% above the prime rate. In special transactions, applicable financing rates may be less than the prime rate if the lessor is permitted to keep the investment tax credit and also expects to realize substantial income on residual or salvage value. Substantial leasing transactions such as those relating to jet aircraft may carry financing rates substantially below the normal equipment-leasing rate schedules.

Most leasing contracts provide that the lessee maintain the equipment. Normally the lessee is expected to insure the equipment in favor of the lessor as well as the lessee, and the lessee is expected to pay personal property and other taxes assessed against the leased equipment. In Ohio, for instance, if the lease contract permits the lessee to purchase the property at lease-end, the lessee must pay the property taxes. If there is no purchase option, the lessor must pay the property tax. If the lessee can contractually shift to the lessor the payment of taxes, the insurance of the leased assets and their maintenance, then the tax deductibility of the lease payments is more assured.

Advantages of Leasing

Several advantages of leasing have continually been emphasized in any discussion of a lease-or-buy decision. These include flexibility, tax considerations, and accounting treatment.

Flexibility. It is stated often that leasing provides greater flexibility than buying as regards the obsolescence of equipment. The line of reasoning is that the lessee can turn in the equipment when it becomes obsolete, putting the risk of obsolescence onto the lessor. If the original cost of the asset is fully amortized during the lease period and there is a fixed obligation to make the lease payments whether or not the asset is obsolete, then it is the lessee that bears the risk of obsolescence. However with such equipment as computers and copy machines, flexibility is provided when the lessor allows the lessee to upgrade the equipment before the end of the lease.

One aspect of the degree of flexibility associated with a lease arrangements is the fact that a lease agreement does not have the restrictive covenants that can be associated with a term loan agreement. Leasing does have the distinct advantage of allowing the firm to utilize assets without a down payment requirement. Further, when a firm acquires an asset and then decides to borrow against that asset, the firm can never borrow 100 per cent of the cost.

Tax Benefits

The lease payment is deductible for income tax purposes. With a purchase, the asset must be capitalized, and the depreciation is tax deductible. The introduction of accelerated forms of depreciation has largely diminished the tax advantage associated with leasing.

One tax advantage that is still associated with a lease arrangement concerns the costs of land. When land is purchased for a building site, it cannot be capitalized and expensed. However, if a firm leases land and a building, and part of the lease cost is contributed to the land, the firm has a definite advantage in the sense that management can write off the cost of both the land and the building. One distinct disadvantage of this arrangement is that in recent years land has appreciated to such a degree that the lessor would have the advantage of the residual value associated with it. In essence, the lessee pays for the land, and the lessor receives the capital gains on any future sale.

The investment tax credit has provided an advantage for both the lessee and lessor. With assets that have lives greater than eight years, a 10 per cent investment tax credit is allowed. If the lessor retains the rights to this credit, the lease payments are usually lower. This would especially be true if the lessee did not have sufficient tax liability to utilize the tax credit fully. The extent to which the lessee and lessor might share in the investment tax credit would be left to negotiations between the two parties.

Accounting Treatment. One of the principal advantages of leasing has been the fact that traditionally the lease commitment did not appear on the firm's balance sheet. This allowed utilization of an asset without the need to record the obligation of a fixed financial commitment. With debt financing, both the asset and the debt obligation would be shown. From 1968 to the present, leases have appeared as a footnote on financial statements. Presently there is a great deal of pressure on the accounting profession to capitalize the lease commitment and show it on the balance sheet. If this occurred, the balance sheet effect of leasing or buying would be the same.

One of the important historical effects of leasing is that it could create a deceptive situation on the balance sheet. Without considering lease commitments, an analyst might find that the asset turnover ratios and the return on assets greatly improved with leasing as compared to financing the purchase of the assets. In addition, the leverage position of the firm would be substantially improved under the lease alternative method of financing. Calculation of the times interest earned ratio from the income statement also shows the position of the firm improved with the lease arrangement.

Those who are responsible for making loan decisions and sophisticated investors should not be fooled (and usually are not) by lease arrangements unless they are totally left off the financial statements of the firm. They recognize the fact that a lease commitment is as serious a fixed cost commitment as a debt payment, and the consequences of not making those payments are the same. If the firm borrows money to purchase equipment and does not make the loan payments, the lender will repossess the equipment and the firm will not be able to continue production. The same result occurs if the lease payments are not made. Thus, astute individuals will calculate the fixed charge coverage ratio, which clearly shows the difference in performance with and without the lease.

In terms of the balance sheet, lending institutions will capitalize the lease payments and place this amount in a revised balance sheet to determine the debt position of the firm more accurately. This is also done in the calculation of the weighted average cost of capital for firms that have the debt section, but the component cost of the lease agreement is in-large lease commitments. Not only is the lease capitálized and added in the debt section, but the component cost of the lease agreement is included on an after-tax basis.

Disadvantages of Leasing

One of the serious disadvantages of leasing is the loss of the residual value of the asset. With equipment that has a high obsolescence factor, this is not an important consideration. However, firms which lease large facilities that include both land and building, can find this an important consideration in the decision to lease or buy. In areas such as Southern California, where the real estate market is dynamic and there has been tremendous appreciation of land values over the past two decades, it is of vital importance. Sometimes the lease will have an option feature allowing the lessee to either renew the lease or purchase the assets. This allows the lessee time to examine the potential residual value issue and make a decision at the end of the lease as to whether the asset under consideration is worth the renewal or purchase.

Another disadvantage associated with leasing is that the implicit cost of leasing is usually higher than the cost of debt financing. Usually this cost differential will run 1 per cent or more.

LONG-TERM FINANCING

We have so far discussed the short- and intermediate term financing needs of the company, how they arise, met and legal aspects of such financing methods. No doubt that small and medium scale businesses are also in need of long-term financing but such financing is more relevant to large-scale business. This section focuses on the market for long-term securities and the types of long-term securities available for use by a firm. It also details on the long-term securities market and the people who are involved in helping firms acquire money.

STOCK MARKETS

Whenever a firm utilizes outside sources of capital, the money and capital markets are involved. Conditions in these markets affect the availability of funds, as well as the cost of obtaining them. They also affect both the financing and dividend decisions of the firm.

Therefore the financial manager must be aware of the mechanics of the money and capital markets. He must consider how the firm's financing decision will affect the external environment, and what effect the external environment could have for the firm. Any changes in monetary policy could affect the financing plans of the company in terms of cost and availability of credit. Government and such bodies formed by Government involved in public financing activities must also be taken into account.

ORGANIZED CAPITAL MARKET

In India organized stock exchanges consist of National Stock Exchange (NSE), Bombay Stock Exchange, Delhi Stock Exchange and the regional stock exchanges such as Jaipur Stock Exchange, Kanpur Stock Exchange, Ludhiana Stock Exchange, etc. Internationally just for comparison, organized stock exchanges in America are New York Stock Exchange (NYSE), in Japan Tokyo Stock Exchange (TSE), in U.K. London Stock Exchange etc.

They are classified as organized because they are tangible in the counter market.

OTC (Over The Counter) Exchange

The organized exchanges act as an auction market, providing a physical facility where buy and sell orders are traded. The over-the-counter market is much more intangible. Many of the stocks of new or relatively small companies are traded in this market. The frequency of activity in any one stock may be much less than on the organized exchanges. To avoid problems of trying to match the buy and sell orders of the investing public, the brokerage firms that deal with over-the-counter stocks will usually maintain an inventory of the stocks. When investors sell, the brokerage firms buy, and when the investors want to buy, the brokerage firms sell.

All security transactions that involve facilities not associated with the organized security exchanges are said to be part of the over-the-counter market. This includes the few brokers who maintain inventories in various over-the-counter securities and the vast number of brokers who act as intermediaries in bringing together the dealers who have the inventory and the investors who want to buy.

However, since most large companies are listed on the exchanges, approximately two thirds of the currency volume of stock transactions takes place on the organized exchanges. The opposite situation exists with the bond market. A number of large corporations have their bonds listed on the BSE bond list, but over 90 per cent of the bond transactions occur over the counter. Bonds are frequently traded among the larger financial institutions, and it is easy for a dealer in this market to set up a transaction between financial institutions for a block of bonds. A similar trend has been emerging in stock transactions. Large blocks of stock are being transferred among large institutional investors without going through the exchanges. This practice has the obvious advantage of eliminating brokerage fees, and it will perhaps become more frequent and important in terms of impact on the organized exchanges.

Considerations of Going Public

Many firms which have become profitable over a period of time reach a stage in their development when the decision to go public and issue common stock is an important consideration. If a firm fits certain requirements depending upon the size of industry its management may consult with an investment banker or such consultancy firm to decide whether or not going public is feasible, given a number of factors.

One of the key questions that must be answered through discussions with the investment banker is how successful the flotation of common stock will be in the existing market conditions. The market for issues can be quite volatile in terms of price and confidence in a particular industry. In some instances, the market may not be willing to participate in the purchase of a new issue. Another factor that must be considered is determination of a discount rate to be applied to the earnings stream of the company in order to fix its value. Frequently this will be accomplished by examining other companies in the same or similar industries that have recently gone public.

Sometimes, however, issues will stagnate on the market, a situation which does not present a good image for the company and can seriously jeopardize its ability to raise future rupees through the equity market. Since going public is one path a firm can take to ensure more equity capital in the future, it is very important that the initial issue be warmly received in the marketplace. This is the job of the consultant, in India such consultancy firms are known as 'managers to the issue'. Much of the firm's future depends upon such a firms ability to perceive the market correctly. Their functions and responsibilities are discussed later in this chapter. The working of these firms are regulated by Stock Exchange Board of India (SEBI). The SEBI specifies the requirements for a public issue of the firm and the Companies Act, 1956 regulates the public issue activity of the company. See Vol. 4, *Corporate Management*.

With the result of efforts of past several years there has been a major achievement in developing a national market system which would link all of the nation's major stock exchanges plus the over-the-counter trading in the exchange-listed stock. This body is how known as National Stock Exchange (NSE). The thrust is to create a single, more competitive system.

One of the principal ways to facilitate the development of a central market system is the creation of an electronically operated linking system. This would allow all parties to compete directly to provide the public with the best prices for securities offered for sale.

INVESTMENT BANKING

In every economy, there is a distinct separation between those who save and those who invest. Generally, the savings and investment functions are carried on independently. Some people will save by putting their funds to work in financial intermediaries, who in turn make these funds available to those who need capital, for plant, equipment, and inventory.

The investment banker is a form of financial intermediary for channeling funds from savers to firms needing them. A corporation needing funds will make available a new security offering. The firm will sell the securities to the investment banker, who will in turn sell them to the general public. For the services provided by an investment banker a fee is paid that is equal to the spread between the price the banker pays for the securities and the price at which the securities are resold to the public.

The investment banker forms a very important link in the relationship between the seller of the securities and the public. Most firms do not utilize the capital markets to a great extent and as a result they are not expert in the sale and distribution of securities to the general public. This effort would be very costly to the firm and would carry substantial risk. Few functions of investment banker are listed below:

(1) providing counsel and advice for the firm,

(2) underwriting the issue, and

(3) distributing the issue.

Advise and Investigation. One of the prime responsibilities of the investment banker is to see that the SEBI requirements for conveying the required information to the investing public are met. To maintain a goods relationship with the public, the investment banker extensively reviews the financial statements, properties, and management of the issuing corporation; the name of the banker will be associated with the issue. In addition to investigating the firm, the investment banker acts as counsel and recommends the appropriate selling price and possible interest rate the issue should carry. The goal is to ensure that the corporation's security offering will be well received by the public, so the investment banker can dispose of the issue quickly and liquidate the funds invested in it. If other groups are brought in to assist with disposition of the issue, the investment banker has the responsibility of investigating the firm on behalf of the other participating members.

Underwriting the issue. When underwriting a particular security issue, the investment banker is taking on the risk function. The investment banking group bears all the risk of possible price fluctuation, from the time the corporation sells the issue to the banking group to the time the issue is fully subscribed to in the marketplace. In this situation, the investment banking group pays the corporation the total amount for the issue, less the underwriting commission. The banking group receives the bonds or stocks and then places them on the open market for sale. It may take from several hours to over six months to sell the issue fully.

During this period, the investment banking group bears the risk that the price of the security will drop. Many investment banking groups have had the market drop out from under them while they were attempting to sell securities on the open market. To the corporation, however, there is no risk; it has already received the funds and is utilizing them. The investment bankers have fully underwritten the offering and bear all the risk.

The banker's commission rate may be higher if, in addition to the usual risk of price fluctuations, there is an added risk in terms of the banker's perception of the difficulty in selling the issue. If the firm considers the underwriting costs to be too high, it may utilize what is termed a *best effort offering*. In this situation, the investment banker will sell the issue on a best effort basis; he or she will try to sell as many of the securities as possible at an established price, and, after a specified period of time, will return the remaining unsold securities to the corporation. In this situation, the investment banker bears no risk and is not responsible for selling 100 per cent of the security offering. For this effort, the investment banker will require a smaller fee. A best effort offering is also used when the issue being sold is of high quality and all that is necessary is a marketing channel to be provided by the investment bankers.

Selling the Issue. The most important function of the investment banker is the actual disposition of the securities to the public market. In the final analysis, this function alone will determine the success of the flotation. This is where the full risk exposure of the investment banker comes to bear. If the issue is not disposed of quickly, a large amount of funds will be tied up in handling an inventory of the security.

To speed up the selling process and help spread the risk, the investment banker usually sets up a syndicate to help underwrite the issue. Much of the issue may be sold by the underwriters salesmen, and some may be given to dealers throughout the country. These dealers receive a discount off the selling price of the securities and perform only a selling function. The spread the dealer gets is less than what the underwriter receives because the dealer is not involved in the investigation or risk- bearing functions.

Process of Public Issue of Shares

Firms that are considering the issuance to the public of bonds, preferred stock, or common stock will usually utilize the services of an investment banker because they do not have the expertise to place the issue on the open market. Once the firm decides to utilize the services of an investment banker, the initial contact is made on either a negotiated or a competitive bid basis.

Negotiated offering. Most firms utilize a *negotiated offering;* the firm that issues the securities selects an investment banker and then works with it to determine the critical features of the issue, such as establishment of a price and time of issue.

Competitive Bidding. On a *competitive bidding* basis, the issuing company will specify the date and time the sealed bids from interested investment banking firms will be accepted. Whichever investment banking firm or group submits the highest bid wins the right to issue the securities.

Preselling Activities. The first step in preselling activities is a series of conferences between the issuing firm and the investment banker. The discussion involves the amount of capital needed, possible types of securities that can be issued, and the terms of an agreement. If the issuing company agrees to some of the preliminary discussions, it will enter into an agreement with the investment banker stating that the flotation will take place.

Once the agreement is developed, the investment banker will initiate the investigation of the firm. This involves an analysis by the engineering staff of proposed asset purchases, if any are to be made. A public accounting firm will audit the financial statements of the issuing company and will also assist in the preparation of the registration statement. A legal firm will be asked to render an opinion of the legal aspects of the flotation. The investment banking firm will also undertake its own analysis of the company. Then a formal agreement is constructed between the issuing firm and the investment banker which outlines all of the details of the forthcoming issue except the actual price of the securities.

The next major step is to get clearance from the SEBI (or any other regulatory body) to issue the securities. Once the registration period comes to a close, the price of the issue is set. With a common stock issue, the price to the investment banker is often set several points below the closing price on the last day of registration. A re-production of front page of a prospectus for an issue of *n* amount of shares for *n* price is given on the following page. The name of the company, and no. of shares offered and the amount offered to public is deliberately withheld.

Selling Activities. It is a common practice for the investment banking firm that deals with the issuing corporation not to underwrite the entire issue but to form a syndicate of other investment banking firms to assist in its purchase and distribution. This is because (1) the original underwriter may be financially unable to handle the entire issue, (2) the original underwriter may want to spread the risk evenly when price fluctuation is likely, and (3) the use of other investment banking firms and their distribution channels will help minimize the selling expense and provide for a broad national distribution effort.

When the issue is finally offered for sale to the public, advertising precedes the date of sale. This includes newspaper advertising and the distribution of the prospectus. For a time, the manager of the underwriting group will help stabilize the price of the issue. This is done for 30 days, during which an order is placed to buy the securities at a specified price in the marketplace. This pegging operation helps prevent a downward shift in the price of the stock by placing a floor on the market price. The manager will acquire an inventory of the stock in hopes the price will shortly rebound so that the securities can be resold.

The investment banking function of market stabilization is of vital importance to the success of the flotation. If the price of the security drops to such a level that it takes months to dispose of the issue, the underwriting group can take a beating in the market. This can seriously jeopardize the future access of the issuing firm to the capital markets. When investment banking firms have had bad experiences with an issue from a particular corporation, they may be unwilling to participate in its future offerings.

Of course, the opposite is also true. A firm that has had bad experience with an underwriter will probably not give it another

PRIVATE & CONFIDENTIAL

FOR EQUITY SHAREHOLDERS OF THE COMPANY

ISSUE OPENS ON November, 1994	LAST DATE FOR RECEIVING REQUEST FOR SPLIT FORMS November, 1994	ISSUE CLOSES ON December, 1994

L E T T E R   O F   O F F E R

OFFER OF EQUITY SHARES OF RS EACH FOR CASH AT PAR AGGREGATING RS.450.00 LACS ON RIGHTS BASIS TO THE EXISTING SHAREHOLDERS OF THE COMPANY ON EQUITABLE BASIS.

HIGHLIGHTS

1. Existing profit making company engaged in the manufacture of complete range of lamps.
2. Company managed by experienced promoters and well qualified team of technicians and professionals trained by
3. Sole selling agent for marketing of energy efficient lamps of in the country.
4. Upgradation, modernisation and cost effectiveness of its existing plant & machinery to improve quality and implementation of ISO 9000
5. Income Tax and Wealth Tax benefits under the Income Tax Act 1961 and Wealth Tax Act, 1957.
6. Easy Liquidity—Listing at and Stock Exchanges.

RISK FACTORS INTERNAL TO THE COMPANY

1. The company has defaulted to the extent of towards the first instalment of redemption of debebntures and lacs towards interest accrued and due but not paid till date on total debentures of lacs as on
2. Clearance from Pollution Control Authorities for the current year and next year yet to be received.
3. Associate Company has been referred to BIFR as the networth has been completely eroded. Further, has defaulted in payment to the financial institutions to the extent of lacs on account of principal and lacs on account of interest. Further, the accounts of company with Bank are overdrawn to the extent of lacs including interest as on and with Indian Overseas Bank to the extent of lacs including interest as on
4. Though the Working Capital Requirements have been assessed by the bankers of the company, viz. the funding requirement for the modernisation and automation of the project to the extent of is based upon the Company's in-house estimates.
5. In the absence of any financial stake either by bankers or financial institutions, the deployment of funds is entirely at the discretion of the Management.
6. As the project is largely funded through equity, the adherence to the implementation schedule solely depends on the ability of the company to raise the resources from the capital market in time.
7. The company is yet to place orders for plant & machinery to the extent of out of a total of
8. There is no authenticated data regarding demand & supply by any reliable agency

Note: Investors are advised to refer to the risk factors, specially towards outstanding litigation/overdue interest/ defaults in payment to Financial Institutions and Banks.

RISK FACTORS EXTERNAL TO THE COMPANY

9. The company may face competition from existing and new units intending to set up manufacturing facilities.

LEAD MANAGERS TO THE ISSUE

REGISTRARS TO THE ISSUE

A reproduction of front page of a prospectus for a public issue.

chance to participate in its issues. The key element, however, is the fact that without the support of the investment banking community, it is highly unlikely that a firm can sponsor its own public offering successfully.

Offering a security issue to the public through an underwriter entails two classes of costs. The first is the underwriter's commission, which is included in the price paid by the public. The other class of costs includes such things as registration, legal, accounting, engineering and printing expenses and state and federal taxes.

Generally, flotation costs vary according to such factors as the type of security issued, the industry, the size of issue, and the underwriting risk. Studies indicate that the larger the issue, the smaller the flotation cost as a percentage of the gross proceeds. The cost of flotation is highest with common stocks followed by preferred stocks and bonds. This spread is due to several factors. Common stock is usually sold in small blocks across the nation and more risk is involved in rapid price movements in common stocks as compared with preferred stocks and bonds. Both factors increase the risk for underwriters.

Flotation costs also vary from one industry to another. Manufacturing firms have higher flotation costs than electric, gas, water, and communication utilities do. This reflects the higher underwriting risks associated with selling security issues of manufacturing firms.

METHODS OF OFFERING OF SECURITIES

There are three distinct groups of investors that can acquire a security issue: It can be sold to the general public; sold to the existing shareholders as a group; or privately placed to large institution. This section discusses these groups and examines the reasons for use of a particular method of distribution.

General Public Offering

In recent years most securities have been offered for public cash sale, with the rest going to financial institutions. Included in this major chunk are both the general public, with no special relationship to the company, and special groups such as officers, employees, customers, and existing shareholders of the firm.

Privileged Subscription and Special Groups

Corporations often offer their securities to officers, employees, and customers. Officers' income can be enhanced with *stock option* plans, which give key executives the option to buy a specified number of shares of common stock within a given period of time at a specified price. This method of distributing securities such as common stock provides an incentive for officers, employees, and sometimes customers to work harder to ensure company success, which will be reflected in the price of the stock.

Pre-emptive Rights. Another way of distributing securities is on the privileged subscription basis. This is accomplished by what is termed a *pre-emptive right,* which gives existing common shareholders the right to maintain their percentage ownership in the corporation. Many states require that the existing shareholder be given pre-emptive rights unless the corporate charter specifically denies them.

When a privileged subscription is used as a means of raising capital, common shareholders receive one right for each share of stock they own. They can use this right to purchase additional shares of stock, within the terms of the specific issue, or can sell the right in the market. If they simply let the rights expire, they lose rupees or additional shares. The subscription time for a rights offering is usually 30 days. Additional rights can be secured from the marketplace. To determine the number of rights it will take to purchase one additional share of common stock, it is necessary to determine the number of new shares that will be issued and then divide this result into the number of old shares.

$$\text{Number of rights needed to buy one new share} = \frac{20{,}000{,}000}{2{,}000{,}000}$$

$$= 10 \text{ rights.}$$

Private Placement

The third form of distributing securities is through private placement. This involves the direct sale of large blocks of corporate securities to large institutional investors. There is some placement of common stock through this method, but the bulk of privately placed securities involves debt instruments.

The capacity for the absorption of offerings by institutional investors did not grow as rapidly as the amount of total debt financing, thus putting a limit on the private placement market.

There is no question that private placement provides a speedy vehicle by which a corporation can dispose of its securities. With a public offering, the firm must file with the SEBI, wait for its approval, and be subject to the risk that the market may have changed by the time the issue is ready to be sold. With a private placement, the issue can be tailored to the needs of the borrower more readily, and thus much of the time involved in a public issue can be eliminated. Since a private placement is negotiated between two parties, the timing in the market is not an important factor.

In addition, with a private placement all of the funds need not be raised at once; rather, financing can be obtained only as it is needed. The borrower will usually pay a commitment fee, but the firm is not faced with the problem of selling the entire issue.

A private placement provides access to the debt market for medium-sized firms. If a public issue were involved, the underwriting costs would be prohibitive. If the company is credit-worthy, there are no problems with private placement.

Usually no underwriting fees are attached. Under certain circumstances, a borrower may call in an investment banker for advice, planning, and negotiating. Under these conditions, there is an advisement fee, but is is substantially less than with a public issue. On the other side of the cost factor is the fact that the interest costs on a private placement are usually higher than with a public offering. Frequently, institutional investors require equity sweeteners in the form of warrants which entitle them to obtain a number of shares of stock at an advantageous price at a later date if the firm is successful.

This section deals with debt instruments that have a maturity of longer than ten years. This is the basis dividing line between ten-year bank term loans, discussed earlier as intermediate-term financing and long-term debt.

LONG-TERM BONDS AND SECURITIES

Since a bond is a long-term contractual relationship between the issuer and the bondholder, the obligations of the issuing corporation must be specified in a written document called an *indenture*. This indenture can consist of several hundred pages. Included are a discussion of the type of bond to be issued, a description of all property that may be pledged, and a statement of the authorized amount of the specific issue and the coupon rate of the issue. In addition, the indenture statement includes protective clauses or *covenants* which outline restrictions on some of the activities of the firm over the life of the bond issue. These restrictions may include future limits on indebtedness restrictions on the amount of dividends a sinking fund arrangement, guidelines for establishing a minimum current ratio requirement or working capital position, and information pertaining to the call privileges.

Bonds are issued in denominations of Rs. 1,000 each, and, before large financial institutions emerged, were usually sold to large numbers of investors. To guarantee that the rights of individual bondholders are being maintained, a *trustee* arrangement is established whereby a third party is given the responsibility. Usually this function is handled by the trust department of a commercial bank.

The trustee has three areas of responsibility. First, the trustee must certify to the issuance of the bonds. This function includes the responsibility of making sure that the legal requirements have been met for drawing up the bond contract and the enactment of the indenture. Second, the trustee makes sure that the corporation carries out all of its responsibilities as listed in the indenture statement. And third, the trustee is charged with the responsibility of taking immediate steps on behalf of the bond-holders if the corporation defaults in payment of principal or interest.

Maturity and Repayment

Most bonds have a finite maturity structure and eventually mature. There are several ways in which this can be accomplished. One method is to let the bonds mature; the corporation makes the final payment, which is equal to the face value of the bond plus the final payment of interest. This payment process can be aided by the establishment of a sinking fund or a serial bond issue. With this form of issue, there is no single maturity for the bond at the end of its life but rather a series of maturities over the life of the bond. For example, a bond might have 25 per cent maturity every 5 years, with the final segment maturing at the end of 20 years.

This process helps alleviate the pressures that would exist if the corporation were forced to utilize its cash account to pay off the bond issue.

Another method is to refund the issue by exchanging the existing issue for another one. This process alleviates the need for the corporation to put up cash at the maturity of the bond issue. And a third method of retiring a bond issue is to convert the bond into another security, provided the issue specified a convertible feature. This action is frequently initiated by calling the existing issue.

Serial Bonds. In a serial bond issue, the total issue may be Rs. 1 crore with a maturity of 20 years, but Rs. 5 lakhs of the bonds may mature each year. An investor is allowed to choose the preferred series. Thus the investor has greater flexibility, and the issue has greater appeal to a wider market.

The investor appeal is derived from the segmentation of the serial issue. The market for debt instruments is segmented in the sense that some investors prefer to invest in shorter maturity issues, while others prefer those with longer maturities. The shorter maturity instruments would normally have a lower interest rate than the longer maturity instruments. This is because more risk is perceived in the long run, and a higher yield is needed to compensate for this risk.

The serial type of bond issue is used when real estate and railroad equipment are used as collateral. The generation of cash flows from these assets is considered to have enough certainty that the issuing corporation can assume the risk of meeting this maturity structure.

Call features. The call feature or call provision gives the corporation the right to call the bond for redemption. If this provision is to be utilized, the indenture will usually specify that the corporation must pay a price for the bond that is greater than the par value. This additional sum is referred to as the *call premium*. The call premium will usually be set equal to one year's interest if the bond is called in the first year. After that, the premium will usually decline at a constant rate.

To the corporation, the inclusion of a call feature in the indenture statement can provide added financing flexibility. If, for example, interest rates declined sharply it would pay the corporation to call the existing issue and float another issue at a reduced rate of interest. This could save the corporation sufficiently in terms of interest expenses. Also, if the covenants in the bond agreement are too restrictive, the call option provides the opportunity for the firm to seek a more favorable financing arrangement. If the firm's financial position has improved since the bond issue was originally issued, it may well be that a new bond issue can be financed with less restrictive protective covenants.

LONG-TERM DEBT INSTRUMENTS

There are various long-term debt instruments that a public firm can utilize to raise long-term capital. The array of bonds is discussed in terms of their priority of claims on the assets of the organization in case of a forced liquidation. This is usually the way they appear on the corporate balance sheet.

Mortgage Bonds

Mortgage bonds place a specific lien on one of the fixed assets of the corporation. The mortgage is the legal document which describes the property that is being collateralized for the bondholders. In most cases, the market value of the collateral will exceed the amount of the bond issue. This provides a margin of safety to the bondholder if the corporation defaults and the trustee forecloses on the property and sells it to repay the bondholders.

Frequently property will have more than one mortgage assigned to it. Another bond issue will be secured by a second mortgage on a parcel of property that already is being used to secure a first mortgage. In the event of liquidation, the first-mortgage bondholders will have to be paid in full before the second-mortgage bondholders receive payment. The first position is classified as a senior mortgage and the second position is classified as a junior mortgage.

Second-mortgage collateralization is seldom used, due to the lack of provision for an asset claim for the bondholders. If it is used, it usually cannotes that the firm is in some financial difficulty. Thus the perception of risk would be higher, and bondholders would demand a much higher yield to compensate them for this risk.

A common feature of mortgages which protect bondholders is a *closed-end or open-end clause*. If the mortgage is the closed-end type, no additional bonds may be issued under that specific lien. To utilize additional mortgage bonds, the firm must secure and mortgage additional property. This feature usually leads to a confusing set of mortgage bonds being outstanding in the corporate capital structure.

An open-end mortgage allows the firm to issue additional bonds under the specific lien. Thus the company can issue different series of bonds at different times using the same asset as collateral. To protect the earlier series bondholders, there are restrictions as to the additional amount of debt that may be secured by the same fixed asset. These restrictions consist of a minimum earning power for the company in relation to the existing bonds, as well as a percentage set in terms of the maximum amount of debt raised in relationship to the total value of the property. Railroads and public utilities have made frequent use of the open-end form of financing. Certainly the open-end arrangement can provide much greater flexibility for a firm's financing capabilities than a closed-end arrangement.

Collateral Trust Bonds

A collateral trust bond is secured by bonds or stocks. If a default should arise, the trustee can sell the collateral and pay the bondholders. The securities are investments in other corporations and are held in collateral trust.

Debentures

Debentures are either secured or unsecured. A secured debenture has a lien on the company's specific assets by way of security. In India, debentures are usually secured by a charge on the present and future immovable assets of the company. In USA debentures are the unsecured bonds of the corporation, as noted above. Because no specific assets are used as collateral for these bonds, the bondholders become one of the general creditors of the corporation. Therefore investors look to the earning power of the corporation as the security base. Though no specific assets are used as collateral, a degree of protection is afforded by the protective covenants that may be included in the indenture document. One of the more important covenants, the negative pledge clause prohibits the corporation from pledging its existing assets to other creditors. Because bondholders have only a general claim on the assets of the corporation, the use of debentures is limited to established and credit-worthy corporations or those firms that have no valuable assets to collateralize.

Subordinated debentures are those unsecured debentures that have a subordinated claim on assets to regular debentures. In a liquidation situation, the subordinated debenture bondholders would receive a settlement only after all the secured and unsecured creditors with priority claims were paid. Subordinated debenture bondholders still have a priority claim to the assets above preferred and common stock shareholders, however. Having subordinated debentures in the capital structure of the firm can have a substantial advantage to senior debt holders in case of liquidation. The reason is that senior debt holders are able to assume the claims of the subordinated debenture bondholders. One of the distinct advantages of issuing subordinated debentures from the viewpoint of the corporation is that since these debentures are subordinated to all existing and future debt, senior debt holders, in evaluating the financial leverage position of the corporation, consider them to function in a way similar to equity capital. Thus subordinated debentures can be increase the equity base and to support future financing. This has the distinct advantage that the fixed obligation of interest is tax deductible to the corporation, instead of the money obligation being paid on an after-tax base in the form of preferred or common stock dividends. Many finance companies have utilized this form of financing instrument in recent years because of the tax advantage generated by the deductibility of interest expense.

Convertible Debentures

Convertible debentures are bonds that can be exchanged at the option of the holder into common stock. Specific terms are established at the time of issue to regulate the conditions under which the conversion will take place. Two of the important aspects of a convertible issue are the conversion ratio and conversion price. The *conversion ratio* establishes the number of shares the holder will receive when he or she converts the bond into common stock. The *conversion price* is the effective price that will be paid for the common stock when conversion occurs.

$$\text{Conversion price} = \frac{\text{Par value of bond}}{\text{Shares received}}$$

The conversion ratio and the conversion price are set at the time the bond is issued. Usually the conversion price is set from between 10 and 20 per cent above the current market price of the common stock. Some issues have conversion ratios and prices established for the life of the issue, while others have what is called a stepped-up conversion price over the life of the bond. This means that as the years go on, the conversion ratio decreases and the conversion price increases. This is done to reflect the natural increase in the price of the stock that might be expected of a growth company.

Most convertible issues have a protection clause which keeps the issue from being diluted through stock splits, stock dividends, or the sale of common stock at a lower price. This means that no common stock can be sold below the conversion price, and if a stock dividend is issued the conversion price must be lowered and the conversion ratio raised by the percentage amount of the stock dividend to compensate for the dilution effect.

Value of Convertible Debentures. The value of a convertible debenture usually consists of two factors: the value as a pure bond, which can be classified as the theoretical value, and the value of the option to convert into common stock.

If the market price of the stock continues to rise, the conversion premium will disappear. This is because the bondholder is aware that the issue will probably be called, and forced conversion will occur. If this is the expectation by investors, they will be unwilling to pay a premium above the conversion value of the debenture issue. To do so could lead to a loss if the issue were called. Thus the debenture sells as though it were common stock.

Warrants

Warrants give the holder an option to buy a stated number of shares of common stock at a specified price and within a specified time period. The warrants are surrendered when the holder exercises his or her option. They are typically used as a sweetener to a debt issue that is either publicly or privately placed. Some issues have detachable warrants. In these cases the warrants can be sold, with the investor obtaining the value of the warrant without obtaining the common stock. This feature can be very important for institutional investors who derive to participate in a debt issue but do not want to obtain the firm's common stock. The investor receives not only a fixed return from the debt instrument but also an option to participate in the growth of the company if the price of the stock should rise. With the use of warrants, the corporation should be able to issue the debt at an interest rate that would be lower than a straight debt issue of comparable risk. If a company is marginal in its credit risk, the use of warrants can make the difference between a successful and unsuccessful debt offering. With the rate of inflation in our economy, many institutional investors demand warrants before they invest in a debt issue of any organization. This protects the investor from inflation with what is termed an *equity kicker*.

At the time of issue, the option price is usually set from 15 to 20 per cent above the current market price of the stock. When the price of the stock rises above the option price, people begin to convert the option into common stock. There are several reasons for this situation. First, if the warrants are about to expire and the price is above the option price, people will convert. Second, warrants frequently have stepped up option prices over time. If the price of the stock is expected to continue to increase, people will use the warrants to purchase stock at the lower price. A third reason is the fact that warrants do not entitle the holder to have voting rights or any rights to dividends. The warrant holder must evaluate his leverage return gain against the fact that as long as he holds warrants he foregoes the receipt of dividend income. This is an important issue when the corporation is paying attractive dividends.

Warrant Valuation

Warrants have both a theoretical value and an actual value in the marketplace. The theoretical value of the warrant is shown in following equation.

Theoretical value = (Market price of common stock –
Option Price) × Number of shares each
warrant entitles owner to purchase.

Assume that each warrant attached to a bond issue entitles the holder to purchase one share of common stock. If the market price of the common stock is currently Rs. 50 per share and the option price of the warrants is set at Rs. 35 per share, then the theoretical value is equal to Rs. 15. This is shown in above Equation.

Theoretical value = (Rs. 50 – Rs. 35) × 1 = Rs. 15.

Typically, the theoretical value of the warrant is the lowest price it will sell for in the marketplace. If for some reason the market price of the warrant goes below its theoretical value, an arbitrage process will take place in the market whereby the warrants are purchased and exercised, and then the stock is sold. This has the effect of eliminating the differential.

Advantages and Disadvantages of Warrants

There are several advantages of warrants, to both the issuing corporation and the warrant holder. The sweetener effect can broaden the market for the issue by attracting institutional investors, allowing an unsalable straight bond issue to be placed on the market, and permitting a lower coupon rate without lowering the price of the issue. In addition, the use of warrants allows a tax-free exchange in installment sale purchases and facility acquisitions. The use of warrants in lieu of stocks allows the firm to save cash because it does not have to pay dividends on the warrants until they are converted. It also can result in the future sale of stock at a higher price than currently exist, due to the premium on the warrants themselves.

For the warrant holder warrants have the advantage that less capital investment is required, compared to investing in stock, and the capital gains potential is much greater. In addition, for investors in high tax brackets the fact that no dividends are paid on warrants is viewed favorably. Further the sale of a warrant dividend as compared to a stock dividend will not result in an immediate reduction in the proportional ownership in the company. If there is a debenture-warrant issue, an investor can borrow a higher percentage on the debenture portion than would be possible with common stock or convertible securities.

There are several disadvantages to issuing warrants, for both the issuing corporation and the warrant holder. The fact that the warrants can be exercised at any time by investors means that the corporation cannot do any effective planning in terms of the cash inflows from the exchange for common stock. This is partially being eliminated by having a call provision attached to the warrant.

Another disadvantage is the dilution effect on earnings per share when the warrants are converted. Prior to the exercise of the warrants, the earnings per share calculation will not include the warrant conversion effect if the price of the stock is below the exercise price. However, earnings per share on a full diluted basis will be calculated if the common stock price exceeds the exercise price.

For the warrant holder, there are no dividends, voting rights ownership in the corporation, or claims on the assets in case of liquidation until the warrants have been converted. If the warrant sells at a substantial premium relating to the common stock and has a finite expiration period, this means unfavorable odds for the holder; 80 to 90 per cent of all warrants expire and thus become worthless. The down side leverage effect has already been discussed, but the risk of loss also exists with a possible increase in the exercise price, the uncertain expiration date if the expiration date is tied to the call or maturity of a bond, the lack of dilution protection, and the possible voiding of warrants if a merger occurs. Finally, those holding warrants which are selling at a large premium relative to the common stock value can lose substantially if another company initiates a tender offer for the common stock and warrants of the corporation.

Finally on the long-term financing we focus on what many call the equity contribution to the capital structure of the firm, how preferred stock, which is classified as a hybrid security, and common stock, which is classified as pure equity, contribute to the financing flexibility of a firm. In India these are known as preference shares and equity shares in that order. Similarly the shareholders of these are known as Preference Shareholders and Equity Shareholders for the purposes of this book we shall stick to the terms 'Preferred stock' and 'Common stock'.

PREFERRED STOCK

Preferred stock is usually considered a hybrid form of security which contains features of both debt and common stock. Legally speaking, preferred stock is like equity because the dividends paid on preferred stock are not tax deductible. Creditors view preferred stock as part of the equity base that is used to help support the leverage position of the firm. To the common shareholder preferred stock is more like debt because the dividends paid to the preferred shareholders must be made before common dividends can be paid. More of the distinguishing characteristics of this hybrid security will be made clear in the following sections.

Claims of Preferred Shareholders

As with other types of financing securities, preferred shares offer holders a claim on income, a claim on assets, and a possible voice in the management of the firm.

Claim on Income. Preferred stock can be issued with or without a par value. The *par value* on preferred stock establishes the face amount of each share and is stated on the corporate charter. The par values on preferred stock are usually Rs. 5, 10 or 100. This amount is important because the preferred stock dividend is usually expressed as a per cent of the par value.

The par value also establishes the bottom price when the issue is first sold in the market. It would never be wise to sell preferred stock below par value in an initial offering. In the first place, it may be prohibited by state law. And in the second place, stockholders can be held liable to corporate creditors for the difference between the par value and what they paid for the stock if the corporation is in an insolvent position. Once the stock is issued, however, it may sell freely in the marketplace without regard to the par value.

To establish a priority of claim on income, shareholders may seek protective features in the issue of preferred stock similar to those found in term loan agreements. There may be a provision to prohibit the payment of dividends on common stock or the purchase of common stock if the current ratio goes below some specified level. Sometimes the earned surplus is frozen at the time of issue, so common stock dividends may only be paid out of earnings accumulated since the issue.

To establish a certainty of income, preferred stock dividends must be paid before common stock dividends. In addition, there is usually a provision that the dividends are *cumulative.* This means that if dividends are not paid, the obligation is carried into subsequent years.

The hybrid characteristics of debt and common stock are evident in the dividend feature. If the preferred dividend is not paid, there is no legal action shareholders can take against the corporation, as with a default in the interest payment on debt. Failure to meet this payment does not make the corporation insolvent. The only agreement is that the preferred dividend will be paid before the common dividend. As with debt instruments, however, the preferred shareholder has a priority claim on income compared to the claim of the common shareholder.

It might seem that if there is no obligation to pay the preferred dividend, the firm should let it slide. This is not to the advantage of the corporation, because if the preferred dividend is not paid there can be no common dividend. And without the common dividend, the price of the common stock will undoubtedly decline. This will jeopardize the capacity of the firm to raise future equity capital through an issue of common stock.

Claim on Assets. Preferred shareholders do have a general claim to the assets of the corporation which takes precedence to the claim of the common shareholder, but there are no specific assets that have been collateralized. Usually in a liquidation, the claim of preferred shareholders is limited to the par value of the stock, plus any accumulated dividends in arrears.

Preferred shareholders usually negotiate with management to ensure that the general level of assets in the corporation is sufficient to maintain their claim and to prevent future investors from obtaining an equal or better claim on the assets. These protective features can be contained in an agreement, which may specify that assets must be twice the amount of preferred stock and debt. If this margin of safety is not maintained, common dividends may be prohibited, or certain voting rights may be granted to the preferred shareholders. The agreement may also control the issuance of additional securities with a prior or equal claim on the general asset level of the firm. This can take the form of a limitation on the issuance of additional debt or preferred stock unless a minimum margin of safety is maintained. For example, there may be a minimum level of interest plus preferred dividend coverage, or a minimum ratio of common stock equity to preferred stock and debt. If these agreements are not met, additional debt or preferred stock may not be issued without the approval of the two thirds of the preferred shareholders.

Participation in Management. Unless there are no specific provisions to the contrary in the corporate charter, preferred shareholders also have comprehensive voting rights. However, most corporate charters limit the voting rights of preferred shareholders to certain restrictions on the payment of dividends and any subsequent issues of prior or equal securities. In these situations, the preferred shareholders would vote in a class; either two thirds or three fourths of the outstanding preferred stock must vote in favor on these issues. Also, the corporation must grant preferred shareholders the right to elect a specific number of directors if it fails to abide by the agreement established between the corporation and preferred shareholders.

Features of Preferred Stock

To make preferred stock a more viable financing instrument and to attract the interest of investors, a preferred issue frequently includes a number of specialized features. Some issues have a number of these features, while others include only one. The number of features included in any issue will depend on the reasons for the issue and the market's risk appraisal of the firm.

Cumulative Dividends

The cumulative feature of dividends is an important aspect of a preferred stock issue. Investors have had bitter experiences with non-cumulative issues of preferred stock; once a dividend is not declared on the preferred, it is forever lost. To maintain the shareholders' claim on the earnings of the corporation, having unpaid dividends carried forward is the main line of protection for the preferred shareholder. This enforces the rule that common stock dividends cannot be paid until all preferred dividends in arrears have been cleared off the books.

Participation

Some issues of preferred stock incorporate a feature which permits shareholders to participate in the residual earnings of the corporation as dictated by a specific formula. For example, 7 per cent preferred issue (Rs. 100 par value) may have a participating feature whereby preferred shareholders can participate equally in any common stock dividends in excess of Rs. 7. If the common stock dividend is Rs. 9, the preferred shareholders can receive an extra Rs. 2 per share in dividends.

This feature combined with a cumulative feature allows preferred shareholders to have not only a certainty claim on income in the amount of their specified dividend but also an opportunity to participate in the growth of the company if the earnings and dividends substantially increase. It can be used as a sweetener for a preferred issue when it is felt that a regular preferred issue may have trouble being absorbed into the market. Today, however, most preferred issues are non-participating, which limits the return to the preferred stockholder.

Convertibility. Convertible preferred stock allows holders to convert these shares of preferred into common stock at a stated price. Many of the issues associated with convertible bonds, also apply to convertible preferred stock.

Convertible preferred is used both as a sweetener to ensure the success of the flotation and as a tool for acquisitions. It is used as a sweetener for a preferred issue when the market perceives greater risk with the issuing corporation and therefore demands a higher dividend yield. The convertible feature allows holders to receive a specified dividend and to participate in any growth of the company. Typically, this means the issuing corporation can place a lower dividend yield on the preferred issue.

In the acquisition of another company, convertible preferred is used for two reasons. First, the exchange of common stock for convertible preferred is non-taxable: it will become taxable only when the preferred stock is sold. If the common stock of the acquired company is exchanged for regular preferred stock, without the convertible feature, a taxable situation results because the exchange is not of "like" securities. The second reason for the use of convertible preferred in an acquisition is that it does not immediately dilute the common stock of the issuing corporation. Though earnings per share have to be reported on a fully diluted basis, it will not dilute the dividend per share or the control effect.

Retirement of Preferred Stock

Though preferred stock has no maturity, it is usually not considered as a vehicle of perpetual financing. Issues of preferred stock therefore incorporate several methods of retirement.

One retirement method is to incorporate a *call feature* in the preferred issue. The call feature is similar to that associated with a bond issue in that it establishes a price above the original issuance price at which the corporation can call the stock. As with a bond issue, the call price will decrease over time. The call feature enables the company to replace an expensive issue of preferred stock with another financing instrument or to force conversion on the convertible preferred stock. Without the call option, the corporation would be able to retire stock only through purchases in the open market, through an advertisement for tenders at a price above the current market price, or through a voluntary replacement of one security for another by the preferred shareholders. These alternatives for retiring a preferred issue that does not have a call option are both expensive and inefficient.

Some preferred stock issues have incorporated a *sinking fund* provision which establishes an orderly process for the retirement of the issue. With these funds, the stock can be retired either through the open market or through the call option. This has the advantage for existing preferred shareholders of increasing the market price through the exertion of demand pressure when the trustee purchases the stock in the open market. It also increases the coverage of the preferred dividend when the number of outstanding shares of preferred stock is decreased.

Because a fixed-rupee sinking fund requirement mean another fixed commitment for the corporation, it increases the financial risk for the firm. A better sinking fund arrangement is a variable fund related to the annual earnings of the firm. When a sinking fund provision is included in a preferred stock issue, the firm should be able to attach a smaller dividend yield. Though there are some preferred issues with sinking fund requirements, they are used much less than with bond issues.

Advantages and Disadvantages of Preferred Stock

Straight preferred stock is not used to the extent it once was, but convertible preferred stock has become quite popular as a tool for mergers and acquisitions. One of the principal drawbacks of preferred stock for the corporation is the fact that the dividends paid are not tax deductible. In terms of the cost of capital, this means that with a 50 per cent tax rate, the explicit cost of preferred stock is twice that of debt financing. At the same time, one of the distinct advantages of preferred stock for the corporate investor is that 85 per cent of the dividends received are tax exempt (whereas all interest received from debt financing is taxable). This allows some select issues of preferred to sell at a lower yield than some corporate debentures even though the preferred stock has a lower priority claim on the assets of the firm.

Thus the tax effect affects preferred stock issues in two ways. The tax-exempt status has increased demand for such issues by the investing public, but the fact that preferred stock dividends are paid out of after-tax rupees has made this instrument less desirable as a financing instrument for the firm. In this situation, the yields on preferred stock generally are higher than on equivalent debt issues.

The use of preferred stock provides a greater degree of financing flexibility for the firm. From the standpoint of the crediiors it adds to the equity base. If earnings have tapered off in one year, dividends do not have to be paid. They may be accumulated, but they do not have the same impact on the insolvency question as the inability of the firm to meet interest payments on a debt issue.

Most preferred issues do not have a sinking fund requirement, and all do not have a final maturity. This allows the company to plan for the retirement of the preferred through repurchase or through refunding.

COMMON STOCK

Common stockholders comprise what is termed the *residual owners* of a corporation. Their liability in the corporation is limited to their investment, and in the event of liquidation they have a residual claim on the assets of the firm after all of the claims of the creditors and preferred shareholders have been satisfied. Common stock has no maturity and can be disposed of by selling it in the secondary market.

Rights of Common Stockholders

The rights of the common stockholders are detailed in the laws of the state in which the corporation is chartered, in the charter of the corporation, and in the corporate bylaws. The major categories of common shareholder rights are discussed below.

Claim on Income. The common shareholder does not have any right to the earnings of the corporation until a dividend is declared by the board of directors. The shareholders have delegated this authority to the board and have exercised their right when they cast their vote for a group of candidates.

The common shareholder cannot force the declaration of a dividend but does have the right to maintain a share in the earnings and assets of the corporation through the vehicle of *pre-emptive rights*. This allows the shareholder to buy a specific number of shares of a new common stock offering that is first offered to existing shareholders before being offered to the general public. If the right is exercised, not only does the percentage share of earnings and assets remain the same, but the voting position of the shareholder relative to other shareholders remains the same. The concept of the pre-emptive right seems fair and logical, yet there are a number of states that do not require it to be included in the corporate charter.

Claim on Assets. The book value of the corporation represents the claim on assets that common stockholders have against the corporation. It is equal to the sum of the capital stock, capital surplus, and retained earnings accounts. The market value of the stock reflects the market's expectation of future cash dividends and earnings to be generated from the assets of the corporation. It also reflects the risk associated with that income stream.

Thus, in evaluating a corporation as a going concern, the firm's earnings capacity as generated by its assets, and not the value of the assets themselves, is of interest. However, when a corporation liquidates, the income stream is dissolved and the book value is used by common shareholders to measure their general claim on the assets of the corporation. In a forced liquidation, the value of the assets that can be used to satisfy the claims of the common shareholders is usually reduced to zero. This is because the claims of the common shareholders are only paid after all claims of creditors and preferred shareholders have been satisfied. In a forced liquidation, the amount of rupees actually received for the assets usually has little relation to their value as shown on the corporate books. When sold, the assets are usually substantially discounted, and the sums received are less than sufficient to cover all claims. In a voluntary liquidation the common stockholders have a much better chance of receiving something, but this still will usually not equal the book value of the corporation.

The protection for the common shareholder comes largely from the discretionary activities of the board of directors in the conduct of the business of the firm. If there is disagreement, shareholders have the right to change the structure of the board of directors. In some cases the directors must secure the approval of the shareholders in undertaking a mortgage or disposing of a significant part of the asset structure of the firm. This restriction may be included in the laws of the state in which the corporation is chartered or in the charter and bylaws of the firm.

Voice in Management. Since the common shareholders of the corporation are the owners, they have the right to elect the board of directors. In a small company, the owners usually directly control the operation of the business; in a large corporation the owners do so only indirectly. The shareholders elect the board of directors, which in turn selects the management team that will actually run the company.

Sometimes the goals of management and the goals of shareholders differ and come into conflict. When this occurs, shareholders may alter the management structure by utilizing their voting power to change the board of directors. Since many large organizations have shareholders spread out over a wide geographical area, management can exercise effective control by controlling only a small part of the stock outstanding. If it is felt that the directors are not acting in a manner that is considered to be in the interest of the shareholders, the shareholders can sue the directors in what is known as a *derivative suit*. These suits are infrequent, since many states require the shareholders to pay the legal costs if they lose.

Use of Proxies. Every common shareholder has the right to cast one vote for every share held. The proxy is a vehicle whereby a person can cast his or her vote for another who is unable to attend the annual meeting of the corporation. The SEC regulates the use of proxies and requires management to provide certain information during a proxy mailing. Prior to an annual meeting, management solicits proxies from its shareholders to vote for a recommended slate of directors. The shareholder who is satisfied with management's performance will sign the proxy and return it by mail. If a shareholder does not return the proxy and does not attend the meeting, the number of votes constituting a majority is reduced.

Since management can disseminate information and solicit votes at the firm' expense, it usually has an advantage in this voting process. However, in certain situations a group of outsiders has attempted to gain control of the corporation through what is termed a *proxy contest*. After filing a registration with the SEBI, which helps prevent the use of false or misleading information, the outside group will try to persuade stockholders to sign a proxy giving it the right to vote their shares.

Management usually has the upper hand in a proxy contest, for they have the use of the firm's resources to manage a proxy fight. However, when earnings and the rate of return have been low, when the dividend payout has declined substantially, and when the stock prices may be reacting adversely, the chances of success for the outsider group are substantially increased.

Right to Inspect the Books. Any stockholder has the legal right to inspect the books and records of the corporation. Usually, this kind of information is limited to the audited financial statements supplied by the corporation in its quarterly and annual reports. To obtain more information, the shareholder may have to take the case to court and show just cause as to why the corporation should make available additional information. This protects the corporation from having to give vital information to competitors.

Shareholders also have the right to obtain a list of names and addresses of all other shareholders of the corporation, which is vital if a group plans to undertake a proxy battle. There is the chance that this right may be abused, so the shareholder may have to take the request to court to demonstrate that the reasons are legitimate. This lessens the possibility of obtaining such a list in order to sell products or even other securities to the shareholders.

Features of Common Stock

This section outlines some of the basic characteristics associated with common stock and clarifies the basic terminology used in the discussion of common stock.

Par Value. Common stock can be issued with either a par value or a no-par value. The *par value* on the stock is a stated figure which appears in the corporate charter but has no economic significance. Most common stock is set with a low par value, for two basic reasons. First, the issuance of common stock with a no-par value can create an extra tax burden for the corporation, because certain states levy annual franchise taxes and state corporation taxes on the par value of stock in corporations chartered in that state. If there is a no-par stock, the state will frequently tax the stock with an assumed par value of Rs. 100. With a low par value stock somewhere in the range of Re. 1 to Rs. 5, the taxes would be considerably lower.

The second reason for setting low par values is that if, on an initial offering, investors purchase the stock at a market value below par, they are liable to the creditors of the company for the difference between the market value and the par value of the stock. If, for example, the par value was set at Rs. 50 and the investors purchased it for Rs. 30, the liability differential is Rs. 20. If in the future a liquidating situation arises, the creditors of the corporation have the legal right to force the equity holders to pay this differential. This is a good incentive for maintaining a low par value.

On an initial offering of common stock, entries in the balance sheet will usually be split between two accounts. If 100,000 shares are issued at a market price of Rs. 30 and the par value of the stock is Rs. 10, the entry in the balance sheet would be:

Common stock (10 par value)	Rs. 1,000,000
Capital in excess of par	2,000,000
Net Worth	Rs. 3,000,000

The capital stock account always records the par value of the stock issued. The capital in excess of par account will record the rupee value that is equivalent to the difference between the market price of the stock and the par value. In this case the capital in excess of par account will record Rs. 20 per share, or Rs. 2 million. If stocks is issued without a par value, it is listed on the books at the market value.

Book Value. The book value of the corporation is equal to its net worth, which includes the common stock, capital in excess of par, and retained earnings accounts. If the corporation has treasury stock, this is deducted from the equity section to arrive at net stockholders' equity. Note that preferred stock is not included in the book value of the corporation. This is illustrated below:

Common stock (Rs. 10 par value)	Rs. 1,000,000
Capital in excess of par	2,000,000
Retained earnings	11,000,000
Total Stockholders' Equity	Rs. 14,000,000
Less: Treasury stock	1,500,000
Net Stockholders' Equity	Rs. 12,500,000

To arrive at a book value per share, we take the net stockholders' equity and divide it by the number of shares outstanding. In this example, assume that there are 80,000 shares outstanding. This gives a book value per share figure of Rs. 156.25 (Rs. 12.5 million divided by 80,000 shares).

Some consider book value to be equivalent to the liquidating value of the company. It is important to keep in mind that in the case of liquidation, most of the assets are sold at prices below what would have been received if the firm were an ongoing entity. This usually leaves nothing for the common shareholders. However, there can be situations where the liquidating value is substantially higher than the book value. This would occur, for example, if the firm has land and mineral rights that have appreciated substantially above the cost value originally placed on its books.

Cumulative Voting. One of the features of common stock that has become prevalent is *cumulative voting* in electing members to the board of directors. Today there are 22 states that require cumulative voting, 18 states that accept it, and 10 states that make no provision for it.

Cumulative voting allows a minority of shareholders to elect a member or members to the board of directors by permitting multiple votes for a single director. An individual who has 500 shares of stock has 500 votes. If five members of the board of directors are to be elected, he or she can cast 100 votes for each of the directors, or, where cumulative voting is allowed, 500 votes can be cast for one director. A minority group of shareholders wishing to determine the number of shares it would take to elect one director could utilize Equation

$$r = \frac{d \times S}{D+1} + 1,$$

where:

r = Number of shares needed to elect a specified number of directors.

d = Number of directors the shareholders desire to elect.

S = Total number of shares outstanding and entitled to vote.

D = Total number of directors to be elected.

To illustrate this concept, assume that a minority of shareholders wishes to elect one member to the board of directors out of the five seats that are available. There are 100,000 shares outstanding which are eligible to vote. The number of shares needed to elect one member is shown in equation

$$r = 1 \times \frac{100{,}000}{5+1} + 1 = 16{,}667 \text{ shares}$$

Note that to elect 20 per cent of the directors, only 16,667 shares of stock, and not 20 per cent of the stock, or 20,000 shares, are required. Cumulative voting thus allows a minority representation on a board of directors.

Equation can be altered to determine the number of directors that can be elected, assuming a group of shareholders has a block of stock. This formulation is shown in Equation

$$d = \frac{(r-1)\,(D+1)}{S}$$

If we assume that a group of shareholders has 35,000 shares, we can substitute this information into the formula and determine the number of directors they can elect. This is shown in Equation.

$$\frac{34{,}999 \times 6}{100{,}000} = 2.1 \text{ directors}$$

Thus, two directors can be elected with 35,000 shares of stock.

Advantages and Disadvantages of Common Stock Financing

The comparative advantages and disadvantages associated with common stock financing can be viewed as an aspect of the analysis of the different forms of financing available to the firm. With common stock, there is no fixed obligation to pay dividends, whereas with bond financing, the interest charges are a fixed obligation, legally binding for the corporation. Common stock also has no maturity, which eliminates the corporation's eventual concern for retirement of the issue. In addition, with the cushion provided against losses by creditors, common stock sales help to increase the credit-worthiness of the corporation by enhancing the debt to equity ratio. Another advantage, from the viewpoint of the corporation, is that the sale of common stock can be executed more easily than debt financing. This is because common stock generally has a higher expected rate of return associated with it than other forms of financing.

Common stock has a number of characteristics that can be considered as disadvantages to this form of financing. When common stock is sold, voting rights are extended with each share. For small and medium-sized firms, the potential dilution of control through the extension of more voting rights can be a serious problem. If the control factor is an issue, management may decide against the common stock vehicle as a means of financing.

Another factor is that the cost structure associated with common stock financing is much greater than that for other forms of financing. Due to the risk associated with common stock in terms of claims on income and assets, the cost of common stock is considerably higher than for debt or preferred stock financing. Also in the flotation of common stock, the underwriting fees are higher than those for an alternative form of financing, because the cost of investigating is higher for an equity issue than for a debt issue. In general, too, stocks, are more risky than other forms of financing, which means that investors must be well diversified in their stock portfolios. Thus the same rupee amount of stock may have to be sold to a wider group of investors in stocks than in bonds. Finally, the dividends paid on a common stock issue are not tax deductible, as with a bond issue. This leads to a higher component cost of capital.

SUMMARY

At the time of incorporation, the total amount at which the enterprise is to be capitalized is determined, based on the nature and size of the proposed operations. In addition to fixed capital requirements for buildings, equipment, etc., funds will be required for promotion and development work, and for working capital sufficient to maintain operations to the point where sales income and earnings will be sufficient to carry the project. Capitalization may take into account the value of patents, secret processes, trade-marks, and similar intangibles, but in a new enterprise there may be no basis for assigning more than nominal values to these items.

State and Federal legal requirements must be taken into consideration, since they affect franchise fees, taxation, security sales, and similar items. Initial capitalization may include plans for future expansion and future marketing of corporate securities.

Classification of stock. Authorized capital stock of a company may be issued in a single classification, *common stock,* or it may include various types of *preferred stock.*

Common Stock carries no special rights or privileges, and bears the full risk of the enterprise. Common-stock holders are the legal owners of the enterprise, and usually exercise control over the business through the voting power of their stock.

Preferred Stock. This class of stock may be preferred as to dividends and assets; it may be convertible into common stock on special terms; a sinking fund may be set up to guarantee safety of the investment; and it may have other rights. However, it may have limited or no voting power, since preferred stockholders do not partake of the same risk as common stockholders.

The division between common and preferred stock is determined by such considerations as who is to control the enterprise, the feasibility of burdening earnings with obligations to pay fixed dividends, tax advantages, ease of sale of securities, and the like. In terms of other gradations of rights and privileges, stocks may be further classified as A and B common, or first preferred, second preferred, and the like.

Par- and No-par-value Stock. Common and preferred stock may have a *par value* (Rs. 10, Rs. 100, etc.) stated in the stock certificate to fix the unit of investment. However, the *real* value of the share is determined by the net assets and earning power of the company, and the *market* value is determined by what investors are willing to pay for the stock, which may or may not be greater than the net asset or book value.

Issued, Unissued, and Treasury Stock. After the enterprise is chartered, part of the stock is issued to pay for property transferred to the company, and part is sold to provide capital funds. The balance of the stock constitutes *unissued* stock to be used in subsequent financing. The latter is not to be confused with *treasury stock,* which is stock lawfully issued by the company and re-acquired by it.

Bond Issues. Bond issues are borrowings based on company promises to repay the loan at stated periods and are backed by a mortgage on all or part of the company's property. They take the form of *bonds, debentures, certificates,* or *notes of issue,* based upon a trust agreement or indenture which contains all the rights and obligations between the company as borrower, the bankers who are to market the issue, the prospective bondholders (represented by the trustee) and the general public. The relationship between the company and bondholders is that of debtor-creditors. While the bondholders have no ownership interest in the company, their rights have priority over those of the stockholders. A temporary failure to pay interest charges or amortization may throw the company into receivership.

Differences Between Debt and Equity Capital. The basic difference between debt and equity capital are maturity, claims on corporate income and assets, and voice in management. While the long-term debts have a stated maturity date on which the principal amount borrowed must be repaid, equity has no such maturity since its life is presumed to be infinite. Again, the bond holder has a prior claim on both the income and assets of a corporation while the equity holder generally has no such claim, and payments to equity holders are not mandatory. Typically, the bond holders have no say in the management of a company so long as all the debts are paid, but the equity holders (the true owners of the corporation) have the only voice in the selection of the board of directors through their voting power.

The use of a high ratio of debt to equity capital (financial leverage) may be beneficial in that it increases the firm's earnings per share (EPS) when its earnings before interest and taxes (EBIT) are increasing, but the danger of a sharp decline in EPS is all too real when EBIT is falling. The reason for this is that with high leverage there is a high fixed charge in the form of the interest the firm *must* pay, no matter what its earnings are.

In order to understand the capital structure of a firm, the debt-equity ratio, the debt-to-total-capitalization ratio, the "times interest earned" (TIE), and total debt coverage must be calculated and analyzed, taking into consideration the record of past years as well as comparisons with the ratios of the industry to which the firm belongs. While neoclassical economists take the position that there is an optimum point in the cost-of-capital curve up to which the debt-equity ratio can be increased, critics of this point of view assert that the total risk for all security holders of a firm is not altered by changes in the capital structure, and that therefore the total value of the firm must be the same regardless of the financing mix.

7

CAPITAL CONCEPTS OF THE FIRM

CAPITAL STRUCTURE

ONCE the firm has decided what kind of investments it wants to undertake and the amount of money what will be needed, it must examine the sources of available financing. Though the firm has a choice of long- or short-term and secured or unsecured instruments, and common stock, preferred stock, debt, or some hybrid security, the overriding decision concerns the relative amounts of debt and equity to be maintained in the firm's capital structure.

Analysis of the financial structure of the firm enters the financial management framework, as shown in Figure 1 of Chapter 1. We shall now analyze the impact changes in the financial structure have on both the firm's ability to raise future capital and the realization of the firm's wealth-maximization goal. Changes in the financial structure will affect the level of operating assets as well as the value of the firm. Decisions which result in changes in the financial structure obviously have risk-return trade-offs that must be considered before the financial package is presented for adoption.

A more detailed view of the capital structure analysis is given in Figure 1. The basic issue is the need to raise more capital. This will generate a new financial structure, since a decision must be made as to the quantity and type (new debt, preferred stock, or

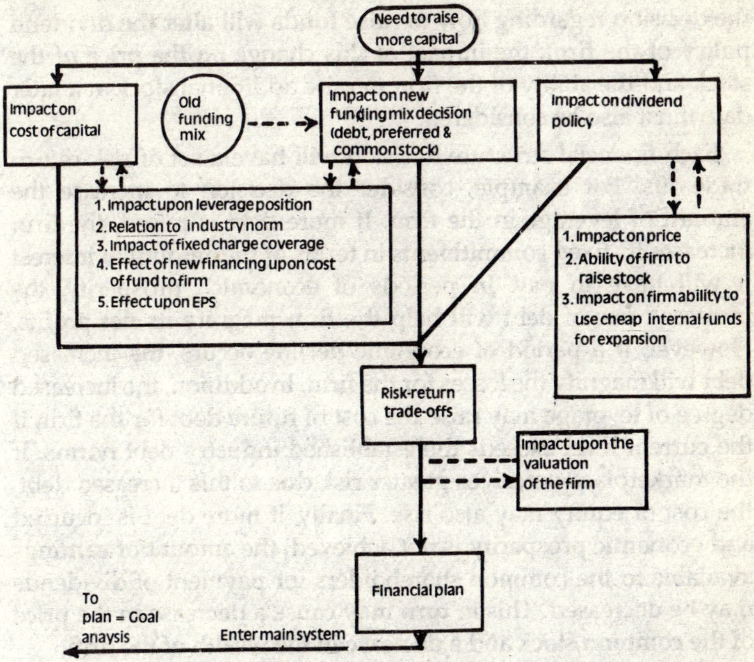

Fig. 1. Financial Structure Subsystem.

common equity) of financial sources needed. This decision will also involve an examination of the past financial structure of the firm. In addition, the analysis will examine the new potential financial structure in terms of how it will affect the leverage position of the firm, how this new leverage position will compare to industry norms, and how the firm will service the new debt or preferred or common equity.

A change in the leverage position of the firm will also have certain implications for the cost of raising this needed capital. Therefore the analysis as to which financing instrument to utilize will include a comparison of the cost components of each instrument. The cost of capital implications extend even further. The analysis must consider not only how the new funding mix will affect the firm's overall cost of capital but also how the future earnings per share will be affected by the new funding mix.

Dividend policy also enters the analysis, since the funds used to pay dividends are a potential source of financing for the firm. If the decision regarding how to raise funds will alter the dividend policy of the firm, the impact of this change on the price of the stock and the ability of the firm to raise additional stock at a later date must also be considered.

Each financial structure decision will have a set of risk-return trade-offs. For example, consider the decision to increase the amount of leverage in the firm. If more debt is raised, the firm increases its fixed commitments in terms of the amount of interest it will have to pay. In periods of economic prosperity, the increased use of debt will help the firm magnify its net profits. However, if a period of economic decline occurs, the increased debt will magnify the losses for the firm. In addition, the increased degree of leverage may raise the cost of future debt for the firm if the current level exceeds the established industry debt norms. If the marketplace perceives greater risk due to this increased debt, the cost of equity may also rise. Finally, if more debt is incurred and economic prosperity is not achieved, the amount of earnings available to the common shareholders for payment of dividends may be decreased. This in turn may cause a decrease in the price of the common stock and a decrease in the wealth of the firm.

Thus the trade-offs between increased risk and the potential increase in return are of concern to all management groups. Each possibility will have an impact on the valuation of the firm. The analysis must consider all ramifications of a capital structure change to determine the impact on the value of the firm. Once this analysis has been completed, a financial plan will be developed. The financial package will be presented to the board of directors for review to determine if in fact the plan meets the goal structure of the firm. If it does, the plan will be initiated. If it does not, a re-examination of the assumptions will be necessary.

FINANCIAL AND OPERATING LEVERAGE

The essential element in analysis of the capital structure of the firm is the effect leverage will have on it. Leverage is defined basically as the firm's utilization of an asset or liability which requires a fixed payment. It is said that leverage is a double-edged sword. When earnings before interest and taxes exceed the fixed obligations, favorable leverage occurs; when fixed obligations exceed earnings before interest and taxes, unfavorable leverage occurs. The examination of the interrelationship between leverage and the value of the firm, begins with the concept of break-even analysis. Although the inter-relation between the leverage and value of the firm are subject matter of this chapter, BE analysis has been given in great detail in vol. 2 of this treatise, *Economic Aspects of Management*. Therefore, only a short discussion shall suffice here.

Break-even analysis is an analytical tool for examining the relationship between the profit and cost structures of a firm. Its use in analyzing the concepts of operating and financial leverage will be explained in this section.

Formally defined, break-even analysis is a device to determine at what point the firm's sales just cover its total costs. The total cost structure of a firm will generally involve two cost classes—variable and fixed costs. Variable costs are defined as those that vary directly with the sales level of the firm. *Operating fixed* costs are defined as those that exist whether or not the firm is in production; these do not vary as output increases.

Cash Break-even Analysis

If a firm is having difficulty selling enough units to break even, the question arises as to whether it will have to shut down. In most cases, the firm can, in the short run, operate below the break-even point, because a large part of the fixed expenses may consist of depreciation, which is considered a non-cash outlay.

Non-linear Break-even Analysis

Up to this point it has been assumed that the relationship between total revenues and total costs is linear. This assumes that revenues and costs increase in the same proportion over all levels of output, which is an unrealistic assumption. It is generally accepted that total revenue increases at a *decreasing rate*. Thus if the firm wants to continue to increase its output, it must at some level start cutting its price. It is also well established that the variable costs increase not proportionally but rather at an *increasing rate* beyond a specific level of output. There is an efficient level of production within a firm, and as the firm exceeds that level, the total cost structure will start to rise. Costs will increase because costs such as repairs and maintenance on equipment rise when the equipment is being pushed beyond its efficient level of operation.

OPERATING LEVERAGE

Operating leverage refers to the degree to which operating fixed costs are used in the operations of the firm. The impact of fixed costs on the profit structure of the firm can be judged with the analytical tool of break-even analysis.

The importance of operating leverage as it relates to profitability can be shown in Figure 2, which considers two firms with different levels of operating leverage. Firm A has fixed costs of Rs. 30,000, variable costs per unit of Rs. 1.50 and a per unit sales price of Rs. 2.50. At this level of operating leverage, the break-even point is 30,000 units of production. Firm B has the same selling price but a higher level of operating leverage in the form of fixed costs of Rs. 60,000. The per unit variable costs have been reduced to Re. 1, due in part to the fact that the firm has more automated equipment than firm A. However, at the same level of output where firm A was breaking even, firm B is still losing Rs. 15,000. The break-even point for firm B is 40,000 units.

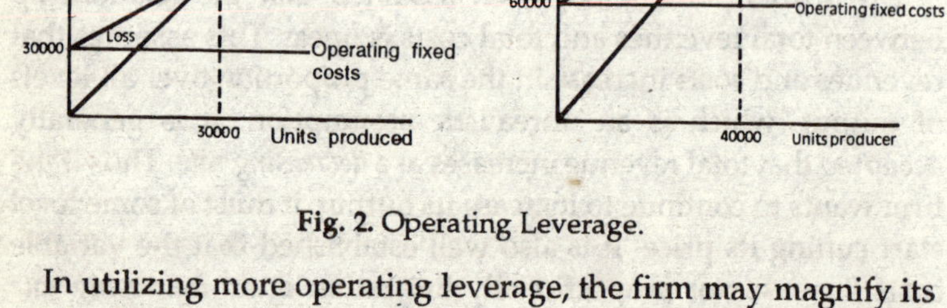

Fig. 2. Operating Leverage.

In utilizing more operating leverage, the firm may magnify its profits, but it may also magnify its losses. Table 1 shows the level of profitability at different levels of production for firms A and B. At 10,000 units sold, firm A is losing Rs. 20,000, while firm B is losing Rs. 45,000. At an output level of 110,000 units, firm A has a profit of Rs. 80,000, while firm B has a profit of Rs. 105,000. Increased leverage will magnify profits at high levels of output but will magnify losses at low levels of production. Once a higher level of fixed costs is assumed, it is difficult to eliminate these costs if sales do not reach the expected level.

Table 1

Effect of Leverage on Profits

FIRM A			
Selling price	Rs. 2.50		
Fixed costs	Rs. 30,000		
Variable costs	Rs. 1.50		
Units sold	*Total revenue*	*Total cost*	*EBIT (loss)*
10,000	Rs. 25,000	Rs. 45,000	Rs. (20,000)
30,000	75,000	75,000	-0-
50,000	125,000	105,000	20,000
70,000	175,000	135,000	40,000
90,000	225,000	165,000	60,000
110,000	275,000	195,000	80,000
FIRM B			
Selling price	Rs. 2.50		
Fixed costs	Rs. 60,000		
Variable costs	Re. 1		
Units sold	*Total revenue*	*Total cost*	*EBIT (loss)*
10,000	Rs. 25,000	Rs. 70,000	Rs. (45,000)
30,000	75,000	90,000	(15,000)
50,000	125,000	110,000	15,000
70,000	175,000	130,000	45,000
90,000	225,000	150,000	75,000
110,000	275,000	170,000	105,000

Degree of Operating Leverage

In addition to examining the impact of operating leverage over a range of outputs, we can also measure the operating leverage effect at a specific level of output. This is called the *degree of operating leverage*. It measures the impact that operating leverage has on earnings before interest and taxes (EBIT) given a change in output. This is shown in Equation 1.

Degree of operating leverage at X units =

$$\frac{\text{Percentage change in EBIT}}{\text{Percentage change in output}} \quad ...(1)$$

Instead of calculating the percentage changes in output and EBIT, we can look at the per unit data as given in Table 1 and calculate the degree of operating leverage at a level of output. This operation is shown in Equation 2.

$$DOL \text{ at X units} = \frac{X(P-V)}{X(P-V)-F}, \quad ...(2)$$

where:

DOL = Degree of operating leverage.

X = Number of units.

P = Price per unit.

V = Variable costs per unit.

F = Fixed costs.

The two equations above show the effect of operating leverage on earnings before interest and taxes. To illustrate the calculating procedure, we can examine the data for firm A and B in Table 1 and calculate the degree of operating leverage at 50,000 units. This is shown for Firm A as:

$$DOL_{50,000} = \frac{50,000\ (2.50 - 1.50)}{50,000\ (2.50) - 30,000}$$

$$= \frac{50,000}{20,000} = 2.5.$$

And for firm B as:

$$DOL_{50,000} = \frac{50,000\ (2.50 - 1.00)}{50,000\ (2.50 - 1.00) - 60,000}$$

$$= \frac{75,000}{15,000} = 5.0.$$

At a level of output of 50,000 units, firm A has a degree of operating leverage of 2.5, and firm B has a degree of operating leverage of 5.0. As the level of output changes, so will the degree of operating leverage. The further from the break-even point, the lower will be the degree of operating leverage.

With a degree of operating leverage of 2.5, if firm A expected to increase its level of output by 10 per cent, Equation 1 indicates that the expected increase in EBIT would be 25 per cent. For firm B, a

10 per cent increase in the level of output would increase EBIT level by 50 per cent. Thus firm B has the higher degree of operating leverage.

The impact of the operating leverage on EBIT will be shown to be even stronger when financial leverage is introduced and the combined leverage effect can be examined.

FINANCIAL LEVERAGE

Financial leverage is defined as the extent to which the firm utilizes limited participating funds obtained at a fixed cost in the hopes of increasing returns to common shareholders. Favorable leverage occurs when the firm invests these funds at a return that is greater than the associated fixed cost. Unfavorable leverage occurs when the return on these invested funds is less than the fixed cost.

Impact of Financial Leverage on Earnings Per Share

Any firm that is considering the use of debt or preferred stock in its capital structure must weigh the impact that the increased leverage will have on earnings per share. Management's object in seeking these funds is to increase the earnings per share. The example below illustrates how debt and stock financing affect this aspect of a company's financial position.

A company attempting to raise Rs. 50 lakhs determines that the funds can be raised through a debt, a preferred stock, or a common stock issue. If the funds are raised through the debt instrument, the firm would pay an annual rate of interest of 7 per cent. If preterred stock is used, the firm would pay an 8 percent dividend. If the funds are obtained through the equity market, 50,000 new shares would be issued at Rs. 100 market price.

The firm has outstanding 50,000 shares of common stock. Table 2 illustrates the impact of these three financing sources on earnings per share by examining them over different earnings levels. Given future uncertainty in the economy, the firm estimates that earnings before interest and taxes (EBIT) could vary anywhere from Rs. 400,000 to Rs. 2 million. In the debt or bond financing alternative, the 7 per cent interest charges of Rs. 350,000 and the 48 per cent tax charge must be deducted before determining the earnings per share (EPS). The EPS will range from 52 paise to

Rs. 17.16 as the EBIT figure increases. In the example, it is assumed that this is the only debt outstanding and the firm has outstanding 50,000 shares of stock. With the preferred stock issue, the impact on earnings per share is more volatile because the preferred dividends are paid on an after-tax basis. Thus the earnings per share will vary from a deficit of Rs. 3.84 to Rs. 12.80. With the common

Table 2

Calculation of Earnings Per Share (in thousands of Rs.)

Bond financing 5 million—7 per cent					
EBIT	400	600	800	1,000	2,000
Interest*	350	350	350	350	350
Earnings before taxes	50	250	450	650	1,650
Taxes, 48 per cent	24	120	216	312	792
Net income	26	130	234	338	858
Number of shares	50	50	50	50	50
Earnings per share#	.52	2.60	4.68	6.76	17.16
Preferred stock financing, 5 million—8 per cent					
EBIT	400	600	800	1,000	2,000
Interest	—	—	—	—	—
Earnings before taxes	400	600	800	1,000	2,000
Taxes, 48 per cent	192	288	384	480	960
Net income	208	312	416	520	1,040
Preferred dividends	400	400	400	400	400
Earnings available to common	(192)	(88)	16	120	640
Number of shares	50	50	50	50	50
Earnings per share	(3.84)	(1.76)	.32	2.40	12.80
Common stock financing, 85 million					
EBIT	400	600	800	1.000	2,000
Interest	—	—	—	—	—
Earnings before taxes	400	600	800	1,000	2,000
Taxes, 48 per cent	192	288	384	480	960
Net income	208	312	416	520	1,040
Number of shares	100	100	100	100	100
Earnings per share@	2.08	3.12	4.16	5.20	10.40

* 7 per cent interest on all debt.

50,000 common shares currently outstanding.

@ 100,000 shares with 50,000 new shares issued at Rs. 100 market price plus the outstanding 50,000 shares.

stock offering, the number of shares would increase to 100,000, and, since there is no interest to deduct, the earnings per share would range from Rs. 2.08 to Rs. 10.40 as the earnings before interest and taxes increase.

The table shows that under certain EBIT levels, the earnings per share under the debt financing alternative is larger than under the stock financing alternative, and at high EBIT levels, earnings per share are higher for preferred stock financing than for common stock financing. This phenomenon can be illustrated in Figure 3 which graphs the relationship between earnings before interest and taxes, and earnings per share for the common stock, preferred stock, and debt financing alternatives. Note that for all levels of EBIT below Rs. 700,000, the common stock financing alternative provides the higher EPS figure, and for all EBIT levels above, this level, the debt alternative provides the highest EPS. The crossover

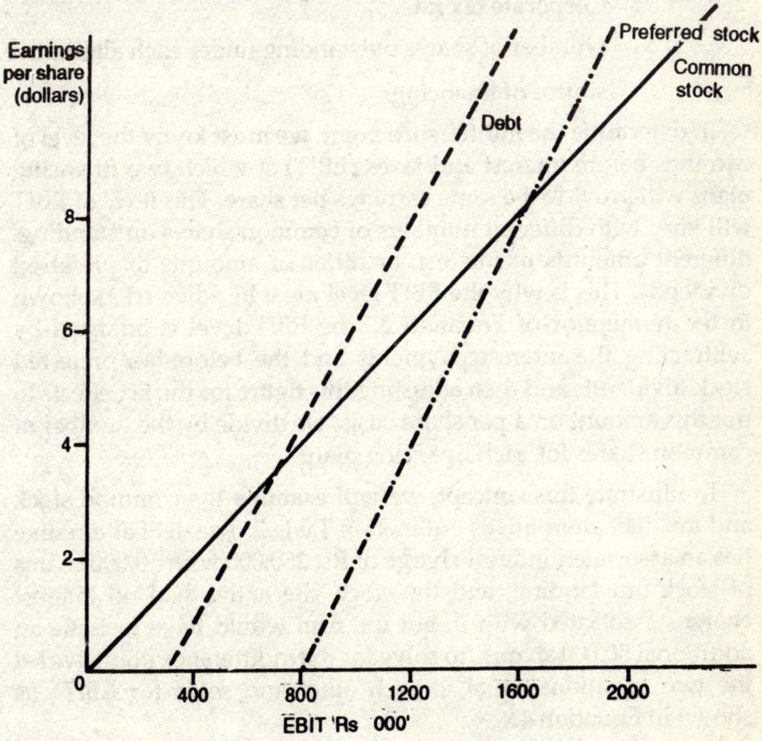

Fig. 3. Indifference Graph.

point is called the *indifference point*. This shows the point at which comparative methods of financing will yield the same results in earnings per share.

To calculate the indifference point between two financing alternatives we equate the two sources of financing, as in Equation 3 and solve for EBIT:

$$\frac{(EBIT' - I_1)(I - t)}{S_1} = \frac{(EBIT' - I_2)(I - t)}{S_2} \qquad ...(3)$$

where:

$EBIT'$ = $EBIT$ indifference point between the two methods of financing.

I_1, I_2 = Annual interest expense or preferred stock dividend on a before-tax basis for the two financing methods.

t = Corporate tax rate.

$S_1 S_2$ = Number of shares outstanding under each alternative source of financing.

To determine the indifference point, we must know the level of earnings before interest and taxes (EBIT) at which two financing plans will provide the same earnings per share. This level of EBIT will vary with different numbers of common shares outstanding, different amounts of interest, or different amounts of preferred dividends. This is why the EBIT level must be adjusted as shown in the numerator of Equation 3. The EBIT level is adjusted by subtracting the interest payments and the before-tax preferred stock dividends and then adjusting this figure for the tax effect. To put this amount on a per share basis, we divide by the number of common shares for each financing plan.

To illustrate this concept, we will examine the common stock and the debt alternatives outlined in Table 2. The debt alternative has an associated interest charge of Rs. 350,000 with 50,000 shares of stock outstanding, and the stock alternative had no interest charges associated with it, but the firm would have to issue an additional 50,000 shares. To solve for the indifference point, we set the two equations equal to each other and solve for EBIT′, as shown in Equation 4.

$$\frac{(EBIT' - \text{Rs. } 350{,}00)(1 - 0.48)}{50{,}000} = \frac{(EBIT' - 0)(1 - 0.48)}{100{,}000}$$

$$(0.48)\ EBIT'\ (100{,}000) - (0.48)\ (350{,}000)\ (100{,}000) =$$
$$= (0.48)\ EBIT'\ (50{,}000)$$
$$48{,}000\ EBIT' - 16{,}800{,}000{,}000 = 24{,}000\ EBIT'$$
$$24{,}000\ EBIT' = 16{,}800{,}000{,}000$$
$$EBIT' = \text{Rs. } 700{,}00$$

As Figure 3 shows, at an EBIT level below Rs. 700,000, the common stock plan provides the higher earnings per share, and at an EBIT level above Rs. 700,000 the bond or debt financing plan provides the higher earnings per share. Below the indifference point, the burden of the interest payments is too great in terms of the effect on EPS; thus the common stock financing plan will have higher earnings per share because there is no interest burden. At high levels of EBIT the fixed interest charges are more than compensated for, however, because the increased number of shares issued on the stock plan is so great that the earnings available to the common shareholders are spread too thin. The result is a lower level of earnings per share relative to the debt alternative.

For the preferred stock versus the common stock alternative, the indifference point is at the Rs. 1.6 million EBIT level. The reason such a level of EBIT is necessary before the preferred stock financing alternative has a higher level of earnings per share is because preferred stock dividends are paid out of after-tax income. The effect is to reduce the earnings per share as compared to the common stock financing plan.

The degree of financial leverage at a particular EBIT level is measured by the percentage change in earnings per share relative to the percentage change in EBIT.

$$DFL \text{ at a certain } EBIT = \frac{EBIT}{EBIT - Y}.$$

where:

DFL = Degree of financial leverage

$EBIT$ = Earnings before interest and taxes

Y = Annual interest expense or preferred stock dividend on a before–tax basis

For the debt-financing alternative at an EBIT level of Rs. 1 million, the degree of financial leverage would be:

$$DFL_{\text{Rs. 1 million}} = \frac{1,000,000}{1,000,000 - 350,000} = 1.54.$$

For the preferred financing alternative at an EBIT level of Rs. 1 million, the degree of financial leverage would be:

$$DFL_{\text{Rs. 1 million}} = \frac{1,000,000}{1,000,000 - 769,231} = 4.33$$

With the debt alternative, a 100 per cent increase in EBIT would lead to a 154 per cent increase in earnings per share. The higher degree of financial leverage associated with preferred stock is due to the higher financial costs on a before-tax basis which act as the *fulcrum* in the leverage analysis.

The double-edged sword concept of financial leverage is clearly demonstrated in this illustration. In periods of high sales and a high EBIT level, the use of debt will magnify the gain to be obtained in earnings per share, compared to common stock or preferred stock financing. The increased earnings per share are the result of the tax effect on the debt interest payments. Because interest is an expense which is deductible before tax, it acts as a tax shield for the corporation. However, in periods of low sales, the interest charges become a fixed burden for the corporation which severely hurt its EPS record, as shown in Figure 3.

The importance of an accurate sales forecast cannot be stressed enough. If the firm expects a high level of sales and it finances this sales growth through a Rs 50 lakhs debt offering, if sales do not reach the level of expectation the firm will face a debt service cost which will impair its EPS record. However, if the firm is correct about the high sales forecast, its profits will be magnified, as shown by the debt line in Figure 3. Note that the debt line is growing much faster than the stock financing line, indicating the magnification of earnings on both the high and low sides.

This type of analysis is not limited to debt or common stock financing. We can also utilize it in analyzing a combination of debt and equity financing alternatives in order to determine the effect of the various combinations on the earnings per share of the firm.

Impact of Financial Leverage on the Return to Equity Holders

Increasing the amount of leverage can magnify the earnings per share of the firm, and thus the shareholder's wealth, when sales are at relatively high levels. The effect on the shareholder's wealth can be more vividly illustrated by examining the impact of leverage on the return to common equity. In the example below we will ignore the effect of preferred stock financing, to simplify the discussion.

One of the ways to examine the relationship between leverage and the return to common equity, is through the use of the earnings power ratio. In developing the concept of the return on total assets and the debt to total asset ratio, we defined the return on total assets as net income after taxes as related to total assets. The effect on the equity holders can be illustrated in Equation 5.

$$\text{Return on net worth} = \frac{\text{Return on total assets}}{1 - \text{Debt/Total assets}} \qquad \ldots(5).$$

Assuming that the return on total assets remains constant, the return on common equity can be increased by increasing the debt to total asset ratio, which is the measure of leverage. This will decrease the value of the denominator, which, when divided into the numerator, will increase the return on net worth.

This relationship is further illustrated in Table 3 which considers Rs. 10 million asset level and various returns on total assets which reflect different levels of economic activity resulting in poor to excellent sales. As the sales level increases, the return on total assets also increases, assuming that the relationship of costs to sales and total assets to sales remains the same. In addition, under each return to total asset column, various leverage levels are examined in order to show the impact on the return on net worth.

For example, if a 6 per cent return on total assets before interest and taxes is expected, the return with no (0 per cent) leverage is 3.1 per cent; with 25 per cent leverage, 2.9 per cent; and with 50 per cent leverage, 2.6 per cent. This decrease is due to the earnings not being high enough to absorb the interest cost, resulting in a negative impact on net income available for shareholders. This is verified in the table, which shows that the return to shareholders decreases as leverage increases at an EBIT level of Rs. 600,000. Above the Rs. 600,000 level, the return to shareholders increases as the leverage factor increases.

Table 3

Effect of Leverage on Return to Net Worth
(Rs. figures in thousands)

	Economic conditions				
	Poor				*Excellent*
	Return on total assets before interest and taxes				
	2.0%	4.0%	6.0%	8.0%	10.0%
0% leverage (10.0 million equity)					
EBIT	200	400	600	800	1,000
Interest	—	—	—	—	—
Earnings before taxes	200	400	600	800	1,000
Taxes @ 48%	96	192	288	384	480
Net Income	104	208	312	416	520
Return on net worth	1.0%	2.1%	3.1%	4.2%	5.2%
25% leverage (2.5 million debt; 7.5 million equity)					
EBIT	200	400	600	800	1,000
Interest 7%	175	175	175	175	175
Earnings before taxes	25	225	425	625	825
Taxes @ 48%	12	108	204	300	396
Net income	13	117	221	325	429
Return on net worth	.2%	1.6%	2.9%	4.3%	5.7%
50% leverage (5 million debt; 5 million equity)					
EBIT	200	400	600	800	1,000
Interest 7%	350	350	350	350	350
Earnings before taxes	(150)	50	250	450	650
Taxes @ 48%	—	24	120	216	312
Net income	(150)	26	130	234	338
Return on net worth	–3.0%	.5%	2.6%	4.7%	6.8%

Note that the double-edged sword is at work again. At low and high levels of profitability, increasing the amount of leverage will magnify the loss potential and magnify the gain potential. Thus, if the firm forecasts a high sales level and increases leverage to 50 per cent, as measured by the debt to total asset level, it will have the highest expected gain. However, if management is wrong in its forecast, the losses will also be magnified as compared to a lower level of leverage.

COMBINED EFFECTS OF OPERATING AND FINANCIAL LEVERAGE

Consideration of the combined effects of operating and financial leverage magnifies the effects of leverage on earnings per share. The two leverage factors together increase the dispersion and risk of forecasting earnings per share. To measure this combined effect, we can multiply the degree of operating leverage by the degree of financial leverage. This will shows the effect that a change in output will have on earnings per share. In essence, earnings before interest and taxes is really X (italicP – V) – F, where X is the units of output, P is the price per unit, V is the variable cost per unit, and F is the fixed cost. Thus:

$$DFL = \frac{EBIT}{EBIT - Y} = \frac{X(P-V)-F}{X(P-V)-F-Y}.$$

Combining the degree of operating leverage and the degree of financial leverage (*DOL* & *DFL*) result in this formula:

$$DOL \,\&\, DFL = \frac{X(P-V)}{X(P-V)-F} \times \frac{X(P-V)-F}{X(P-V)-F-Y}$$
$$= \frac{X(P-V)}{X(P-V)-F-Y}$$

Note that the fixed financial costs, Y, is increase the degree of combined leverage over operating leverage alone.

VALUATION OF THE FIRM

The firm has to make investment, financing, and dividend policy decisions that will be structured in such a way as to maximize the stockholders' wealth, since the risk-return trade-offs inherent in these decisions will affect the price of the stock.

To formulize the concept of valuation, we can express the functional relationship in the value of the firm as shown in Equation 6.

Value of firm = Function of (invstment mix, financing mix, dividend policy). ...(6)

Thus the firm must manipulate its investment, financing, and dividend policy decisions in terms of their risk and return trade-offs in such a fashion as to maximize the value of the firm. Not only must each of these decision variables be analyzed internally, it must also be examined in light of the interrelationship between the three decision variables.

This chapter discusses the concept of valuation of the firm. It will describe the various methods of valuing bonds and stock and show how to determine a value for a corporation. The next two chapters will explore in detail the impact of the financing decision on the cost of capital and the importance of the dividend policy in determining the value of the firm.

The concept of value can mean different things to different people. In the field of finance, there are many approaches to the valuation of a firm and thus many meanings of the term *valuation*. Brief descriptions of the differences between some of the major concepts are given below.

Liquidation Value Versus Going Concern

A firm's liquidation value is associated with what it would receive from sales of its assets, including the plant, equipment, inventory, and accounts receivable. If the assets were sold and the money utilized to pay the debts, the amount left over would be considered the liquidation value of the firm. In terms of establishing a value for an organization, the liquidation value of assets would be the minimum value acceptable by an organization.

Unless a firm is in a great deal of financial trouble and the fear of failure is on the horizon, no owner would accept the liquidation concept as a means of establishing a value for a firm. The owner would contend that the firm consists of much more than pure assets; people are what make the organization successful. Management skills are utilized to produce an efficient level of operation and a profitable sales level established by successful sales people. The firm should be valued as a *going concern*. If the going-concern value has been established, the difference between it and the value of liquidating assets would be the contribution made by the people in the firm.

Book Versus Market Value

In the recording framework established by the accounting profession, all assets listed in a corporation's balance sheet are carried at cost or market, whichever is lower. As time elapses from the date of purchase, assets can appreciate tremendously if the level of economic activity consistently grows. *Book value* refers to the difference between the assets recorded as cost and liabilities, as listed on the firm's balance sheet. Market value reflects the salable value of the assets.

Market Versus Intrinsic Value

The differences between the concepts of market and intrinsic value were pointed out above for use in analyzing bonds and stock. *Intrinsic value* represents the true value of the security, based on such factors as assets, earnings, and dividends. Once the intrinsic value for a security has been established, it can be compared to the *market value*, which reflects the current value of that security. If the intrinsic value based on hard data exceeds the current market value, it would be wise to buy the security in hopes that the market would soon recognize its true worth. By the same token, if the market value exceeds the estimated intrinsic value, the security is said to be over evaluated, and it would not be a good investment.

A similar comparison can be made of the valuation of business organizations. Basically, the same kind of forecast cash flow data are utilized by all. By applying the appropriate discount rate or capitalization rate, it is possible to determine the value of a business or asset. This quantitative figure represents the intrinsic value of the asset or organization. If the asset or firm were up for sale, its intrinsic value could be compared with the asking or market price. Then a decision would be made as to whether to invest, depending on whether the intrinsic value is above or below the market price.

VALUATION OF A BOND

In determining the intrinsic value of a security, the primary interest is in evaluating the capitalized income stream that would be generated over the life of the security. In the case of bonds, the income received consists of annual interest payments plus the principal amount when the bond matures. The capitalization rate applied to the income stream will differ in various bonds, depending on their risk profiles.

Relationship of Short- and Long-Term Interest Rates

As the economy moves through the expansion and contraction phases of a business cycle, the structure of interest rates will accordingly increase and decrease, to a degree. As the economy expands and the demand for business expansion loans increases, the interest rates on business loans will also increase. Conversely, when the economy is contracting and businesses do not want to expand, there is a low demand for funds, and interest rates decrease.

Interest rates schedules are so structured that when the rates on low-risk bonds increase or decrease, the whole structure of interest rates moves in the same direction. The market for bonds is segmented into short-term bonds, which are characterized as low-risk securities, and longer term bonds, which have a higher risk factor. As we might expect, the low-risk securities have a lower interest rate, due to the perceived lower risk. This interest rate can be considered as the rate of return the investing public demands be paid by the government or corporation for the public's investment in the bonds. Table 4. presents a three-year array of rates for bonds (both short-term and long-term) and for other money market instruments.

Thus, increased risk can be perceived as one moves from short- to long-term securities and from federal government bonds to bonds of quality corporations and then to bonds of smaller corporations. As the risk perceptions increase, so will the required return of the bondholder. This is because an investor recognizes the opportunity cost associated with an investment. If he or she invests all the money in one security, he or she foregoes the opportunity of investing in another. Thus, it is logical to require a higher return if the investor community perceives a greater risk in a particular bond.

Table 4

Money Market Interest Rates and Yields

	1986	*1985*	*1984*
Federal Reserve discount rate	5.25%	5.50%	7.7%
Federal funds rate	5.05	5.82	10.51
Government securities yields:			
3-month bills	4.98	5.80	7.84
6-month bills	5.26	6.11	7.95
1-year bills	5.52	6.30	7.71
3 to 5-year notes	6.94	7.55	7.81
10+ U.S. bonds	7.61	7.19	7.56

	1986	*1985*	*1984*
Commercial paper:			
90-119 days	5.24	6.26	10.05
4-6 months	5.35	6.33	9.87
Corporate bond yields:			
Aaa	8.43	8.83	8.57
Baa	9.75	10.61	9.50
Business loans:			
Prime rate	6.35	7.26	10.50
Mortgage rate	8.76	8.75	8.71

Relation Between Short- and Long-Term Interest Rates Over Time

We would expect that over time, long-term interest rates would generally be above short-term rates, due to the risk relationship between the two classes of bonds. To a large extent this is historically true.

If you were on the other side of the picture and were supplying short- and long-term funds, which would you rather have supplied in 1968? Long-term securities would be preferable. If you could lock a customer into a long-term agreement before interest rates were expected to fall, as a lender you would be much better off.

Thus there is a shift in demand from long-term to short-term debt. On the supply side, there is a shift from short-term to long-term debt. In this situation, there is a great deal of demand for short-term loans but the supply is diminishing. Whenever demand exceeds the available supply, the price will go up. Therefore the short-term interest rates increase substantially. Since there is little demand for long-term debt and there is substantial supply of these loans, the rate on long-term debt will decrease. This will create a situation wherein short-term rates rise relative to long-term rates, and eventually, if the pressure remains heavy, the shot-term rates will rise above the long-term rates.

This section has shown how bonds can be evaluated to determine their intrinsic value. We have examined the way in which the discount rate is determined in terms of the current yield and yield to maturity and have seen the interrelationships between various interest rates and how short- and long-term rates relate to each other over time.

VALUATION OF COMMON STOCK

The concept of valuation of common stock is basically the same as with bonds. The individual is interested in the capitalized value of a specified income stream. The only difference is that with common stock, the certainty of receiving that income stream is not as great. Thus, a higher risk factor enters the analysis of common stock valuation.

Valuation Models

If investors were asked what they expected to receive from an investment in common stock, they would probably reply that they expected to receive dividend income plus some price appreciation when the stock is sold. The value of the stock would be determined by the discounted value of the dividend income stream and the ending or selling price of the stock. If it is assumed that the capitalization rate, *k*, is given, and that stock will be held for one year, the value would be expressed as in Equation 7.

$$\text{Present price} = \frac{\text{First-year-dividend}}{(1+k)} + \frac{\text{Price in 1 year}}{(1+k)} \quad \text{...(7)}$$

If we further assume that the company will pay Rs. 2 dividend, that the price in one year will be Rs. 50, and that the capitalization rate is 10 per cent, then the present price or value can be determined as in Equation 8.

$$\text{Present price} = \frac{\text{Rs. }2.00}{(1.10)^1} + \frac{\text{Rs. }50.00}{(1.10)^1}$$
$$= \text{Rs. }1.82 + \text{Rs. }45.45 = \text{Rs. }47.27 \quad \text{...(8)}$$

Further examination of Equation 7, shows that the price in one year is really nothing more than the current price, growing by some growth rate, *g*. We could thus rewrite Equation 7, expressing this relationship as:

$$\text{Present price} = \frac{\text{First-year divided}}{(1+k)} + \frac{\text{Present price (1 + Growth rate)}}{(1+k)} \quad \text{...(9)}$$

If, according to generally accepted theory, a stock price is based on expected future dividends and the risk of these dividends as perceived by the investor, and if the investor is holding the stock for a longer period than one year, the valuation analysis must also consider the dividend income stream beyond the first year, plus the terminal price of the stock at the time of sale. However, the terminal price of the stock is dependent upon what subsequent buyers expect to receive in terms of the dividend income stream and the terminal value when they, in turn, sell.

This process continues to infinity because each subsequent buyer of the stock is willing to pay a price for it which is based on his estimate of the expected dividend stream and the terminal value of the stock. Thus the current value of the stock can be expressed in an equation which evaluates all future dividends and the final terminal value of the stock.

$$P_0 = \frac{D_1}{(1+k)^1} + \frac{D_2}{(1+k)^2} + \frac{D_3}{(1+k)^3} + ...+ \frac{D_\infty}{(1+k)^\infty} + \frac{P_\infty}{(1+k)^\infty} \quad ...(10)$$

where:

P_0 = Current price of the stock.

D_1 to D_∞ = Expected future dividends from year 1 to ∞.

P_∞ = Price of the stock or terminal value at ∞.

k = Appropriate discount or capitalization rate.

Since the terminal value will depend upon an investor's expectation of future cash dividends to be received, Equation 10 be expressed as the summation of all future expected cash dividends from now until infinity.

$$P_0 = \frac{D_1}{(1+k)^1} + \frac{D_2}{(1+k)^2} + \frac{D_3}{(1+k)^3} + ...+ \frac{D_\infty}{(1+k)^\infty} = \sum_{t=1}^{\infty} \frac{D_t}{(1+k)^t} \quad ...(11)$$

This equation, which states that the value of a stock is equal to the discounted value of all future dividends, may be acceptable for those firms that pay dividends, but can it apply to firms that do not pay them? The theory that maintains that dividends totally determine the value of the stock would contend that a firm which is not paying dividends today is building up its retained earnings base and will at some future point be able to pay substantial dividends. Thus, in terms of Equation 11, the first few values of D_t would be equal to zero, but at some future point we would be able to calculate the discounted value of dividends and determine the current value of the stock.

The Discount Rate

Up to this point we have considered the discount rate, *k*, as a given. How this rate is determined is of consideration.

An investor in common stock is expecting a return. If firm pays cash dividends, the investor will express the return in the form of the cash dividends plus the terminal value of the stock sold. The terminal value is the capital gains that the investor will receive, representing the difference between the price paid for the stock and the price he or she could receive by selling the stock. The value, *k*, is always expressed in terms of a percentage and is thus broken into the two components of dividends yield and capital gains yield.

If it is assumed that a firm will pay Rs. 3 dividend, that the current price of the stock is Rs. 50, and that it is estimated that the stock will be sold for Rs. 55 in one year, the total yield can be calculated as in Equation 12.

$$\text{Dividend yield} = \frac{\text{Dividends}}{\text{Price}} = \frac{\text{Rs. } 3.00}{\text{Rs. } 50.00} = 0.06, \text{ or 6 per cent}$$

$$\text{Capital gains yield} = \frac{\text{Price increase}}{\text{Current price}} = \frac{\text{Rs. } 5.00}{\text{Rs. } 50.00}.$$

$$= 0.10, \text{ or 10 per cent}$$

Thus, the total expected return is equal to the dividend yield plus the capital gains yield:

$$\text{Total yield} = \frac{\text{Expected dividends}}{\text{Current price}} + \frac{\text{Expected price increase}}{\text{Current price}}$$

$$= 6 \text{ per cent} + 10 \text{ per cent} = 16 \text{ per cent} \qquad ...(12)$$

To formalize this more exactly, the rate of return on a share of common stock can be expressed as:

$$k = \frac{D_1}{P} + g,$$

where:

k = Total yield or rate of return to be received by an investor.

D_1 = Dividends to be paid per share at the end of year 1.

P = Current price per share

g = Expected growth rate in the price of the stock

The rate of return or total yield can be viewed in two different ways. The first approach would classify this yield as the rate of return that will be received by investing in the stock. It is defined as the expected dividend yield plus the expected price appreciation to be received over the period the individual is investing in the stock.

The second way to view *k* is as a *required rate of return* which an investor can demand the firm to pay in exchange for his or her investment in the stock. The reason *k* is considered a required rate of return is that the investor has a perception of the risk and is aware of the opportunity cost of the investment, as noted above. The firm he or she is considering investing in has risk associated with it, as compared to other firms in the same industry. If the investor views all firms in the industry as belonging to an acceptable risk class for investment, he or she will want to invest where the money will receive the highest return. Thus he or she will calculate all the returns for the companies in the industry. The required rate of return, *k*, thus is the highest rate paid by a firm in that industry, since an investor will want to select the investment or firm with the highest return for the same degree of risk.

An example will help illustrate this concept. Consider that an investor is willing to accept a level of risk associated with the steel industry and has classified all firms in the steel industry as belonging to one risk class. The investor wants to invest where the highest return for the given level of risk can be obtained. Firm *A* in the industry has a 7 per cent expected rate of return while firm *B* has a 10 per cent expected return. It so happens that firm *B* provides the highest return of any firm in the steel industry. The investor therefore will establish the required rate of return as 10 per cent, recognizing that whatever firm is invested in, he or she will have to forego the opportunity of investing in other firms. With the required rate of return set at 10 per cent, the investor will not invest in firm *A* unless this firm increases its rate of return or yield to 10 per cent. If other investors feel the same way firm A will have to pay a rate of return of 10 per cent in terms of dividend yield and capital gains in order to attract investment in its firm. Eventually an equilibrium position between the two firms will be reached. The rate for *A* will rise as the price drops when people sell, while the rate of return for firm *B* will drop as the price rises. The price rise for firm *B* is a result of the increased demand for the firm's stock.

Thus investors will select a risk class of firms with which they feel comfortable and then will select the firm that offers the highest return for the given level of risk. This is because investors feel that their return should be equal to a risk-free rate of return plus a premium return for the risk they are willing to accept for investing in a firm. The risk-free rate would be the rate associated with investments in 90-day Treasury bills. The difference between this risk-free rate and the rate the industry is paying is the risk premium rate required to attract investment into the industry.

In addition to the above general valuation model, where the assumption as to future dividends could vary, we may now consider to simplify the process of evaluation by taking into account the exact nature of growth assumptions of dividends. Some of these are listed below:

1. Zero Growth. When the growth of dividend is expected to be zero the valuation of shares is same as for a perpetuity.

2. Constant Growth. Usually the dividends and earnings as in the previous assumption, do not remain static but increase or decrease. We may assume the growth as equivalent to growth of Gross National Product (GNP). In general, the value of future dividends, D_t, can be expressed as:

$$D_t = D_0 (1 + g)^t \quad \text{...(13)}$$

3. More than Normal Growth. It is also not uncommon for a firm to experience supernormal growth because of its products largely in demand. This occurs frequently in the dynamic growth part of the life cycle of the firm. (see vol. 3 of this treatise, *Economic Aspects of Management*). If suppose a firm grows at 20% for five years and then slows down to a rate of 10%, both the growth rates are to be considered. The solution to the current problem lies in the fact that the value of the stock is equal to the discounted value of dividends for the first five years, growing at a super-normal growth of 20% plus the discounted value of all future dividends, growing at the normal rate of 10 per cent.

VALUATION OF THE WHOLE FIRM

In addition to evaluating specific securities, such as debt and equity instruments, it may be necessary to evaluate the whole firm. Determining a value for a firm may involve the liquidation value of the assets in case of a possible bankruptcy, or it may involve the valuation of an ongoing firm for possible acquisition. In the analysis below, we will discuss only the valuation of the whole firm as an ongoing concern.

In the case of a public company, the firm's value is the summation of the market value of common stock and the market value of debt. If the firm has both types of securities, the valuation formula would be:

$$V_L = V_S + V_D,$$

where:

V_L = Value of a levered firm.

V_S = Market value of the common stock.

V_D = Market value of debt.

If, for example, the public company had Rs. 3 million of debt and a market value of Rs. 5 million for common stock (Rs. 50 per share × 100,000 shares), then the market value of the company would be Rs. 8 million.

If the interest is in acquiring a private company, the problems are more complex because there is no market value of common stock. If, for example, a firm is for sale and the owner is asking Rs. 2.5 million rupees, an intrinsic value for the firm can be determined to guide the investor, in the manner described below:

The approach is similar to the present value approach used above for capital budgeting decisions. The first step is to determine the future stream of net cash flows that the proposed investment will yield over time. The second step is to find the present value of this cash flow stream and compare it to the required initial investment. If we were using the net present value method, we would discount the cash flows at the cost of capital.

In evaluating an ongoing firm, we will estimate future net income after taxes rather than future net cash flows. We assume that (1) cash expenditures for the replacement of plant and equipment over time will just about equal the noncash expense of depreciation, (2) the stream of income will continue indefinitely, and (3) the income stream will be constant.

The investors' decision as to the price they are willing to pay for a firm is based on three factors. First, they are willing to pay a higher price for a higher after-tax income stream. Second, the risk associated with that stream must be considered. Third, they are willing to pay a higher price for a firm that has the capacity to lever—through debt—this future income stream.

Given this information, we can express the general valuation formula for a levered firm as:

$$V_L = \frac{Y(1-t)}{k} + (R)(t), \qquad \text{...(14)}$$

where:

V_L = Value of a levered firm.

Y = Net operating income before interest and taxes.

t = Corporate tax rate.

k = After–tax capitalization rate for an unlevered firm.

R = Rupee amount of total debt.

In this equation we are stating that the value of a levered firm will be higher the greater the after-tax stream of earnings, the lower the discount rate, and the higher the debt capacity of the firm.

Determination of Expected After-tax Income

The first step in determining tax-adjusted expected operating income is to determine expected net operating income before interest and taxes. This is usually based on the historical earnings of the firm. In examining past earnings it is important to select a period that can be classified as a "typical period", which would include both bad and good years. Also we must take in consideration any strong earnings trend—either upward or downward—that is visible in recent years. This can be accomplished by applying more weights to recent years' earnings.

Assume that, after examining the past earnings of the company, we have estimated net operating income before taxes and interest to be Rs. 300,000. If the corporate tax rate is 48 per cent, our estimate of tax-adjusted earnings which is one part of the valuation formula would be as shown in Equation 15.

$$Y(1-t) = \text{Rs. } 300{,}000\,(1-0.48) = \text{Rs. } 156{,}000 \qquad \text{...(15)}$$

Determination of the Discount Rate

The discount rate used to capitalize tax-adjusted earnings reflects the risk associated with the business. Here risk is defined as the variance in the range of possible outcomes of earnings which occurs about the expected return. Usually the discount rate is determined by examining other firms in the same industry. If we are dealing with an unlevered firm we examine other unlevered firms by applying the first part of the valuation formula, $V = (Y[1-t])/k$. Therefore:

$$k = \frac{Y(1-t)}{V} \qquad \ldots(16)$$

Note that Equation (16) expresses the valuation of the firm in terms of the whole entity. We can make a simple adjustment and express this equation on a per share basis:

$$k = \frac{Y(1-t)/\text{Number of shares}}{V/\text{Number of shares}} = \frac{EPS}{P}. \qquad \ldots(17)$$

Thus for companies with common stock outstanding, we can express k as the ratio of earnings per share to price per share of the stock. This is the *price-earnings multiple*, or *P/E ratio*. If we are determining a value of an unlevered firm in a primarily unlevered industry, we can examine a number of the unlevered firms and determine a capitalization rate. If we perceive that the firm's risk differs from that of other firms, we can adjust the discount rate in either direction.

If we are determining a discount rate for a levered stream of after-tax earnings from examining other levered firms, we cannot use the price-earnings ratios of these firms. This is because the P/E ratio reflects not only the business risk exposure of the firm but also the financial risk associated with leverage. Firms apply different degrees of financial leverage, and we must compensate for this by using the general valuation formula as shown in Equation (14) and solving for k.

To accomplish this, it is important to examine firms that are in the same risk class as the firm being evaluated. This risk class may be defined in terms of similar products, cost structures, or market positions.

Estimating the Firm's Debt Capacity and Calculating the Total Value of the Firm

In determining the debt capacity supported by the expected stream of earnings, we again have to examine other firms in a similar risk class. Their revenue streams and their ability to service the debt, as well as their debt ratios, must be considered, and investment bankers who can provide guidelines as to proper debt levels, given a specific level of risk, should be consulted.

If the firm the investors are interested in buying has existing debt, the effect on the price they are willing to pay can vary. If we determine that the firm is not utilizing its debt capacity, the value we will calculate for the firm will undoubtedly exceed its market value. If the investors decide to purchase only the assets of the firm and not to assume any of the existing debt, then the maximum purchase price they are willing to pay is our determination of V_L. If they purchase the common stock of the corporation, or purchase the assets and assume a certain portion of the debt, then the maximum purchase price they are willing to pay is V_L minus the market value of the debt assumed.

The foregoing section on the capital structure of the firm examined how the firm can alter its leverage position and discussed some of the general implications this change will have for its profitability structure. The second provided an overview of the effects of debt and equity on the value of the firm.

We shall now examine the impact of changes in the capital structure on the cost of raising funds, and how this can affect the capital investment decisions of the firm. The concept of the cost of capital, how this cost is measured, how the concept can be utilized to minimize the firm's structure,and how the cost of capital can be related to a required rate of return to be used as a cutoff point in capital investment decisions are the points of consideration in the following paragraphs.

Formally defined, the cost of capital for a corporation is *that rate of return which must be earned on invested capital so that the value of the common stock remains unchanged*. This definition varies slightly for the individual components of the capital structure of the firm.

COMPONENT COST STRUCTURE

This section examines the components of the capital structure, such as long-term debt, preferred stock, and equity, or common stock, and analyzes the cost of capital implications for the capital structure of the firm of using each form of financing.

The Cost of Debt

Debt financing is one of the more frequently sought forms because it is one of the least costly. In terms of the cost of capital definition, the firm must make sure that when it borrows funds, the rate earned through use of the debt-invested funds is equal to or greater than the cost of this debt. Thus, the *cost of debt must be equal to the rate of return earned on debt-invested funds, so that the earnings available to the common shareholder remain unchanged.* This means that the explicit component cost of debt is equal to the rate of return earned by investors, or the interest rate on debt.

Thus the cost of capital is really a minimization concept in the sense that a minimum rate of return that must be earned on invested rupees is specified. Of course, a higher rate of return, above the cost factor to the firm, is much more desirable. Initially we may define the *cost of debt* as the interest rate the firm has to pay to the lending source, whether it be to a bank or for a new debt issue the firm has placed with the public market.

This will be referred to as the cost of debt because this is what the firm has to pay annually to its debt investors for borrowing the sum. The firm must earn such a rate of return on its debt-financed investments that the earnings available to the common shareholders remain unchanged. If less than an estimated per cent return were received on the investment, the earnings available to the shareholders (earnings per share) would decline, and this could have an adverse effect on the price of the stock.

The Cost of Preferred Stock

Preferred stock (or preference shares) is frequently referred to as a hybrid security which is somewhere between debt and common equity. It is similar to debt in that it pays a fixed commitment or annual dividend, and, in case of liquidation, the claim to the assets of the corporation by preferred holders has priority over the claims of the common shareholders. It is similar to equity, or common stock, in that if the dividends are not paid, the result is not corporate bankruptcy. To the investor, an investment in preferred stock is less risky than one in the common stock of the corporation, but more risky than an investment in its debt securities.

The Cost of Using Retained Earnings

Equity capital usually consists of two components. The first is the amount of funds available in the form of net income that may be used to pay dividends or may be retained in the business for asset purchases. The second source of equity capital is the amount of funds raised by a new common stock issue. This section deals with the cost associated with using retained earnings as a source of financing; the cost of issuing new common stock is discussed in the next section.

The definition of the cost of retained earnings is the rate of return that must be earned on equity-invested capital so that the total yield available to the common shareholders remains unchanged. The cost of retained earnings simplifies to the *rate of return that stockholders expect to earn on the common stock of the firm.* This expected or required rate of return can be determined from the valuation formula for common stock described in the preceding chapter. It was stated that the value or price of a share of common stock is equal to:

$$P_0 = \frac{D_1}{k-g} \quad \text{...(18)}$$

where:

P_0 = Current price.

D_1 = Expected dividends.

k = Stockholders' required rate of return.

g = Growth rate.

If dividends are expected to grow at a constant rate, we can solve for k, the required rate of return, as in Equation (19).

$$P_0 = \frac{D_1}{k-g}$$

$$P_0\,(k-g) = D_1$$

$$(k-g) = \frac{D_1}{P_0}$$

$$k = \frac{D_1}{P_0} + g. \quad \text{...(19)}$$

Thus the required rate of return is equal to the dividends yield plus the growth rate of dividends, which will reflect itself in future prices. If, for example, a firm plans to pay Rs 2.40 dividend, its current price is Rs 40, and it has an expected growth rate of 6 per cent, we could calculate the rate of return earned on this stock as:

$$k = \frac{\text{Rs. } 2.40}{\text{Rs. } 40} + 0.06 = 0.06 + 0.06 = 0.12 \text{ or } 12\% \qquad \ldots(20)$$

With a dividend yield of 6 per cent and a growth rate of 6 per cent, the rate return earned by investors on this stock is 12 per cent.

This rate of return paid by the corporation becomes a required rate of return to the investor who applies the opportunity cost doctrine. If 12 per cent has been the historical rate of return on the stock, the investor will expect this to continue. If it decreases, he or she will re-evaluate the position in the stock and possibly sell.

Investors classify firms by risk classes and then seek the firm that pays the highest return in the given risk class. If the firm continues to make investments that yield 12 per cent, the rate of return to the common shareholder will remain unchanged, and the investor will yield 12 per cent. If, however, the firm yields less than 12 per cent, this will lead to a revaluation of the required rate of return and possibly a decrease in the price of the stock.

This situation can be illustrated by extending the previous example. The growth rate of earnings, dividends, and stock price was expected to be 6 per cent. The stock price at the beginning of Year 1 was Rs. 40. At the end of Year 1, the earnings were Rs. 4.80 per share, and since the firm pays 50 per cent in dividends, the dividends were Rs. 2.40. The remaining Rs. 2.40 was retained to be invested in Year 2. From Equation (20), the rate of return for Year 1 was calculated to be 12 per cent ($k = (\text{Rs. } 2.40/40) + 0.06 = 0.12$). The stock price, growing at the 6 per cent growth rate, would be Rs. 42.40 (1.06×40) at the end of Year 1. This price increase results from the fact that the firm is expected to earn a 12 per cent return on the Rs. 2.40 per share reinvested capital.

To explain more fully, assume the firm will have net income of Rs. 4.80 again at the end of Year 2 (unless investment is made). The firm retains from Year 1 Rs. 2.40 per share for this investment. It will need to earn a 12 per cent return on this reinvested capital during Year 2 in order to justify the price at the beginning of Year 2 of Rs. 42.40. The earnings, therefore, at the end of Year 2 would be Rs. 5.088 per share: Rs. $4.80 + (0.12 \times \text{Rs. } 2.40)$. A 50 per cent dividend would be Rs. 2.544. Earnings and dividends have grown by 6 per cent, which was the expected rate at the beginning of Year 1. The stock price at the end of Year 1 was Rs. 42.40. This can be verified:

$$P_1 = \frac{D_2}{k-g} = \frac{2.544}{0.12-0.06} = \frac{2.544}{0.06} = \text{Rs. } 42.40.$$

Therefore, for the price to be Rs. 42.40 at the end of Year 1, the firm must be able to invest the retained funds at 12 per cent.

Consider the result if the company expects it can only reinvest this Rs. 2.40 per share retained earnings at 6 per cent. The earnings at the end of Year 2 would be Rs 4.944: Rs. 4.80 + (.06 × Rs. 2.40). A 50 per cent dividend would be Rs. 2.472. Earnings and dividends have only grown at a 3 per cent rate. The stock price at the end of Year 1 was supposed to be Rs. 42.40, but this cannot be verified:

$$P_1 = \frac{D_2}{k-g} = \frac{2.472}{0.12-0.03} = \frac{2.472}{0.09} = \text{Rs. } 27.47.$$

Since the retained funds are not expected to be invested at 12 per cent, the value of stock will decrease as long as investors feel that the firm will not earn that 12 per cent in the future.

The Cost of Issuing New Equity Stock

It will be found that the cost of issuing new common stock or external equity is slightly higher than the cost of internal equity or retained earnings. This is because the price that the stock is sold for in the market is not the price the firm receives. As with preferred stock, when new common stock is issued, firms utilize the services of investment bankers to help place it; for their services, the bankers are paid a commission, which is referred to as the flotation costs of underwriting a new equity issue. The price the firm is interested in to determine its cost of equity for a new issue is the *net price*, which is the market price of the stock less the flotation costs. The cost of external equity is found with Equation (21).

$$k_e = \frac{D_1}{P_0(1-F)} + g \qquad \text{...(21)}$$

where:

k_e = Cost of external equity.

D_1 = Expected dividends in one year.

P_0 = Market price of stock.

F = Flotation costs expressed as a per cent.

g = Growth rate of dividends, earnings, price of stock.

The formulization for the cost of external equity is basically the same as the one for the cost of retained earnings or internal equity. It states that the cost of equity is equal to the expected dividend yield plus the expected growth of earnings, dividends, and price. Only in the case of a new issue or external equity will the denomination, P, become the net price per share the corporation will receive in cash when the new issue is sold.

WEIGHTED AVERAGE COST OF CAPITAL

When examining the cost of capital for a firm, we are not always interested in examining the cost of a single component such as debt or preferred stock or equity but may want to know the total cost of capital to the firm, considering all forms of financing. The cost of long-term debt, preferred stock, and equity, considered together, is referred to as the *average cost of capital*. But is it appropriate to simply add the three costs together and then divide by 3 to arrive at an average? The answer is no. Very seldom do the three forms of financing contribute equally to the capital structure of a firm. If they do not, it is unfair to state, for example, that the cost of preferred stock contributes equally to the overall average cost of capital for the firm, when in fact there is hardly any preferred stock in the capital structure.

A good way to measure the average cost of capital for the firm accurately is to derive what is termed a *weighted average cost of capital*. This technique applies weights to each source of financing in terms of its contribution to the capital structure of the firm; the average thus is a simple weighted average.

Calculation of the Weighted Average Cost of Capital

The calculation process to derive the weighted average cost of capital is quite simple. Assume that a firm had in its balance sheet Rs. 35 million of debt, Rs. 15 million of preferred stock, and Rs 50 million of common equity. Further assume that the average before-tax rate for all debt is 6 per cent; that the preferred stock has a dividend yield of 8 per cent, and that the component cost of equity is equal to 12 per cent. Table 5 shows how the weighted average cost of capital for this firm is calculated.

Table 5

Calculation of Weighted Average Cost of Capital

Type of financing	*Balance sheet figure (Rs)*	*Balance sheet figure in % form*	*Component costs*	*Weighted average cost of capital*
Total debt	35,000,000	35%	3.1%	0.0108
Preferred stock	15,000,000	15	8	0.0120
Common equity	50,000,000	50	12	0.0600
	100,000,000	100%		0.0828 = 8.28%

We first list all the rupee amounts of debt, preferred stock, and common equity. Next, these dollar amounts are converted into per cent form by expressing each as a percentage of the total financing for the firm. These percentage components become the weights for the weighted average. Next, we list the component costs for each source of financing. To arrive at the weighted average cost of capital, we multiply the percentage weights by the component costs and then sum the answers. For this illustration, the weighted average cost of capital is equal to 8.28 per cent.

The Cost of New and Historical Capital

The historical data on which the illustrations of the calculation of the cost of capital have been based are derived by looking at the past balance sheets of a corporation and pulling out information on capital structure and associated costs. This is fine for certain situations, but there are times when historical data are not adequate.

Table 6

Calculation of Average Cost of Capital Over Varying Debt Levels

	Per cent of total	*Component cost*	*Weighted cost**
Debt	0 %	4.0%	0 %
Equity	100%	14.0	14.0
Total	100%		14.0%
Debt	10%	4.0	0.40%

		Per cent of total	*Component cost*	*Weighted cost**
Equity		90	14.2	12.78
	Total	100%		13.18%
Debt		20%	4.0	0.80%
Equity		80	14.5	11.60
	Total	100%		12.40%
Debt		30%	4.5	1.35%
Equity		70	15.0	10.50
	Total	100%		11.85%
Debt		40%	5.5	2.20%
Equity		60	16.0	9.60
	Total	100%		11.80%
Debt		50%	7.0	3.50%
Equity		50	18.0	9.00
	Total	100%		12.50%
Debt		60%	9.5	5.70%
Equity		40	21.5	8.60
	Total	100%		14.30%

*We divide the product of per cent of total with component cost by 100 to obtain a percentage; figures rounded to nearest hundredth.

One of the primary applications of the results of a cost of capital analysis is in the capital budgeting process of selecting among alternative investments. In utilizing cost of capital information in capital budgeting, the concern is with the cost of obtaining new funds, whether they be debt, preferred stock, or common equity. In periods of rising interest rates, the cost of new capital or the *incremental cost of capital* will be higher than the historical weighted average cost of capital.

In using incremental costs, the same logic applies as in using the weighted average cost of capital. If a firm uses debt it is using up this source of cheap funds, since as the new level of debt increases, the firm's leverage position moves toward or beyond the industry norm. This will jeopardize the firm's access to future debt capital markets. A good example of this is the firm that uses too much debt. At some future time it may need more capital, but the only market open to it will be equity, because the market will not absorb another debt issue from it. If the equity market is not available, due to a decline in the price of the company's stock or a general decline in the stock market, the firm could be in considerable trouble in terms of its ability to raise the needed capital.

This is a perfect illustration of why it is important for a company to maintain a proper balance between debt and equity. If this is done (as in the example with the firm with a 45 per cent optimal leverage ratio), the firm will have access to both markets. If one market is in a period of decline, it can turn to the other as a source of funds.

If the firm is interested in utilizing cost of capital information for capital budgeting decisions, which involve new projects or investment alternatives, the analysis should also include new cost data. Then it is possible to compare rates of return on these projects with the cost of capital for raising new capital to undertake investment alternatives.

Firm's Efforts Towards Optimal Capital Structure

We have so far dealt with the means by which a firm can strive to achieve an optimal capital structure which will minimize its cost of capital. In practice, however, an optimal capital structure cannot always be maintained. This could be due to such factors as the unavailability of required amount of capital, the existing external financial environment, and the timing of financial need.

If, for example, the optimal capital structure of a firm is 40 per cent debt and 60 per cent equity, it is unlikely that in reality the firm would always simultaneously seek 40 per cent debt and 60 per cent equity. On the contrary e.g. a firm having optimum capital structure requiring Rs. 10 crore for some specific investment might use either debt or equity to raise the entire amount. Recognizing that its capital structure had deviated from the optimum, for the next financing increment at some future time it would try to use the other source of capital to bring its capital structure back into line. Because firms raise capital at discrete intervals, there is a tendency to create a temporary non optimal capital structure. Thus at any one time a firm may not be at an optimal capital structure position, but it strives for this and is usually a little above or a little below it, given the financing instrument most recently used.

Striving to maintain this equilibrium is important because this is what gives the firm a viable access to the capital markets, and this, in essence, guarantees the survival of the firm. A firm that is active and engaged in new investments needs capital. The advantage of maintaining an optimal or close to optimal capital structure is that this guarantees the firm the widest possible access to the capital markets. If, for example, the firm let its debt structure get out of hand, its access to the capital markets would be limited, and this could stop the firm from taking advantage of new investment opportunities.

Consider an Example. A firm that has a 40/60 optimal capital structure for which it should strive, but instead it has utilized the debt vehicle to such an extent that its true capital structure is 55 per cent debt and 45 per cent equity. Recognizing that it is out of alignment, for the next financing effort the firm plans to use the equity market. However, when the time for raising this capital arrives, the equity market has collapsed and the price of its stock has dropped enough that the firm no longer wants to use this vehicle. It turns to the debt market but finds that since its capital structure is so far out of line, the market will not accept another of its debt issues. With no viable financing source, the firm probably will have to forego the planned investment opportunity.

If the firm had maintained a close approximation to the optimal capital structure, this might not have happened. If one of the markets were bad, the other possibly could be utilized. It is important to remember that a single firm dies not have control over the debt and equity market; to a large extent, the market is controlled by external factors. Therefore the firm has to maintain an optimal capital structure and make sure that it maintains financing viability in all markets, so that if one is closed for effective financing, the other can be utilized.

RETURN ON CAPITAL

Rate of Return on Capital is widely used to appraise the effectiveness of management performance, to select the contents of an investment portfolio, and to make decisions regarding new product development and acquisition of plant and equipment. Unfortunately, the term means different things to different people. Some refer to it as 'rate of return on investment.'

Definition

Return on capital is the relationship, usually expressed as a ratio or percentage, between the income (or "profit" or "interest") from an enterprise or undertaking and the related investment or capital commitment.

Background

While ratios between interest and principal have been computed as long as man has loaned money. Modern applications of this concept may be divided into three historical periods. The first of these periods used the ratio between the income as displayed on the contemporary income statement and divided it by the assets or equity as shown on the balance sheet. This computation developed in the nineteenth century, predominated in security analysis during the first half of the twentieth century, and may still in the 1980s be seen in connection with regulation of public utilities and analyses made in connection with the purchase and sale of shares of common stock (or equity capital of the firm). It is referred to here as the *mercantile rate of return.*

A second approach to capital budgeting reflects the time preference concepts of the bond and money markets. It was not until 1951—that the method began to be used by financial management in connection with capital budgeting decisions (decisions involving the long-term commitment of capital). For capital budgeting decisions involving bonds and bank loans, the "arithmetic" of discounted cash flow computations and present value computations had been in use centuries earlier. But the attempt to apply the same kind of arithmetic that had been used for fixed-obligation bonds to the wider class of problems involving uncertain cash flows. During the fifties, the use of this approach to capital budgeting was more common in business literature than in the corporate board room, but the method became increasingly popular during the sixties, and is widespread in the seventies. It is referred to here as the **industrial rate of return.**

Over the years, a technique widely used has been the estimation of the time that would elapse before the cash inflows (or the reduction in outflows) resulting from an initial outlay of cash will equal that outlay. This is known as the *pay-back period*, or "payout" or "pay-in" period. While not strictly speaking a return-on-capital computation, the reciprocal of the pay-back period will often be an excellent approximation to the rate of return on capital computed by the industrial method, and this is considered later in the discussion of the various methods.

In 1959, there has been a trend toward a third approach to the solution of capital budgeting problems by the use of Linear Programming techniques. While this approach does not yet seem to have played a major role in actual capital budgeting decisions, it is certain to do so in connection with large industrial projects and military and space procurement expenditures. This linear programming approach selects the best projects and the best courses of action in terms of some stated objective (say to maximize equity at some later date). While it does not usually involve a direct computation of return on capital, it does permit the capital analyst to detect the binding constraints or bottlenecks to his maximization efforts, and it may thereby permit an indirect computation of a "quasi" return on capital. It is here termed the *bottleneck rate of return,* and is discussed in some detail in the concluding section of this entry, under the head, *Emerging Techniques.*

The Mercantile Rate of Return

The mercantile rate of return is the ratio (expressed in percentage form) between some figure appearing on the contemporary income statement and some figure appearing on the contemporary balance sheet. For illustrative purposes, a simplified income statement for a hypothetical company for the year ending December 31, 1990 and the related balance sheets at the beginning and end of the year are presented in Tables 7 and 8 respectively. Referring to the figures given there, the mercantile rate might be computed as follows:

$$\begin{aligned} \text{Rate of Return} &= \frac{\text{Income}}{\text{Average Assets}} \times 100 \\ &= \frac{1330}{(4982 + 6312)/2} \times 100 \\ &= 24\%. \end{aligned}$$

This mercantile method of computing rate of return on capital has also been referred to as the "accountant's method" (a lamentable libel on a proud profession!) and the "financial- statement method."

Table 7

Mercantile Accounting Income Statement
Year Ending December 31,1990

Revenues		Rs. 4,200
Less: Cost of sales	Rs. 2,500	
Depreciation	370	2,870
Income		1,330

Table 8

Mercantile Accounting Balance Sheet
December 31

	1990	*1989*
Cash	Rs. 1,000	Rs. 1,000
Receivables	4,200	
Inventory		2,500
Equipment	1,852	1,852
Accumulated depreciation	(740)	(370)
Assets	6,312	4,982
Contributed capital	5,352	5,352
Retained income (loss)	960	(370)
Equity	6,312	4,982

Assets are chosen as the base when it is desired to measure the performance of management in using the total amount of property entrusted to its control. Thus, for internal management purposes and from the point of view of the entity as a whole, the important thing may be the effectiveness with which management makes use of the total assets of the company. In contrast, stockholders' equity may be the base of the computation when appraising not only the overall use of the assets, but also the extent to which financing methods were advantageous from the point of view of the stockholders.

The two approaches may be distinguished by the terms "return on assets" and "return," or "yield," on "equity."

To illustrate the distinction, suppose the corporation had been partly financed by the issue of 10% bonds and that the liabilities and equity section of the balance sheet was as follows:

	12/31/90	12/31/89
Bonds payable	Rs. 2,000	Rs. 2,000
Contributed capital	3,352	3,352
Retained income	960	(370)
Liabilities and Equity	6,312	4,982

Let the concluding part of the income statement be the following:

Income before interest expense	Rs. 1,330
Less: Interest expense	200
Income	1,130

The computation of return on assets would be identical to the previous computation. It would be the ratio of total income (Rs. 1,330) earned from the use of all assets (averaging Rs. 5,647) without considering the amounts of that income available for the different types of investors and without considering the extent to which those assets had been financed by particular classes of investors. In contrast, emphasizing the interests of stockholders, it would be necessary to relate the net income available to stockholders with the stockholders' equity, specifically:

$$\text{Return on Equity} = \frac{1130}{(2982 + 4312)/2} \times 100 = 31\%$$

Trading on the Equity. Return on assets and return on equity may be used to understand the effect of "trading on the equity." Where bondholders are paid a lower rate of return on their investment than the rate of return earned on total assets, stockholders will benefit. Stockholders, in effect, will receive the benefit on the extra return earned on the assets financed by bondholders. The following *leverage factor* may be computed to assess the extent to which return on equity is improved over return on assets as a result of trading on the equity:

$$\text{Leverage Factor} = \frac{\text{Rate of Return on Equity}}{\text{Rate of Return on Assets}}$$

$$= \frac{0.31}{0.24} = 1.3$$

Where this leverage factor is greater than 1 (as in the example), the stockholders may have benefited through use of the funds supplied by bondholders at a lower rate of return than that earned on the assets. To determine whether stockholders have really benefited, however, it is further necessary to assess or attempt to weigh the greater risk that may be incurred by the company as a result of the greater fixed obligation imposed by the interest and principal on the bonds.

Some companies use gross assets (that is, assets before deducting the depreciation taken on these assets in prior years) instead of net assets in computing return on assets. Such companies justify their use of gross assets by their desire to prevent the rate of return from rising as the net book value of depreciable assets is reduced by depreciation. Undepreciated cost provides an unchanging base and, so long as annual income is constant, the rate return is stable.

This viewpoint involves certain preconceptions not only about the stability of future earnings but also about what rate of return ought to be: Should the figure for rate of return be stable from year to year because it is stable or because the accountant expects it to be stable and therefore adopts conventions that make it stable? Some accountants have argued that the relevant investment base should instead be assets net of accumulated depreciation allowances, since it seems inconsistent to compare a profit figure from which depreciation *has* been deducted with an investment figure from which the accumulated depreciation *has not* been deducted. There are also many other variations regarding the rate base and dealing with matters such as whether the assets should include excess or idle assets, assets still in construction, assets financed by short-term sources of credit, etc.

There are also many variations in the income figure employed for the mercantile rate of return. Thus some companies do not deduct taxes because they are anxious to measure those things under the control of management, and they feel that taxes, while somewhat subject to managerial control (tax planning), are more under the control of Congress than of management. There are also variations in practice regarding the inclusion of dividend income, interest income, and "other income" and "other expenses" in computing net income for the rate of return calculation.

Whatever variations exist with regard to the capital base and the return on that capital, certain common features seem to be evident in the mechanics of computation. Thus, most companies attempt to get a "representative" figure for the capital base in the sense that it is the average of the relevant balance sheet magnitude at the beginning and end of the year, or it is a thirteen-point average of the balance sheet magnitude at the beginning of the year and at the end of the following twelve months. Furthermore, most companies "annualize" their income statement figure; thus, net income for two months would be multiplied by 12/2 to get its annual equivalent.

E"Du Pont Analysis" of Return on Capital and Sales. Some companies make use of the "du Pont analysis" of return on capital, named after the company that pioneered in its use. While income and capital determine the rate of return on capital, the du Pont analysis introduces a third factor—sales—that may be used to assist in judging the adequacy of income and capital. Note from Fig. 4 that:

$$\frac{\text{Income}}{\text{Capital}} = \frac{\text{Income}}{\text{Sales}} \times \frac{\text{Sales}}{\text{Capital}}$$

The first factor on the right-hand side of the above equation may be referred to as the *profit margin* and the second as *turnover*. Such a breakdown of return on capital into two factors permits introduction into the analysis of the very important element of sales volume. Further, it permits the breakdown of return on capital to be handled in ratio terms.

If this ratio approach is not taken, then the analysis takes place in terms of total investment and total income and, because of differences in the scale of business, these total rupee figures are not comparable from business to business. By introducing sales, both income and investment are reduced to ratios, and these ratios are somewhat comparable.

To illustrate this du Pont approach, consider the three companies for which certain information is summarized in Table 9. Assuming all three companies are in the same industry, why is it that companies *B* and *C* have earned only 1% on capital when company *A* has earned 20%? Income and investment figures alone shed little light on the question because of disparities in size between company *A* and the other two companies. Thus it is impossible to say whether *B*'s low rate of return in comparison with *A*'s is attributable to its larger capital or to its lower income. The fact that companies *B* and *C* have identical income and capital

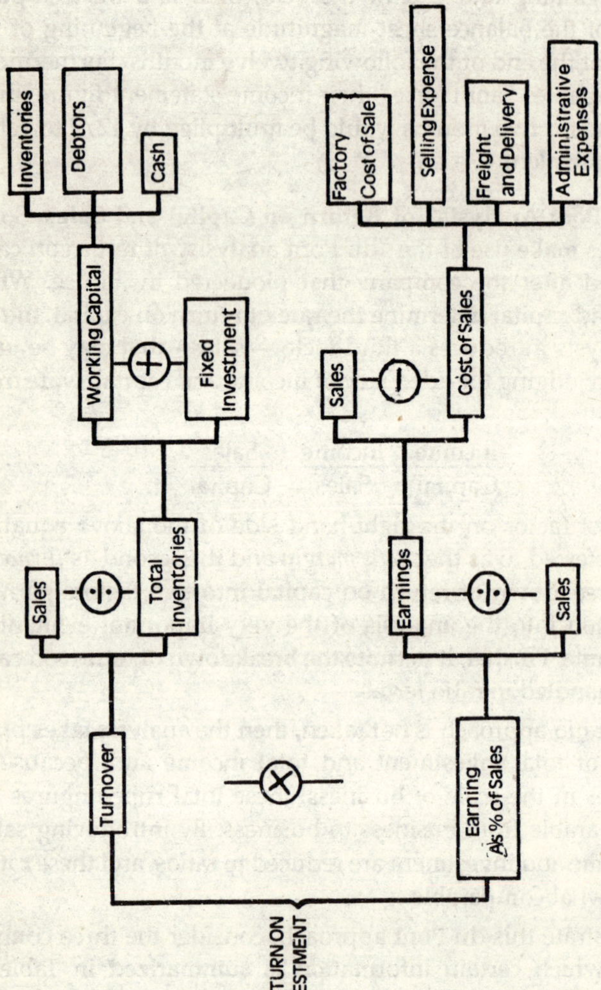

Fig. 4. Du Pont Analysis of Return on Capital.

suggests that the same conditions underlie the low rate of return, but, as shown below, this conclusion is erroneous.

Table 9

Du Pont Analysis of Return on Capital

(Rupees)

	Company A	*Company B*	*Company C*
1. Sales	1,000,000	500,000	10,000,000
2. Income	100,000	50,000	50,000
3. Capital	500,000	5,000,000	5,000,000
4. Income as a % of sales (line 2/line 1, × 100)	10%	10%	0.5%
5. Turnover (line 1/line 3)	2	.1	2
6. Return on investment (line 4 × line 5)	20%	1%	1%

Introducing sales to measure level of operations helps to disclose areas for more intensive investigation. For example:

Company *B* does as well as company *A* in terms of profit margin, for both earn 10% on sales. But *B* has a much lower turnover of capital than does *A*. Whereas a rupee of capital in *A* supports two rupees in sales each period, a rupee in company *B* supports only ten paise in sales. Perhaps the analyst should look carefully at *B*'s investment. Is the company keeping inventory larger than necessary for its sales volume? Are receivables being collected promptly? On the other hand, company *C*'s turnover is as high as that achieved by company *A*, but *C*'s margin on sales in much lower. If *A* can earn ten paise of profit on a rupee of sales, why does C earn only half a paise? Are its operations inefficient, its material costs too high, or does its location entail high transportation costs? The du Pont analysis will not categorically answer these questions, but it may point the investigator in the right direction.

Industrial Rate of Return

The industrial approach to the computation of return on capital examines the relationships among the cash inflows and outflows relating to long-term commitments of capital. It has two main varieties: the *rate of return* approach and the *net present value* approach.

Using the rate of return approach, the analyst designates as the industrial rate of return *that rate of interest which will discount or accumulate the cash inflows and outflows from a project or undertaking to zero at some particular reference date.* Designating the cash flows of year *i* as R_i (where R may be positive if it is a cash inflow or negative if an outflow), the industrial rate of return is that interest rate r (expressed in decimal form) which solves the following equation for given R_i:

$$0 = \frac{R_0}{(1+r)^0} + \frac{R_1}{(1+r)^1} + \frac{R_2}{(1+r)^2} + \ldots + \frac{R_n}{(1+r)^n}$$

where the cash flows commence at time 0 and continue through time *n*.

To illustrate this approach using actual numbers, suppose a new company is formed to carry out an industrial undertaking that requires it to make the following disbursements and cash commitments at time 0:

Required minimum cash balance	Rs. 1,000
Purchase of initial inventory	2,000
Purchase of depreciable assets	1,852
Disbursed and Committed at Time 0	4,852

At time 1 there will be a further disbursement of Rs. 500 in connection with an additional purchase of inventory. While there will be various receipts in the next few years they will be promptly reinvested in inventory. At time 6 the equipment will be worn out and the project completed and the company will be able to withdraw from the venture with Rs. 9,400. (These are the same cash flows implicit in the illustration of the mercantile rate of return and the reader should have no difficulty in relating the cash flows at time 0 and at time 1 with the 12/31/1989 balance sheet previously presented.) It will be found that these cash flows can be discounted to zero through use of a 10% discount factor, as verifiable by substitution in the foregoing equation, as follows:

$$0 = \frac{(4.852)}{1.1^0} + \frac{(500)}{1.1^2} + \frac{9{,}400}{1.1^6}$$

(The 10% is arrived at by trial-and-error use of percentages obtained from financial tables of Net Present Value. (see vol. 3 of this treatise and section below).

An accounting interpretation consistent with this rate of return approach can be had through industrial accounting. Designating time 1 as the year ending December 31, 1990, the relevant operating statement or statement of receipts and disbursements appeaı s in Table 10. Over the life-span of the project or undertaking, the net income from the project will be the same—Rs 4.048—whether one considers mercantile accounting and the mercantile rate of return or whether one considers industrial accounting and the industrial rate of return. The manner in which that income will be considered to have been realized or earned will, however, differ. In mercantile accounting and the mercantile rate of return, income is earned when a sale is made. In industrial accounting and the industrial rate of return, income is assumed to be earned through the passage of time in the same manner that interest is earned on a savings and loan account. The earning of income in years 1 and 2 may be computed as follows using the industrial approach:

Table 10

Industrial Accounting Statements of Receipts, Disbursements and Cash Commitments Years Ending December 31 (Drafted As of December 31, 1990)

1994	expected future net receipts and released cash commitments	Rs. 9,400
1990	net disbursements	(500)
1989	Net disbursements and cash commitments	(4,852)
Anticipated Income		4,048

Year 1 income: 10% of 4,852	Rs. 485
Year 2 income: 10% of (4,852 + 500 + 485)	584
Total Earned in Years 1 and 2	1,069

These figures may readily be related to the balance sheets drafted at the end of year 1 and 2 as seen in Table 11.

Table 11

Industrial Accounting Balance Sheet

	12/31/90	12/31/89
Expected future net receipts	Rs. 9,400	Rs. 9,400
Less: Unearned income	(2,979)	(3,563)
Assets	6.421	5,837
Contributed capital	5,352	5,352
Retained income	1,069	485
Equity	6,421	5,837

As in the case of the mercantile rate of return, the industrial rate of return may be employed either to assist in making decisions ("capital budgeting") or to assist in appraising the past performance of management in reaching goals ("control"). But note the perils of using one method for the accept or reject decision with regard to a particular project, and using another to post-audit that decision and to assess its desirability once the project has been chosen. Using the discounted cash flow approach to capital-budgeting, for example, management might be led to expect a 10% return on this project and a post-audit of the decision at the end of year 2 might, even if the project is exactly on target, suggest that the project is actually earning 24% if the mercantile approach is employed. If capital budgeting relies on the discounted cash flow approach, then a meaningful appraisal of past performance in implementing capital budgeting decisions can only be had through the type of numbers generated by industrial accounting.

Net Present Value. As an alternative to the rate of return approach discussed above, many capital analysts prefer the *net present value* approach. The net present value approach relies in part upon determining a "cost of capital" rate. This cost of capital may be defined as the rate at which the company would be disposed to finance the additional projects. It may also be defined in alternative opportunity cost terms. Suppose, in the present case, that those who provide the capital to finance this project could easily earn at least 8% on their money in several other ventures of comparable risk.

Using 8% for discounting purposes, the net present value of the project may be computed as follows:

9,400	discounted 6 years at 8% has a present value of	Rs. 5,924
(500)	discounted one year at 8% has a present value of	(463)
(4,952)	expended or committed at time 0 has a present value of	(4,852)
	Net present value at 8%	609

Whereas the rate of return approach leads to acceptance of projects if they have an industrial rate of return greater than the cost of capital, the cost of capital approach leads to acceptance of those projects for which the net present value is positive when the cash flows are discounted through use of the cost of capital rate. (Both approaches usually lead to acceptance and rejection of the same projects.)

Industrial accounting may again be employed to give an effective post-audit of capital budgeting decisions implemented by the net present value approach. The operating statement would be identical to that already shown in Table 10. One version of the appropriate balance sheet is shown in Table 12. In this version, assets are carried at the amount of the initial disbursements and capital commitments when compounded two years at the cost of capital rate:

Investment at time 0	Rs. 4,852
Earned income in year 1 = .08 × 4,852	388
Investment in year 2	500
	5,740
Earned income in year 2 = .08 × 5,740	459
Asset at end of year 2	6,199

This version, a conservative one, does not recognize the net present value as being earned until the sixth year, at which time its compound amount at 8% (namely Rs. 966) will be considered earned income. Another and less conservative approach would be to consider the net present value of Rs. 609 as earned income when the project is commenced. While the conservative approach shows the assets at the compound amount of the past investment, the less conservative approach carries the assets at the present value of future expected receipts when discounted by use of the cost of capital rate.

In the above discussion and illustration, it has been assumed that all cash flows occur at a moment or point in time and that interest is compounded once a year. While these assumptions simplify the arithmetic and comport well with the bond and banking markets where coupons are clipped once a year and interest may be added to the account at December 31, they depart from the more general world of business where money flows in and out continuously and is immediately available for reinvestment. For decisions involving capital budgeting in this more general world of business, it is often useful to use instead tables which assume

Table 12

Industrial Accounting Balance Sheet
December 31, 1990

Expected future net receipts	Rs. 9,400
Less: Unearned income	3,201
Assets	6,199
Contributed capital	5,352
Retained income	847
Equity	6,199

continuous cash flows and continuous compounding. Table 13 is a part of extensive tables of the present value of Re. 1 assuming continuous cash inflows and continuous compounding, prepared by The Atlantic Refining Company, and published in National Association of Accountants Research Study No. 35. "Return on Capital," 1959.

Table 13

Continuous Interest Table
Discounting Performance After Reference Point Which Occurs Uniformly Over Individual Years

	10%	*20%*	*30%*
From 0 to 1 year	.9516	.9063	.8640
From 1 to 2 years	.8611	.7421	.6400
From 2 to 3 years	.7791	.6075	.4741
From 3 to 4 years	.7050	.4974	.3513
From 4 to 5 years	.6379	.4072	.2602
From 5 to 6 years	.5772	.3334	.1928

To illustrate the use of such a table, suppose a company is considering making a large initial investment in a project which is expected to require a further net cash disbursement during its first year of Rs. 10,000 and which should then result in a net cash inflow of Rs. 100,000 during the second year, a further cash inflow of Rs. 200,000 during the third year, and no further cash flows thereafter. Assuming the company's cost of capital is 15% compounded continuously, then the present value of these cash flows (before considering the initial cash disbursement) would be computed as follows:

Rs. 200,00 × .6879	Rs. 137,580
100,000 × .7993	79,930
	217,510
10,000 × .9286	9,286
Present value	208,224

If the project requires an initial disbursement of less than Rs. 208,224 it may be worth considering.

While past discussions have tended to treat the expectations of future cash flows as single-valued expectations, there has been an increasing tendency to treat these expectations as a probability distribution. With this interpretation in mind, the figures appearing in Tables above may be thought of as "expected values," given perhaps by the arithmetic mean or the mode or the median. These expected values may than be "surrounded" by confidence limits, and the distance of these confidence limits from the expected values may be used to indicate the degree of risk.

Pay-Back

The *pay-back period,* as stated earlier, is the period of time that will elapse before the cash inflows (or the reduction in outflows) resulting from an initial outlay of cash will equal that outlay. For example, if a company will have to disburse Rs. 1,449,480 for the purchase of a plant and if the net cash inflows from the operation of that plant will be Rs. 600,000 per year, then it will take about 2.4 years before the cash inflows from the operation of the plant will "return" the initial investment. In this case, the pay-back period, or pay-back, is 2.4 years.

The reciprocal of the pay-back period will often be an excellent approximation to the rate of return on capital computed by the industrial method. If, for example, the cash inflows of Rs. 600,000 were expected to continue into the indefinite future, the rate of return computed by the industrial method would be 41%. The reciprocal of the pay-back period is, in this case, 1/2.4, or also 41%. This reciprocal of the pay-back period will only serve as a good approximation to the industrial rate of return if the cash inflows will continue for considerably longer than the pay-back period—say twice as long. If the cash inflows of Rs. 600,000 were only expected to continue for three years, then the industrial rate of return would be only 15%, computed by the method previously described. The reciprocal of the pay-back period, 41%, would here be a very poor approximation to this industrial rate of return. The pay-back approximation of 41% is, however, an excellent approximation to the industrial rate of 40% that applies if the cash inflows continue for $8\frac{1}{2}$ years.

Another requirement for a meaningful use of the pay-back approximation is that the expected cash inflows must be relatively uniform in amount from year to year; thus, where the cash inflows during the initial year or two of a project are very low but the cash inflows in later years are very high, the pay-back approximation would not be a reliable guide to rate of return.

Given these limitations, pay-back is to the industrial rate of return what a slide rule is to a computer. Pay-back is a quick, convenient calculation that may be used for small and incidental capital budgeting decisions (say the decision to buy a bookkeeping machine) whereas the industrial rate of return should be used for the big decisions.

Pay-back is also frequently used as a measure of the risk or uncertainty involved in a particular investment. However, while it is true that the pay-back period is an estimate of the period during which the initial outlay of cash is expected to be recovered, this period tells little about risk. It may well be true that the shorter the period of capital commitment, the less the risk of loss on that capital commitment. Risk should be measured by the extent to which future cash inflows may differ from their expected values. Since the pay-back period is an estimate of the period of capital commitment and since it is based on expected (possibly arithmetic mean) values, it cannot be used as a reliable indicator of the dispersion of future expectations around that mean value.

NEW TECHNIQUES

Linear Programming

Linear Programming offers new and powerful insights into the capital budgeting process and into the concept of rate of return. In particular, models developed by Charnes, Cooper, and Miller and by Weingartner are particularly directed toward the capital budgeting process and result in the computation of a type of rate of return. See vol. 3 of this treatise for detailed discussion on Linear programming.

The "Bottleneck Rate of Return"

But there is another and possibly more significant manner in which this model and comparable models may throw light on capital budgeting problems. For every direct or "primal" problem in linear programming, there is another derived or "dual" problem. Without dwelling on the mathematical aspects of the dual problem, it is worth noting that the dual problem results in the calculation of "shadow prices" or "dual evaluators." These "dual evaluators" may be considered "price tags" which measure the severity of the primal constraints and help to identify which primal constraints are "binding" or "bottleneck" constraints.

Thus the "price tag" relating to the first financial constraint is Rs. 0.80, and it suggests that if the company had Re. 1 less available for purchase of inventory in the first period (that is, if purchases in the first year were limited to what could be purchased with Rs. 499 rather than Rs. 500), then the total net cash inflow would be less by not only the Re. 1, but also by a further Rs. 0.80. Again without going into the rather detailed manner in which the receipts and disbursements would change, it should be noted that the Rs. 0.80 may be thought of as the incremental or marginal "profit" from the 500th rupee. It may then be argued that the Rs. 0.80 is somewhat akin to an interest rate and that the Rs. 0.80 plus the 500th rupee may be thought of as a compounded amount. Charnes, Cooper and Miller have said that such dual evaluators have the "dimensions of compound interest" and have referred to these rates and amounts as "compounded rates of accumulation," "compound internal yield rates," and "internal discount factors."

While neither the linear programming approach to capital budgeting problems nor the "bottleneck" rate of return seems to have been used extensively in practice as yet, nevertheless they offer such penetrating insights into the funds allocation process that their future in the practical world of capital budgeting seems secure.

8

WORKING CAPITAL MANAGEMENT

FINANCIAL manager devotes most of his time managing working capital. It involves the greatest percentage of the financial manager's time in terms of the day-to-day operations of the firm, and one of the main reasons for this is that current assets historically represent more than 60 per cent of the total assets of the firm.

For smaller firms, working capital management is an even more important area. A large part of the fixed assets of small businesses, such a plant and equipment, can be rented or leased. Since a small business has difficulty in utilizing the long-term capital markets, current liabilities are a vital instrument of financing for it. To avoid a liquidity crisis, they must have proper management of their working capital position.

These exists close relationship between sales growth and the increase in current assets needed to support a sales increase. The immediate need to pay labor expenses and increase the investment in accounts receivable and inventories can present a financing problem to a firm with little access to the long-term capital markets and limited access to trade credit and other accruals. The pressing need for capital for short-term purposes make the proper management of working capital for the small firm a critical issue. The same issues can face large corporations, which supposedly have access to the long-term debt and equity market in addition to the short-term sources of financing.

CURRENT ASSET FINANCING

In determining the appropriate level of investment in current assets and an appropriate levels of current liabilities the first step is to examine the general relationship between sales and fixed and current assets. There also must be a general insight into the options for financing changes in the structure of current assets.

Determining the Level of Current Assets

Any decision to maintain or alter the structure of current assets and current liabilities will be accompanied by certain risk and return trade-offs. A firm considering expansion generally has a schedule giving the capacity of the plant, but often the implications of varying the level of current assets in the balance sheet are not carefully examined.

When a firm decides to increase its level or sales, it must recognize the need for an asset base consisting of current and fixed assets to support the sales growth. It may be that existing facilities of plant and equipment are adequate for the next several years, but there will have to be increased commitments to the cash, accounts, receivable and inventory accounts. Similarly, when a firm experiences a permanent sales decline, the asset base should be decreased; the existing asset structure will be too large and will not be needed to support a lower level of sales.

The relationship between sales and the current asset accounts is illustrated in Figure 1, which assumes there are three possible current asset levels the firm can maintain, and the fixed asset investment remains constant over these levels. It is further assumed that the firm manages the investment in accounts receivable and inventories efficiently, so that these investments are in reality predetermined. The current asset section of a balance sheet omits the investment in cash and marketable securities, which can vary significantly. Accounts receivable and inventories can vary more directly with changes in the sales level, when managed efficiently, but the level of cash and marketable securities can vary widely. Thus cash and securities comprise more of a decision variable for management than the other two current assets.

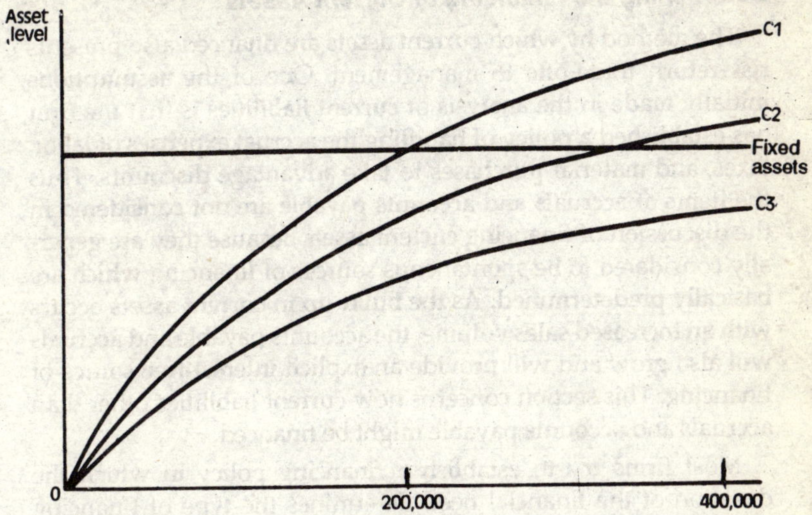

Fig. 1. Graph indicating the Current and Fixed Asset requirement at various sales levles.

In Figure 1, alternative 1 is associated with a more conservative management approach in that over all three output levels, the firm will maintain a higher current asset level than it would for alternative 2. The risk-return trade-offs are related to the fact that a wider margin of safety in avoiding insolvency (inability to meet the firm's obligations) exists with alternative 1, which always maintains a higher current asset balance and a higher liquidity factor.

However, alternative 2 provides a larger rate of return on assets for the firm because it carries a smaller current asset balance. Alternative 2 also incorporates the opportunity cost doctrine; as more rupees are invested current assets, these rupees cannot be utilized for other potentially more profitable investment opportunities. Thus alternative 1 provides a greater liquidity cushion to allow the firm to meet its current obligations if cash flows decline unexpectedly. This reduces risk, especially when other assets cannot be converted into cash except at a substantial sacrifice in price. Alternative 2, on the other hand, reduces the investment in current assets, which increases the rate of return on total assets but at the same time increases the risk exposure to the firm.

Determining the Financing of Current Assets

The method by which current assets are financed also presents risk-return trade-offs to management. One of the assumptions initially made in the analysis of current liabilities is that the firm has established a policy of handling the accrual expenses of labor, taxes, and material purchases to take advantage discounts. Thus the items of accruals and accounts payable are not considered in the discussion of financing current assets because they are generally considered to be spontaneous sources of financing which are basically predetermined. As the build-up in current assets occurs with an increased sales volume, the accounts payable and accruals will also grow and will provide an explicit interest-free source of financing. This section concerns how current liabilities other than accruals and accounts payable might be financed.

Most firms try to establish a financing policy in which the duration of the financial need determines the type of financing sought. A general observation is that long-term needs should be financed with long-term sources, and short-term needs should be financed with short-term sources. Fixed assets are considered a permanent need and are financed with long-term capital. Current assets generally fluctuate with sales, depending on the seasonality of the business, and the financial need also fluctuates. Within the category of current assets, a firm would not generally draw down to a zero cash accounts receivable, or inventory balance. In this case, a segment or part of the current asset category would become a permanent fund requirement which should therefore be financed with a long-term source of capital.

This situation is illustrated in Figure 2, which graphs the financing requirements of the firm over a period of time. In this figure permanent fund requirements consist of both the fixed assets and the amount of current assets considered to be a permanent feature of the balance sheet. The short-term fund requirement is indicated by the wavy line; it is suggested that this requirement should be funded with short-term capital. The rationale for this is that if long-term sources are utilized to finance short-term needs, the firm will be incurring a cost on funds that are not needed.

A good example of an industry with a cyclical short-term need for funds over the course of a year is the canning industry. During the spring and summer large sums must be laid out for the picking

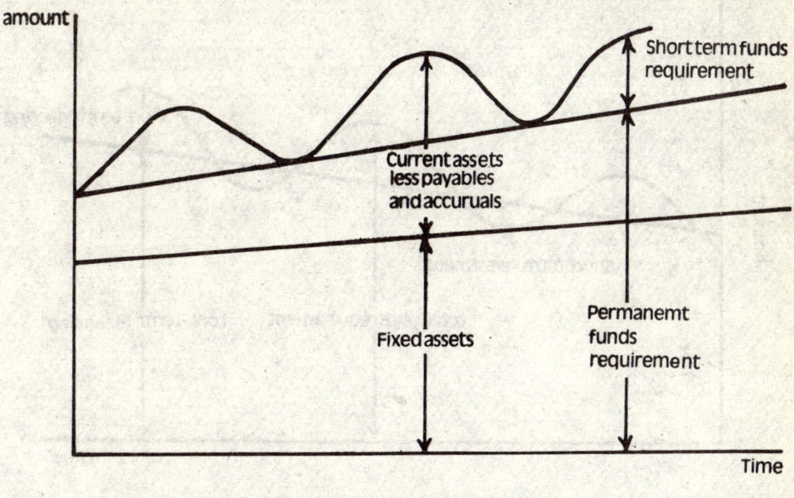

Fig. 2. Financing requirement over time.

and processing of the fruits or vegetables. A peak in needed financing is reached during this period: when the season is ended, the financial need also declines. It will exist on a declining scale until all of the accounts receivables are collected. Short-term financing such as a one-year bank line of credit serves this requirement. However, it is apparent that if long-term financing were utilized, there would be many months during the course of the year when interest would be paid on unneeded capital.

Unfortunately, the decision as to the breakdown of short- to long-term uses of financing is not as simple as it may seem. This is especially true when conditions of uncertainty are encountered. Swings in the business cycle may make short-term financing difficult or even impossible to obtain. Also, uncertainty pertaining to the expected receipt of cash flows may jeopardize the repayment of short-term bank loans.

Because of such conditions of uncertainty, management may decide to utilize a specified amount of long-term financing for short-term needs. This situation is illustrated in Figure 3. It is recognized that short-term loans are more risky than long-term loans in terms of both the ability of the firm to repay and the availability of future short-term funds. In addition, the monthly

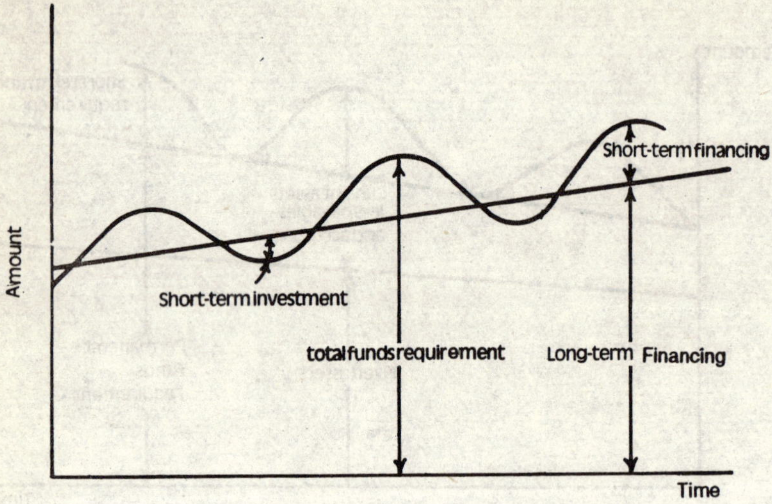

Fig. 3. Long-term and short-term financing requirements.

payments on a loan of longer maturity will be less than on a short-term maturity loan which acts as a buffer in case of a decline in expected cash inflows.

However, ever the long run, a firm will often pay more for long-term than for short borrowing. usually this provides enough incentive to utilize short-term financing instruments for short-term needs.

A firm generally has two choices to decrease the risk of cash inadequacy. It can either increase the maturity structure of its debt, which will decrease the monthly amount of payments, or it can decrease the maturity of its current asset base.

RISK-RETURN TRADE-OFFS

The decisions concerning how to finance current assets and the appropriate level of current assets are interdependent. A firm that maintains a relatively higher level of liquid current assets is better able to finance current assets (less payables and accruals) with short-term debt. If the short-term need is financed with equity rather than debt, the need for liquidity could be less; equity does not incur an interest expense but may have a constant dividend requirement.

Under conditions of certainty, where all future cash flows are exactly known, the firm could successfully match financial need with a maturity structure of debt that corresponds with future cash inflows. Thus it can eliminate low-yielding liquid asset balances and unneeded long-term financing. However, when conditions of uncertainty are present and future cash flows are subject to fluctuations, the firm can provide a safety margin of liquidity by either increasing its level of liquid assets or by lengthening the maturity structure of debt. These two solutions are not necessarily mutually exclusive, however; many combinations can be analysed.

Deriving Uncertain Cash Flow Information

The first step in determining the appropriate level of liquid asset balances and the financing necessary to achieve these levels is to utilize the cash budget for a selected period and develop a liquid asset balance statement under varying assumptions of sales collection and expense fluctuations. For each new assumption, a new set of liquid asset balances can be developed. From this, management develops a subjective probability distribution which shows the probability such a fluctuation will occur. These balances are thus treated as subjective random variables.

Utilizing Financing to Maintain Liquid Asset Balances

Management generally considers it undesirable to have a negative liquid asset balance at the end of any month. The problem is whether or not management has the options available to guarantee a positive liquid asset balance. Associated with any option is an opportunity cost, or the cost of alternative options.

The analysis could become quite complex with the addition of mortgage loans and other forms of debt, which would require consideration of all kinds of possible combinations and the associated opportunity costs. The analysis may be simplified to demonstrate a technique that can be utilized to match sources of debt with desired liquid-asset monthly ending balances.

In analyzing which financing alternative to select to achieve a specified asset balance, the opportunity cost involved in that instrument must be considered. One technique that can be utilized to do this is for management to specify the probability levels of zero or negative balance that would be at an acceptable risk level and compare them to the opportunity costs involved. For example, if management specifies that it would tolerate a 2 per cent chance of having a zero or negative liquid asset balance, this can be achieved with the alternative which has associated with it certain opportunity cost which, compared to the other alternatives, is quite a high cost for always having only a 2 per cent probability of a negative balance.

Thus, management must develop its own risk-preference structure and agree upon a risk-tolerance level (probability factor) that is acceptable when compared to the opportunity costs involved. Once this decision is made, management can then select the appropriate financing instrument and achieve the set of liquid asset ending balances that would be specified by the liquid asset balance projections.

CASH AND LIQUID SECURITIES

Now we share examine the various categories of current asset investment: cash and marketable securities, accounts receivable, and inventory. Our objective is to show the ways to manage these current asset accounts more efficiently. An optimal level of investment is sought by examining the benefits of holding rupees in these asset forms, and comparing the benefits with the costs involved in establishing and maintaining a specified current asset level.

CASH MANAGEMENT

As greater emphasis has been placed on the problems of proper cash management, financial managers have become much more sophisticated in their analysis of establishing an optimal cash-holding policy. The goal is to minimize the investment in cash while at the same time protecting the firm against sudden, unforeseen cash drains. The investment in the cash account is minimized so that more rupees can be diverted from idle balances into investments in earning assets.

Motives for Holding Cash

The rationale for a firm holding cash has four aspects; (1) the transaction motive, (2) the precautionary motive, (3) the speculative motive, and (4) the financial motive.

There is an obvious need for the firm to have a specified amount of cash on hand to meet the ordinary needs of the business in making purchases and paying bills. This leads to what is termed the *transaction motive* for holding cash. Some firms, such as utilities, have an inflow and outflow of cash that can be accurately estimated and synchronized, so the cash account can be relatively low compared to that required in other industries. In industries where the cash inflow and outflow cycle cannot be measured accurately, a higher cash balance will be required. Many firms have a high degree of seasonality, which can give rise to an increased need for cash when purchase requirements are increased or when cash inflows taper off. Firms dealing with agricultural products or consumer product firms that are subject to holiday activity are examples of seasonal business which may require extra funds at various times during the year.

A second motive for holding cash is the *precautionary motive.* Firms subject to seasonality or prone to swings in the business cycle are subject to conditions of uncertainty in a synchronized schedule of cash inflows and outflows. These firms may decide to hold a sum of cash in reserve specifically to take care of unforeseen cash requirements or to meet the periodic need to obtain cash on short-term notice. If interest rates are unusually high, or if the money supply is tight and loanable rupees are not available, it is wise to have a certain amount of funds set aside for such needs.

The third motive for holding cash is called the *speculative motive.* Firms often have investment opportunities that would put them into a profitable situation if they had enough cash to take advantage of them. For example, in 1979 a firm had an opportunity to receive as much as a 30 per cent discount on inventory purchases if it could pay cash. Buying materials at a 30 per cent discount would substantially reduce the cost of goods sold and increase the overall profit rate. Unfortunately, the firm did not have the cash to take advantage of this unusual opportunity. It attempted to obtain Rs. 30,000 financing for this purpose, but the tight money supply and increased interest rates during 1979 created financing difficulties, and the opportunity was lost.

One of the factors the firm must consider with the speculative motive is the opportunity cost associated with allowing cash to sit idle. In many instances, the opportunity loss will be greater than the gains that could be achieved by holding cash for speculative purposes.

The fourth motive for holding cash is called the *financial motive.* Firms often utilize accumulated cash reserves for the purchase of capital assets or the retirement (or refunding) of bonds or preferred stock. In accumulating cash for these purposes, the firm must evaluate the opportunity cost associated with holding idle cash balances. This opportunity loss is equivalent to the return obtained by investing these funds. This cost or loss would then be compared to the cost of using debt or equity sources for capital asset investment or the retirement of preferred stock or debt issues.

If the firm has sinking funds attached to a debt or preferred stock issue, there is no choice but to hold these accumulating cash balances. However, this feature of the issue must be evaluated in terms of its cost at the time the firm is contemplating putting an issue on the market with an attached sinking fund.

Receipt Patterns

One way the efficiency of cash management can be increased is through improvement in the firm's receipt stream. This is primarily accomplished by accelerating the collection process or reducing the time between when the customer pays the bills and when the firm can actually use these funds. Two techniques which help improve the cash inflow position of the firm are described below.

Concentration banking. When a firm decides to utilize a form of concentration banking, the decision calls for the establishment of centers of collection strategically located throughout the country. We have all received bills which require us to send payments to the home office, which may be located many states away. A firm that utilizes this method of collection will have a long delay before it can actually use these funds.

The period of delay between the time an individual pays a bill with a check and the time the funds are physically withdrawn from the person's checking account is called the *float period.* The payment must go through the mail, be received by the corporation, deposited in its checking account, and then completely cleared through the banking system. This process can take days, especially when a weekend is included. This means that an individual actually has use of these funds for some time beyond the mailing date of the bill. If the firm could cut this time process, it could increase the daily cash receipt balances. If this were possible, the firm could invest some of these funds and receive a return which can accumulate to a considerable amount when large sums of money are involved.

Concentration banking can help eliminate the float period by having the prayer of the bill send the payment to a collection center in his or her geographic area. When the payments are received, they are deposited in a local bank near the collection center. Surplus funds in excess of compensation balances can be transferred periodically to the corporation's main bank. Usually a concentration bank is not only a receiving bank but also is responsible for disbursements in that geographic region. In these cases surplus funds may not be transferred, but rather are used regionally.

This system of decentralized billing and collection has several advantages to the firm. First, it reduces the time it takes for the customer to receive a bill, as compared to a mailing from the home office, and payments are received much earlier and can be deposited sooner in the regional bank. Second, payments received in one specific geographical area can be cleared through the banking system much more quickly. Third, if the firm can decrease the float period by two or three days a month, it could utilize these funds for two or three days by investing in marketable securities. By doing this over the course of a year, a considerable amount of interest can be earned.

One of the factors that must be analyzed in the use of a concentrated banking system is the cost versus the benefit to be received. The monetary benefits would come in the form of interest received from the investment of surplus funds. The cost involved concerns the *x* charge for a wire transfer of funds from a regional to a centralized bank, if that is necessary. Also, most banks which perform this service require compensating balances. If these compensating balances could be used profitably by the corporation, an opportunity cost is involved which must be calculated and weighed against the gains from interest income.

Lockbox systems. A collection system which utilizes lockboxes can speed up the collection process even faster than the use of concentration banking. With concentration banking, payments are received at the collection center and are then deposited in a bank after processing. The time from receipt of payment to deposit in the bank is eliminated with a lockbox plan. The operating procedure is for the company to make arrangements with a local bank to handle the business within a specific region. The company then rents a post office box to which all payments within that geographic region are mailed. The bank picks up the mail from the post office box several times a day, and payments are immediately deposited, with all checks being microfilmed. The firm receives a deposit slip with a list of payments, along with any other material found in the envelopes.

The lockbox system offers the advantage of allowing checks to get to the bank and become part of the corporation's usable cash balances sooner than if payments were first handled by the firm's main or regional collection center. For providing this service, banks will charge a higher fee structure than if they simply received the checks for processing. Thus, the cost is substantially greater for this type of service. The payment for these services often comes in the form of higher compensating balances being required. When the average payments are small, this method of reducing float is not feasible.

Not only must a marketing feasibility study be done to ascertain the best location for a lockbox installation, but a cost-benefit study must be undertaken. The degree of profitability is dependent on such factors as the geographical distribution of customers, the size of the average pay-enough cash on hand to meet the payments. Thus we are only concerned with the negative part of the distribution in determining an optimal decision rule for daily balances. If at times excess funds are available, they can be transferred to the purchase of marketable securities.

One way to decide on the appropriate level of cash to have on hand is to determine what probability of running out of cash is acceptable to the management group. If management agrees that having a 3 per cent chance of not having enough funds on hand is tolerable, all we have to do is read the rupee amount of the cash balance that it associated with that probability level.

If management wanted a larger balance, there would be a smaller chance of having insufficient funds. Similarly, if a higher probability level were acceptable to management, we could maintain a smaller cash balance. The decision as to the appropriate decision rule or probability level to accept is dependent on such factors as management's aversion to risk, the tightness of the existing money supply in the nation, and the relationship that exists between the firm and the bank.

One technique that has been utilized by a bank is to extend a line of credit to a firm so that when an overdraft situation exists, the appropriate amount of funds will be extended. This is beneficial to a company that does not have marketable securities in sufficient quantity to meet this need.

Quantitative techniques are now being employed to solve the problem of proper cash balances. Linear programming models have been developed which take into account a multiple banking relationship, with numerous receipt and disbursement accounts. By analyzing the results of the linear programming analysis, management can determine the marginal cost of service for each bank. With the information obtained from these models, management can evaluate its position with each bank and possibly the firm will be put in a better bargaining position when future borrowing situations arise.

LIQUID SECURITIES

Marketable securities are considered as "near- money" investments which serve a liquidity need for a firm. They are termed *near-money* because they have varying yields and fluctuations in market price. The main reason corporations hold marketable securities is that they can sell them for approximately what they paid for them when the need arises. Evidence suggests that corporations hold these securities as a reserve for meeting future liquidity needs. They act as a reserve while at the same time they allow the firm to get a return on these balances. When a cash need arises, the firm will dispose of some of the marketable securities. When there is surplus cash, additions will be made to the marketable securities portfolio.

Formerly corporations sought investments primarily in short-term government securities. Now, however, the investment portfolio is much more varied, providing a potential for a greater return on the investment. Once the amount of the liquid asset balance has been determined for a corporation, the balance between cash and marketable securities must be divided. This decision can be made by management judgement, or models (discussed in the next section) can be utilized. After the decision has been made as to the rupees contribution to marketable securities, management must decide how the investment should be split among a number of alternative marketable security investment opportunities.

Factors in Selecting Marketable Securities

When the considering an investment in marketable securities, the financial manager is primarily interested in three factors: (1) the degree of default risk involved in the investment, (2) the future marketability of the security, and (3) the maturity structure of the securities.

Default risk. The possibility of the borrower being unable to make payments of interest or principal is considered the default risk. If the market place determines that one security has a higher degree of default risk than another, possible investors in it will demand a risk premium. The greater the possibility of default, the greater the financial risk and the greater the premium in terms of yield demanded by investors.

Marketability. The degree of marketability of a security refers to the investor's opportunity to convert the holdings into cash. The price received from the sale and the time involved in selling the security are two important factors that have to be considered. The investor who lowers the price enough can dispose of these assets quickly, but the course this is not the objective of holding marketable securities.

Corporations want to dispose of marketable securities in a short time, but also at a price that is close to what they paid for the security. The greater the marketability of the security, the greater the probability of making large transactions at or near the quoted price. If a security is rated as having a poor degree of marketability, the investor's required yield on that security will be higher. Thus a risk premium is considered when there is a higher default risk, and also when there may be difficulty in the marketability of the security. Both of these factors add to the required investor's yield.

Maturity. The maturity structure of the marketable security is an important aspect of the analysis whether to invest in one or another type of security. The reason for this is the risk associated with changes in the value of the security as interest rates fluctuate over time.

Even though there is greater risk in holding long-term securities, it must be remembered that they generally carry a greater yield, compared to short-term securities. Again, the risk-return trade-offs must be kept in mind. A financial manager who decides to hold marketable securities to maintain a reserve of near-money must limit the risk exposure because he has to be able to dispose of part of his portfolio of marketable securities on short notice. This is why firms usually limit their marketable securities investment to those with shorter maturities.

MANAGEMENT BETWEEN CASH AND MARKETABLE SECURITIES

Having examined the reasons for holding cash and the rationale for investing in marketable securities, the remaining consideration in the management of cash and marketable securities is the division of funds between the cash account and the investment in securities.

As is evident from previous discussions a firm has to have enough cash on hand to meet transaction demands for cash and also to satisfy precautionary needs. To maximize the wealth of its shareholders, the firm should minimize the investment in cash and invest all excess liquid asset balances in marketable securities. While the firm will receive interest from these investments, there are transaction costs involved in switching from cash to marketable securities and then back to cash when the need arises. If the firm faced conditions of certainty where future cash needs were known, it could invest in marketable securities as long as the interest revenue exceeded the transaction costs. If all required payments were known with certainty and there were no delays in exchanging marketable securities for cash, and, further, if no transaction or inconvenience costs were involved, ideally, the firm would maintain a zero cash balance. There would simply be a transfer of marketable securities into cash when bills were due.

With conversion delays, however, the firm almost certainly needs to maintain a cash balance.

Description of the Decision Model

Under conditions of uncertainty, the concept of probabilities must be brought into the analysis and applied to the estimated cash requirements. We will consider a one-period analysis which examines a firm's cash requirements on a weekly basis because the firm experiences wide fluctuations in cash balances over time. With a wide degree of dispersion of cash flow estimates and a high degree of correlation of the cash flow over time, more frequent analysis is desirable.

Analysis of the Decision Model

An outline the analysis process involved in making a decision as to the proper investment level in marketable securities may be prepared keeping the following factors in mind. They key to the analysis is to examine the net expected earnings for each alternative and select the alternative that has the highest net earnings figure. The net expected earnings calculation involves an analysis of the interest revenue, the costs of selling and buying marketable securities, and the probabilities of various cash balance levels over the next week.

The analysis is continued through the investment in marketable securities, the level which considers all the possibilities of having to sell marketable securities. The conclusion from this analysis is that the highest net expected return considering all costs and returns is received by the firm maintaining a substantial investment in marketable securities. By changing some of the assumptions concerning the expected return on the investment and/or assumptions pertaining to the cost structure of buying and selling the securities, the results could change significantly. It should further be pointed out that there are numerous other models to help analysts determine the distribution of funds between cash and marketable securities. This section has served as one illustration as to what can be accomplished in the area of cash and marketable securities management.

CREDIT AND COLLECTION POLICIES

Accounts receivable is the vehicle by which business organizations extend open-account credit to their customers. Because a firm foregoes immediate cash for a sale when it records an accounts receivable, the management of this aspect of the firm is very important.

This chapter describes the role of accounts receivable in financial management and suggests how accounts receivable can be managed effectively. While general credit and collection policies for a firm are examined first and then the extension of credit to individual accounts is discussed these two aspects are definitely interrelated. A liberalization of the credit policies of a firm always involves the trade-off between increased profits on sales that may arise from a more liberal policy and the increased cost of carrying added accounts receivable. A thorough analysis of credit extension to a customer helps reduce the risk of bad-debt losses and the potential of slow payments. These factors affect the investment in accounts receivable and help determine the firm's accounts receivable policies.

Though business cycle swings are uncontrollable factors, the general credit policy of the firm does have several controllable variables. The credit standards the firm sets, the credit period established, the discounts given, the level of default risk that is acceptable, and the collection policy are all controllable.

One of the most important investments firm makes is in its accounts receivable. The level of this investment is dependent on the rupee amount of credit sales and the time between making the sale and collecting the funds payment. The time between sale and payment is dependent on such factors as general swings in the business cycle and the credit policy of the firm. Changes in economic conditions are an uncontrollable variable for the firm; when a recession hits, for example, the firm's customers may be forced to delay payments. If this continues for an appreciable period the level of investment by the firm in its accounts receivable will increase substantially.

Credit Ratings

One of the major decisions a firm must make is the level of risk it is willing to accept in extending credit. If a firm accepts credit sales only from the strongest customers in terms of credit-worthiness, it will reduce its bad-debt experience and the expenses of the credit department. At the same time, however, it will be giving up a large volume of sales and potentially credit- worthy customers. If industry competition establishes or maintains more liberal credit standards, customers will purchase from other firms rather than one that has restrictive credit standards.

In such a situation, the firm's solution is to liberalize its credit standards to the point where the profitability generated from the additional sales acquired by accepting more customers is equal to the additional cost incurred in accepting additional accounts receivable. The costs of accepting additional accounts receivable include: (1) increased costs of the credit department, (2) increased potential for bad-debt experience, and (3) increased investment in accounts receivable. The costs related to the credit department include the clerical expenses involved in screening accounts and servicing them. The increased probability of bad-debt losses will decrease the profitability of additional sales. To get a net profitability figure for calculation purposes, however, we can assume that there will be no bad-debt losses and that other credit department expenses have already been deducted. The increased investment in accounts receivable is due to higher sales, with more accounts receivables, and the potential of a longer collection period. This can create an opportunity loss in terms of utilizing these funds in the production cycle or using them elsewhere. This opportunity cost can be increased if the firm has to borrow funds to carry the production cycle while funds are tied up in accounts receivable.

Terms of credit

The terms of credit refers to the time for which credit is extended and the discount which may be given for early payment. A typical type of credit terms is 2/10, net 30; a 2 per cent discount is given off the sales price if the payment is received within 10 days, and the entire amount is due 30 days from the invoice date if the discount is not utilized. With terms of net 60, for example, no discount is given and payment is due 60 days after the date of invoice.

The credit period. The credit period is the time a customer has to make payment for goods purchased. The net 30 part of a credit term expression refers to the credit period. To stimulate sales, a firm may consider lengthening the credit period for its current customers. The viability of this decision would include an analysis of the trade-offs between the profitability generated from the additional sales versus the cost incurred in increasing the investment in accounts receivable. One of the critical parts of the analysis would be a decision as to what incremental sales can be expected and what the competition might contemplate in terms of a reaction.

Cash discounts. Like increasing the length of the credit period, altering the cash discount entails more thought because if more people take the discount, there will be a definite reduction in the profits realized per unit sold. It is important in this kind of analysis to make sure that the return on these funds generated by a speedup in collections more than offsets the cost of initiating or increasing the allowable discount. If the analysis is affirmative, the firm should alter the cash discount policy.

Another way to alter the discount is to change the discount period. If a firm considers increasing the discount period from 10 to 15 days, for example, there is a dual effect. If the discount period is lengthened five days, some customers who formerly did not take the discount will do so, and this can lead to a reduced average collection period. However, customers who have regularly paid on the tenth day now have five extra days, and this can lengthen the average collection period. The firm must evaluate the payment habits of its customers and determine the net effect in terms of numbers of customers and rupee volume if additional customers take advantage of this new policy. To initiate this policy, the marginal rupee gain of increasing the average collection period must outweigh the marginal rupee loss that will occur if existing customers take an additional five days to make their payments.

The maximum length of the cash discount period would only be as long as the two-way turnaround time of the transaction for the book-keeping operations of the two firms involved. The cash discount period should in essence be equivalent to cash. If a customer cannot pay a bill within 8 or 10 days, it is questionable whether it can pay it within 15 days. This is considered in the analysis when the marginal gains are compared to the cost of extending the cash discount period.

Default risk

Up to this point we have assumed of situations, where there were no bad-debt losses. Now we consider the full impact of increasing sales demand by lengthening the credit terms, which will increase not only the slowness of payments but also the proportion of receivables that may default in payment. Even when bad-debt losses are considered, as well as slowness in receivables, in this example, the additional profits expected far exceed the required rate of return on the incremental investment in receivables. The firm should go ahead with the relaxation of credit standards.

Sources of Credit Information

A number of sources of information concerning potential customers are available, but it is important to keep in mind that an expense is associated with collecting the information. A firm has to weigh the cost of obtaining information against gains to be received by having the credit information. For small customers, limited information is used in making the extension of credit decision, because the cost of getting extensive credit information is not worthwhile compared to the profit potential in the account.

Time is another factor which is considered in the decision as to the extent of credit check necessary. Shipments of material to customers cannot be help up for long while the credit check is in progress.

Financial statements. One of the best and cheapest sources of credit information is the financial statement supplied by a potential customer. In addition to the balance sheet and income statement, aging schedules of receivables and payables can also be requested. Put together, they provide a great deal of historical information concerning the profitability and financial activity of the potential customer. If a customer is unwilling to submit these financial statements, the supplier can rightfully assume that the financial position of the potential customer is week. This in itself is good grounds for rejection of a credit application. If a supplier has the time and personnel to evaluate them, periodic statements submitted by customers can provide a review of the customer's financial position as a basis for determining whether credit should be extended, contracted, or ended. Audited statements are preferable to unaudited statements.

Credit reports. Firms that grant credit also can have access (for a fee) to credit reports on potential customers from credit reporting agencies. A credit report is a fairly comprehensive analysis of a company. All financial obligations are listed, along with highlights of its financial position and a historical account of the firm in the form of a business and product description. A trade check is also done in which existing suppliers provide information on promptness of payment, whether payments are past due, and whether discounts are taken. Much of the information in these reports is obtained directly from the company, so the details of the report in large part depend on the firm's willingness to be examined.

In addition, credit ratings are also available on a vast number of business firms. Subscribing for this-service grants access to information on credit-worthiness. The service indicates the size of the company's base and a credit evaluation of companies in certain size classifications. Dun & Bradstreet also indicate when insufficient information is available to make a credit appraisal.

Credit Bureaus. These are business service organisations which fill a specific need for retail and professional persons in their trade areas. They also benefit consumers who are able to obtain credit privileges rapidly and efficiently. The primary function of a credit bureau is to gather, assemble, file and report credit history and facts on individuals in order to assist credit grantors in determining the worthiness of consumers who apply for credit.

More specially, credit bureaus can be described as business organizations that systematically collect and file identification data (name, social security number, address, etc.). pay habits (whether payments are current in the time period reviewed by other creditors). and public record (civil judgments, bankruptcy filing, etc.). Factual, impartial reports are then available to credit grantors who have a business need for such information.

In 1803, the very first "credit bureau" was organized by merchant tailors in London. Fifty-seven years later, the idea came to the United States and a bureau was formed in Brooklyn, New

York. From these modest beginnings grew an industry which serves credit grantors and consumers throughout most of the free world.

The consumer credit system is based on the theory that the majority of consumers are responsible individuals who can be sold the goods and services they need today on their promise to pay tomorrow. That this is correct is borne out by statistics which reveal that approximately 70% of credit users will pay promptly. Another 25% will become slow-payers, and will require some follow-up activity. Of the remaining 5%, some may eventually pay, but many will never pay at all.

Credit grantors are interested in making profitable credit sales and holding credit losses to a minimum. Since losses due to extension of credit to consumers who do not pay must be passed on to all consumers by increasing the price of goods or services, it is in the public interest that credit grantors have a reliable, unbiased central source for the credit history of applicants.

The law requires, among other things, that credit grantors certify that they have a permissible purpose for each credit report they obtain. These purposes are listed in the law. In order to ensure that all the requirements of the law are observed, credit bureaus require a contractual agreement with each credit grantor before they will furnish reports.

The bureau gathers its information from several sources. Information on paying habits is secured from credit grantors who furnish the data. Some creditors generally provide information only in response to a specific request. For example, the credit bureau in a small town may call a tire store, state that a consumer has given it as a credit reference, and ask how payments were made. Computerized credit bureaus have the capability of being able to accept complete accounts receivable tapes from automated credit grantors.

Employment information is verified by contacting the consumer credit applicant's employer when requested to do so by the credit grantor. Public record information is obtained from the court house records and district courts. Bureaus generally obtain data regarding civil court judgments, divorce actions, tax liens, and bankruptcy filings. Some bureaus gather real estate data, chattel mortgages, marriage license filings, and other data affecting a person's ability to pay.

The information is held in strict confidence in compliance with the Act. This law also gives consumers the right to learn the nature and substance of all information about them on file in a credit bureau. Consumers also have the right to dispute data and request that they be re-checked. Credit bureaus are required by law to interview consumers about their files and to provide trained personnel to conduct these interviews.

Each individual file, whether on a computer or in a file jacket in a manual bureau, contains only items that are pertinent to his or her credit history. Every entry must be of the type that can be verified by documentation somewhere. This may be a creditor's ledger, an employer's records, or a file in the country clerk's office. Credit bureau files may contain no hearsay or statements of opinion.

Credit reports are furnished in several ways. Computerized credit bureaus offer their largest credit grantor users the privilege of installing a terminal in their offices so reports may be produced quickly. Security safeguards are built into such arrangements to ensure that reports are drawn only for authorized reasons. Oral reports, read from the bureau's terminal or from the manual file in a non-automated bureau, comprise the bulk of reports furnished. Type-written reports or "hard copies" from computers are produced when the credit grantor has a need for a permanent record of the report, such as home mortgage loan and car purchase applications.

In addition to providing reports on a local level, credit bureaus exchange information upon request for two purposes: (1) to transfer the credit records of individuals who apply for charge accounts in other communities, and (2) to transfer the credit records of those who move to other communities.

Checking through banks. Some suppliers' banks have credit departments that will undertake credit checks for the firm. By contacting the potential customer's bank, it can obtain information on such items as averages cash balances, outstandings loans, and the bank's experience in dealing with the client in terms of loan repayment promptness. A supplier contacting a potential customer's bank will not have the same success in gathering this information as can be achieved through a bank-to-bank contact.

Prior company experience. In deciding whether the amount of credit granted to an individual customer should be increased, the supplier's past experience with that account is an important indication. Examination of the promptness of payment will indicate the ability of a customer to handle a larger credit volume. Sometimes a supplier can exchange information with others who supply the same firm and can check its payment habits with other suppliers. Information can be obtained on the length of time the account has been in effect, the size of the line of credit, and the record of prompt payment.

Credit insurance. A firm has the option of using credit insurance, which can protect it against large bad-debt losses. Insurance companies granting this type of insurance restrict the coverage to specified risk levels as established by the D&B ratings. These companies frequently require coinsurance, which requires the participation of the firm in the amount of 10 to 20 per cent of its bad-debt losses. This protects the insurance company from too liberal credit extension policies by a firm buying the insurance. The cost of this insurance varies with the estimation of the degree of risk involved. Usually it is calculated as a percentage of sales. The decision to utilize this form of protection will in large part depend on estimation of the degree of risk the firm is being subjected to and the capacity of the firm to bear this risk.

Use of computers in receivables management. Credit analysis has been assisted greatly in recent years by the availability of computers. They have the capacity of providing up-to-the-minute data on any internal account. All the data recorded on a company's receivables ledgers can be transferred to the computer by punch cards or tape. With a push of a button, management can obtain information on recent billings, payments, discounts taken, and unpaid balances. An aging of all the accounts can be quickly obtained which will break down receivable balances into those that are current, those that are 30 days old, 60 days old, and so on.

One of the uses of the computer in the credit departments is that it can flag a delinquent account and send delinquent letters at once. The credit manager is immediately made aware of the situation, whereas notice might otherwise be delayed for a considerable time. Accounts that are reaching their credit limit are also flagged so management can evaluate the account to determine if an extension of credit is appropriate, given the information provided by a credit review.

INVENTORY MANAGEMENT

Like accounts receivables, inventories represent a large portion of a firm's assets. On average, the inventory to sales ratio runs between 14 and 24 per cent, while inventory as a percentage of total assets ranges from 20 to 35 per cent. The size of the inventory indicates that a substantial investment can be made in this asset account. Therefore it must be managed efficiently so that the investment does not become unnecessarily large. This chapter will demonstrate the importance of managing this category of assets and illustrate some methods or tools that can be utilized to improve efficiency.

In manufacturing firms, inventories consist of three elements: raw materials, work in process, and finished goods. Each of these elements plays an important role in the production and sale of products. A smooth production process goes from the ordering of raw materials through the creation of semifinished goods (or work-in-progress inventory) to the final product, which is stored in finished goods inventory. There must be sufficient raw or semi-finished materials on hand to carry the product through to its final state.

Production personnel want ample materials on hand; sales personnel want ample finished goods so they do not face stock-outs and have to place back orders. The financial manager should strive to maintain a proper balance of inventory to guarantee that there are sufficient quantities on hand to meet the needs of production and sales, while at the same time an over abundance does not result in an unnecessary investment in the inventory account.

The amount of inventory any particular firm maintains will depend on such factors as the level of sales, the length of the production cycle, and the durability of the product. Petroleum producers maintain small inventories because they deal in a primary resource; vegetable dealers handle highly perishable products; and heavy machinery manufacturers have a large investment in inventories because a long time is needed to manufacture the product. All firms have rationales for setting specified levels of inventory. There is no question, however, that many firms could examine their inventory levels more closely and reduce their investment in the three types of inventory.

Larger firms have recently been employing computers and operation research techniques to assist in controlling their inventories. The compute stores all information pertaining to a specific item, and as each sale is recorded in its memory banks, preprogrammed order points automatically key the computer to order when the inventory is reduced to that level. Department stores have made great use of this technique with the assistance of punched cards as sales slips which are later fed into the computer. Even with such sophisticated tools, the human factor is still needed to guarantee that the system operates efficiently. An order for 120 garbage cans at one installation was misread by the computer as 12,000 garbage cans. The computer filled the order with all the cans in stock and back ordered the rest.

Management realizes that a certain amount of materials and products must be on hand to meet the inflow and outflow demands of the production cycle. In addition, it is desirable to maintain a level of safety stock which provides a margin in case of an unusually large order or delivery delays of necessary supplies. Despite these needs, management cannot order as much as it wants and maintain as large an inventory as it can because there are costs associated with inventories. Even though the firm may be able to obtain discounts by ordering large quantities of supplies, other costs are incurred when a large inventory accumulates.

Thus, management must weigh the inventory needs of the firm with the costs associated with inventory accumulation. It might try to keep enough inventory on hand at all times to minimize the total costs of maintaining that inventory level. The cost of inventory to a firm is usually divided into two classifications:

1. Those costs associated with carrying the inventory.
2. Those costs associated with ordering inventory.

Carrying costs usually include four items: (1) the cost of tying up money in inventory, which can be related to the cost of capital;

(2) the cost of insurance on inventory; (3) the inventory property tax levied; and (4) the depreciation and obsolescence factor.

The second category of costs includes those related to shipping, receiving, and ordering. These include the cost of placing an order, the expenses associated with shipping and handling the inventory, and the discounts that can be lost.

A third category of costs which we will not deal with directly is the cost of running short of inventory. This is a difficult category to measure. Included in this category would be the cost involved in the loss of sales due to stock-outs, the loss of customer goodwill, and potential disruption in production schedules.

Attempts to minimize these costs and to determine an average inventory balance to be maintained are illustrated in Figure 4. In this illustration, the optimal inventory is determined and the shapes of the cost curves are shown. Carrying costs are upward sloping; as inventory balances increase, insurance, storage, and tax expenses rise sharply. Ordering costs, such as shipping and handling, quantity discounts, and placement costs decline sharply as the amount of inventory increases. Summing up the two gives the total costs curve. The minimum point on the total costs curve would be the desired inventory balance.

This type of analysis can be utilized not only for inventory but also for other asset accounts such as cash, marketable securities, and fixed assets. Associated with investments in each of the asset accounts are the cost trade-offs as suggested in Figure 4.

Raw materials and work-in-process inventory needs are known with a degree of certainty, due to their dependence on production schedules, but demand for products and the subsequent usage of inventory are not known with certainty. Finished goods inventory is the category that is subject to the greatest degree of fluctuation and uncertainty. In addition, there is usually a degree of uncertainty associated with the placement of a raw materials order and the actual time the order will be received by the firm. These uncertainties suggest that it is unwise for a firm or plant to allow its inventory to be depleted completely before new orders are received.

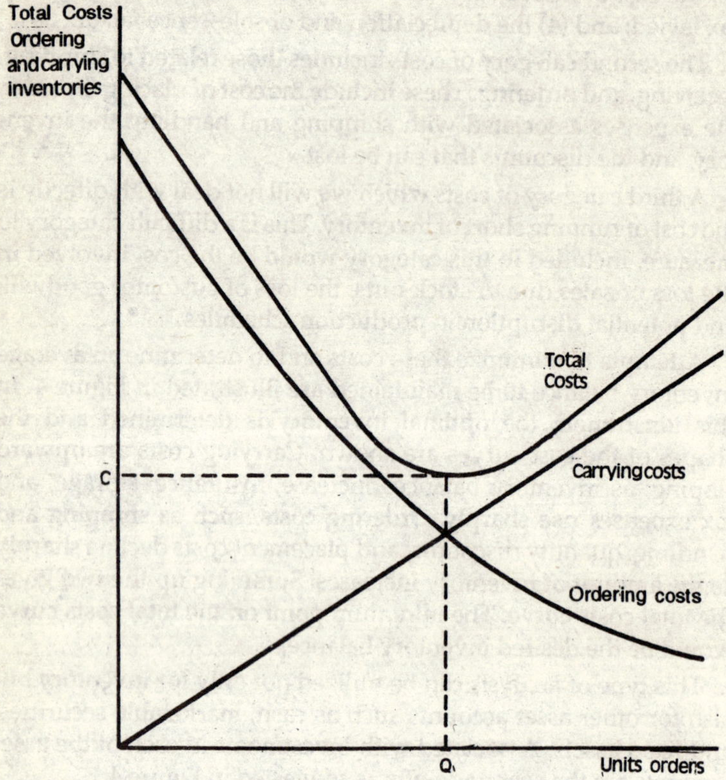

Fig. 4. Optimum level of inventory.

Determining the Level of Safety Stocks with Probabilistic Information

To protect itself from conditions of uncertainty, a firm usually maintains a level of safety stocks in all three inventory categories: raw materials, work in process, and finished goods. The opportunity cost associated with stock-outs in raw materials and work in process is a slowdown in the production cycle. For finished goods inventory, the opportunity cost associated with stock-outs could be lost sales. The level of safety stocks on hand will be determined by a comparison of the cost of a stockout versus the cost of carrying additional inventory.

Determining The Level Of Safety Stocks Using The Order Point Formula

Many analysts find that the probabilistic approach illustrated above is unduly complex and sometimes unfeasible for a multi-period problem. An alternative way to establish a level of safety stock is the order point system, whereby an order is placed once a certain level of inventory is reached. This order point is defined as the level of inventory, given the lead time required to procure additional inventory, where the remaining inventory would be completely exhausted if a new order did not arive on time.

We can illustrate this concept with the example of a firm which has determined its EOQ to be 1,000 units. Assume that the lead time to obtain additional inventory is estimated to be 10 days. With demand of 18,000 units per year, this means that 18 orders will be placed every year, or one every 20 days. This is a daily usage of 50 units.

With the assumption that there is a lead time of ten days from when the order is placed to when it is received, we will have to order when inventory is reduced to the multiple of lead time times daily usage. With an EOQ of 1,000 units, the ordering point would be at 500 units (50 units a day, ten-day lead time).

With a safety stock level of 500 units to protect the firm against a further ten-day delay in delivery beyond the lead time, maximum inventory is increased to 1,500 units: the EOQ of 1,000 units, plus the 500 units of safety stock. Thus the initial order is 1,500 units. Subsequently the firm will order the EOQ whenever the inventory falls to 1,000 units: the safety stock of 500 units, plus the 500 units expected to be used during the lead time. Note that once the order point is reached, the firm could accelerate its sales toward a zero inventory level and use up its safety stock. The maximum usage represents an increase in the daily usage. this new usage figure would be 100 units per day, which is found by dividing the inventory left by he lead time period of 10 days.

FINANCIAL INVENTORY CONTROL

The proper control of inventory is a duty of the financial manager. which cannot be stressed enough. This chapter provides insight into a few of the inventory control methods the manager can use. The availability of the computer has made great progress in the maintenance of proper control of this asset account. Operations research approaches are also useful to inventory control.

The techniques for inventory controls we have presented have not distinguished between the various types of inventory. To control the inventory process properly there could be separate control systems for raw materials, work in process, and finished goods. In addition, there might be separate control systems for different lines of products within the firm. Frequently a few products will account for the vast percentage of a firm's annual sales. The rest of the product lines may be large in number but account for only a small percentage of sales. The firm will have to maintain more careful control of those products that move quickly by maintaining the proper ordering point level, including a proper safety stock factor. Items in inventory that do not move quickly should be analyzed to determine the minimum investment the firm has to make in them so that surplus capital can be diverted to other productive investments.

The direct physical control of inventory is not the responsibility of the financial manager, but the investment of funds in this asset account certainly must have his scrutiny. This requires familiarity with inventory control techniques so investments in inventory can be managed efficiently. The firm's goal of maximizing the wealth of the shareholders can be aided by recognizing the opportunity cost of tying up funds in inventory. If high opportunity costs are associated with this investment in current assets, the likelihood is great that the optimal level of average inventory will be low.

Another factor the financial manager must consider is uncertainty concerning the lead time between placement of an order and its actual receipt. If the lead time is low the level of safety stock can also be reduced, which will have the effect of reducing the rupees investment in inventory. If a large opportunity cost is associated with inventory investment, there is a greater incentive to reduce the lead time for orders. This may induce the financial manager to search for suppliers that can supply goods quickly, as well as to apply pressure to existing vendors to improve their delivery schedules. The emphasis in this area is directly related to the comparative trade-off between the opportunity cost in holding inventory versus the added cost involved in reducing the lead time on deliveries.

9

DIVIDEND POLICY

THE objective of stated dividend policy for a firm is to determine how new income after taxes will be distributed among the shareholders i the form of dividends or reinvested in the form of additions to retained earnings. The additions to retained earnings can be one of the most useful financing tools for the firm seeking to raise capital to undertake new investments. Often a firm is unable to pay out as much as is desired in the form of dividends and at the same time retain as much as it wants for investment opportunities. In these instances, these two alternatives uses of net income are in conflict.

If management increases the contribution to retained earnings, investors may view the decrease in dividends adversely in terms of the price of the stock, even though the funds could yield a higher growth rate for future earnings per share. If dividends are increased, this takes funds away from investment opportunities that could increase the future earnings per share. To maintain the objective of maximizing the wealth of the shareholders, management must determine the proper mix of dividend payout and retention of earnings.

This chapter examines the issues involved in maintaining a dividend policy and also demonstrates how to determine the optimum mix of retained earnings and dividends.

INFLUENCES ON CORPORATE DIVIDEND POLICY

Many factors enter into the decision as to how much amount should be paid out annually to stockholders in the form of dividends. This section discusses the factors that influence dividend policy.

Legal Implications

Over the years, legal statutes have become quite explicit in dealing with corporate dividend policy. Dividends must be paid out of current earnings or from earnings previously accrued as reflected in the retained earnings account. Today, state laws emphasize three rules for dividend policy:

1. The **net profit rule** states that dividends must be paid from past or current earnings.
2. The **capital impairment rule** prohibits the payment of dividends from the capital account to protect shareholders and creditors.
3. The **insolvency rule** states that the corporation may not pay dividends when insolvent. This means that dividends may not be paid when liabilities exceed assets.

The legal rules act as boundaries within which a corporation can operate in terms of paying dividends. Within these boundaries are many financial factors that have an impact on the dividend policy of a firm.

Liquidity

A firm that may be growing and quite profitable may not be able to pay a specified cash dividend because of lack of cash on hand. The net income figure visible on the year-end income statement represents the increase in retained earnings on the balance sheet. To offset the increase in retained earnings, assets will increase in the form of current or possibly fixed assets required to conduct business. If there is insufficient cash or if there are sufficient pressures for liquidity due to the high growth rate of the *firm*, management may not be able to declare a cash dividend. The issue is the amount of cash management must have to carry on the daily routine of the business.

Restrictions in Loan Agreements

When a firm borrows money from banks or from individuals through a bond issue, the legal document that accompanies the loan may in many instances have restrictive clauses pertaining to the payment of dividends. The intent of these restrictions is to protect the lender in terms of the firm's ability to service the debt obligations. Examples of these restrictions are: (1) the payment of dividends can be made only out of current earnings, (2) the payment of dividends cannot be made when the ratio of current assets to current liabilities decreases to some level, and (3) the establishment of a sinking fund is required to guarantee the retirement of debt out of current earnings. A similar restriction associated with a preferred stock issue is that common stock dividends cannot be paid until all accrued preferred stock dividends have been distributed. These are a few examples of restrictive clauses pertaining to the payment of dividends which affect the dividend policy of the firm.

Continued Access to the Capital Market

A firm that is well established and has a record of profitability will be able to raise debt or equity capital on relatively short notice. A firm that has this ability can pay a cash dividend even though management feels that there will be substantial cash needs in the near future. Ready access to debt and equity financing instruments allows management to feel secure in its ability to pay both the cash dividend and the corporate obligations. The impact of the cash dividend is, therefore, not as great on the liquidity position of the firm. A smaller firm that does not have quick access to the debt or equity markets probably will not be able to pay the cash dividend if there are foreseeable heavy future cash drains.

Rate of Return and Investment Opportunities

If the firm is growing rapidly, there will be a large demand for capital. When current earnings are a primary source of funds, management may feel that internal expansion and continued growth take precedence over the payment of cash dividends. This would especially be true if the rate of return the firm earns on its assets is in excess of what the individual shareholder could expect to receive by taking dividends and reinvesting those amounts elsewhere.

Control

With cash being utilized to pay dividends, it may be necessary for a firm to look to the equity market for additional rupees of capital to finance future expansion. Percentage control of the stock becomes an issue when a group of shareholders is unable to purchase a percentage of the new issue to maintain its percentage of ownership of the corporation. This situation can be of critical importance for the management, which may wish to maintain 51 per cent control but may not be able to if more stock is issued. Under these circumstances, management may withhold the payment of cash dividends in order to retain the necessary funds for investment purposes.

Tax Implications for Shareholders

The tax status of the owners of the corporation will in many cases influence the dividend policy of the firm. In a closely held corporation with owners in the high income tax brackets, little or no dividends, which would be taxed at the normal income tax rate, may be desired. Rather, the owners would prefer to take the income out of the corporation in the form of capital gains, which would be taxed at a much lower rate. In cases of public corporations where the owners are in a high tax bracket, an immediate conflict will arise due to the fact that these individuals will not want cash dividends, while those in the lower tax brackets will want them.

STABILITY IN CORPORATE DIVIDEND POLICY

This section examines the relationship between corporate earnings and the dividend policies of domestic corporations. Patterns of dividend payout are discussed, followed by an explanation of why corporations seed to maintain dividend stability.

Established Dividend Trends

Historical records of corporate dividend policy indicate that corporations to a large extent follow a stable dividend policy.

Over a long history of dividends a corporation is generally locked into a pattern which establishes a certain level of dividend payment. If the dividend policy is abruptly decreased, repercussions could be expected which would result in a decrease in the price of the stock. Since decreases are to be avoided, corporation; have established the policy that an increase in the level of dividend payments will only be made after earnings have clearly reached a permanent higher level. Dividend increases, therefore, lag behind upward shifts in earnings.

Explanation of The Stable Dividend Policy

There are numerous reasons why a firm establishes a historical pattern of a stable dividend policy. All of them have the objective of maintaining the confidence of investors in the corporation.

Elimination of investor uncertainty. There is no question, for most analysts, that dividends carry an informational content concerning future earnings. If dividends fluctuated as widely as earnings data, investors could easily interpret this as indicating that the firm has no notion as to where its earnings are going in the future. Even if a fluctuating dividend policy results in the same average amount that would have been received under a stable dividend policy, the uncertainty factor for the investor could easily lead to a higher discount factor being applied to the firm than if a stable dividend policy were maintained. This higher discount factor would mean a higher required rate of return by the investor and, therefore, a higher cost of capital requirement for the firm.

dividends as a source of income. Many people rely on dividend payments as a source of income. People anticipating retirement will invest in firms that have a history of strong dividend payments. If the firm abruptly reduced its dividend, these investors would sell their stock and invest in another firm that has a substantial dividend payment record. Thus in a firm like L & T, which has a long history of stable dividends, a large proportion of its investors are dependent on the dividend as a source of income. If L & T were to initiate an erratic pattern of dividend payments there would probably be a sharp decline in the price of the stock as the income-oriented investors sold their shares.

Widening the investor community. Some of the largest investors in business are financial institutions such as banks, savings and loan associations, insurance companies, pension funds, trustees, and other organizations. Because of their fiduciary responsibility as a guardian of other people's money, certain legal restrictions are placed upon the ability of these organizations to invest in corporations. They cannot invest in corporations unless the corporations are on a legal list prepared by various government agencies. It is desirable for a corporation to be placed on these lists because it widens their investor groups to include not only individuals and corporations but also large financial institutions. One of the requirements for these lists is a stable dividend policy. If an erratic pattern of dividend policy were initiated, a corporation could be removed.

A stable dividend policy maintained by a firm also helps to establish stability for the market price of its stock. This is desirable for institutional investors who are seeking a specified return rather than potential capital gains. While no definitive empirical study covering stocks in general has found a direct relationship between a stable dividend policy and stable market price trends, there is evidence on individual stocks to suggest that the market price is supported on the down side by a stable dividend policy. In other words, the stable dividend sets a market price floor for the individual corporate stock.

Methods of dividend payout. Three distinct forms of dividend policy are utilized by corporations today. In the *constant dividend* policy followed by a large number of firms, a constant dividend is paid annually. An example is Burroughs's long-standing 50 cent annual dividend. A stable dividend policy utilizes this form of dividend payment.

A second type of dividend structure utilizes the *constant payout ratio.* The payout ratio is defined as the percentage of available earnings paid out as dividends. A firm which has a 50 per cent payout ratio, for example, will always pay out 50 per cent of its earnings in the form of dividends. Thus, if in one year a firm has Rs. 30 in available earnings, Rs. 15 will be paid in the form of dividends. If in the next year the firm has only Re. 1 in available earnings, the firm will pay only a 50 paise dividend. The problem with this format is that the payout ratio may be constant, but the rupee annual dividend can widely fluctuate with the historical level of earnings. As a result, most corporations do not use this technique of dividend payment.

A third type of dividend policy utilizes a *small regular dividend plus an extra year-end dividend.* With this policy, a small regular quarterly dividend is paid, and then, if the firm has extra funds at the end of the year, a bonus dividend is declared. This policy provides extra flexibility for the firm because it can retain the funds and not pay the bonus dividend if there are heavy cash demands, or it can distribute the bonus dividend. The stable dividend policy is maintained for the smaller quarterly dividends.

The only problem with the third technique is that if a history of large, tear-end bonus dividends develops, investors will begin to expect it. Thus the firm could get locked into this format, which becomes nothing more than a stable dividend policy at a higher rupee level. If the firm did not pay the bonus dividend one year, the repercussions could be as great as if it had deviated from its stable rupee dividend.

PAYMENT OF DIVIDENDS

Most companies that pay dividends pay them quarterly. If the *regular quarterly dividend* is Rs. 4.00, a corresponding *regular annual dividend* could be Rs. 16.00. Annual reports of corporations may often express the pride the firm takes in having maintained a stable dividend over several decades. This section will review the mechanics of the dividend paying procedure.

Dividend Distribution Procedure

The procedure for declaring and paying a dividend starts with a meeting of the board of directors. For example, at a meeting on August 16, the directors could declare a Rs. 4.00 quarterly dividend to all holders of record on September 15, with the payment to be made on October 3. September 15 is then the holder-of-record date, on which the corporation closes its stock transfer books and makes a complete list of all stockholders as of that date. If notification is given to the company of a transfer of title of the stock before September 15, the new owner will receive the dividend, However, if notification is on or after September 15, the old shareholder receives it.

To guarantee the dividend to a person purchasing the stock before September 15, the brokerage industry has established a policy that the right of the dividend remains with the stock until four days prior to the holder-of-record date. At that time, rights to the dividend no longer go with the shares of stock. This procedure is used to allow ample time to notify the company of the transfer of the stock. The date that the right to the dividend is eliminated is called the *ex-dividend* date, and this stock is said to be traded ex-dividend. Thus, a person who purchases the stock prior to September 11 will receive the dividend, If the stock is purchased on September 11 or later, the seller and not the buyer will receive the dividend. On October 3, the *payment* date, the corporation will mail all dividend checks to the shareholders of record.

STOCK DIVIDENDS AND STOCK SPLITS

From a management point of view, stock dividends and stock splits are used to try to enhance the value of the stock to the shareholders. Though it is often said that the two are similar in nature, they are used for different purposes, and from an accounting point of view they are quite different.

Stock Dividends

A stock dividend can be defined as the payment of additional stock to the shareholders. The percentage ownership of each shareholder remains unchanged, and in fact the dividend represents a recapitalization of the company. To illustrate the effect of a stock dividend on the capital structure of the firm, take the example of a company that has the following capital structure.

Common stock (Rs. 10 par, 800,000 shares)	Rs. 8,000,000
Capital surplus	4,000,000
Retained earnings	20,000,000
Net Worth	Rs. 32,000,000

Now assume that the company pays a 10 per cent stock dividend, which would amount to an additional 80,000 shares being issued. Also assume that the stock will sell for Rs. 40 at the fair market value. For each ten shares owned, the stockholder will receive an additional share of stock. With this information, the balance sheet can be recast as:

Common stock (Rs. 10 par, 880,000 shares)	Rs. 8,800,000
Capital surplus	6,400,000
Retained earnings	16,800,000
New Worth	Rs. 32,000,000

This example shows that with the 10 per cent stock dividend, a total of Rs. 3,200,000 is transferred from the retained earnings to the common stock and capital surplus accounts. The common stock account. Which lists all entries at Rs. 10 par, increased by Rs. 800,000 and the capital surplus increased by Rs. 30 per share, or Rs. 2,400,000. Notice that throughout the transaction, the total net worth of the company remained unchanged. Since there are more shares outstanding, the earnings per share figure will decrease, but since the investor has more shares, the total earnings allotted to an individual investor will remain unchanged.

To the investor, a stock dividend can have either of two effects. In the first case, if the firm pays the stock dividend in lieu of a cash dividend, the per share market price of the stock would be expected to go down, but the investor's total investment in the company would remain unchanged. This can be illustrated by an example of an investor holding 50 shares in the company in the example above. Originally, the investment was equal to Rs. 2,000. With a 10 per cent stock dividend, the per share price should drop from Rs. 40 by (1 – 1.00/1.10), or Rs. 3.63. there would be a new market price of Rs. 36.37, but when multiplied by his total new holdings of 55 shares, his total value is still Rs. 2,000. Under these circumstance, the issuance of a stock dividend has no effect on the value of holdings in the corporation.

The second effect is that the stock dividend can be of value to an investor when it is issued in addition to a prior cash dividend. Under these circumstances the total cash dividends to be received will increase, due to the increased number of shares held by the stockholder.

For the company issuing the stock dividend, there are two primary reasons it is done. First, the stock dividend may be issued to conserve cash, while still appeasing the investors' need for dividends. This can be done to take advantage of investment opportunities by retaining a larger per cent of annual earnings, which would reduce the dividend payout ratio and resulting cash dividend. Another possibility would be that the corporation may be in a liquidity crisis and needed to conserve cash to pay outstanding obligations.

The second reason for the company to issue a stock dividend would be to help reduce the price of the stock and make it more attractive to investors. Many feel that there is a reasonable trading range for stock, and if the price substantially exceeds that range the trading activity may decline. For some companies this range is around Rs. 60, and a stock dividend may be necessary to bring the per share price back to this acceptable trading range.

One of the great disadvantages of stock dividends is that with periodic small stock dividends, investment analysts do not always adjust the earning per share figure. They adjust only for significant stock dividends or stock splits. Therefore, earnings per share for the year a dividend is issued will be higher than they should be. In the future, when earnings growth is measured, the growth rate will be less using the unadjusted earnings as the base point than if the earnings had been adjusted. This could have the effect of creating a downward bias in the price-earnings multiple, or P/E ratio.

Stock Splits

In a stock split, the number of shares is increased as with a stock dividend, but there is a proportional reduction in the par value and the price of the stock. In the preceding example, assume that there is a two-for-one split. Initially, the capital structure was:

Common stock (Rs. 10 par value, 800,000 shares)	Rs. 8,000,000
Capital surplus	4,000.000
Retained earnings	20,000,000
New Worth	32,000,000

After the two-for-one split, the capital structure would be:

Common stock (Rs. 5 par value, 1,600,000 shares)	Rs. 8,000,000
Capital surplus	4,000,000
Retained earnings	20,000,000
New Worth	32,000,000

With a stock split, only the data in parentheses for the common stock account changes. In this case, the par value was cut in half and the total number of shares outstanding was doubled. As with the stock dividend, the total value of new worth remains the same. Though the accounting treatment of the two is different the effect of increasing the number of shares is the same. The stock split is generally used to substantially increase the number of outstanding shares when management wants to reduce the per share market price. It is generally accepted that anything greater than a 25 per cent increase in the outstanding number of shares is considered a stock split, and anything under the 25 per cent figure is a stock dividend.

As with a stock dividend, the stock split does not change the total value of the holdings of the shareholder. However, in large splits the corporation may decrease the per share dividend. In many instances, this decrease in the per share dividend will still mean that the total cash dividends received by an investor will remain unchanged or possibly even increase in total cash value. For example, if the holder had 50 shares and previously received a Re. 1 dividend but with a two-for-one split would receive a 60 paise dividend, the total cash value of the dividends would increase from Rs. 50 to Rs. 60.

The biggest positive factor for the investor when a stock split occurs is that once the stock is brought back to a reasonable trading range, more interest may be generated in it, and the price could start to climb back to the price level experienced prior to the split. This was the experience frequently for holders of IBM stock throughout the 1960s.

One recent study attempted to measure the influence of the stock dividend or split on the market price of the stock in a more exact fashion. The goal was to see if there was measurable informational content about the future price performance of the stock and if information on the market period, size of the new distribution, and the terminology describing the new distribution explained related stock price movements. One of the major conclusion was that the firm should relate the costs of the distribution to the firm and shareholders very carefully before they initiate new stock distribution in excess of 20 per cent. The results of the study indicated that stock prices are not dramatically affected by such distribution, whether they are in the form of splits or dividends, and the type of market (bull, bear, or no change) did not affect this conclusion.

RESIDUAL THEORY OF DIVIDEND POLICY

This part of the chapter provides an insight into some of the theory that has been developed concerning the interrelationship between the payment of dividends, the retention of earnings, and the value of the firm.

Development Technique

The residual theory of dividend policy implies that the dividend decision should be made after the investment alternatives have been selected. It is in essence a summary of the section on capital structure in the sense that it incorporates the concepts of average cost of capital, incremental cost of capital, and the marginal efficiency of investment curves to make the investment, financing, and dividend decisions of the firm simultaneously.

The premise upon which the theory is based is the logical relationship existing between the firm's investment opportunities and the investment opportunities of the individual stockholders. If the firm can earn a rate of return that is greater than what the individual investor would earn if the earnings were paid out in dividends, then it would be to the advantage of the investor for the firm to retain all of the earnings for reinvestment purposes. If the individual had investment opportunities greater than the rate of return the firm could earn on reinvested earnings, then the firm should pay out all the earnings in the form of dividends. If the rate of return for the firm and the rate of return for the individual stock-holder were the same, then the investor should be indifferent between dividends and earnings retained by the firm. These three situations can be summarized as follows:

If $r > k$, then investors prefer retention of earnings by the firm.

If $r < k$, then investors prefer that earnings be paid in the form of dividends.

If $r = k$, then investors are indifferent between dividends and reinvested earnings.

In these statements r is equal to the rate of return that the firm can expect to earn on its assets, and k represents the required rate of return or the rate of return that the individual investor can earn elsewhere for the same degree of risk. Thus they demonstrate how the firm can maximize the value of the individual shareholder. If management distributes the earnings where they will derive the most benefit in the eyes of the investor, and if the investor accepts the above logic, then the value of the stock will be maximized.

The first step in developing the residual dividend is to utilize the concept of the weighted average cost of capital to establish an optimal capital structure—debt and equity mix—for the firm so that it can operate at the minimum point on its average cost of capital curve. This establishes an optimal debt ratio the firm will use as a guide when it undertakes new financing; it will raise the funds in that proportion of debt and equity.

Utilizing information developed on the average cost of capital, we can take an example and find its optimal capital structure and average cost of capital curve (Figure 1) To map out the average cost of capital curve, we are not given the component cost information but rather the cost of capital relationships between debt and equity. Assume that, in fact, the optimal amount of debt in the capital structure which will allow the firm to operate on the minimum point of its average cost of capital curve is 40 per cent. If it needs to raise additional financing for investment projects, the firm would want to raise the funds in the proportion of 40 per cent debt and 60 per cent equity.

The second step is to develop a weighted incremental cost of capital curve that can be utilized as an investment cutoff point.

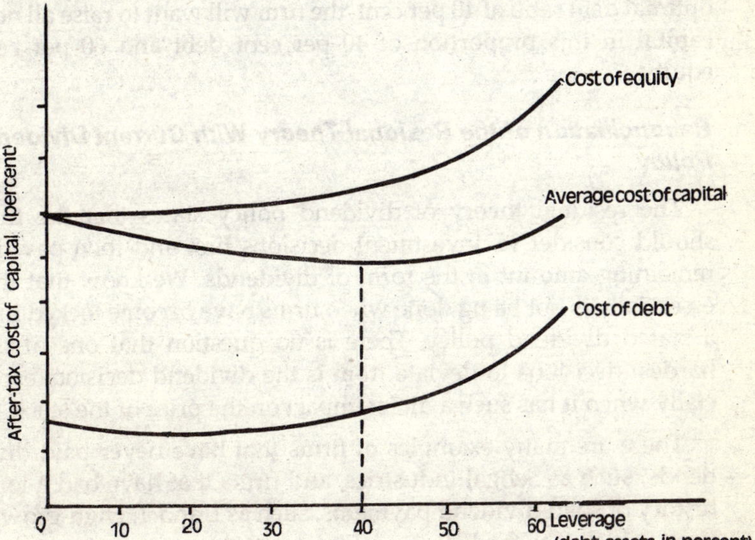

Fig. 1. Average Cost of Capital

Earlier we observed that as long as the firm operates at its optimal capital structure, and as long as it uses projected earnings that would go into retained earnings as the equity source of capital, the weighted incremental cost of capital will be constant. Also, the weighted incremental cost of capital will be equal to the minimum average cost of capital because all new capital is raised in the optimal debt to equity proportion.

If the firm raises more equity capital beyond the projected earnings amount that would go into retained earnings, it must issue more common stock, and the cost curve will rise. This is because the cost of external equity, or issuing new common stock, is higher than the cost of internal equity, or retained earnings.

The third step is to bring into the analysis the investment array schedule that the firm has developed for the next three years. The firm has considered numerous investment opportunities for this period and has used the internal rate of return technique of ranking investment alternatives.

The fourth step is to bring the three concepts together and demonstrate how the dividend decision becomes a residual decision. Assume that the firm has Rs. 75 million from projected earnings available for investment purposes. With knowledge of the optimal debt ratio of 40 per cent, the firm will want to raise all new capital in this proportion of 40 per cent debt and 60 per cent equity.

Reconciliation of the Residual Theory With Current Dividend Policy

The residual theory of dividend policy states that the firm should consider its investment decisions first and then pay the remaining amount in the form of dividends. We know that this essentially is not being done when firms have become locked into a stated dividend policy. There is no question that one of the hardest decisions to deviate from is the dividend decision, especially when it has such a direct impact on the price of the stock.

There are many examples of firms that have never paid dividends, such as Sehgal Industries, and firms that have had a long history of solid dividend payments, such as L and T. High-growth firms which face the IRR_1 investment schedule often were started under the express assumption of not paying dividends.

What would happen to a firm such as L and T if it decided to substantially cut its dividends to take advantage of investment opportunities? The price of the stock would drop. Investors would want to sell not only because they would not be receiving dividends, but also because of the strong feeling that dividends reveal something about future expected earnings. If dividends decline, then the expectations are that future earnings may do so also.

Investors have different reasons for investing in corporations. Some invest in growth firms for capital gains, realizing that dividends will not be paid for a long time. Other people invest in firms that pay large dividends and thus provide a definite income stream. In the middle are people who invest for both a dividend stream and a capital gains yield.

If a corporation undertook a substantial revision in its dividend policy, there would probably be a shift from one type of corporate investor to another. For example, if a corporation which had paid a substantial dividend decided to reduce it and conform more to the residual dividend policy, shareholders who wanted nothing more than dividend income would sell their stock. People who were afraid that the decrease in dividends meant a decrease in future earnings would also sell. The immediate effect would be a decrease in the price of the stock. However, as other investors saw that the firm was utilizing this money to make profitable investments which would be reflected in higher future earnings per share, they would invest in the firm's stock to receive both a dividend yield and the potential of capital gains. Thus, a shift would occur from share-holders who are purely dividend oriented to those who are satisfied with a lower dividend yield and the potential for some capital appreciation.

The same thing would happen if a corporation which had paid zero dividends changed to a substantial dividend payout policy. Many investors would infer from this that the company did not have good investment prospects, and the growth in earnings per share could not be maintained. This could lead to a decrease in the P/E ratio and the price of the stock. These investors would probably sell their stock and look for other companies with high growth prospects. However, other investors would invest in the firm because it would now fit their investment qualifications.

A price decline will occur in both instances. The real question is whether a firm can withstand the price decrease and wait until the investor shift is completed and the stock again rebounds. This especially is a problem when the firm has to go to the equity market for more funds. It would not want to issue new common stock if the price were substantially depressed. Once a dividend policy is established, it is difficult for a firm to increase or decrease the dividend, considering the price consequences that would result.

CONFLICT IN THE THEORIES ON DIVIDEND POLICY

Over the past several years, a substantial argument has developed in the academic literature on dividend policy concerning the relevance of dividends in determining the value of a company's stock. These agruments have been centralized into two basic factions. One believes that the risk associated with expected dividend payments is much less than that associated with the capital gains that would result from the retention of earnings. Their analysis suggests that the earnings stream of firms with a low dividend payout factor will be capitalized at higher rates than those that pay out a larger percentage of their earnings in the form of dividends.

Merton. H. Miller and Franco Modigliani hold a different view of the value of dividends. They feel that investors should be indifferent between returns distributed in the form of dividends or of capital gains; the value of the firm is based solely on the earning power of its assets, and the way the earnings stream is divided is not of significance. They believe that changes in dividend policy reflect changed expectations about future earnings. Any change in the price of the stock is caused by the informational content dividends can convey about future expected earnings.

Many of the empirical tests that have been employed to prove one or the other theory are subject to a number of statistical biases. Most studies, however, do seem to indicate that there is a relationship between the dividend payout factor and the value of the firm. Since no conclusive empirical test has yet been made, the two sides assume different positions in arguing about which factors make dividends relevant or not relevant. Some feel that dividends have less uncertainty attached to them than retained earnings, but the preference for dividends may be offset by the higher tax bracket associated with dividend payments. Others feel that the lower uncertainty associated with dividends is the dominant factor.

The importance of dividends versus capital gains as related to the value of the firm may in reality be an individual decision. Because of the different assumptions as to the stockholder's tax status and preference or need for current income, it is very difficult to make generalizations. Given these individual investor differences, plus the different investment opportunity sets of firms, the construction of an optimal dividend policy can be expected to vary considerably from firm to firm.

10

BUSINESS COMBINATIONS

THE goal structure of a firm is essentially based on maximizing the wealth of the shareholders. The means used to achieve this goal is growth, and the firm has the option of either internal or external growth. This chapter will discuss the opportunities of growing externally through business combinations. The financial manager must be able to analyze a prospective combination in order to evaluate its desirability in relationship to the goals of the firm. Because of the complexity of combinations, he or she must be familiar with not only the financial aspects but also the accounting and legal factors involved. Assistance should be sought from professional such as attorneys and CPAs in order to ensure success.

NATURE OF BUSINESS COMBINATION

Businessmen generally use the term *merger* in describing a business combination, although technically there are several different kinds. A merger is a combination of two or more firms in which one firm is fused into the other. The acquired form loses its corporate existence, and the surviving firm obtains all assets and liabilities. This is distinguishable from a consolidation, in which two or more firms combine to form a totally new corporation. Both old firms cease to exist. Generally, firms of about the same size will consolidate, whereas firms of significantly different size will merge.

Several other terms often used in considering business combinations are *parent-subsidiary* and *acquisition.* A parent-subsidiary relationship exists when two or more firms remain in operation as legal entities even though one is owned by the other. Acquisition refers to a situation where the identity of the acquired firm is not maintained, usually following a purchase.

In order to simplify the discussion, the term *business combination* will be used in describing external growth.

Reasons for Business Combinations

There are many reasons, both business and personal, why external expansion is attractive to firms. Growth itself creates larger size and opportunities for *economies of scale.* External expansion also provides growth very quickly and possibly at less cost. Because production capacity, product lines, and marketing outlets are already developed, there is assurance of an immediate income flow. Time costs and research costs are avoided, as well as the competitive battle to secure a market share.

If a firm is able to achieve operating economies through a merger, a synergistic effect occurs whereby the combined companies are worth more than the sum of their parts. This is often referred to as the two-plus-two-equals-five effect. If a firm acquires another firm in the same industry, operating economies can result from the consolidation of duplicated facilities in the marketing, research, purchasing, and administrative areas. For example, operating economies can be achieved in a merger between two airlines simply by eliminating the duplication of existing facilities and runs. In an industrial company, synergism can occur not only with the elimination of the duplicated facilities but also with a rounding out of the product line in the hopes of increasing the total demand for the products of both companies.

Arguments have been advanced that the only true justification for a merger is to achieve operating economies when the objective of the firm is to maximize the wealth of the shareholders. It is contended that the other benefits associated with mergers can be achieved by investors on their own. Conglomerate mergers—a merger of two companies in unrelated product lines—are especially singled out as examples of mergers that lack economic justification, unless it is clearly illustrated that the acquiring company can manage the assets of the acquired company in a more productive fashion. In the absence of operating economies, the only other reasons that can justify a merger are imperfections in the capital markets or irrational behavior on the part of the investors.

External expansion results in *management acquisition*. Qualified, aggressive management is often hard to find, and combination can provide this essential ingredient with a minimum of problems. Combination also leads to diversification and a reduction of risk. Expansion can reduce earnings instability by opening up new areas and strengthening present lines. Since the acquired firm is already producing, their is less risk of loss, and the larger a firm becomes, the better able it is to absorb the risks of future expansion.

Business combination might be the *necessary alternative to achieve growth*. Internal growth might be too slow, and similar facilities might be impossible to duplicate because of the patents, processes, and people involved. External expansion might also be *necessary for proper financing*. Stock may be accepted more readily by a selling firm than by the general investing public. In addition, combination with highly liquid firms allow a business to grow even further by utilizing this liquidity.

Business combinations *improve the value of securities*. Larger, growing firms have earnings capitalized at lower rates, which produces higher market values. The stocks have better marketability, thus reducing risk and allowing for a higher price-earnings ratio. Taxes also influence external growth. Acquiring a firm with a tax loss carry forward can prove to be very beneficial, since it can be used to reduce present tax liability. In addition, inheritance and estate tax pressures can be relieved by the more marketable nature of a larger firm's securities.

Personal reasons influence the desire for external expansion. Owners might gain a large profit from a business combination, as well as further power and prestige. In addition, an owner of a firm who is retiring might want not only to see the firm carry on but also to obtain a more marketable security.

Types of Combinations

There are basically three types of corporate growth—horizontal, vertical, and conglomerate. Horizontal combination involves two or more firms in the same type of production or in marketing the same product. The firm is basically enlarged, allowing for economies of scale since duplicate facilities can be eliminated. Also a broader product line can be offered.

Vertical growth involves two or more firms in different stages of marketing or production of a single product. The combination moves forward to combine with a consumer of the product or backward to combine with a supplier. Economies are realized by controlling purchasing and distribution.

The danger in both horizontal and vertical growth is that it is centered on the same product and is subject to the same business and cyclical fluctuations. Conglomerate growth involves two or more firms whose products are not related. Such diversification broadens the product base, reduces risk, and balances cyclical fluctuations. Management problems can arise, however when firms in unfamiliar fields are combined.

Combination Procedures

A business combination should not be rushed into. Like any large investment, it requires careful planning and analysis. In the first step the firm determines clear corporate objectives and evaluates its own strengths and weaknesses. This is necessary in order to establish its long-range goals and the criteria to meet them. The firm will save a great deal of time and money by knowing just where external expansion fits into its plans.

After criteria are established to determine the type of firm needed, a careful search must be made for the right firm. an appraisal must be made of the firm to determine its suitability. Attorneys, accountants, and business consultants should be called in to assist in the analysis and negotiations. Management, especially top executives, should participate in the negotiations, and the board of directors should be kept well informed. The board must ratify the final plan, after which it is submitted to the stockholders for their approval. Once the required percentage approves, the combination can take place after the appropriate papers of incorporation are filed with the state.

Dissenting shareholders can contest the price paid for their stock, in a combination. A suit can be filed, and the court will establish the fair market price for the shares. Since this payment must be in cash, a large number of dissenting shareholders can create a significant cash drain on the firm. These problems provide an incentive to make the original offer very attractive in order to minimize dissent.

Another potential problem which must be considered carefully throughout the negotiations is the impact of federal antitrust laws on the combination. This subjected is discussed more fully in the Appendix to this chapter. Tremendous costs are involved in challenging an antitrust case, and it is preferable if antitrust problems are foreseen.

TERMS OF A BUSINESS COMBINATION

Earnings

Since the goal of a firm is to maximize the long-run wealth of the existing shareholders, as we have often stated, business combinations should result in an increase in the market price of the stock. Market values are determined by future earnings and dividends, but since future values are difficult to predict, investors, shareholders, and manàgement consider the impact of the combination on present earnings per share as particularly significant.

To illustrate the impact on earnings, suppose the relevant data for two firms interested in a business combination were:

	Company X	*Company Y*
Total earnings	Rs. 100,000,000	Rs. 40,000,000
Shares outstanding	10,000,000	5,000,000
Earnings per share	10	8
Market price	160	160
P/E ratio	16	20

Company X plans to purchase company Y by exchanging stock for stock. The ratio of exchange will be based on the market price of the two securities; in this case these are equal, so it will be 1:. The impact of the combination on earnings per share (EPS) is shown below.

	Shares owned after merger	EPS	
		Before	After
Company X shareholders	10,000,000	Rs. 10.00	Rs. 9.33
Company Y shareholders	5,000,000	8.00	9.33
	15,000,000		

Total earnings of Rs. 140 million with new shares outstanding of 15 million yields an EPS of Rs. 9.33. Thus Company Y's shareholders experience an accretion, while Company X's shareholders face a slight dilution. The effect on the future stock price is dependent on earnings and the P.E multiple. The P.E multiple is less certain to predict, since it is dependent on the growth in earnings, risk in earnings, money supply, interest rates, market multiplier, investor confidence, and an industry effect. If the P/E jumped to 20, the new stock price of Rs. 186.60 would benefit all shareholders. If it remained at 16, the new price of Rs. 149.28 would benefit none of the shareholders. Generally, even though stockholder wealth is of primary interest, the difficulty of accurately predicting the stock market price means negotiations will concentrate most heavily on the impact on earnings per share.

The preceding example assumed a 1:1 exchange ratio. Suppose the market price for Company X was Rs. 160 but for company Y it was only Rs. 80. This would yield an exchange ratio of 1:2, or two shares of Y stock for one share of X stock. Further assume that the earnings for Company Y are only Rs. 20 million. the effect on earnings would then be slightly different;

	Shares owned after merger	EPS		
		Before	After	Relative
Company X shareholders	10,000,000	Rs. 10.00	Rs. 9.60	Rs. 9.60
Company Y shareholders	2,500,000	4.00	9.60	4.80
	12,500,000			

The important point is that the new earnings per share after the merger must be put on a relative basis which takes into account the exchange ratio. This will permit an accurate comparison to be made.

If the business combination in the initial example were to be determined on an exchange ratio based on earnings rather than market prices, the relative earnings position of each set of shareholders would remain unchanged, as shown below;

	Shares owned after merger	*EPS*		
		Before	*After*	*Relative*
Company X shareholders	10,000,000	Rs. 10.00	Rs. 10.00	Rs. 10.00
Company Y shareholders	4,000,000	8.00	10.00	8.00
	14,000,000			

When the exchange ratio is based on earnings, the ratio is 8:10, or Company Y shareholders receive eight new shares for every ten of their old shares ($8/10 \times 5,000,000 = 4,000,000$). New EPS is Rs. 10 per share, but Y shareholders only hold eight tenths as many shares. Therefore, on a relative basis, their EPS has remained unchanged.

Most frequently, the exchange ratio for a business combination will be based on market share value as shown in the first two examples. Unless the firms are similar, the combination will create both an accretion and a dilution in earnings per share for the firms involved. In the first example, company X shareholders had an EPS of Rs. 10 before the merger and only Rs. 9.33 after the merger. The resulting dilution of 67 paise was caused by an increased number of shareholders sharing a relatively smaller total earnings. Company Y shareholders experienced the opposite effect of accretion from the same transaction; EPS went from Rs. 8 to Rs. 9.33. If a firm only considered this initial impact on EPS, the accept-reject decision for a combination would turn solely on the question of accretion or dilution. This however does not take into account the future growth of earnings created by the combination. Earnings growth rates will be different for each firm before the merger. If Company Y had a higher growth rate than Company X, the latter might be willing to accept an initial earnings dilution in order to benefit from future higher earnings caused by a higher growth rate. The growth rate for the combination can be estimated as the weighted average of the individual firm's growth rates, with the weights based on earnings contribution.

To continue the initial example, assume that company X has a compound annual earnings growth rate, (G_e) of 8.2 per cent, while this rate for company Y is 31.8 per cent. The weighted growth rate for the combination can be calculated as follows:

	Earnings	*Percentage*	G_e	*Weighted*
Company X	Rs. 100,000,000	71.47	8.27	5.857
Company Y	40,000,000	28.6	31.8	9.10
	Rs. 140,000,000	1007		14.957

The shareholders for Company X suffer an initial dilution from Rs. 10 to Rs. 9.33 per share, but the earnings growth rate increases from 8.2 per cent to 15 per cent.

This relationship can be graphed (Figure 1) in order to show how many years it will take for shareholders of company X to benefit from this higher growth rate in earnings. The longer the duration of dilution, the less favorable a combination appears during negotiations. A similar analysis can be made from the viewpoint of company Y shareholders. There would be an initial earnings accretion from Rs. 8 to Rs. 9.33, but because of a lower growth rate, after a period of years dilution would result.

This relationship between earnings and growth rates is also important because of the impact on the future P/E ratio. A higher growth rate in earnings is one variable which will increase the P/E multiple and therefore increase the price of the stock. The critical elements in a combination therefore are the size of each firm's earnings, their earnings growth rate, their P/E ratios, and the exchange ratio. The first three elements are factors which cannot be changed. The fourth element, the exchange ratio, is the key bargaining element which is manipulated by both parties during the negotiations.

Other Quantitative Considerations in Determining Terms

There are other quantitative considerations in determining the terms for a business combination. *Dividends* represent the actual income received b6y the shareholders. However, the dividend decision should be kept separate from the combination decision. Future earnings are the key variable. Altering the dividend payout ratio can be used to make the offer more attractive, but care must be taken to ensure that such a change would not jeopardize the

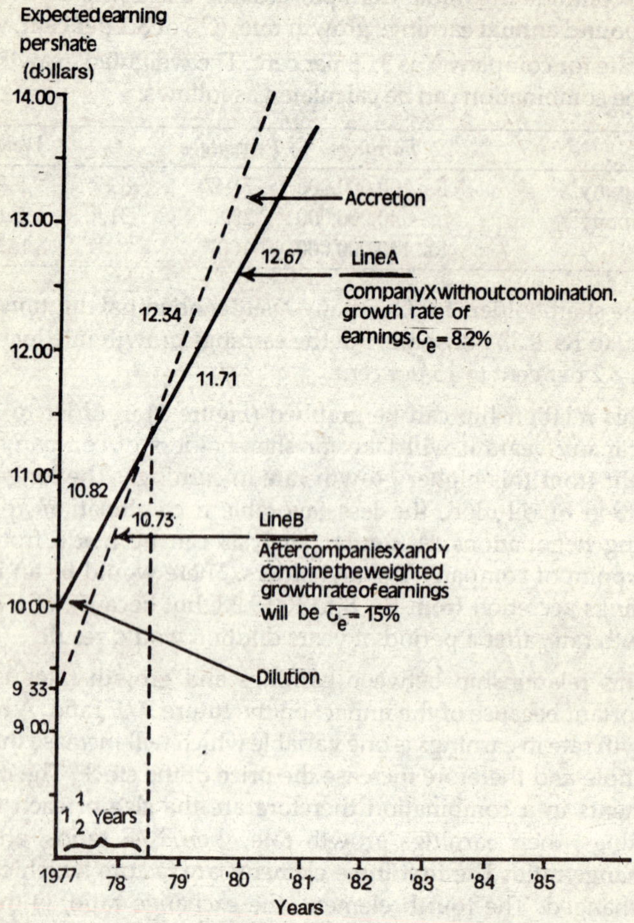

Fig. 1. Projected Earnings per Share, with and without merger for Company X

stockholders' wealth. Generally, the more growth oriented a firm is, the less is the role dividends will play.

The *market value* of the common stock, along with *earnings per share,* are the two major concerns in planning the terms of a business combination. Market value helps establish the exchange ratio to be used. It is felt that the price of a firm's stock represents the intrinsic value of the firm, combining the earnings potential, dividend future, and risk associated with that firm. One problem which must be considered is that if an exact exchange ratio based on stock price is used, there is no immediate incentive for the shareholders of the acquired firm to accept. Therefore, the exchange rate will often be increased in order to account for either an added incentive or an additional value to the assets if the stock is underpriced.

The market price and exchange ratio also influence the P/E multiple. If both firms are large, there will be less of an impact on the P/E ratio than if one is large and the other small. If there is one high P/E ratio and one low P/E ratio, the combination can prove especially advantageous, since EPS will increase for one firm and market value should increase for the other. Because of this relationship between market value and earnings, firms can grow and increase stockholder wealth solely by combinations. However, the test of success is in utilizing and managing the new combination in order to maintain the improved value.

Two other factors do not have very much importance in business combinations, although they are often discussed. *Book value* per share represents the historical investment value in the firm. Generally, this value is far below the current value, but if it happens to be above the market value, it might be a better indicator of the actual value of the firm. Proper management could realize the true earning potential of the assets, which indicates that the market value is underpriced. The other factor is the *net current asset* or *working capital* per share figure. This plays a more important role in determining the terms of a combination when the element of liquidity is of particular importance. A firm with excess liquidity or borrowing power is particularly attractive to a firm in need of liquidity. The liquidity ratio can give the analyst a feeling for this extra advantage in situations where it constitutes the reason for the combination.

Qualitative Consideration in Determining Terms

Although earnings per share and market value are the two most important determinants of the terms of a combination, they are not the only factors considered. There are qualitative factors surrounding a combination which make it more or less attractive. Many of these factors have already been discussed. Factors such as operating economies can be quantified to some degree, but others, such as improved management, expanded product line and sales expertise, and reduced risk cannot be assigned a value.

The desired result of any combination is to create a synergistic effect. Synergism refers to the fact that the two firms, when combined, generate a greater profit than the sum of profits if the firms had remained separate. Economies of scale and better management can reduce costs, while a broader product line, new technology, and a more efficient marketing system can increase the profit margin. A sounder firm will generate lower risks and higher market values.

The bargaining process during negotiations seeks to reach the best combination of both the quantitative and qualitative factors. Each party will be seeking the best price plus the best strategy for running the new combination. Management must understand the interrelationships among all of these variables in order to optimize the synergistic effect as well as to create an attractive enough offer to assure the combination will take place.

ACCOUNTING FOR A BUSINESS COMBINATION

The completion of a business combination results in a new firm. The financial statements must follow the regulations of the Securities and Exchange Commission, which are based on the recommendations of the professional accounting community. Opinions 16 and 17 issued by the old Accounting Principles Board provide the accounting framework for business combination. Essentially two accounting methods are available—pooling of interest, and purchase. Each has its distinctive characteristics.

Pooling of Interest

In order to be classified and handled as a pooling of interest, a firm must meet six requirements.

1. The acquired firm's stockholders maintain an ownership position in the surviving firm.
2. The basis for accounting for the assets of the acquired entity is unchanged.
3. Independent interests are combined; each entity has had autonomy for two years prior to the initiation of the plan to combine; no more than 10 per cent ownership of voting common stock is held as inter-corporate investments.

4. The combination is effected in a single transaction; contingent payouts are not permitted in poolings but may be used in purchases.
5. The acquiring corporation issues only common stock with rights identical to its outstanding voting common stock in exchange for substantially (90 per cent) all of the voting common stock of the other company.
6. The combined entity does not intend to dispose of a significant portion of the assets of the combining companies within two years after the merger.

The key to a pooling of interest is that substantially all of the ownership interests (which includes both debt and equity owners) of the firms engaged in the business combination will continue their ownership interests in the new firm. This continuity of ownership means that no economically significant change has resulted from the combination. The owners are the same, the assets are unchanged, and the tax basis for the assets is the same.

To account for a pooling of interest, the two balance sheets are simply added together, no matter whether the purchase price was above or below the book value. Since there must be continuity of ownership, the combination cannot be paid for with cash.

Firms favor a pooling of interest treatment because its accounting treatment does not influence future earnings per share as a purchase does. Goodwill is not considered in the accounting procedure. In the past, the one disadvantage to a pooling was the potential distortion of earnings caused by a sale of assets after a combination for higher than their book value. This problem has essentially been solved by the requirement that assets may not be sold for at least two years after the combination.

To demonstrate the pooling-of-interest concept, consider the combination of Company X and Company Y. Table 22-1 shows the pre- combination balance sheets of the two firms, along with other financial data which has been presented before. Based on market share price, the exchange ratio would be 1:1 or 15,000,000 new shares for Company XY. At a price of Rs. 160 per share, the total market value is Rs. 800 million. Assuming that this combination meets each of the six requirements, the new firm, XY, would have a balance sheet which consists of the sum of the two individual balance sheets. (See Table 2).

Table 1

Percombination Financial Data (in thousand)

	Company X	*Company Y*
Current assets	400,000	225,000
Fixed assets	600,000	375,000
Total Assets	1,000,000	600,000
Current liabilities	150,000	100,000
Long-term debt	250,000	100,000
Common stock, Rs. 10 par	100,000	50,000
Capital surplus	300,000	250,000
Retained earnings	200,000	100,000
Total Liabilities and Net Worth	1,000,000	600,000
Total earnings	100,000	40,000
Shares outstanding	10,000	5,000
Earnings per share	10	8
Market price	160	160
P/E ratio	16	20

Since the exchange ratio is on a 1 : 1 basis, there are no changes to the capital accounts. If the exchange ratio for some reason had been otherwise, say 2 : 1, there would be a change in the capital accounts. With a 2 : 1 ratio for Company Y, shareholders would receive two shares for each of theirs, or a total of 10,000,000 new shares. Company X shareholders would also receive 10,000,000 shares if their exchange ratio were 1 : 1, so total shares would be 20,000,000. At a par of Rs. 10, the common stock account must be Rs. 200 million. Since the two accounts only sum to Rs. 150 million, the additional Rs. 50 million must come from capital surplus. this change is shown in Table 3 (the rest of the balance sheet is the same as in Table 2).

Table 2

Pooling Interests, Postcombination Financial Data (in thousand)

	Company XY
Current assets	Rs. 625,000
Fixed assets	975,000
Total Assets	Rs. 1,600,000
Current liabilities	Rs. 250,000
Long-term debt	350,000

	Company XY
Common stock, rs. 10 par	150,000
Capital surplus	550,000
Retained earnings	300,000
Total Liabilities and Net Worth	Rs. 1,600,000
Total earnings	Rs. 140,000
Shares outstanding	15,000
Earnings per share	Rs. 9.33

Table 3

Change in Capital Accounts (Pooling of interest)

	Company X	*Company Y*	*Change*	*Company XY*
Common stock, Rs. 10 par	Rs. 100,000	Rs. 50,000	+ Rs.50,000	Rs. 200,000
Capital surplus	Rs. 300,000	Rs. 250,000	– Rs. 50,000	Rs. 500,000

The effect on the market price (as described earlier) is much harder to predict than earnings. Also, the combination does create a dilution-accretion problem, but in addition other factors such as growth rates are determinants of acceptability. In fact, any business combination which uses market price to establish the exchange ratio and which has companies with different P/E ratios will experience the dilution-accretion effect.

Purchase

The second method for accounting for a business combination is known as a purchase. A purchase involves a combination in which all or substantially all of the ownership interest in at least one of the firms is eliminated. Cash or securities is generally the medium used in such a combination. A purchase ensures that the assets of the acquired firm will have new owners, and these new owners must consider the purchase of the assets as an investment. The assets must be fairly appraised so that the actual values of tangible assets are recorded. Care must be taken to adjust for undervalued inventories, overdepreciated assets, unrecorded patents, and similar misstatements.

The purchase price paid by the acquiring firm will very likely not equal this acquired net worth. Since the purchase is an investment, any difference must be accounted for. This difference between the purchase price and the adjusted book value is called *goodwill.*

Goodwill represents the amount paid by a firm to acquire the right to above-normal earning power. Many view goodwill as the value placed on a going concern with an earning history, and growth potential. The old Accounting Principles Board recommended that goodwill be written off over time against income, but not for a period longer than 40 years (2.5 per cent per year). This is the reason firms prefer pooling of interest over purchase accounting. For tax purposes, goodwill amortization is not deductible from earnings before tax. Therefore, it must be deducted after tax which reduces the reported income in the future years.

The example of Company X and Company Y will help illustrate the accounting effects of a purchase. Assume that X plans to buy Y with stock on a 1:1 basis (see Table 1). Company Y shareholders would thus receive 5,000,000 shares at Rs. 160 per share, or a total investment of Rs. 800 million. Also assume that the assets of Company Y are understated, and the assessed valuation is determined to be Rs. 300 million in current assets and Rs. 500 million in fixed assets. Since Company X is purchasing these assets, it will want to use the assessed valuation after the combination is complete. Company X is also assuming Company Y's liabilities of Rs. 200 million, so the net assets or book value of Company Y will be Rs. 600 million (total assets minus liabilities).

Table 4 shows the result of the business combination. The difference between the purchase price of Rs. 800 million and the book value of Rs. 600 million is the Rs. 200 million representing goodwill. Goodwill is included on the balance sheet as an intangible asset and will be amortized over time. If the purchase is by stock, appropriate adjustments must be made to Company X's capital accounts to reflect the increase in stock. In this case, 5,000,000 shares at Rs. 10, or Rs. 50 million, goes to common stock and 5 million shares at Rs. 150, or Rs. 750 million, goes to capital surplus.

Note that all accounts are not simply added together, as in a pooling of interest. The asset accounts must be adjusted in order to reflect their true assessed value. The liability accounts are added together if the firm is assuming all liabilities. The capital accounts reflect the change in the number of shares used for the purchase. If

Table 1

Purchase Accounting for A Business Combination (In Thousands)

	Company X	*Company Y*	*Adjustments to Company Y*	*Adjustments to Company X*	(1 + 4) *Company X after purchase*
Current assets	Rs. 400,000	Rs. 225,000	+ Rs. 75,000	+ Rs. 300,000	Rs. 700,000
Fixed assets	600,000	375,000	+ 125,000	+ 500,000	1,100,000
Goodwill	—	—	—	+ 200,000	200,000
Total Assets	Rs. 1,000,000	Rs. 600,000			Rs. 2,000,000
Current liabilities	Rs. 150,000	Rs. 100,000		+ 100,000	Rs. 250,000
Long-term debt	250,000	100,000		+ 100,000	350,000
Common stock, Rs. 10 par	100,000	50,000		+ 50,000	150,000
Capital surplus	300,000	250,000		+ 750,000	1,050,000
Retained earnings	200,000	100,000			200,000
Total Liabilities and Net Worth	Rs. 1,000,000	Rs. 600,000			Rs. 2,000,000
Total earnings	Rs. 100,000	Rs. 40,000		+ 40,000	Rs. 140,000
Shares outstanding	10,000	5,000		+ 5,000	15,000
Earnings per share	Rs. 10,00	Rs. 8,00			Rs. 9.33
Market per share	Rs. 160,00	Rs. 160,00			
P/E Ratio	16	20			

Purchase price = Rs. 800,000

Book Value of Assets (assessed) = 600,000

Goodwill = Rs. 200,000

cash were used, Company X's capital accounts would not change. The retained earnings accounts are *not* added together, Company X's retained earnings must remain unchanged, and Company Y's retained earnings become part of the addition to capital stock and paid-in surplus. This is based on the accounting concept that one company cannot increase its retained earnings by buying another. (Remember that in a pooling of interest the ownership interests continue so that retained earnings can be added.)

The impact on earnings—both dilution and accretion—is the same as previously discussed. Of course, if the purchase were by cash, the result would be an accretion for all parties involved. The impact on market price will be as uncertain as with a pooling.

TRANSACTING A BUSINESS COMBINATION

There are two ways a firm can acquire another in a business combination—by purchasing the assets or purchasing the stock. If the former method is used, cash or stock is used to acquire all or part of the assets of the other company. If all of the assets are acquired, the selling firm becomes merely a shell, with cash or stock as its only asset. It can then continue in existence and invest, or it can dissolve and pay a liquidating dividend. If only part of the assets is purchased, the selling firm remains in existence. Whether the buying firm uses cash or stock will have a significant income tax effect. The advantage to the purchase of assets is that it is easier. Only the board of directors of the buying firm need approve the purchase. Note, however, that the shareholders of the selling firm still need to give approval.

In a purchase of the common stock, the selling firm ceases to exist, and the surviving firm assumes all of the assets and liabilities. The use of cash or stock will present income tax considerations. Approval for such a purchase must be granted by both sets of shareholders.

HOLDING COMPANIES

To achieve a successful business combination, one firm does not always have to acquire 100 per cent ownership of another. A holding company is a firm which owns sufficient stock in other firms to have a controlling interest. Although at least 51 per cent ownership would seem necessary in reality only 10 to 20 per cent is required in large publicly held firms. This results from the wide distribution of stock. There are advantages and disadvantages similar to those in other forms of business combination, but the holding company technique also has some unique aspects.

One advantage is that a holding company can control by fractional ownership, which requires a significantly smaller investment. Also, a smaller price per share will generally be paid, and no approval from shareholders is required. A holding company can purchase the shares on the open market without creating the problems of negotiations, legal disputes, and management resistance. Another advantage is that each firm in the holding company is a legally separate operating unit. The firms are not legally interconnected, so obligations of one do not become obligations of the others. This tends to reduce the overall risk.

A major disadvantage concerns the multiple taxation of profits. The holding company receives dividends as income from the controlled firms. If 80 per cent or more of the stock is owned, the Internal Revenue Service will not tax the dividend and a consolidated return can be filed. If less than 80 per cent of the stock is owned, 85 per cent of the dividends can be deducted before tax, but 15 per cent is taxable. If the corporate tax rate is 48 per cent, the effective tax rate on total dividends is 7.2 per cent. Therefore, the holding company has to pay a partial tax, and the shareholders of the holding company have to pay tax on the dividends they receive. This results in double taxation of the same income.

Another major disadvantage to a holding company is the increased risk due to pyramiding. In pyramiding, a holding company controls firms which are themselves holding companies which control more firms. Due to its ability to control by partial ownership, the original firm at the top of the pyramid can control a tremendous amount of assets for only a very small investment. Suppose holding company. A owns 30 per cent of the stock of three holding companies, B, C, and D. Assume this 30 per cent is the controlling interest. Then suppose each of the three owned holding companies controls three operating firms by controlling 30 per cent of their stock. Because of pyramiding, the original firm. A controls the nine operating firms with an investment of only nine paise on a rupee (Re. $\times 0.30 \times 0.30 =$ Rs. 0.09).

By partial ownership. A has leveraged its position. As with all types of leverage, it is a double-edged sword. When the operating firms are profitable, the return to the shareholders of A will be greatly multiplied. However, when losses occur and dividends cannot be paid to the holding.

SUMMARY

A firm can grow by internal or external means. Business combination is a general term to describe the more specific types of combination of merger and consolidation. A merger is a combination of two or more firms, with one firm being fused into the other. A consolidation is a combination in which two or more firms form a totally new corporation, and both firms cease to exist alone. Firms of similar size usually consolidate, and those of different sizes usually merge. A parent-subsidiary relationship exists where both firms continue in separate existence but one owns the other.

There are many advantages to external expansion. Increased size can create economies of scale in operations. Combination can be done quickly and is less costly and can enable a firm to acquire top management. It can also lead to diversification and a reduction of risk as well as an improved securities positions. External growth might be the only avenue to expand, as well as the most profitable method. Taxes and personnel reasons also influence growth by business combination.

There are three types of growth—horizontal, vertical, and conglomerate. Horizontal combination involves two or more firms who produce or market the same product. Vertical combination involves two or more firms engaged in different stages of producing and marketing the same product. Conglomerate combination involves two or more firms whose products are unrelated.

Management must first evaluate its own goals, together with its own firm's strengths and weaknesses. Only then can a set of criteria be developed to analyze and evaluate a potential business combination. After negotiations have been conducted and a combination agreed upon, the board of directors must approve the plan, and then the stockholders must vote on it. Dissenting shareholders can file suit to contest the price paid for their stock. Management must at all times be aware of and plan for the antitrust implications present in all combinations.

A business combination will have an impact on earnings per share, in most cases creating some dilution or accretion. Although stockholder wealth is a long-run goal, it is very difficult to predict future earnings and future stock price accurately. Investors, shareholders, and management place particular significance, therefore, on the present impact to earnings.

Market price is most commonly used to determine the exchange value for the combination, since market value is thought to express the intrinsic value of the firm. When the P/E ratios of the firms involved differ, there will be an earnings accretion and dilution, This effect on earnings is not the only deciding element, however. A significant factor concerns the growth rate in earnings. One firm might be willing to accept an earnings dilution if an increased growth rate could be obtained. Other factors such as dividends, book value, and new asset values per share are usually not too important in determining the exchange ratio in a combination.

Quantitative factors must be weighted with qualitative factors in order to determine the final price during negotiations. All parties hope that a synergistic effect will result from the combination, producing a greater combined profit level than the firms could have achieved separately.

There are two accounting methods for a business combination—pooling of interest and purchase. Pooling of interest essentially adds the two balance sheets together and maintains the ownership interests. A purchase takes into account goodwill. Firms prefer a pooling of interest since with a purchase, goodwill must be amortized and deducted from future income on an after-tax basis, thereby reducing reported earnings.

A combination can be carried out by buying either the assets or the common stock. Both methods can utilize cash or stock for payment, which creates important tax problems. The seller prefers stock since it is a non-taxable transaction until the stock is sold; cash is immediately taxable. The buyer, however, prefers a cash purchase since it can raise the depreciable value of the assets and achieve a larger future tax shield.

An alternative to direct negotiations is a tender offer. A firm can by-pass the other firm's management by appealing directly to the stockholders to submit or tender their shares for a fixed price. The SEC requires a 30-day notice on a planned tender offer.

An alternative to owning another firm fully is to have partial ownership. a holding company, with as little as 10 or 20 per cent ownership, can control many operating firms. A pyramid can be established which will leverage the profits of the holding company. As with any leverage situation, however, it will magnify not only profits but losses.

11

BUSINESS FAILURE ANALYSIS AND REMEDIES

Failure is concept antithetical to business, yet its potential importance to the firm means the financial manager must be familiar with all of the alternatives available to counter financial problems. On one side, the financial manager of a going firm which extends credit must be aware of the Firm's rights and remedies regarding a debtor-customer who has experienced some form of financial difficulty. (Experience gained in collecting such debts becomes part of the information used to update a firm's accounts receivable management and credit policy). On the other side of the coin, no firm is entirely safe from the hazards of failure. The financial manager must be aware of the potential for failure and be able to deal with the many problems which arise out of financial difficulties. With legal assistance and a rational decision process the firm can foresee such problems and provide for them in furthering its goals.

OVERVIEW OF BUSINESS FAILURE

There are many definitions of failure in a business context; the meaning varies, depending on who is using the term and why. Economic failure can mean that the rate of return on investment is less than the firm's cutoff rate or is less than other similar investments. Economic failure can also mean that revenues do not cover costs, or the average return on investment is less than the firm's cost of capital.

The financial manager uses a definition of business failure which has two aspects, both of which relate to insolvency. Insolvency is inability of a firm to meet its current obligations. The first type of failure is called *technical insolvency,* or insolvency in the equity sense. Here the firm has a positive net worth position and assets are greater than liabilities, but because of illiquid assets and an inadequate cash flow, it cannot meet its current charges.

The second type of failure is called *insolvency in bankruptcy.* It represents the more severe situation where total liabilities exceed a fair valuation of total assets, and there is a negative net worth. The firm cannot fulfill its obligations in full no matter how liquid the assets. Although the layman usually associates failure with bankruptcy, the financial manager must recognize the problem as twofold and must be able to respond to both situations.

Causes of Failure

Most authorities agree that management is the major cause of financial failure. Dun and Bradstreet has found that in approximately 90 per cent of the cases, management inefficiency, in the from of lack of experience or incompetence, was the cause of failure. Other listed causes are neglect, fraud, and disaster. Of course, the causes of failure will vary within an industry. In addition to the above general classifications, the economic environment, excessive competition, investor expectations, credit conditions, and governmental regulations will also affect the failure or success of a firm.

Dun and Bradstreet has also found that new firm are more likely to fail. In 1969, approximately one third of the failures occurred within the first three years, 53 per cent within the first five years, and 77 per cent within the first ten years. Two of the probable reasons for this trend are a young firms inability to withstand competitive pressures and to meet the many financial and economic requirements in times of stress.

PREDICTION OF FAILURE

Financial failure, except in a catastrophe, does not happen overnight but is created by a gradual succession of poor management decisions. The financial manager, in either a creditor or a debtor situation, would like an early warning system which would make it possible to predict potential failure. Such a predictive modes could then be used to seek rational solutions to the difficulties. There is no magic crystal ball in any realm of financial management, since it operates in an environment of uncertainty, but some research has been done on the use of financial ratios to predict business failure.

William H. Beaver's 1966 study tested the predictive ability of 30 financial ratios on a sample of firms that had failed. His research revealed that the financial ratio with the best predictive ability was the cash flow to total debt ratio, and the second best ratio was net income to total assets. The ratios showed a tendency for deterioration several years in advance. Beaver also conducted research on the ability of changes in stock prices to predict failure and found that investors tend to adjust stock prices in relationship to the financial condition of the firms, based on the likelihood of failure as shown by ratio analysis.

A more recent study by Edward I. Altman utilized a multiple discriminate analysis to devise a predictive model of failure. Beginning with 22 financial ratios and a paired sample of bankrupt and non-bankrupt firms, Altman used a computer to choose the five ratios which, when considered together, not individually, provided the best predictive model. This model was found to be:

$$Z = .012X_1 + 0.14X_2 + .033X_3 + .006X_4 + .999X_5.$$

The five ratios used are as below in Equations:

$$X_1 = \frac{\text{Working capital}}{\text{Total assets}} \qquad \ldots(1)$$

Equation 1 is a relative measure of the net liquid assets of the firm, relative to the firm's total capitalization. A potentially failing firm experiencing losses will also probably be experiencing a disinvestment in current assets. This ratio was found to have more predictive value than the current or quick ratio. Of the five ratios in the model, it was found to be the least significant. (X_1 as a percentage, such as 10 per cent, is expressed as 10.0 in the model.)

$$X_2 = \frac{\text{Retained earnings}}{\text{Total assets}} \qquad \ldots(2)$$

Equation 2 is a cumulative measure of profitability over time. It is a ratio biased against younger firms, but statistics have also shown that younger firms have a higher propensity for failure. (Express X_2 as a percentage, such as 5 per cent, as 5.0 in the model.)

$$X_3 = \frac{\text{Earnings before interest and taxes}}{\text{Total assets}} \qquad \ldots(3)$$

Equation 3 is a measure of a firm's basic earning power on its asset base. Of the five ratios, it was found to be the most important. (Express X_3 as a percentage, such as 7 per cent, as 7.0 in the model.)

$$X_4 = \frac{\text{Market value of equity}}{\text{Book value of total debt}} = \frac{\text{Market value of all shares}}{\text{Current and long-term debt}} \qquad \ldots(4)$$

Equation 4 is the inverse of the familiar debt to equity ratio. It measures how much the firm's assets can decline in value before liabilities exceed assets. (Express X_4 as a percentage, such as 200 per cent, as 2.0 in the model.)

$$X_5 = \frac{\text{Sales}}{\text{Total assets}} \qquad \ldots(5)$$

Equation 5 is the familiar capital turnover ratio, which measures the ability of the assets to generate sales. By itself, the ratio has no predictive value, but in the model it was the second most important element. (Express X_5 as a factor, such as 200 per cent as 2.0 in the model.)

Altman applied his predictive model to a sample of companies and to a secondary, independent sample and found it to be a considerably accurate predictive tool within a two-year period before actual bankruptcy. He found that if $Z > 2.99$, the firm was clearly not going to fail. If $Z < 1.81$ the firm was going to go bankrupt. The area in between, $1.81 < Z < 2.99$, Altman called the "zone of ignorance", indicating that the model cannot accurately predict within this range. However, he felt that $Z = 2.675$ was as good a dividing line as possible.

The model was developed using older data on companies with assets between Rs. 700,000 and Rs. 25,900,000. Therefore it must be used with care in applying it to new situations. However, it did effectively demonstrate the potential for predicting failure. This implies that a similar model adapted to a firm's own industry can help the financial manager recognize a problem early enough so that preventive measures can be implemented.

There are several areas in which the model can be used. On the creditor side, the firm can use it in credit evaluation, loaning practices, and accounts receivable management. As a going concern, it can use the model in its investment and valuation analysis. The model can also be used as an internal predictive tool to foresee financial failure. Both large and small firms can use the advance warning to find a solution to the problem. This notice is particularly important for larger firms where merger is the only feasible solution. A merger must be consummated will before bankruptcy or liquidation in order to maintain some bargaining power and to gain the full tax advantages of a merger.

Although a predictive model will aid in recognizing possible failure, the financial manager must know the various remedies available and the advantages of each. The remedies range from a totally private voluntary solution to a court imposed, involuntary solution, with a full spectrum in between. The more privately and voluntarily the problem is handled, the lower the costs, in terms of both money and time. However, it is often impossible to reach a reasonable solution agreeable to all, and a firm must seek relief via legal assistance and possibly the court system.

Determining the Seriousness of Potential Failure

The financial manager must decide how serious the failure or potential failure is; a temporary insolvency situation will require less drastic measures than a total insolvency, for example. The valuation techniques discussed in Chapter 15 can then be used to aid the decision process. The going-concern value of the firm must be compared with liquidation value. The going- concer value consists essentially of the capitalized value of the firm's earning potential, and the liquidation value depends on the type of assets the firm has, the market for those assets, and the opportunity costs available for any funds generated by liquidation.

Generally, If the liquidating value exceeds the going-concern value, it will be in the best interest of the owners and creditors to liquidate. Of course, failure affects many other segments of the business environment, such as employees, customers, and suppliers. A quantitative valuation must be balanced with the qualitative effects of failure in a cost-benefit analysis. Time will always be a crucial variable throughout such an analysis.

VOLUNTARY SETTLEMENTS OF FINANCIAL PROBLEMS

After the financial manager has diagnosed the problem, whether from a creditor or debtor viewpoint, he or she must seek a solution through one of the available remedies. Initially, the various voluntary settlements should be considered, since they are usually quicker, less expensive, and, overall provide for a more harmonious process.

When potential failure faces a firm, the first thought is to preserve the firm and the management. If the financial manager's valuation analysis shows this is possible, then he or she can attempt to work out an internal, voluntary reorganization. Examples would range from a change in the firm's credit policy and current asset management principles to a debt re-adjustment and recapitalization. The latter, however, are longer-range solutions which take time to analyze and implement. The firm actually facing failure does not have this immediate option because of the lack of time.

Extension and Composition

Two voluntary remedies which can be supplemented quickly are extension and composition. Both are informal, out-of-court settlements which are governed by state law, but the financial manager should seek the assistance of counsel in applying either of these remedies. An *extension* extends the length of time creditors must wait for payment of their obligations. A *composition* consists of a voluntary agreement between the debtor and at least two creditors to reduce the creditor's claims and to accept a partial pro rata payment in full discharge of the total claim. Often creditors will agree to a combination of these two remedies.

In order to take advantage of these remedies, a firm generally must only be in temporary insolvency, and, most importantly, must be a basically sound firm with a high potential for recovery and future economic stability. Typically, the debtor will meet with the creditors to explain the difficulty and express the desire to work out a compromise. The major creditors will form a committee to work with the firm in developing an acceptable plan. Often, outside adjustment firms are brought in to assist in drawing up a plan. The plan, when finally agreed to and signed by all parties involved, becomes a binding contract. As part of the agreement, the creditors can initiate controls on the firm's management in order to ensure a proper recovery; they can even assume operating control of the firm if mismanagement presents too large a problem.

The advantages to a voluntary settlement are numerous. The proceeding is informal and held in a more congenial, compromising atmosphere. Creditors are often hesitant to press bankruptcy proceedings, since it would adversely influence their relationship with the debtor and their other customers. A voluntary proceeding is simpler to negotiate and understand, and the expenses are minimized. The creditor will typically get a higher return than in other proceedings, since many administrative and legal costs are avoided, and it has the advantage of maintaining close relations with a good customer.

The major disadvantage to both a voluntary extension and composition is that the agreement is in no way binding on any creditor who does not desire to participate. Obstinate creditors who withhold their consent to the plan can seek any other legal remedies and thus can jeopardize the success of the agreement. In practice, if only creditors holding a small amount of debt are holding out, the other creditors might agree to pay them off and avoid the nuisance. This means that the remaining creditors assume these obligations. Another potential problem is that the operating management of the firm is usually left in control after the agreement, thereby increasing the likelihood of renewed problems. However, creditors can develop controls as part of the agreement in order to protect their interest from mismanagement.

SUMMARY

Financial failure will affect almost all business firms, either as creditors trying to collect the credit extended or as debtors trying to meet their obligations. Failure comes in two forms, both related to inability to meet current obligations. In technical insolvency the firm cannot meet its debts because of illiquid assets and inadequate cash, but the firm's assets still exceed its liabilities. In insolvency in bankruptcy, total liabilities exceed assets. In both situations, the financial manager must be aware of the alternative remedies available and the procedures to follow in order to find a solution to the difficulty.

The primary cause of business failure is management, either through lack of experience or incompetence. Other direct causes of failure are neglect, fraud, and disaster. Several elements which also have a significant effect are the economic environment, competitive environment, and governmental regulations. Age has also proven to influence the probability of failure, with over three fourths of the failures occurring within the first ten years of a firm's existence.

Some research has indicated that a model based on financial ratios can be a very good predictive tool for business failure. Such a model can be used in credit evaluation, in investment analysis, and as an internal predictive tool to foresee financial failure. Being able to predict financial difficulties will ultimately help in avoiding failure.

When a firm is facing financial difficulties, a valuation of the firm must be made. A comparison between the going-concern value and the liquidation value will help determine which remedy to pursue. This is tempered by the qualitative costs to other segments of the business community, such as employees, customers, and suppliers.

If it is found advantageous to maintain the firm, management can seek either a judicial or nonjudicial solution, voluntarily or involuntarily. The more voluntary a solution is and the less the courts are used the quicker and less expensive the remedy will be. However, these easier alternative are often not a possibility because of other constraints. This is the primary reason an established procedural system has been set up to deal with failure.

To maintain the firm, two of the simplest solutions are extensions and compositions. An extension simply extends the length of time for payment of the debts, and a composition is an agreement by the creditors to accept less than total payment in full satisfaction. Neither procedure is binding upon creditors who do not agree to the plan.

The largest number of failures that reach the judicial stage result in liquidation and are handled as straight bankruptcies by the federal district court. The procedure, either voluntary or involuntary, is formal, costly, takes a very long time, and returns a relatively small amount, to the creditors. The advantages of the process are that it provides an orderly method to liquidate the assets of a failing firm, and it deals fairly with all creditors.

12

EMPLOYEES BENEFITS AND FINANCIAL PLANNING

INTRODUCTION

FINANCIAL management in a corporate enterprise is concerned with the Planning and Controlling of the firm's financial resources. The objective of employees are generally to maximise their benefits. The cost of the company is monetary one. The company can maximise benefits to employees only when the corporate objective is in harmony with their interest. The benefits to the employees are either statutory or as per customs of company. This study is concerned with the financial aspects of employees benefit. We discuss first the nature of statutory and customary benefits and the related financial aspects in the following paragraphs.

NATURE OF BENEFITS

Statutory Benefits

Law has made it obligatory upon the company to provide certain basic financial social security to all its employees ignoring the category, status and the class to which they belong. The following are the statutory benefits which in ordinary course of the corporate operations fall within the nature of regular costs, observing proper allocation of funds and financial arrangements.

Statutory benefits which accrue to an employee in corporate sector have been provided in the following statues:

1. Employees' Provident Funds and Family Pension Fund Act, 1952, and Employees' Family Pension Scheme, 1971.
2. Employees' State Isurance Act, 1948.
3. Facilities under the Factories Act, 1948.
4. Payment of Bonus Act, 1965.
5. Payment of Gratuity Act, 1972.
6. The Maternity Benefits Act, 1961.

The readers are supposed to have studied the main provisions of the above enactments in their intermediate course. Nevertheless, our chief concern here is to explain fully the benefits admissible to the employees which need to be given special treatment by a finance manager.

Employees' Provident Fund. An important consideration for the Finance Manager of a Corporate unit is to ensure that enough provision is made by the unit to meet the commitment of contribution under the Employees' Provident Fund Scheme framed under the Employees' Provident Funds and Miscellaneous Provisions act, 1952. The contribution payable by the employer under the Scheme is normally 8-1/3 per cent of the basic wage, dearness allowance (including any cash value of any food concession) and retaining allowance, if any, actually drawn during the whole months. In certain specified industries employing 50 or more persons the contribution payable by the employer is 10 per cent. In both cases, a matching contribution is to be paid by the employee. It is the responsibility of the employer to pay both the contribution payable by him and also in respect of the employees employed by him or through a contractor. The employer shall not be entitled to deduct the employee's contribution from the wage of a member or otherwise to recover it from him. The employer has the duty to deduct the employees contribution from his wages before paying the employee his wages and shall, together with his own contribution as well as an administrative charge of such percentage of pay for the time being payable to the employees other than an excluded employee, pay within fifteen days of the close of every month by separate Bank drafts or cheques to the fund. The employer is also duty bound to furnish to the Commissioner of Provident Fund within twenty days of the close of the month, a monthly consolidated statement showing recoveries made from the wages of each employee and the amount contributed by the employer is respect of each such employee.

Final Withdrawal. Full accumulations with interest thereon are refunded in the event of death, permanent disability, superannuation, retrenchment or migration from India for permanent settlement abroad/taking employment abroad, voluntary retirement etc. full accumulations with interest thereon are refunded in following cases also:

(*i*) Where a factory or other establishment is closed but certain employees who are not retrenched are transferred by the employer to other factory or establishment not covered under the Act;

(*ii*) Where a member is discharged and is given retrenchment compensation under the Industrial Disputes Act, (14 of 1947);

Table 1

Period of membership of the Fund	*Percentage of Employers' Contribution and interest thereon refundable*
Less than 3 years	25%
3 years or more but less than 5 years	50%
5 years or more but less than 10 years	75%
10 years or more	100%

Note: Now, with effect from 1.4.1990 full withdrawal of Employer's contribution is allowed in all above cases.

(*iii*) The Government of India have also directed that the Provident Fund accounts, should be settled immediately by payment of both the employee's and employer's share of contribution in full in respect of those members who cease to subscribe to the Fund as a result of an establishment going out of the purview of the Act under Section 16(1)(a) thereof. In other cases, the member's own share of contribution together with interest thereon is refunded along with the employer's contribution with interest thereon depending upon the length of membership as indicated below:

The Employees' Family Pension Scheme. In exercise of the powers converted by Section 6A of the Employees' Provident Funds and Miscellaneous Provisions Act, 1952, the Central Government has framed a Family Pension Scheme and brought it in operation with effect from the Ist March, 1971. No separate contribution are payable under the scheme by the employers' and the employees. However, out of the Provident Fund contributions a sum representing 1-1/6% of the employees' pay along with an equivalent amount of 1-1/6% is to be remitted by the employer by a separate Bank draft or cheque for credit into the Family Pension Fund. The cost of the remittance if any is to be borne by the employer. The Central Government also contributes @ 1-1/6% of the pay of the members of the Family Pension Fund. The term pay includes the basic wage, dearness allowance (including the cash value of any food concession) and retaining allowance, if any. All the moneys belonging to or standing to the credit of the Family Pension Fund account are kept in deposit with the Central Government in the Public Account (on which the Central Government allows interest).

Rate of family Pension is prescribed in paragraph 28 of the Employees' Family Pension Scheme, 1971 comprising the following ground rules:

(1) In the case of member who being a member of the Family Fund dies during the period of reckonable service before attaining the age of 60 years, family pension shall be paid at the rates specified in the Table 2 subject to the condition that he has contributed to the Family Pension Fund for a period of not less than 3 months.

Table 2

Pay of the member on which contribution to the family Pension Fund is payable	*Monthly rate of Family Pension*
Up to Rs. 300	Rs. 225 (Fixed)
Exceeding Rs. 300 but not exceeding Rs. 650	Rs. 275 (Fixed)

Pay of the member on which contribution to the family Pension Fund is payable	*Monthly rate of Family Pension*
Exceeding Rs. 650 but not exceeding Rs. 1200	40 per cent of pay subject to a minimum of Rs. 300 and a maximum of Rs. 450
Exceeding Rs. 1200 but not exceeding Rs. 1600	35 per cent of pay subject to a minimum of Rs. 450 and a maximum of Rs. 510.
Exceeding Rs. 1600	30 per cent of pay subject to a minimum of Rs. 510 and maximum of Rs. 750.

Note: The minimum services for entitlement for family pension and lump sum payment of death of employee under Employees Family Pension Scheme, 1971, has been reduced from 1 year to 3 months. Further, the lump sum payment has been increased from Rs. 2,000 to 5,000. The notification shall be deemed to have come into force with effect from 1st April, 1988.

If at the time of death during the period for which contribution to the Family Pension Fund was received of reckonable service a member was not in receipt of full pay, the rate of full pay last drawn by him during that period shall be taken into account for the assessment.

In the case of part-time employee who was a member of the Family Pension Fund while serving in more than one establishment covered under the Act, the rate of Family Pension shall be determined with reference to the aggregate of the full pay last drawn by him in such establishments on which contribution to the Family Pension Fund were recovered.

In the case of a piece-rated or a daily rated employee, who was a member of the Family Pension Fund, the rate of full pay last drawn by him during the period for which the contribution to the Family Pension Fund was recovered, shall be determined by taking into account his average earning in the twelve months preceding that in which he dies.

(2) Where an employee who has been a member of the Family Pension Fund for a period not less than 7 years dies during the period of reckonable service, the above rate of family pension shall be subject to the following modifications:

(*a*) for a period of 7 years from the date of death or, till the date on which the member of the Family Pension Fund would have reached the age of 60 years had he remained alive, whichever period is shorter, the family pension payable shall be at the rate specified in the table plus 20% of pay of the member as determined for the purpose of sub-paragraph (*i*) subject to a maximum of twice the family pension mentioned in the Table 2;

(*b*) the family pension payable after the expiry of the period referred to in clause (*a*) shall be the same as in the Table 2.

Ad hoc relief to those drawing family pension is given from time to time in terms of notifications issued by the Central Government. Thus, the amount mentioned in the Table is not static, it keeps on increasing so as to maintain the real value of the pension.

Other benefits under the Employees' Family Pension Scheme are:

Life Assurance Benefit. Where a member who has contributed to the Family Pension fund for a period not less than 3 months while in reckonable service, a lump sum of Rs. 500 is payable to him/her family as Life Assuance benefit.

Retirement-cum-withdrawal Benefit. The retirement-cum-withdrawal benefit becomes payable to the member either on attaining the age of 60 years or on cessation of membership from the Family Pension fund before attaining the age of 60 years for reasons other than death provided that the member has contributed to the fund for a period of not less than three months.

The retirement-cum-withdrawal benefit rates are as under:

Last Pay	*Benefit available*
Pay upto Rs. 690	Rs. 110 (for one years' membership) to Rs. 9,000 (for 40 years' membership).
Pay from Rs. 691 to Rs. 1130	Minimum Rs. 112 to Rs. 181 (for one years' membership) Maximum Rs. 9,000 (for 40 years' membership)
Pay from Rs. 1131 to Rs. 2500	Minimum Rs. 182 to Rs. 400 (for one years' membership) Maximum Rs. 9,040 to Rs. 19,835 (for 40 years membership).

Besides *ad hoc* relief is also given to family pensioners from time to time.

Employees Deposit Linked Insurance Scheme. This scheme was introduced in 1976 by the Government through Amendment in act in order to provide life insurance benefit to employees of any establishment or class of establishment to which this act applies. Under this scheme, on the death of an employee while in service, who is a member of the Employees Provident Fund or of the exempted Provident fund, the person(s) entitled to receive the provident fund accumulations, is paid an additional amount, equal to average balance in the provident fund account of the deceased during the preceding three years or during the period of his membership, whichever is less if the average balance was not below Rs. 1000 during the said period. The maximum amount of benefit payable under this scheme is Rs. 10,000.

Employees' State Insurance. Employees State Insurance Act, 1948, applies mainly to factories in the notified areas/centres. The provisions of the Acts can however be applied by the appropriate Government to any other establishments or class of establishment, industrial, commercial, agricultural or otherwise.

The benefits available, under the provisions of the Act, to the insured persons or their dependents are noted as under:

(*a*) *Sickness benefit*: Whereby insured person is entitled to a periodical payment in case of his sickness.

(*b*) *Maternity benefit*: An insured women employee in case of confinement or miscarriage or sickness arising out of pregnancy, confinement, premature birth of child or miscarriage is entitled to such periodical payments.

(*c*) *Disablement benefit*: An insured person who suffer disablement as a result of an employment injury is entitled to a periodical payment is called disablement benefit.

(*d*) *Dependants' benefit*: If an insured person dies as a result of an employment injury his dependants are entitled to periodical payments known as the dependents, benefit.

(*e*) *Medical benefit*: Medical Benefits are made available for treatment from sickness for the insured persons. This benefit has since been extended also to the family members of insured persons.

(*f*) *Funeral expenses*: A lump sum payment specified by the government. time to time is admissible to the eldest surviving member of the family of an insured person towards the expenditure on the funeral of the deceased insured person. In the event of the deceased insured person leaving no family behind him, such payment is made to the person who actually incurs the expenditure on the funeral.

The responsibility for the payment of contributions to the ESI corporation rests upon the employer. He has to deposit his contribution as well as the employees' contribution which he can deduct from wages. The contribution payable by the employer is 5% of wages whereas that payable by the employee is 2.25% of his wages. No contribution is payable by an employee drawing less than Rs. 6 per day.

Benefits under Factories Act. Apart from the provisions for providing facilities for the health, safety and welfare of the employees who work in the factory, the employer has to pay in monetary terms by way of annual leave with wages admissible to the employees under Chapter VIII of the Factories Act, 1948. The Act safeguards any right to which a worker may be entitled under any other law or under the terms of any award agreement, including settlement or contract of service. Provided if such award, agreement including settlement, or contract of service provides for a longer annual leave with wages than provided in the above chapter, the quantum of leave which the worker shall be entitled shall be in accordance with such award, agreement or contract of service but in relation to matters not provided for in such award, agreement, or contract of service or matters which are provided for less favourably therein than, the provisions relating to (1) annual leave with wages; (2) wages during leave period; (3) payment in advance of wages in certain cases; and (4) mode of recovery of unpaid wages becomes applicable.

Benefit of Bonus. Bonus is payable to the employees of an establishment employing 20 or more persons and falling within the purview of the payment of Bonus Act, 1965. Bonus payment is made out of the allocable surplus, computed, under the Act. In case of Non-banks, it is 67% of the available surplus in an accounting period. In other case, 60% of the available surplus is the allocable surplus. Available surplus is the total sum that remains out of gross profits after deduction of the following items:

(i) any amount by way of depreciation is admissible in accordance with the provisions of Sub-section (1) of Section 32 of the Income-tax Act or in accordance with the provisions of the Agricultural Income-tax as the case may be;

However, where an employer has been paying bonus to his employees under a settlement or an award or agreement made before 29th May, 1965, and subsisting on that date after deducting from the gross profits notional normal depreciation, then, the amount of depreciation to be deducted under this clause shall, at the option of the employer continue to be such notional normal depreciation.

(ii) any amount by way of development rebate or development allowance which the employer is entitled to deduct from his income under the Income-tax Act;

(iii) any direct tax, subject to the provisions of Section 7 of the Payment of Bonus Act, which the employer is liable to pay for the accounting year in respect of his income, profit and gains during that year;

(iv) such further sum as are specified in respect of the employer in the Third Schedule. In the case of a company the further sum to be deducted are specified as under:

(a) The dividends payable on its preference share capital for the accounting year calculated at the actual rate at which such dividend are payable;

(b) 8.5% of its paid-up equity share capital as at the commencement of the accounting year;

(c) 6% of its reserves shown in its balance sheet as at the commencement of the accounting year including any profits carried forward from the previous accounting year.

In case, the employer is a foreign company under the Companies Act, 1956 (Section 591 thereof), the total amount to be deducted under this item shall be 8.5% on the aggregate of the value of the net fixed assets and the current assets of the company in India after deducting the amount of its current liabilities (other than any amount shown as payable by the company to its Head

Office whether towards any advance made by the head office or otherwise or any interest paid by the company to its head office) in India.

Thus taking into consideration the above aspects, the available surplus in respect of the accounting year shall be the aggregate of (A) the gross profits for that accounting year after deducting therefrom the sums as referred to above at item (i) to (iv); and (B) an amount equal to the difference between—(i) the direct tax,calculated in accordance with the provisions of Section 7, in respect of an amount equal to the gross profits of the employer for the immediately preceding accounting year; and

(ii) the direct tax, calculated in accordance with the provisions of Section 7, in respect of an amount equal to the gross profits of the employer for such preceding accounting year after deducting there from the amount of bonus which the employer has paid or is liable to pay to his employees in accordance with the provisions of this Act for that year.

Section 7 of the Payment of Bonus Act, 1965 is reproduced below:

Calculation of direct tax payable by the employer

Any direct tax payable by the employer for any accounting year shall, subject to the following provisions, be calculated at the rates applicable it the income of the employer for that year, namely:

(a) in calculating such tax no account shall be taken of—

   (i) any loss incurred by the employer in respect of any previous accounting year and carried forward under any law for the time being in force relating to direct taxes;

   (ii) any arrears of depreciation which the employer is entitled to add to the amount of the allowance for any following account year or years under Sub-section (2) of Section 32 of the Income-tax Act;

   (iii) any exemption conferred on the employer under Section 84 of the Income-tax Act or of any deduction to which he is entitled under Sub-section (1) of Section 101 of that Act, as in force immediately before the commencement of the Finance Act, 1965 (10 of 1965);

(b) where, the employer is a religious or a charitable institution to which the provisions of Section 32 do not apply and the whole or any part of its income is exempt from tax under the Income-tax Act, then, with respect to the income so exempted, such institution shall be treated as if it were a company in which the public are substantially interested within the meaning of that Act;

(c) where the employer is an individual or a Hindu undivided family, the tax payable by such employer under Income- tax Act shall be calculated on the basis that the income derived by him from the establishment is his only income;

(d) where the income of any employer includes any profits and gains derived from the export of any goods or merchandise out of India and any rebate on such income is allowed under any law for the time being in force relating to direct taxes, then, no account shall be taken of such rebate;

(e) no account shall be taken of any rebate other than development rebate or investment allowance or dévelopment allowance or credit or relief or deduction (not herein before mentioned in this section) in the payment of any direct tax allowed under any law for the time being in force relating to direct taxes or under the relevant annual Finance Act, for the development of any industry.

If the allocable surplus in any accounting year exceeds the amount of maximum bonus payable to the employees in the establishment under Section 11 then, the excess shall, subject to a limit of 20% of the total salary or wages of the employee employed in the establishment in that accounting year be carried forward for being set on in the succeeding accounting year and so on upto and inclusive of the fourth accounting year to be utilised for the purpose of payment of bonus, in the manner illustrated in the Fourth Schedule of the Act.

In case where for any accounting year, there is no allocable surplus or the allocable surplus in that year falls short of the amount of minimum bonus payable to the employees in the establishment under Section 10, and there is no amount or sufficient amount carried forward and set on under Sub-section (1) which could be utilised for the purpose of payment of minimum bonus, then, such minimum amount or the deficiency as the case may be shall be carried forward for being set-off in the succeeding accounting year and so on upto and inclusive of the fourth accounting year, in the manner illustrated in the fourth Schedule. The Fourth Schedule is reproduced below.

THE FOURTH SCHEDULE
(See Sections 15 and 16)

In this Schedule, the total amount of bonus equal to 8.33 per cent of the annual salary or wage payable to all the employees is assumed to be Rs. 1,04,167. Accordingly, the maximum bonus to which all the employees are entitled to be paid (Twenty per cent of the annual salary or wage of all the employees) would be Rs. 2,50,000.

Year	*Amount equal to sixty per cent or sixty-seven per cent, as the case may be, of available surplus allocable as bonus*	*Amount payable as bonus*	*Set on on set off of the year carried forward*	*Total set on or set off carried forward*	
	Rs.	Rs.	Rs.	Rs. of (year)	
1.	1,04,167	1,04,167**	Nil	Nil	
2.	6,35,000	2,50,000*	Set on 2,50 000*	Set on 2,50,000	(2)
3.	2,20,000	2,50,000* (inclusive of 30,000 from year 2)	Nil	Set on 2,20,000	(2)
4.	3,75,000	2.50,000*	Set on 1,25,000	Set on 2,20,000 1,25,000	(2) (4)
5.	1,40,000	2,50,000* (inclusive of 1,10,000 from year 2)	Nil	Set on 1,10,000 1,25,000	(2) (4)
6.	3,10,000	2,50,000*	Set on 60,000	Set on Nil 1,25,000 60,000	(2) (4) (6)

7. 1,000,000	2,50,000* (inclusive of 1,25,000 from year 4) and 25,000 from year 6)	Nil	Set on 35,000	(6)
8. Nil (due to loss)	1,04,167** (inclusive of 35,000 from year 6)	Set off 69,167	Set off 69,167	(7)
9. 10,000	1,04,167*	Set off 94,167	Set off 69,167 94,167	(8) (9)
10. 2,15,000	1,04,167* (after setting off 69,167 from year 8 and 41,666 from year 9)	Nil	Set off 52,501	(9)

Notes: * Maximum

** Minimum

! The balance of Rs. 1,10,000 set on from year 2 lapses.

According to the Payment of Bonus Act, 1965, a minimum bonus which shall not be less than 8.33% of the salary or wage earned by the employee during the accounting year or 100 rupees (60 rupees in the case where the employee is below 15 years of age whichever is higher) is payable to every employee in respect of each accounting year, whether there is allocable surplus or not. In case the allocable surplus exceeds the said amount of minimum bonus payable to the employees, an amount in proportion to the subject to a maximum of 20% of such salary or wage. Adjustment of customary or interim bonus paid to the employees is allowed against the bonus payable under the Act. Further, the employer is entitled to deduction of certain amounts from bonus payable under the Act from the employees who is found guilty of misconduct causing financial loss to the employer.

The payment of bonus is not compulsory for the period of first five years of a new establishment. But if in any accounting year even before the expiry of the above limit of five years it makes profit, it is required to pay bonus for that particular year.

years to PRA enable it to set up an Educational Development Group. The main objectives of the Educational Development Group are: "(i) to stimulate the development and improvement of pre-retirement education and increase awareness of its value and purpose; (ii) to give guidance and support to provides of PRE (employers, adult educators and voluntary organisations); (iii) to identify and disseminate appropriate teaching materials and examples of goods practices; (iv) to promote greater general awareness of the needs of people in middle and later life and encourage the development of better ways of meeting them".

The experience of USA in the area of imparting pre-retirement education are little different than those of UK as discussed above. A survey conducted in 1976 by Prentice-Hall and American Society for Personnel Administration revealed that in USA mostly retirement preparation assistance is in the shape of financial assistance and basic health insurance information. This survey also revealed that 75% of the responding 269 companies have pre-retirement planning programmes. More than half offer individualised counselling, 1/3 conduct group counselling sessions and the remainder have both types programme by 1980. Some of these companies are IBM, Zenith Radio Corporation, Chemical Bank, Amplex Corpn., Sears, Roebuck, Dow Chemicals, Texas Power & Light, Koppers, Polaroid, United Airlines, American Airlines, Eastern Kodak, Lever Bros., General Electric, Lockhead, etc. Evidence is available that earlier to above survey the Equitable Life Associates conducted a survey in 1950, Hewitt and Associates conducted similar survey in 1952. It was reported that 13 of the 355 companies had pre-retirement planning programmes in 1950 of one kind or other. Hewitt had reported that only 2.7% of the Companies out of 657 companies with workforce of 2.5 million had offered educational or lecture programme regarding retirement. At University level, research started on the subject of formal retirement preparation programme at Michigan and Chicago. By 1970, American Association of Retired Persons (AARF) published a series of book-lets on subjects like health, income, financial planning, use of time, housing and location, legal affairs etc. for information on continuous basis to retired persons for their rehabilitation. Besides there are private organisation like Retired Advisers Inc. (RAI) and Retired Services Inc. (RSI) that provide written material for retires and prospective retirees.

James W. Walker & Marriet L. Laxer in their book "The End of Mandatory Retirement" (John Willey & Sons, 1978) have revealed that in 1974 out of 800 responding companies 704 offered retirement education programmes viz. 371 offered financial information, 170 basic information on supplementary benefits under companies and health and insurance plans, 103 provide general counselling 60 supplies written materials and counseling on personal basis.

In India, education on retirement or pre-retirement education or retirement planning are the subjects not considered important either at the government level or in the private organisation. There is not even a single scheme which may be cited as a beginning of the era of retirement planning in India. The only exception is the defence services where some systematic programme for the exposure of retirement defence personnel whereby guidance is given to them in the direction of their rehabilitation.

Based on the experience of the developed nations of world, retirement planning or pre-retirement educational programmes should be adopted in India by governments of the States and the government of the Centre besides the private limited companies and the public corporations. Retirement education could become one of the prominent activity of the Adult Education Centres and the educational institutions particularly those devoted to advance management education and training. Part-time course could be commenced in these centres for the guidance of the senior executives of the limited companies and corporations who should be guided to take up In-Company or Out-of-Company programmes for educating and informing those employees who seek premature retirement or for the superannuated retirees. Educational programme should cover and if literature for publicity and educating the retirees is published should comprise of the following areas:

(1) *Financial planning*: establishing the need for finance for retirees, their sources of income, items on which to spend money, budget for income and expenditure, etc. This is the urgent need in Indian circumstances for such planning as majority of retirees lack social security measures adequate to their retirement needs. Particularly in the private sector organisation where no retirement pension is provided, immediate action is required for looking after the retirees. Even public sector undertakings who have been given

the importance of a pace-setter for the private sector has lagged behind in this area of social benevolence. How to save money, protect the savings and invest them in less risky high return bearing occupations.

(2) Augmenting sources of income for the retired person on retirement is most important requirement for the survival of the retirees and their dependent and cultural programmes, family and other matters.

(3) Meaningful use of time in leisure and in social activities, in self development and cultural programmes, family and other matters.

(4) Setting house and location or the place where retiree may spend his time, climate considerations, cost of living, amusements and recreation for happy pass-time etc.

(5) Health care and safety: It is the health that faces the challenges of retirement and aging. Medical checkup at periodic intervals is essential, light exercises and walking etc.

(6) Legal affairs retirement places time at retiree's disposal but demands of aging and old age fatigues do not allow him to move into litigations. Help of lawyers to look after his income resources, taxations, property protections and other related matters is essential.

Like-wise there may be other fields which should be covered under the pre-retirement education plan as may be revealed on the basis of experiences. But in the above areas literature could be created to solve the problems of the retirees.

With a view to make a start of pre-retirement education in India, it may be worth consideration that the Associations of employers in private sector, banking industry and financial institutions and investment bodies should take similar steps with a view to expedite the establishment of machinery which could plan, evaluate and assist the retired people in the setting up of activity of commercial or industrial nature as may be permitted keeping in view the experience and expertise of such retirees.

Plea for Retirement Benefits

In the wake of strong support to computer technology expressed by the government in recent years, rethinking is required to be done on the aspects of employees' retirement benefits particularly in the organisations and enterprises where computer technology can be adopted for public convenience, safety and economy. It is in this context that the employment policy as well as the retirement policy throughout the country will have to be reviewed for making adjustments for adoption of computer technology because in these situations it is likely that the work force whether managerial, administrative or in ranks with blue or white collars has got to be reduced and human labour or human skill saving devices, i.e. the computers will replace them in sizeable number. For example, in financial institutions, banking, insurance companies, and other alike institutions computer technology can be adopted without much delay for better, accurate, quick results. People manning positions in these organisations will have to be induced to acquire new skills matching to the computer technology adaptation and those who are constrained to improve may be motivated to vacate the positions voluntarily to give way to the youths with modern knowledge matching with the change.

The issue of this change over is not simple in the present circumstances particularly when there exist already a heavy back log of unemployment of both educated and technically qualified youths besides the skilled and the unskilled labour. Many new issues emerge in such a situation. Trade Union have their own say before any change at any organisational level is contemplated. This situation was faced in the banking industry recently when the Indian Banking Association had to decide upon the computer based clearing system. If the Trade Union leaders are convinced of the wider public interest and adequate compensation for the affected members resulting from the change over, the problem meets a ready solution. But the question of the general change over involving the entire economy, the whole industrial and commercial setup, present a different problem. The main clash exists between the old and new blood. This clash has been experienced in the developed nations like USA and UK and is, at the advent of adoption of new technology is discernible in India also. Experience of the developed nations if has to serve as a guide then reconsideration will have to be given to incentive plan for the early retirement. The most favourably thinking goes to hold the solution to the problem of transition into technological era lies in managing the change with the induction of new blood which is

Payment of Gratuity. Gratuity is a retrial benefit given as a lump sum amount to an employee by his employer on the termination of the employment. To be eligible to receive gratuity under the Payment of Gratuity Act, 1972, an employee should have rendered continuous service for not less than five years on superannuation or retirement or resignation. When termination is due to death or disablement due to accident or disease, the completion of continuous service of five years is not necessary.

In the case of death of an employee, the gratuity is payable to his nominee or his heirs/as the case may be. The amount of gratuity payable to an employee should not exceed twenty months wages. For every completed year of service or part thereof in excess of six months, the employer shall pay gratuity to an employee at the rate of fifteen days' wages based on the rate of wage last drawn by the employee concerned. The maximum amount of gratuity shall not exceed Rs. 50,000. In case of piece rated employee, daily wages shall be computed on the average of the total wages received by him for a period of 3 months immediately preceding the termination of his employment, and, for this purpose, the wages paid for any overtime work shall not be taken into consideration. In seasonal establishments, gratuity is payable to the seasonal employees at the rate of seven days' wages for each season. To other employees, the usual rate of 15 days wages for every completed year of service applies. The gratuity can be fully forfeited in the following circumstances:

(i) riotious or disorderly behaviour;

(ii) dismissal; and

(iii) moral turpitude.

The gratuity of an employee can also be partially forfeited to the extent of damage of employer's property after giving a reasonable opportunity to the concerned persons.

The Maternity Benefit. The Maternity Benefit Act, 1961, regulates the employment of women in certain establishments for certain periods before and after child birth. The Act also provide maternity and certain other benefits. According to the Act maternity benefit, is payable to a female worker for 12 weeks i.e. six weeks up to and including the day of her delivery and six weeks immediately following that day. Minimum period of service required to be put in employment is 160 days in the twelve months immediately preceding the date of her expected delivery with the employer from whom the woman may claim the above benefit. In the event of death of a woman employee, the maternity benefit shall be payable only for the days upto and including the day of her death. In case the child survives the women employee who dies after giving birth within the six weeks period following the date of delivery, the employer shall be liable for the maternity benefits, for the entire period of six weeks post to delivery of child. In case such child also dies during the said period then the benefit will be given only for the days to and including the day of the death of the child. The Maternity Benefits Act, 1961 does not affect the continuance of payment of maternity benefit where the Employees' State Insurance Act, 1948 is applicable.

Payment of medical bonus: Every woman entitled a maternity benefit under the Maternity Benefit Act shall also be entitled to receive from her employer a medical bonus of Rs. 25 if no pre-natal confinement and post-natal care is provided for by the employer free of charge.

Customary Benefits

Besides the above statutory benefits the employer also provide certain benefits to its employees which may be adopted as per customs prevalent in the industry or the social environment. These benefits are generally provided by a corporate unit to build its image in the industrial or commercial world depending upon its earning capacity, profitability and management attitude towards employees welfare. These benefits are listed below:

(1) Leave Fare Concessions or Leave Travel Grants: This benefit is admissible in certain corporate sectors of standing to its employees where by the employees are encouraged to take annual leave once in two years or so and spend the leave period at leisure at some hill station or visit those places carrying commercial or historical importance, or visit their home towns or religious places as they like to visit with the members of family and dependents. The employer company allows reimbursement of travel expenses depending upon the admissibility of class of travel or mode of transport to the category of employment one belongs.

always easy, possible, and successful. The old become adamant to change and cannot deliver the desired results even fresh training in the requisite area of technology despite the fact that such training is expensive and scarce. The best policy is suggested by the experts is the review of incentives for early retirement which serves two ends viz. "old timer working population will go to production activity by engaging themselves in promotion and management of new units; and new trained persons will man their jobs more efficiently and better equipped and modern knowledge of know-how and work process".

Technological transition is a continuous process and if such steps are not taken India will remain many generations behind the new world due to educational lag, technological transition lag, and for want of trained people and modern equipments. This is the first stage of technological transition and is bound to continue with advancement of science and technology and so is the process of retiring the old and replacing them by youths will continue. This is how in USA and other developed nations of West Europe the technological transition is taking place. In American private organisations the practice exists under which attractive premature retirement benefits to their employees along with the intensive guidance to take up production activities is provided. Guidance covers introduction to special agencies which provide money, guidance for promotion of industry, technological help, marketing facilities and managerial know how and entrepreneurial training and advance refresher courses.

Retirement benefits available in India are not much encouraging as compared to the other nations of the world. A review of existing retirement benefits is necessary to carry the discussion further for evolving a plan for premature retirement incentives.

In India, Central Government Civil Service Rules particularly the pension schemes launched in 1950 and 1964 are the main guidelines deserving reconsideration and setting example for the public sector undertakings, banks, financial institutions, as well as the private sector organisations particularly the corporate sector.

Under the existing government rules, the retirement has been stipulated on completion of 30 years qualifying service. This is known as compulsory retirement. There is also provision for voluntary retirement permitted on completion of 20 years qualifying service. In the latter case of retiree is given five years benefit for calculating pension which is reckoned on the basis of qualifying service and the over all benefit does not extend beyond 30 years service period. The benefit which an employee normally gets on retirement from government service are the pension, service gratuity and death-cum-retirement gratuity where admissible. Pension includes gratuity except when the term pension is used in contradistinction to gratuity. The Central Government Pension rules apply to government servants who retire or retired or discharged or allowed to resign from service or dies including civilian government servants in the Defence Services. State Government and Railways have their own pension rules as such Central Government rules do not apply to them. Besides there are also certain classes of persons who are also not governed under the said pension rules viz. (a) pensions in casual and daily rated employment; (b) pensions paid from contingencies; (c) persons entitled to the contributory Provided Fund; (d) members of all-India services; (e) persons locally recruited for services in diplomatic consular or other Indian establishments in foreign countries; (f) persons employed on contracts except when the contract provides otherwise; and (g) persons whose terms and conditions of service are regulated by or under the provisions of the constitution or any other law for the time being in force.

There are various types of pension schemes viz. (1) Superannuation Pension: admissible to one who retires on attaining age of compulsory retirement; (2) Retiring pension: admissible to those who retire or retired in advance of the age of compulsory retirement or who is declared surplus opts for voluntary retirement as per existing provisions; (3) Invalid pension: admissible to those who retire from service on account of any bodily or mental infirmity which permanently incapacitates him for service on medical ground; (4) Compensation pension: this is the type of pension which is allowed to a person who is discharged on abolition of permanent post. It is an alternative option in the form of pension. (5) Compulsory retirement pension: it is admissible in the event when retirement is inflicted as a penalty i.e. pension or gratuity or both at a rate not less than 2/3 and not more than full compensation or gratuity or both is admissible to such person on the date of his compulsory retirement; (6) Besides, compassionate allowance equal to 2/3 of pension or gratuity or both which would have been admissible on retirement. Compensation pension is admissible to that government servant who is dismissed from service whose gratuity or pension is forefieted. Provision of commutation of pension is available to a government servant for a lump sum payment not exceeding 1/3 of his pension. However, commutation or pension is not allowed to the government servant under departmental or judicial proceedings instituted before or after the date of his retirement during tendency of such proceedings. On death of the government servant, the committed value is payable to his/her heir. Extra- ordinary pension benefits are also provided to government servant where death or injury is sustained attributable to service or aggravated by service other than a industrial worker or members of armed forces. Option is available for a civil servant in government either for a pensionary scheme or contributory provident fund benefits. Government of India has made available pensionary benefits to industrial employees since 1960 with option either to retain existing contributory provident fund benefits.

With the availability of pension for a person while in government service there are number of restrictions which have been placed in the matter of re-employment of such persons. These restrictions may be analysed from the angle of disincentives to take up economic activity on retirement. Precisely these restrictions are discussed below:

(1) Restriction on commercial re-employment after retirement: Previous permission/sanction of the government is required before a person accept commercial appointment within two years of his retirement. By commercial appointment/employment it is understood such employment in any capacity including that of an agent,under a company, cooperative society, firm or individual engaged in trading, commercial, industrial, financial or professional business and includes also a directorship of such company and partnership of such firm, but does not include employment under a body corporate, wholly or substantially owned or controlled by the government or setting up practice either independently or as a partner of a firm, as adviser or consultant in matters in respect of which the pensioner has no professional qualification or the matters in respect of which the practice is to setup or is carried on are relatable to his official knowledge or experience or the pensioner has professional qualifications but the matters in

respect of which such as are likely to give his client an unfair advantage by reason of his previus official position or the pensioner has to undertake work involving liaison or contract with the offices or officers of the government. For example, a government servant belonging to Indian Revenue Service or had been member of any other Central Service Group A, retired from a post under the Department of Revene and Insurance in Ministry of Finance, cannot set up practice before two years from the date of such retirement. However, this restriction is not available for employment in University as the same is not a commercial employment.

(2) Another restriction is in the form of disentitlement of a person who is a government servant for two pensions in the same service or post at the same time or by the same continuous service. A government servant on re-employment cannot have a separate pension or gratuity for the period of his re-employment.

(3) Besides, pension is also subject to future good conduct of the pensioner and can be withdrawn by serving requisite notice.

(4) Pension can be withheld for serious crime or offence committed by the pensioner under Official Secret Act, 1923 for grave misconduct which includes the communication or disclosure of any secret official code or pass word or any sketch, plan article, model, note, document or information such as mentioned in Section 5 thereof prejudicing the interest of general public or the security of the country.

(5) Permission of the government is required for a pensioner belonging to Central Service Group A to take-up any employment outside India in any local authority, corporation or other institution which function under the supervision and control of a government outside India or an employment under an international organisation of which government of India is not a member.

The above restrictions are of objective nature and could be relaxed in suitable cases where the government policy towards encouragement of pre-mature retirement is reviewed with the sole objective of solving the unemployment problem linked with the initiation of new economic activity taken up by the pre-maturedly retired persons.

Gratuity is not pre retirement benefit equally important as pension and is admissible to the government servant as per rules.

Gratuity is of two types viz. Terminal Gratuity which is allowed to a person who retires on superannuation or is discharged from service or is declared invalid for further service provided that he rendered satisfactory service. For unsatisfactory service the amount of gratuity could be reduced. The government of India has enhanced the amount of Gratuity could be reduced. The government of India has enhanced the amount of Gratuity from Rs. 30,000 to Rs. 50,000 for the total tenure of service depending upon the entitlement of a person. Another form is Death Gratuity which is available to the family of a temporary or quasi-permanent government servant who dies in service. It is admissible as per prescribed rates.

Many public sector corporations, banks, financial institution and investment bodies follow the government plan of gratuity and contributory provident fund instead of pension. Nevertheless there is hardly any provision in these organisation for voluntary retirement benefits.

Nor withstanding the above, even the pensionery benefits provided by the central government or state government are not much inducive to persons thinking in terms of premature retirement for taking up any industrial or commercial activity as revealed under the foregone discussion. In the circumstances the entire matter relating to the policy framework o. .etirement or the benefit accruing on retirement or on early/premature retirement, deserve a passionate review and reconsideration with a view to create more attractive incentives for the aspirant retirees. Even in private organisation need exist if the options for pensions are created for the general welfare of the retired pensioners. In the connection, experiences of developed nations will pave a way for the guidance in this direction.

The example of USA's firms is more glaring. Private pension plans exist as non-contributory but solely financed by employers as well as those contributory by both employer and the; employee. William C. Greenough and Francis P. King in "Pension Plans & Public Policy". Columbia University Press, New York, have stated that in 1970 in USA, 79% were non-contributory pensions and 21% contributory pensions plans which existed in the private sector firms. These pensions are available after full retirement age of 65 years of age. A study of Corporate Pension Plan prepared by

Banker Trust Company, USA in 1975 had reported that 77% employees were of more than 10 years service after full years of retirement age. A substantial number of plans require 30 years service for entitlement of full pensions. Earlier retirement provision do appear in the multi-employer plans. Monthly Labour Review in July, 1970 issue had reported that 6% of the employee preferred earlier retirement at the age of 55–59; 3% preferred at the age of 60–61 years, 8% at the age of 62–63 years, and 69% at the age of 65 years. The pension plans are mostly provided by large private employers i.e. 54% of all members of pension plans were with employers of more than 10,000 employees, 82% were with employees of more than, 1,000 employees. However, Pension Reforms Act, 1974 imposed a limit that pension benefits should not provide income which exceeds 100% of final pay together with social security.

For self-employed persons incentives are given by US government. For example, pre-tax funds can be created for later years and all gains can accumulate tax-free, Keogh Act, 1962 was passed in USA to cause incentives to self-employed persons to set aside a minimum of US $ 2,500 p.a. as a tax deductible contribution to a retirement plan from business income. Under 1981 Tax Act, the maximum deductible amount has been raised to $ 15,000 p.a. plus $ 2,000 as voluntary contributions as deductible. Accumulations, thus, grow and no tax is paid. On retirement of the individual, tax is paid when he withdraws the money so accumulated. At this moment, he has a lower tax bracket because of reduced total income and is thus benefited to a maximum extent. Roll-over is possible of this accumulated sum to a qualified retirement plan or a corporation or individual retirement account (IRA). Besides Keogh Plan, there is individual Retirement Account another plan that allows an individual who is not covered by any other plan to set up his own tax exempt retirement account. Any wage earner can now set aside $ 2,000 p.a. or 1% of income, whichever is less, for retirement investments. In the case of spouse working, upto $ 4,000 can be set aside. It carries same advantage of tax deductibility as Keogh Plan.

In Canada, Provincial Pension Benefits Act and Federal Pension Benefits Act, 1967 apply to Government units and private units. It is not compulsory for an employer to establish or maintain a pension plan. However, if an employer does so, is required to meet funding standards and certain Rules on the vesting of pensions, investments and related matters. Entitlement for pension is at the age of 45 years provided the person has had 10 years continuous service with the employer or has completed 10 years of membership in the Plan whichever occurs first. An employee who has worked for less than 10 years for his employer but has worked for at least 10 years for several employers under a Multi-employer Plan, is entitled to a vested benefit.

In France, private pension are growing social security measures regulated under Ordinance of Oct. 4, 1945. At the age of 55 years a person becomes entitled to a pension in private enterprise. There are different kinds of pension plans obtained in France viz. the cadres plan (Confederation General des cadres) CGC is important others are AGIRC (Association General des Institutions de Retraites de cadres), UNIRS (Union National des Institutions de Retraites des salaries), ARRCO (Assocation des Regimesole Retraites Complimentaires). All these plans cover 8 million employees of more than 6,00,000 employers.

In West Germany, private pension system is voluntarily promoted with the difference that not only large employers but 2/3 of the firms having 50 employees have pension plans and 1/3 of the small firms do have pension plans.

In Netherland, Dutch workers participate in private pension plans. 2.3 million employees out of 3.9 million workers participate in 85 industry-wide multi-employer pension funds.

In Sweden and other European nations private pension plans exist. Amongst all the advanced nations in the world the old age benefits provided by social security are maximum in Italy amounting to 80% of pay regardless of income; in Spain, the retirement benefits range from 80–100% of pay upto a fairly high ceiling. In Luxembourg, Portgal, Belgium, Substantial old age benefits are provided as reported in the 1978 Report from the Conference Board's Division of Management Research, "Rethinking Employees' Benefits Assumption."

In Japan, in 1970, 3.4 million workers out of 20 million workers were covered under private pension plans. Benefits are paid with minimum 20-25 years of participation. The large Japanese companies having private pension plans have more generous schemes than the State-run plans. As in Europe, private Japanese pension schemes supplement compulsory government administered pension plans which cover the entire population. As reported by the Economist, May, 1983 (p. 89) under, "Re-employment & Pension Plan-Aging of Japanese Social Security" in Japan, a pensioner on retirement at the age of 60 gets a maximum of 44.2% of their earnings in the year before they retire as against the persons retiring at the age of 65 years and getting between 44% and 41% of earning in West Germany, Sweden, Britain, and USA. Japanese have eight State run person insurance schemes. On these two biggest, one-known as the Employee's Pension Scheme-includes the employee of the companies with more than five workers, cover both workers and their dependents and account for 43% of the population. The other is organised on a rational basis,takes in the self-employed workers in small firms and all their dependents and covers 47% of the population. Rests are small funds schemes covering seamen, farm and fishery workers, teachers, employees of public corporations and so on.

Referring back to U.K. large companies provide for private pensions on the same line, more or less, as discussed in the case of Canada and USA. However, for those persons who are self-employed, private organisations run pension schemes which are different to those of Japan. The most common of these pension schemes are the two as discussed by Malcolm Craig in "Successful Investment Strategy" Woodhead-Faukner, Cambridge, 1984. First one is traditional plan 'with profit' pension scheme which offers steady growth and guarantee a basic pension in the retirement years; and the second one is "Unit Linked Scheme" which is major growth centre. The money paid into this scheme is reinvested by the funds investment managers into ordinary shares in U.K. and overseas, gilt-property, local authority bonds and other investments. These schemes are sold directly to public by market oriented institutions such a Abbey Life and Hambros. Besides over the past few years, the company pension market has been developing leaps and bounds as reported by Diana Wright in "Self-investment at a Premium" in Administrator, May, 1982. Favourable tax and other considerations viz. legislation have allowed 'Pension Industry' to grow fast. Small self-administered pension scheme in the corporate sector is better source of investible funds as low allow 50% of the funds to be utilised by the companies.

(2) **Encashment of Leave Salary**: Sometimes the employees are given the benefit of encashment of their earned leave who do not want to avail it and want to put more time in work. Generally this benefit is linked with Leave Fare Concession to enable an employee to enjoy fully his part leave with the encashed amount of leave by meeting his other expenditure in addition to the travelling expenses granted by the employer. The benefit is made available as one months leave may be allowed to be encashed in one year or two years period depending upon the facility allowed in a particular company.

(3) **Holiday Home**: Companies establish holiday home at different places of interest where the employees would like to spend their holidays while availing of the leave fare concessions and encashment of part of their leave. These holiday homes provide comfortable place to stay with kitchen facilities to the employees and the members of their family. Hotel accommodation is costlier and holiday home provide the substitute accommodation for a stay. Thus the facility provides monetary benefit to the employee in terms of saving the money which they are likely to spend on hotel accommodation or other stay arrangements while in transit to spend their paid holidays.

(4) **Medical Reimbursement Benefit**: Monthly lump sum is paid to employees to meet the medical expenses of the self and/or family members or dependent parents. In addition to, employees are paid ex-gratia in the circumstances when they have to meet heavy medical expenses to save their own life or the life of their family members. These facilities may be provided in addition to the free medical aid provided by the company to its employees by paid medical consultants during or after office hours.

(5) **Subsidised Accommodation Benefit**: Companies provide subsidised accommodation to their employees in the cities where rented accommodation is costly and beyond the reach of the employees at the nominal deduction from their salary towards the rent for such accommodation.

(6) **Conveyance Allowance**: Companies do provide to their employees either free transport by bus or car from their residence to the place of work and back or award a lump sum monthly

allowance differing according to the status and position and category of employment for maintaining their own conveyance being utilised for office purpose. Their benefit is in addition to the salary an employee gets per month. Some employers provide this facility of conveyance maintenance allowance or direct reimbursement of actual conveyance expenses incurred by the employees.

(7) **Subsidised Canteen Facilities**: Subsidised canten and retail purchasing facilities are also provided by the employers for the employees which are to benefit the employees to take their balanced meals in the office premises at minimum expenses and purchase essential items of their daily consumption at lesser prices. Retail shops of the mills sometimes allow concessions to the employee on purchases of the mill manufactured goods.

(8) **Children Education Allowance**: This benefit is also made available by the employers to the employees for one or two children to keep their norms of family planning fully realised and to ensure that the employees with their short families maintain their efficiency and health properly.

IMPLICATIONS OF WELFARE SCHEMES ON SHORT-TERM AND LONG-TERM FINANCES

All welfare schemes and the benefits being provided by a company entail cost in terms of finance. To enable the company to meet these cost from short-term and long-term arrangements the following criteria is generally suggested.

The company should create fund and go on crediting every year out of its profits to build a reserve for meeting the expenditure towards welfare schemes for the employees. The reserve fund should not be ploughed back in the company in financing its operational programmes but should be invested in liquid securities.

Statutory benefits in the shape of provident fund, Employees State Insurance and Gratuity are regulated under the provision of the statutes and the regulations made therein and as such the company has to make arrangement both short-term as well as long-term to meet their requirements.

For customary benefits which a company provide for its employees, provision should be made through annual budgets for meeting these costs. Some of these costs are of regular nature and therefore should be treated along with other administrative costs.

From the point of view of finance manager, a short-term view of these benefits would affect the liquidity position of a company and warrants the availability of funds to meet out the workers. needs ensuring a smooth running of the operations. On the long-term side, the finance manager, as referred to above, has to create long-term reserve to meet the financial commitments particularly for the retirement benefits of the employees nearing the age of retirement.

PROVIDENT FUNDS AND PROVISIONS OF THE COMPANIES ACT, 1956

According to Section 418 of the Companies Act, 1956 all moneys contributed to provident fund constituted for its employees or the money received or accruing by way of interest or otherwise to such funds shall be deposited within fifteen days from the date of contribution, receipt or accrued in the following manner:

1. in the post office savings bank account or
2. in a special account to be opened by the company for this purpose in the State Bank of India or in a scheduled bank;
3. where the company itself is a scheduled bank, in a special account to be opened by the company for the purpose either in itself or in the State Bank of India or in any scheduled bank; or be invested in the securities mentioned or referred to in clauses (a) to (e) of Section 20 of the Indian Trust Act.

With regard to payment of interest on the above deposits sub-section (2) of Section 418 specifies that notwithstanding anything to the contrary in the rules of any provident fund to which Sub-section (1) applies or in any contract between a company and its employees no employee shall be entitled to receive, in respect of such portion of the amount to his credit in such funds as is invested in accordance with the provisions of Sub-section (1), interest at a rate exceeding the rate of interest yielded by such investment.

Further, under Sub-section (3) it has also been provided that an employee will continue to the right under the rules of a provident fund to obtain advance from or to withdraw money standing to his credit in the fund, where the fund is a recognised provident fund within the relevant provisions of the Income-tax Act, 1961.

In case where a trust has been created by a company with respect to any provident fund referred to in Sub-section (1), the company shall be bound to collect the contributions of the employees concerned and pay such contributions as well as its own contributions, if any, to the trustees (within the fifteen days from the date of collection) but in other respects, the obligations laid on the company by this section shall devolve on the trustees and shall be discharged by them instead of by the company.

It has been held in *Desikachari v. Pirrie* (AIR 1940 Mad. 184) that where the amount of the provident fund lying in deposit in a bank to the credit on the company has not been invested in the authorised securities as provided in this section, the company is guilty of a breach of trust and the bank with the knowledge of this must be held to have participated in the breach of trust.

The employee whose contributions have been so deposited in the Bank is entitled under Section 419 on request made in this behalf to the company, or to the trustees referred to in Sub-section (4) of Section 418 as the case may be, to see the banks receipt for any money or security such as is referred to in Sections 417 and 418 of the Act.

Penalty for contravention of Sections 417, 418 and 419 has been stipulated under section 420 of the Act which may be inflicted on any officer of a company or any such trustees of a provident fund as is referred to in Sub-section (4) of Section 418 who knowingly, contravenes, or authorises or permits the contravention of, the provisions of Sections 417, 418 and 419 of the Act. Such persons shall be punishable with imprisonment for a term which may extend to six months or with fine which may extend to one thousand rupees.

RETIREMENT BENEFITS AND FINANCIAL IMPLICATIONS

Need for Pre-retirement Education

In India, every year a number of employees in public sector, State and Central Government Services, municipalities and other local bodies, army services and private sector organisations retire. Majority of these retired persons, post retirement, face work-free

From the above discussions, it transpires that India lags much behind in the area of retirement benefits to the employees in government as well as in private sector. There is enough to be done and accomplished in the direction of introducing pension schemes by the private employers to their employees. On the part of the government too is required to relax retirement rules so that an employee may seek retirement prematurely on sound and attractive incentives and take up freely the commercial or industrial activity to add to GNP and create new avenues for employment. The public sector undertaking have to give lead to private sector particularly by quickly introducing retirement pension schemes on superannuation as well as on voluntary basis after completion of minimum period of service so that the people with will, zeal, experience and skill could take up production activity and add to the generation of new sources of GNP and employment in the economy.

SAIL have recently implemented the scheme of voluntary retirement for their employees. The basic objective of the scheme is to:

1. achieve optimum manpower utilisation.
2. improve the average-mix of the employees and
3. Improve the over all skill level.

The scheme is applicable to all regular/permanent employees of the company. Any regular employees who has completed 10 years of the service in the company or 40 years of age is eligible to seek voluntary retirement.

A retired employee is basically entitled to number of benefits. These are:

1. Full provident fund contribution of employer with accretion there to in the account of employee to provisions of Provident Fund Rules applicables to the employees.
2. Gratuity for each completed years of service or part there of as admissible under gratuity rules.
3. Leave salary for the unavailed earned leave. The quantum of leave salary will not exceeds the maximum limit to which earned leave can be accumulated under the leave rules applicable to the employee.

4. Transfer benefits for self and family as admissible under the TA rules on super annuation.
5. Ex-gratia payment equivalent to 45 days emoluments (Pay + DA) for each completed year of service or the monthly emoluments at the time or retirement multiplied by remaining months of service left before the normal date of retirement whichever is less. For example, an employee who has completed 24 years of service and has got only one year of service left for normal retirement, will get an ex-gratia of only 12 months of emoluments and not 36 months emoluments.
6. One month/three months notice pay as per service conditions: Other public sector units are also considering the above proposal for their employees.

In private sector, DCM has also introduced attractive scheme of voluntary retirement for the employees of the company.

With a view to boost India's economy to the stage of 'take off' of economic development to match the development and achievements of the developed nations, a new generation of entrepreneurs is required who may be innovating and imitating. The persons who could be released from jobs in private and public undertakings or Central or State Government services on pre-retirement plan could form an army of such entrepreneurs and besides creating avenues of new employment and new activities of productions could take the economy ahead to the aspirations of "21 st" Century of electronic stage. Therefore, the government should bring effective legislation and take result bearing measures to ensure adoption of retirement benefits, inducement for premature retirements to aspirant employees who could be motivated to take up production activity on small or medium scale basis.

Future Projections and Provisions in the Accounts

Theoretically, a pension plan or other retirement benefit plan for an employee may be funded by a trust fund known as self-administered plan or by an insurance company known as insured pension plan or by a combination of both. Under the self-aaministered plan, contributions are paid to the trustee company who has full freedom and flexibility in investing the funds as per the provisions of the plan; whereas in the case of insured pension plan payments are directly made to a insurance company or to trustees for onward payment of premium to a insurance company. In U.S.A., maximum number of the companies follow self-administered plans. There are other types of plans in vogue in USA but this is the most familiar one which favourably compares to the plan which has been followed in these concerns where the provident fund and pension schemes have been statutorily implemented. Divestment of funds is the main attraction in the plan which keeps off the management from tampering with the funds.

Three broad factors affect the cost of a pension programme to a company according to J.B. Cohen and S.M. Robbins viz.,(1) the nature of the benefits; (2) the cost of a programme may be affected by the method of funding employed; and (3) cost is influenced by the actual experience of the company in operating under the programme. In the first category the cost will depend upon the nature of benefits; i.e. more liberal the benefits, the greater will be the cost. "Pay-as-you-go pension plans" are the example of this type of plans. In these plans, costs, exclusive of administrative expenses, are the same as the amount of benefits disbursed. In the second category, advance funding arrangement is made and the costs of the benefits may be measured by the contributions the company makes in the form of premiums to an insurance company or payment to a trust fund.

James A. Hamilton and Dorrance C. Bronson in "Pensions" have discussed number of methods for funding the pension benefit schemes used by the companies as noted below:

(1) **Current disbursement method**: During the early years of the plan these disbursements start out at less than 1% of the active payroll and eventually reach a peak. The major drawback of this method is the absence of any reserve to provide a payment base in an emergency.

(2) **Terminal Funding method**: Funds are set aside to provide for an Immediate life time pension as each employee retires. Early payments under this method exceed actual pension requirements and thus a reserve is created which the company could use in an emergency which is not available under the first method. Company's later contributions to pension funds are below actual

pension payments, as the company earn interest on the balances in the reserve. The main drawback of this method is that the reserve established in only applicable to the employee already retired and provides no projection to those still on the active pay-rolls who are looking forward to retirement in the future time.

(3) **Level Annual Method**: This method takes care of the above drawback visible in Terminal funding method. Company, as per this method, pays a level contribution at the beginning of each year to the pension fund or on an annuity contract. The payment is based on the age of the employees so that at the start of the plan i.e. one-year amount is needed for those reaching the year of retirement. Company's contribution are highest in the first years when the plan is installed and stabilise at a much lower level afterwards.

(4) **Past Service Reserve and Level Contributions for Future Service**: In this method the Company decides first to meet in full its past service liability. It does so by making a substantial extra payment in the first year of the plan. Thereafter, it funds its future costs as in the prior method by level contribution.

It transfers from the introduction of above methods that for any given pattern of benefits, payment will vary with the funding method selected. "Costs will be affected if benefits are increased and by the actual experience of the company. The death rate of active employees determines the number who eventually will receive the benefit while the rate among retired employees establishes the cut-off time for receipt of the benefits. The effect of mortality must be considered in conjunction with death benefits because increased retirement costs from a low death rate among active employees may be offset by reduced death benefits. Management must evaluate liberal death benefits in the light of the additional costs imposed. Besides, the turnover of employees also influences costs. In non-vested plans, the amount save through employee withdrawals either increases the benefit payments or lowers contribution costs. Because pension costs are reduced by the interest earned on the funds invested, a successful investment policy is of considerable importance."

Selection of method of funding: Finance manager has to select and recommend the method of funding a plan which will benefit to his company. He is guided in this decisional process by a number of bench marks. He has to consider of initial stage the importance of the pension plan as long-range programme with heavy costs upon the company in the later stage if no pre-arrangements are made. Therefore, advance funding is more desirable than pay-as-you-go-plan. For small companies self-administered plan are good as they cannot take advantage of buying individual policies from the insurance companies. Larger companies have a wider choice to make on relative advantage of each method.

Secondly the finance manager should consider the cost of acquisition and administration. The major acquisition item is the commission paid which is largest in individual contracts then group permanent contracts or group annuity contract. Similarly, administration expenses are higher in individual contract than the other categories.

Thirdly, managerial responsibilities be also taken into condera-tion which pension plan to create because specialised talents are required to develop and manage an investment portfolio.

Fourthly, tax aspects be taken into consideration with respect to tax incidence of qualified pension plans.

The Pension Plan Balance Sheet. Pension Plan Balance sheet provide information to the actuary to judge the cost of the plan. Pension Plan Balance Sheet looks as under:

Assets	*Liabilities*
PV Pension Fund	*PV* expected from Past service
PV contributions for future services	*PV* expected future service cost
Deficit/Surplus	
Total Assets	To *PV* expected Benefits-Total Liabilities

From the above Balance sheet, it may be observed that on the liabilities side, there are two principal liabilities i.e., (1) Pensions that have already been earned by current employees and retired employees; (2) Pension which are expected to be earned by the employees through their future service. The sum of these two numbers measures the present value of all the pension commit-ments.

On the asset side, there are two main assets viz., (1) the amount put aside by the company in the pension fund; (2) value of the regular contributions to the fund that the firm plans to make in the future for its current employees. If all goes well, the value of the fund and the planned contributions should be sufficient to cover the liabilities. But assets, will be less than liabilities in case either the pension benefits are increased or the investments in pension funds do not perform upto the desired level. This deficit will be the balancing item which the company will have to make some time.

Actuary does the entire accounting for pension funds and divides the plans liabilities into two parts:

PV expected benefits for past service

+ *PV* expected future service costs

= *PV* expected benefits

As per the definitions of what is due to past and what is due to future, the *PV* expected benefits are arrived at. Some actuaries like to think of the proportion of payments that have accrued as a result of past service. In that case "*PV* expected benefits for past service = *PV* accrued benefits". The other opinion could be that all employees have so far earned is the pension that they could secure if they left the company today and in that case "PV expected benefits for past services = PV vested accrued benefits." For these employees who are fully vested the two definitions are the same. For employees who are only partially vested, their past service earns them less if they leave the firm today than if they stay on. Therefore, *PV* vested accrued benefits is less than *PV* accrued benefits.

On the assets side, first asset is "pension fund", which is a result of past contributions of a company. These funds are vested in trust and invested in a diversified portfolio of securities. These are generally reported as accounting costs as the market valuation of securities is controversial. Thus, the assets to the fund do not cover the benefits that have accrued, the company has an unfounded liability as under:

Unfunded liability = *PV* accrued benefits (–) *PV* Fund assets. This liability must be reported in a footnote to the company's Balance Sheet. The methods of calculating the unfunded liability may be different in different set-up and organisations.

The second assets in the pension plan balance sheet is the stream of contributions to cover future services. This is generally known as "normal costs". The pension fund should be large enough to cover any benefits resulting from past services and future normal costs should cover benefits resulting from future service. Accrued benefits costs method is recommended by actuaries with the idea that the company should contribute each year in present value of any benefit that have accrued in that year.

The above discussion relates to the normal situation when everything goes well which seldom happen. Things may go wrong viz. there may be decline in the value of securities in the pension funds; or employee turn-over may be lower than predicted; or union may negotiate increased pension benefits. In these circumstances, the actuary has to adjust the accounting by increasing the estimate or normal cost to bring the balance-sheet back into balance. If it is not done then balance sheet would show a deficit resulting from the excess of *PV* of expected benefits over *PV* of assets in the pension funds. Therefore, the actuary does the above adjustment.

One can imagine a system in which pension plans are not funded. The company does not make any provision but waits a person to retire and pay pension out of current income. This system can work so long company continues to grow or prosper but fails when the company is put into difficulties.

13

CORPORATE BORROWING

INDUSTRY normally requires short-term, mid-term and long-term finances. In our country, besides commercial banks, there are other specialised institutions that provide financial assistance to industry. The basic difference between a term loan and a working capital loan is that the term loan is for a fixed period and is to be paid back out of the cash generations from the operations whereas the working capital loan is to be paid back from the sale of current assets.

Term Loans

When appraising a term loan proposal, the basic question that is to be determined is whether enough profits can be expected to be earned during the currency of the term loans for repaying the principal instalments and the interest on the loans.

In recent years, the institutional set-up in India for the provision of medium and long-term credit for industry has been broadened. A number of specialised institutions has been started all over the country. These have been described in Study Note III and are listed below for ready reference.

1. The Industrial Financial Corporation of India (I.F.C.):
2. State Financial Corporations:
3. Life Insurance Corporation of India (LIC):

4. The National Small Industries Corporation. (NSIC):
5. The Industrial Credit & Investment Corporation of India (ICICI):
6. National Industrial Development Corporation (NIDC):
7. Industrial Development Bank of India (IDBI):
8. Industrial Rehabilitation Bank of India (IRBI):
9. Term lending by Banks:

Appraisal of Term Loans

A financial institution has to carefully evaluate an application for a term loan before it is granted. This is because a term loan is a long term commitment of a substantial amount of funds. In a way, when it grants a loan, the financial institution participates in the venture itself since it acquires a part of the risk by committing its own funds substantially. The repayment of the loans and the interest payments, no doubt, have priority over the money that is to be paid to the shareholders. Yet to commit substantial sums of money in a new business undertaking requires a very careful analysis of all aspects of the project. The appraisal techniques of a term loan, therefore are different than the conventional methods by which banks appraise short-term loans. Apart from the security, the technical institutions look for managerial competence, basic viability of the project, demand of the product and technical excellence of the project.

The financial institutions operating at the national level have devised more or less common procedures of appraising long-term loans and have a single proforma which may be submitted to any institution. Before a concern applies for loan, it must possess a Letter of Intent or other sanction from the Government such as registration with Director General of Technical Development (DGTD) or No Objection Certificate from the State Government. It must also have foreign exchange requirements sanctioned by the Government as also a clearance for the technical and foreign collaboration agreement, if any. In case clearance is required under the MRTP Act, this must also be obtained. These, together with filled application form and the detailed project report constitute the basis on which the financial institutions appraise term loans. Normally, the financial institutions first scrutinise the application at a preliminary level. If they are satisfied, they issue the detailed application form.

This application proforma for term loans is quite broad in its coverage and includes the general particulars of the company, its promoters and the management. In case it is existing company, particulars of present production facilities; production, sales, raw materials, inventories, executives, labour, research and development, existing capital structure and finance are also sought. In case it is a new project or in case an existing company seeks loans for a new project, details are sought regarding technical features, foreign technical collaboration and financial participation, estimated cost, installed capacity, particulars of land and building, plant and machinery, margin for working capital, the proposals for financing, production, sales, the future market profitability and cash flow etc. Separate details are required regarding the security offered. The annexures to the application form contain details regarding existing and projected unit cost of production, past balance sheet, cost and profitability analysis, sources and uses of funds, estimated cost of the scheme and particulars about machinery etc.

The financial institutions generally conduct feasibility study on many aspects i.e., technical, commercial, economic, financial, social and managerial. These broad aspects of appraisal are briefly discussed below:

1. **Technical Feasibility**. This has the following aspects:

(i) Review of infrastructure facilities, i.e. land, housing, transportation, raw materials, supplies, fuel, power and electricity etc.

(ii) The location of the project, judged from the point of view of economy and workability.

(iii) The proposed size of the plant and capacity level.

(iv) In case the technical know how has been imported from a foreign country, its suitability and workability in the Indian conditions.

(v) The project schedule in detail. The financial institutions are extremely keen that the project schedule is drawn up in a manner that the project can be completed as stipulated. This is because delay increases costs substantially in view of the inflationary trends, delay also increases the financial cash losses. All these result in acute shortage of working capital funds. As an example, a sugar plant of a certain capacity which could be set up at a cost of Rs. 250 lakhs in 1975, could in 1985 be set up only at a cost of Rs. 820 lakhs. Thus, a delay in the project schedule can upset all the calculations.

2. **Economic feasibility**. This examines the market potential of the product proposed to be manufactured. It is important to analyse whether or not the output of the new unit will be absorbed in the market. These projections are basically dependent upon the market forecasts for the product. For this purpose, the overall demand forecasts of various important categories of products are regularly developed by various agencies. The planning Commission, while formulating the plans, also has certain basic estimates of the demand and production of certain commodities. The financial institutions go into demand projections and examine whether or not the demand for the product will be there. The projection of demand, since it deals with future, is a highly complicated matter. It depends on a number of factors and statistical forecasting models are required to forecast demand for various products. Although such demand forecasts are basically approximations, they are important since they denote the broad trends regarding a project.

3. **Commercial Feasibility**. This refers to an examination of the commercial aspects of and arrangements for the project. The financial institutions to examine the arrangements made by the applicant for procurement of machinery and raw materials and for sale of goods. They ensure that such arrangements are purely commercial in nature and do not tend to benefit the promoters or their relatives. In this regard, if all the machinery is supplied by a single supplier, the financial institutions go into the details. However, if the machinery and the raw materials are to be supplied on the basis of competitive bidding, it is preferred by the financial institutions. Similarly, arrangements for sale of finished goods are looked into.

4. **Financial Feasibility**. This refers to an appraisal of the financial structure and the expected financial results of the project. The following basic issues are examined:

(i) Estimates of the cost of the project are examined to ensure that the estimated costs cover all items of expenditure and the assumptions made behind such costs are realistic in nature. Thus, where an applicant does not provide for the possible inflation and its impact on costs, the financial institutions require him to change his cost estimates.

(ii) The sources of finances are examined in depth. The financial institutions are very keen that the total financial requirements cover not only the cost of fixed assets but also contingencies, working capital and initial cash losses. As we have already emphasised, initial cash losses and pre-operative expenses tend to mount in the case of a delay in the project. This eats into the working capital available to the firm. If a financial institution finds its client in such a situtation it has to give more credit to client to tide over these difficulties. Otherwise, the institution is in the danger of losing even the initial sum of money. It is, therefore, important at the very beginning to ensure that adequate provision for contingencies, working capital and initial cash losses has been made, taking into account the possible delays in the completion of the project.

(iii) The financial institutions also examine the pattern of financing the project. They prefer that owners should commit their own funds substantially by way of subscription to share capital. Unsecured loans from promoters are allowed only in restricted circumstances and with the condition that the promoter would not withdraw the amount of money without permission of the institution and would charge the same rate of interest as charged by the financial institution. Also, the company cannot pay interest to the promoters unless interest has been paid to the financial institution. Similarly, deferred payments in the case of large scale projects are not considered to be very sound, since machinery purchased on such payments is seldom cheap. Public deposits can at best be considered as supplementing working capital requirements as a stop gap arrangement. Financial institutions are keen that a proper debt equity ratio is maintained. This is because this ratio, if sound, offers them a certain amount of security. The norms are that where project is of less than Rs. 5 Crores and is not in a backward area, atleast 20 per cent of the cost should be provided by the entrepreneurs. If the project is in a backward area and of less than Rs. 5 crores, 17.5 per cent of the cost could be provided by the entrepreneurs. For technical, personnel and professionally, qualified engineers etc., at least 15 per cent of the cost of the project is required to be provided by promoters. The financial institutions normally wish to maintain a debt-equity ratio of 60:40. However, in extreme cases, specially in cases of overruns etc., they may allow a debt-equity ratio of 70:30.

(iv) In the case of an existing company, the impact of the new project on the level of production, net earning, borrowings, costs etc., is seen. The level at which the project is likely to break even is also examined.

(v) The debt-service capacity and the repayment schedule are also looked into. The repayment, schedule is drawn up as per the financial projections. Repayment, obviously, is to come from internal accruals and, therefore, usually a stipulation is made in the loan agreement the applicant will not declare a dividend higher than a certain rate without the consent of the financial institutions. The repayment schedule is also dependent upon the cash flow projections of the undertaking.

5. **Managerial Assessment**. An important part of assessment conducted by the financial institutions is to examine the competence skill and reliability of management. Assessment is made by the financial institutions regarding managerial skills keeping in view the professional qualifications, abilities, past record and integrity. Obviously, financial institutions would put a premium on a management with a record of competence and honesty.

CORPORATE TAXATION AND ITS IMPACT ON CORPORATE FINANCING

The establishment of a new business involves a number of considerations including those arising from the provisions of the Direct Tax Laws and particularly the Income Tax Act. the decision to set up a new business in a particular form of organisation or at a particular place, and also the choice of the nature of the business and the type of activities to be undertaken require that a number of tax consideration, should also be taken into account before arriving at the appropriate decision from the angle of sound financial management. The discussion in the following pages is intended to briefly ouline the important aspects of tax considerations which must be taken into account by taxpayers while arriving at the appropriate decision. It may, however, be noted that the discussion is only intended to point out those aspects which must be taken into account and is not meant to be a source of elaborate guidance to entrepreneurs in the matter of tax planning for a new business.

Any one proposing to set up a new business must decide in advance the following important areas in order that he is in a position to take the full benefit of the tax concessions and reliefs granted under the Income-tax Law.

Form of Business Organisation

Under the Income Tax Law, a taxpayer may carry on the business in the form of a sole proprietorship concern, a partnership firm, a company, a Hindu Undivided Family (HUF), a trust or other associations of persons as the form of business organisation. The most obvious factors that must be taken into account in deciding about the appropriate form of business organisation are the provisions for allowance and disallowance of expenses and the rates of tax applicable to the total income of the assessee, which may be estimated, say, for a period of 10 years taking into account, the volume of the business are the expected turnover, margin of profit, etc. While considering the choice of the appropriate form of business organisation, it is also essential to take into account the relevant provisions of the Income Tax Act relating to clubbing and aggregation of income, so that, additional tax burden is not attracted in case where Section 64 of the Income Tax Act becomes applicable. For instance, in order to avoid the applicability of Section 64(1) to club the income of the husband and wife who may carry on business in partnership firm, it may be advantageous for the assessee to carry on business in the form of private limited company or a trust.

In the case of a HUF, a company, trust or other association of persons, a reasonable amount of remuneration paid or payable for the services rendered by the ultimate owner of the business is permissible as a deduction, and to that extent, the income from the business gets, reduced; consequently, the tax liability also would be worked out on a reduced total income whereas in the case of a partnership firm or a sloe proprietorship concern, even a reasonable amount of remuneration is not admissible as a deduction and consequently the assessee may not be in a position to take the benefit of allowances in respect of remuneration for the services rendered in computing the taxable income. Further, the rates of tax applicable to a company are generally flat rates and thus a company having a total income of say, Rs. 1 lakhs or less may have to pay a comparatively larger amount of tax than an individual a trust, a HUF of an unregistered firm having similar amount of income, because, in the case of these taxpayers, the rates of tax increase progressively along with an increase in the amount of income liable to tax. Closely-held non-industrial companies should, however, distribute the statutory percentage of their distributable income so as not to attract the liability to additional income-tax in all cases where they would otherwise be liable to additional income tax.

Nature of the Business

The Income Tax Law provides special tax concessions and reliefs for certain types of business and every taxpayer should choose that business which he is in a position to carry on while at the same time availing himself of the full amount of benefit arising from the tax concessions provided under the law. Broadly, 'business' for this purpose may be classified as trading and manufacturing business or a combination of both. A tax payer who intends to carry on only trading business will find himself at an advantage if he carries on trade across the borders of the country by exporting his goods and services to foreign countries. This would enable the assessee to get a weighted deduction under Section 35B on account of export markets development allowance, in computing his business income. Besides, the Ministry of Commerce and the Foreign Exchange Regulation Act provide a number of tax concessions for exports. Thus a person who intends to carry on trading business, would do well to export the goods even though he might find good market for the product at the same price within the country.

In the case of manufacturing activities, tax payers will have to choose between the various types of manufacturing activities resulting in the manufacture or production of goods. The activities of mining, generation and/or distribution of electricity or any other form of power and manufacturing or processing of goods are treated as industrial activities and a taxpayer carrying on industrial activities would be entitled to the special tax concessions on account of:

(a) investment allowance,

(b) higher depreciation allowance in the form of initial depreciation and extra shift allowance,

(c) rehabilitation allowance,

(d) amortisation of expenditure on scientific research related to the business,

(e) amortisation of preliminary expenses and expenses on prospecting for minerals,

(f) amortisation of the cost of patents and copyrights,

(g) the benefit of tax holiday,

(h) deduction in respect of profits and gains derived from the industrial undertakings established in a backward are;

(i) deduction in respect of profits and gains from the industrial undertakings established in rural areas; and

(j) deduction in respect of profits derived from the publication of books etc.

The profits derived from manufacturing activities in the case of closely held companies would suffer tax at comparatively lower rate that those applicable to the profits derived from trading activities. Further, if the assessee's manufacturing activities also involve the carrying on of certain agricultural operations (e.g. growing of sugarcane and manufacturing sugar, growing of tea leaves and processing them etc.) the amount of income attributable to the agricultural activities representing the agricultural income of the assessee is totally exempted from income-tax in the hand of the taxpayer. Thus while deciding the nature of the business, the benefit of tax exemption available in respect of certain types of income such as agricultural income, income from poultry or dairy farming or growth of mushrooms, income from new industrial undertakings and income from the publication of books etc., should also be taken into account. Where the assessee is a co-operative society. Section 80P of the Income-tax Act grants further deductions from the gross total income depending upon the nature of the business from which the income is derived. These tax concessions should also be taken into account before deciding about the nature of the business proposed to be set up by any taxpayer as they effectively increase the rate of return on the investment.

Location

While deciding about the choice of the place from which new business should be carried on, the assessee should by and large be guided by the general financial and commercial consideration involved in the matter of location of any business such as the availability of raw materials, availability of suitable facilities for transport and communications nearness to the markets etc. Besides, tax considerations would also play a vital role in this regard. This is because of the fact that Section 80HH of the Income-tax Act provides special tax concession for industrial undertakings and hotels which are established in backward areas, at any time on or after 1.1.1973. The tax concessions are given in the form of deduction from gross total income of a sum equal to a certain proportion of the points and gains derived from the new industrial undertaking or hotèl established in the backward areas. The benefit of tax exemption is available for a period of 10 assessment years after and relating to the first accounting year in which the hotel or the new industrial unit established in the backward area starts functioning or commences production or as the case may be. The list of backward areas for this purpose is given in the Eighth Schedule to the Income-tax Act. New industrial undertakings in the small scale sector established in rural areas are entitled to a similar tax exemption of a sum equal to a certain proportion of the profits derived from the new industrial unit with effect from 1.4.1978. This, however, is subject to the conditions specified in Section 10HHA.

The industrial undertakings which are established in backward areas are also entitled to the benefit of tax holiday under Section 80J of the Income-tax Act in addition to the deduction available under Section 80HH or 80HHA as the case may be even industrial undertakings which are previously established in non backward areas would be entitled to the benefit of deduction under Section 80HH if they are shifted to a backward area specified in the Eighth

Schedule. The other conditions which will have to be fulfilled to get the benefit of tax exemption are specified in Section 80HH and 10HHA. An industrial undertaking which shifts its business from any urban area to a rural or backward area with the prior permission of the Central Board of Direct Taxes is also entitled to the benefit or tax credit certificate under Section 280ZA.

or idle future, i.e. they have no plans to work for economic gains and also no happy past time. No counselling is done by the employers before a person retires to enable him to utilise his retired life in terms of time, energy and money resources in a planned way. In USA, UK and other West European countries proper education and training is imparted to persons retiring from jobs as a systematic and planned retirement package programme as a routine course of retirement planning followed in majority of the business organisations and other institutions. All possible information and knowledge is passed on to the employees seeking pre-mature retirement or retiring after superannuation. In companies where such guidance is not available within the organisation, external experts are engaged who have specialisation in counselling on financial planning for the retired persons, planning for substitute work either as second career placement in another job or taking up personal pursuits.

Education in the area of retirement planning prepares a person with confidence to face change involving shift in work situation, change in rewarding pattern for the work and much more than these is psychological adaptation to aging. If a person has a necessary plan to engage himself in work on retirement from active job situation he has a role to play in the society and while busy in the role playing he can avoid aging. The sad part of the retirement life is the aging factor which makes the retired persons subject to emotional stress which is normally reflected in "irritable behaviour, mean temper, rigid forgetfulness, suffering anxiety, depression and uninvited grief". These ailments occur during the period of post transition from adulthood to old-age and are unavoidable and inevitable natural phenomenon. But careful retirement planning may induce a person to be psychologically more prepared to face the problems of old age. This transition makes a person sad, passive, inactive, and repulsive with acute negative outlook towards life as if he has nothing more to accomplish in life but to wait for death. Education of retirement planning makes him a positive thinker with self-identification and a definite role to play in changed circumstances and environment.

The benefits of pre-retirement education are many. A retired person with pre-retirement education musters self-confidence and enforces his inner strength to maintain will-power. With the growing age, old persons experience diminishing strength, distaste for learning, repletion in memory and gross reduction in capacities of making judgments and perception. Proper guidance given to old people from time to time unable them to dispel these negative forces and provide avenues where they could utilise their competence of interactive capacities which definitely grow with aging. Education of retired way of life definitely makes a man more active than to his age, a person may be bald or wrinkled faced but may feel more smart and active in personal and interactive life. There are some people who do not need any pre-retirement education for a happy and active post retirement life but their background is entirely different as they are not normal persons, they have different outlook towards life and self-interest.

For example, a person may feel young with his active interest in social life, family life of his own or his children or grand- children, community activities, and personal financial independence. Personal financial independence is a matter of concern to all particularly those who have no retirement pension benefits or sources of income to cater their living requirements. Specially for such persons retirement planning is a necessary course of life which should be taught through a well guided process of education means. All retired persons irrespective of their rank or status in active life can attain the state of happiness through creative life if they are well exposed to pre-retirement education phased out in a systematic way.

In this direction, India may learn from the experiences of the some of the well advanced nations. To cite instances below from the experiences and efforts being made in U.K. and U.S.A. in the direction of pre-retirement planning and education in public and private organisations as a routine part of service conditions of the employees.

In U.K., Government have taken steps to foster 'Pre-retirement Education' (PRE), on sound footings having learnt lessons from the experiences of the private agencies like Pre-retirement Association (PRA) and other bodies who have been active in the field and nurtured the retirement planning ideas and ideals for past twenty years. Department of Education and Science (as reported by Gecil Kellehar, who runs regular retirement planning courses for ICL and Norfolk Education Department, in Administrator—January, 1984 p. 29) is providing a grant of £ 75,000 p.a. for three